Black H

White Rider

For July

AAcorn Books
Micaville, North Carolina

Black Horse, White Rider

by

Jack R. Pyle

AAcorn Books
Micaville, North Carolina

Cover concept by Margo
Cover design by Morris Publishing
Cover photographs,
Courtesy Brunswick-Golden Isles Visitors Bureau
Page design by Crispin Tovar

Published by:

AAcorn Books
P. O. Box 647
Micaville, NC 28714
aacorn2@excite.com

ISBN: 0-9663666-6-2
Library of Congress Control Number: 2001132845

Printed in the United States of America by:

Morris Publishing
3212 E. Highway 30
Kearney, NE 68847

This book is dedicated to
all the women back through the centuries
who were undereducated
because "too much learning could
cause their brains immeasurable harm";
to the women who lost children
because the sire
was considered more capable
of seeing to a child's needs; and,
to all those people
of color
who were the black horse.

Other books of fiction
by Jack R. Pyle:

Pieces of the Puzzle - The Poties Town Quartet and Other Stories

After Many A Summer

The Sound of Distant Thunder

The Death of Adam Stone

and

Non-fiction, written with co-author Taylor Reese:

Raising With the Moon
The Complete Guide to Gardening -
and Living -
by the Signs of the Moon

You and the Man in the Moon -
The Complete Guide to Using the Almanac

Acklowledgments

The librarians in the Research Section of the Library in Brunswick, Georgia were always more than helpful, always thinking of still another book that might help shed light on the Georgia of yesterday.

When I explained my mission–the story I intended to tell–they larded me with wonderful reference material. If I had never been lucky enough to have visited the Sea Isles of Georgia, the reference material they furnished might have been enough, but, fortunately, my love of this section of the Atlantic coast was well-nourished before I undertook the research needed for this book.

On one of my days of intensified research, a period of blustery, rainy, bitterly cold January weather—weather to chill the soul—I found the welcome inside the Library as warm as the missing-that-day Georgia sun. The stack of books heaped on my table made me keenly aware of the pride these folks put in their heritage.

Ladies, thank you for helping to tell my story.

My appreciation, too, to all of the people of the State of Georgia for the many courtesies, for the wonderful tales of the past that have been handed down through the generations, and for the Southern hospitality that I found at every turn in every road.

I still have Georgia on my mind.

jrp

BLACK HORSE, WHITE RIDER

Chapter One

Elizabeth Chadwycke had been sitting at the window for a long time. The letter lay in her lap. How dare he pressure me, she thought. Her cup of chocolate grew cold.

She could ring for another cup, but it would not obliterate the coldness she felt toward Byron Greenleaf, a brother-in-law removed by a bitter divorce.

And yet he was not removed, was he? His letter revived it all–all the grief, the bitterness, the hate.

Her fingers smoothed the creases her anger had put in the letter after the first hasty reading. It was dated May 12,1866 and it was Byron's careful hand. Each letter flowed with the beauty of the marsh grasses that surrounded the western edges of Greenleaf Island, and yet the flow was as restrained and controlled as he always was.

It had been almost twenty years.

"*My dear Elizabeth,*" the letter began, "*I have no right to ask favors. I knew the grief you had because of my brother while I stood by doing nothing to help you, but time has a way of making beggars of us all. I ask nothing for myself. Nonetheless, I am aware of the responsibilities that lie at my door. My own circumstances make it impossible for me to live up to the accountability I know is mine alone. For that reason, I am begging for your forgiveness. I want you to do for me what I did not do for you those many years ago, before the war brought havoc to a spot we both loved."*

Yes, Byron could have stood up to Clay and Aunt Mattie. Was that the weakness he spoke of, or was it the fear that Clay might expose his secret? Elizabeth looked back at the letter. *"I am aware of the willfulness and pride that runs deep in the Greenleaf blood. I need not tell you of this. You experienced it from both Clay and Aunt Mattie, and, perhaps to a lesser degree, from me."*

Her hand trembled. She had needed his help back then, if only his shoulder to cry on, but her memories of Byron centered more on the sunshine that bathed the jut of land where his offices were on Greenleaf Island. In her mind, as clearly as if she were there, she could see the tabby building bleached by sun and salt air so that the lime, sand and shell of its walls grew whiter as the years passed.

Slavery had been abhorrent to Elizabeth every day of her life, and yet, when she arrived at Greenleaf Plantation for the first time, she had virtually bathed in the adulation that greeted the master's return with his new bride.

The boat from Savannah was named for the river that brought the riches of the land from the interior of Georgia. It dumped those nutrients from upriver on the islands and the savannahs where the river met the sea.

As the *Altamaha* chugged in, the water was alive with boats. The arrival of the coastal steamer was always a period of great activity for Darien, Georgia. This time it brought even more animation. The smaller boats, many fashioned from logs, bobbed on the choppy waters. It was a vivid picture she would always remember: a warm Southern winter's day, the blue sea reflecting the blue sky, with sunshine bathing the vivid colors the boatmen wore. There was laughter and singing. There were smiles of joy and welcome.

"Oh, Clay, I didn't know it would be like this." She saw a young man with a pole balancing his log craft. His smile showed large white teeth. She heard him clearly, "Oh, Massa, me glad to see you, Massa." And from down at dockside, a large woman in two shades of red said, "Oh, skin-so-white Missus, you look so fine, you look so fine."

Then it started, almost like a Greek chorus, the chant, "Mistah Clay, Mistah Clay. You come home, you come home."

Where was the cruelty and repression? The noises around her were wild, but joyous. There were whistles, grunts, laughter, shouts, but it was all so gay; it was all a holiday. She was sure Papa would have called it pagan, but to Elizabeth it was a party, a wild and riotous party.

As the memory faded, Elizabeth glanced down at the letter again. Whatever Byron's part in the war might have been, he was now—a little more than a year after Lee's surrender—back in Philadelphia, back once again under the dominion of Matilda Greenleaf. Aunt Mattie.

This was irony. For the first time since her marriage to Clay Greenleaf nearly twenty-three years ago, she had managed to bring her life into focus. Her second husband, Spencer Chadwycke, had been buried for more than two years. This comfortable home in Sudbury Square in Boston was a part of her legacy. Until the arrival of the letter, she had managed to achieve tranquility. The bloody part of the war was in the past. She had no further need to write the articles, the leaflets, and suffer the rigors of traveling to speak for the end of slavery. It was over. She had no further need to even think about the intolerable conditions she had seen at firsthand during her stay at Greenleaf Island.

Now this, a letter from Byron. An unwanted letter. Not with news of her daughters, but one filled with words that picked at the scabs of almost-healed wounds. This letter kept dragging her back through the years, forcing her to look at the things she had left on the trash heaps of the past.

Every day since the divorce from Clay Greenleaf, her mind had been torn by the loss of the girls. And today, with the arrival of the letter, her heart was all but wrenched from her body. Nausea crawled up her windpipe. Her eyes ached with dry tears. She looked at the letter again. What had Byron said about her two daughters?

"The girls are fine. They were taken to Aunt Mattie before the worst of the war came to our part of the coast." She paged through the letter. There was no further mention of Mary or Ann Frances. Mary had always been independent, but Ann Frances, little Frannie, was of a different stripe. What had those years under the guidance of Clay and Aunt Mattie done to her? What had it done to both girls? She had not seen either of them in over twelve years. They were young ladies now. Frannie would be twenty-one in just over a week and Mary, only ten months older, would be almost twenty-two.

She had not seen either girl since the courts had awarded them to Clay when they were eight and nine. Who had been a mother to her girls? And just what had Byron told her about the girls in his letter? Nothing. Nothing that helped. Nothing at all.

She reread the brief mention of Clay. *"Clay is dead. His death was a waste, but war is a waste. I will send additional information of your daughters and Clay with Gordy."*

The letter was not about her girls, it was about Gordy. *"He means more to me than I can say, Elizabeth. I feel a great sense of responsibility for him,"* the letter went on. *"While I am still alive I wanted to prepare him for what lies ahead. He is intelligent, sensitive and, in time, can do a lot for his people. But, alas, dear Elizabeth, I am unable to do more for him than I have already done. My health in these recent years has been failing. It was a difficult journey for me to Philadelphia, but I knew I had to get Gordy to you. I will depend on you to see that he has the best education available."*

She put the letter down. Was he thrusting this burden on her conscience? What did she owe Gordy—or Byron? Her opinions on slavery were well known. Her articles, her abolitionist tracts, her speeches had been widely distributed. They were even circulated in the South. Byron's letter contained no specifics. Perhaps she would find more detail in the "additional information" he had briefly mentioned.

What kind of a man might Gordy be? He was a mulatto. His mother was Jude, the cook on the rice island, and his father was Jonathan Rigby, the white overseer Elizabeth first met when she arrived at Greenleaf Island the winter of 1844. Would he be like his father?

The letter brought back the image of Gordy's father. Another scab—one only recently healed. If she had ever had the urge to kill, it would have been Jonathan Rigby. Her hatred of him was still alive. Byron had managed to exacerbate this still fevered wound with these flimsy five pages.

She glanced outside through the bay windows. Spring had come to Boston. The buds on the maples were ready to leaf. It was a time of renewal for the world, but was she ready for it?

The pages burned in her hand. Because of the letter, this year Spring could be a renewal of something old. A revisitation. She was not at all sure she wanted that.

The letter said Gordy would arrive at 11:00, *"providing the train meets its schedule."* It was ten minutes past.

As she reached the foyer, the doorbell sounded. She heard scurrying in the hall behind her. "It's all right, Margaret. I'll get the door. I'm expecting a guest. Would you tell Mrs. Conroy that there will be two for lunch? Serve it in my upstairs sitting room, please, Margaret."

She hesitated briefly, brought her shoulders back, and then crossed the marble foyer to the large oak front entrance.

Chapter Two

After lunch, Elizabeth invited Gordy to sit in the other winged chair in the large bay that protruded from the front of the house on all three floors.

"It's time for a serious talk, Gordy. Byron's letter told me what he has in mind, but there's one thing that's more important, at least to me."

There was a quick look of fear in Gordy's eyes, but it was gone as she continued."What Byron wants is one thing, but the more important thing is, what do you want? Why are you in Boston?"

"Well, Miss Elizabeth—"

"We must get something clear, Gordy. You may call me Mrs. Chadwycke or Elizabeth, but the days of 'Miss Elizabeth' are over. Conditions for black people are still chaotic, but, in time, all people, black and white, will be equal."

"Equality is not everywhere, Mrs. Chadwycke."

"I know, Gordy, but it will come. We must be patient. With Mr. Lincoln dead, President Johnson appears to be working to impede the process. Luckily, nothing is forever."

With the hint of a smile in her voice she said,"You have decided to call me Mrs. Chadwycke. That much is settled. Gordy is what I called you at Greenleaf. You're grown man now, but I can still see the boy I knew. Unless you object, it's Gordy. And there's one more detail. You will soon have full citizenship, so you'll need a full name. Gordy may have been suitable on

Greenleaf Island, but not for Harvard. You know who your father was, don't you? Your mother told you, or Byron has?"

"My mother told me. It was Mr. Jonathan."

"Then we have a start. You are Gordon Rigby, son of Jonathan Rigby. You can have a third name, a middle name."

"Could it be Byron?"

"You admire him, don't you?"

"I love him, Mrs. Chadwycke. When it was forbidden to teach black people, Mr. Byron taught me. Everyone thought I was learning only enough to keep the records, but Mr. Byron taught me to read, write, and to do more than simple arithmetic. He said one day I'd be free. He wanted me to help others as he had helped me."

"Byron thought that? I didn't know."

"He said it had to be. He said,'They know it, Gordy, they know it. Change is coming. They speak one way, but they can feel the shift in the tide.' Yes, ma'am. He knew."

Gordy had brought a locked leather case full of papers. Since his arrival, it had not been moved from the door of her sitting room.

"I'll get into Byron's box later," Elizabeth said. "Perhaps it will answer the puzzles I have, but for now, let's talk about you and my first question. I may know what Byron wants; I may think I know what you want, but I must hear it from you, in your own words.What do you want from your stay with me here in Boston?"

Those last words out of her mouth surprised her. She had been considering what she might do with Gordy while he was enrolled at Harvard, but now, without thinking of the words as they were uttered, the die had been cast. She had said "...stay with me here in Boston."

Her heart knew what her mind had not grasped. Gordy said nothing.

"Don't you know what you want?"

"Yes, ma'am, I know, but—" His embarrassment was clear.

"You think it might sound pompous? Promoting yourself as the Lord Protector of all the black people in Georgia?"

"Yes, ma'am, something like that."

"I understand, Gordy, I truly do. When I took the girls from their father—when I ran away from Greenleaf Plantation—I wanted to obliterate all injustice. I knew what I wanted to do, and yet I couldn't give form to it either."

How well she remembered. If she ever needed Papa, it was then.

"I tried to say it once to my father," she said. "I thought a clergyman would understand. Papa laughed at me. He laughed! He gave me a lecture on 'cleaving to my husband.' Then I came to Boston, to my father's sister. Aunt Florence had more compassion in an instant than Papa could muster in a century. She understood. She encouraged me. I don't think my writing or my speaking won any battles for the Union, but I do think I made a difference in the lives of the people who read my tracts or who heard me.

"So, yes, I do understand, Gordy. Perhaps you can't make a miracle by yourself, but you can make a difference. Don't be afraid to say how you feel."

"I believe I can teach, Mrs. Chadwycke. Mr. Byron has faith in me. There is a need. There is suffering in Georgia now—some of it is worse, much worse, than before." As he spoke his eyes focused on the place, that lush island, where his mind had gone. Quietly he added, "So I must move. I must learn quickly."

Elizabeth could see the fire she had known in herself. Gordy was a man with a mission. In that instant, she knew she would help him.

"Then it's settled," she said. "I'll go with you. You will enroll at Harvard tomorrow, and you'll live here. You can move at your own pace. I know it will be swift. I'll be here to support you as Aunt Florence supported me. You brought only a satchel, Gordy. Where is your clothing, your valise?"

"At the station. I didn't know about lodging."

"I'll send for it." As she spoke, she pulled the bell cord. "Your room will be at the end of the hall on the left. It has the morning sun. Perhaps you'd like to look it over."

There was a knock at the door. "Come in, Margaret."

Elizabeth stood. As she spoke, there was the slightest gesture that dismissed them both. "Mr. Rigby will be staying with us, the guest room at the end of the hall. See that he is comfortable there. And ask Mr. Conroy to help him with a desk from Mr. Chadwycke's study. Gordy will be a student at Harvard. He'll need a desk."

When they had gone, Elizabeth unlocked the neat black case she had left just inside her door. How like Byron it was. There were a number of packets—letters, papers, deeds—each labeled and tied with coarse cotton thread. Why so many records, she thought, and why send them to me?

She untied the string. The top sheet in the first packet was a note. "*The fiscal condition of the estate is poor, but not hopeless,*" it said. "*Clay converted a large part of the gold I had been holding into paper money on his last trip home from the war. He considered treasonous all my arguments against this patriotic but foolish conversion. That paper money is worthless according to the news I have been getting out of Washington. It's now only paper.*"

The note continued, but Elizabeth was not ready for the finances of Greenleaf Plantation. She put the bundle aside.

Another packet contained only deeds and contracts—proof of ownership that might be required at some later date. Why send these to me? Why not keep them in Philadelphia until they are needed? She retied the thread and put it aside.

There was a packet of childish drawings, school papers, and valentines. The note read: "*Dearest Elizabeth, I know how you missed the girls after Clay took them from you. There was nothing I could do, but I made this effort. Here is a collection of the trivia that meant something to them as they were growing up. I believe it may mean something to you, too.*"

Tears blurred her vision. It was clear to Elizabeth now. Byron may have kept her at a distance when she lived on the island, but he loved her, he had compassion for her, or he would not have gone to so much trouble. He must have been a veritable pack rat collecting these bits, these fragments from the life she was unable to share with her children.

The cruelest thing Clay had done was to take the girls away. Byron must have understood how she felt when they were wrenched from her. She picked up a valentine from Frannie to Uncle Byron. The colors spilled over beyond the lines. There was Mary's spelling paper with one hundred marked at the top. How kind of Byron. She felt his love for her as she touched the children's papers. It was something she would not forget.

She blinked back the tears and picked up his note. "*At any rate, none of this collection would still be in existence once you arrive here. Our house has not been touched—I believe because I continued to live in it—but many of the houses you know well have been vandalized. The Hamiltons were burned to the ground, as were the Wrights. Once I leave here for Philadelphia, nothing will last for long. You will be shocked when you see the conditions that exist.*"

There was more of the memorabilia, much more, but the tears came too fast. These papers rekindled the horror of the day the children were taken. She retied the packet and put it aside.

Then she saw the envelope at the bottom of the case marked: "*Elizabeth Chadwycke, Personal.*" It was made from coarse brown paper and sealed with the wax impression of Byron's unusual signet ring. She opened it.

"*Dearest Elizabeth,*" the letter read. "*There is so much to explain, and so little time. My health has deteriorated alarmingly. Dr. Masters—he replaced Dr. Barnes since you were in Darien—has been unable to determine the cause. For now, I want you to understand why I ask you to take on a responsibility you could refuse to bear. I would gladly see to Gordy's further education, but, alas, dear sister-in-law, I am not able. Gordy knows how ill I am, though we never discuss it. He wants to stay with me. I have forbidden it. I shall soon be completely paralyzed."*

The last word made her stop reading. Paralyzed? How dreadful. Or, was this just another Greenleaf manipulation? She knew that family, she knew them well. Better to question everything. But, after a time to reflect on those questions, questions that seemed to be without answers, she went back to her reading.

"This condition started before the war ended for us with Sherman's virtual rape of Georgia before he got to Savannah. At first I gave the bouts of numbness in my limbs little credence. It was an annoyance. I thought it might be nerves, brought on by what was happening to Georgia, and by what was happening to our people. Because of the war, my ordeal at Greenleaf was a greater responsibility than I had ever shouldered."

Elizabeth's strong sense of reasoning told her that this much at least was true. Who else but Byron would be capable? She read on.

"As you know, the workers on Greenleaf Island were kept in ignorance. Clay was not alone in refusing to let them be taught even the most fundamental things. Most of the planters were of the same opinion. It was widely believed that educating the blacks would turn them into uncontrollable rabble.

"Because of their lack of skills, our people were unable to cope with the ordinary aspects of life. They looked to me. As the war progressed, we became isolated by the Union's blockade of our shoreline. It was useless to plant rice or cotton. There was no market, so we had no money for food for the more than three hundred souls here and at the rice ponds."

She stopped reading. More than three hundred? That many? Her mind wandered back to the island she had known so long ago. She could see sunlight dappling through the gnarled branches of the giant spreading oaks and the bower they formed over the shell road leading from one of the slave quarters to the other. She could not remember anything like three hundred people, black or white. As she glanced out the window and beyond Boston toward the Charles, her mind brought back another river, the black, serpentine river through the marshes that connected the main house and its island to the rice island. She remembered the mounds of earth around each rice pond. There were two separate communities on the rice island for slaves. A hundred people living there? Or was it more? On Greenleaf Island there were three more slave communities. Perhaps the figure was correct.

It was a bittersweet memory. Those were people in bondage. How could she remember any part of her stay as pleasant? But there were pleasant aspects to it. She had gone there as a bride, and the islands, once you got to know them and understand them, were beautiful.

She rubbed her eyes, put her glasses back on. "*I was slow in realizing the need,*" the letter continued. "*There was considerable want before it became clear to me that we were going to have to be self-sufficient or die. I managed to get every family at Greenleaf to plant a garden. We did well with corn, potatoes, yams and a variety of other vegetables. We put goats on one of the unused islands, and we had pigs.*

"*There is no need to dwell on it, but it did require my best efforts. I was on a horse for a good part of each day, going from one of the quarters to another, helping our people understand what had to be done. They had to be made to realize that we had no source of food from outside.*

"*It was not the fault of the blacks or the whites. We had all become complacent. We grew bountiful cotton and rice; we produced so much that buying what we needed was the only way we knew. You will recall how I would list our needs. The factoring house did the buying. With the arrival of the boat in Darien, we had our supplies and food for our people. There was no need for gardens then. We, Clay and I, felt we needed every available hand for field work. We had to produce the bounty that earned the gold that was required to pay our debts. We may not have been aware of it, but it was a treadmill. We were slaves to it as much as our people were slaves to us."*

There was irony in that last statement. How dare he compare his lot with that of the workers at Greenleaf Plantation? Slaves indeed! And yet, there was a parallel. The Greenleafs were victims of the system. But, were they slaves? Certainly not. Byron could quit at any time. More Greenleaf hyperbole. They were good at that. She read on.

"I believe I pushed myself too hard—that coupled with my fear for Clay. He had rounded up a raggle-taggle group of volunteers and had gone off to bring the war to a quick close. I am sad to say Clay did not return. His personal things are in a separate packet. Some of it you may want; some you may wish to give to the girls. Clay did not die as he might have hoped, charging into the Union forces. He died trying to make the best of a retreat, a rout I have been told, even before the battle for Atlanta was over. His 'army' fell apart. They ran. He was cut down as he attempted to rally them."

Clay dead. How many times had she made that wish, but now that it was a fact, she had a rush of guilt. She picked up the letter again.

"I am rambling, Elizabeth. There seems to be so much to tell you—it has been so long—and I find it difficult to organize all the details in my mind. There was a time when I was good at organization, but not now. My thoughts wander and I have a fear that I am not making any manner of sense at all.

"Before I lose all capacity for organization, let me tell you about Gordy. He must be educated. He will be—along with you—the salvation of the people of Greenleaf Island."

She stopped. It was necessary to reread the last line. She could understand Byron's desire to have an educated Gordy return to help the people now bereft of direction, but what had that to do with her? Byron was presuming beyond limits just by sending Gordy to Boston. But, this new twist was too much. She had been gone from those islands for more than two decades. Why should she be responsible for the salvation of anyone there?

"We all have a responsibility: We, for keeping our people ignorant and in bondage; you, dear Elizabeth, for your part in overthrowing a system that was at least working. Nothing is working now." She read the last part of that sentence again. *"...for your part in overthrowing a system that was at least working."* His point was not lost.

She continued reading: *"When you think this over, I know you will wish to finish the job you wanted to do long ago when Clay forbad you to teach anything but the fundamentals of hygiene to our people. Now that the winds have turned, you will be able to start your school. All of us must help. We must make these people ready to pick up the reins for themselves. They must be free, as Mr. Lincoln's proclamation promised—whatever that may mean—and it will mean different things to different people."*

She put the letter down and rang for Margaret. Her lips were a thin line and her hands were clenched. Well, Byron, she thought, I'll help with Gordy's education, but I've given enough of my life to emancipation. I'll not be going back to the coast of Georgia. Not for you. Not for anyone.

Margaret knocked and entered. "Yes, ma'am."

"There's a storm coming, Margaret. There's a chill in the air. I'd like the brandy and a pot of tea."

Digging through the past cools the blood, Elizabeth thought as Margaret closed the door. She picked up the letter again. *"But I digress,"* it read. *"I must speak of Gordy. It is difficult to lay my soul bare, dear Elizabeth, even with you, whom I trust completely. What I tell you now I believe you know, though in our many philosophical discussions it was never said. And yet I believe you knew what was never spoken.*

"Gordy has worked with me since he was ten. I saw him

one day on a work crew. He is a strong young man now, but on that day he was a slightly built lad who was not doing well in the fields. I asked to have him assigned to me. Rigby was amenable because looking at the boy was a sore point for him. You must know, since the resemblance is clear, Gordy is Rigby's son, a child of Jude, the cook on the rice island."

She remembered Jude. One of her tracts had been written about Jude, and about her union with Rigby. Had Jude wanted the relationship? One thing sure, if she had not, it would have made no difference to Rigby, no difference at all.

"Gordy was a joy to be around, alert and eager to learn," the letter went on. *"I taught him to read and write. Clay was furious; he thought education, especially of a mulatto, might create trouble. Teaching Gordy violated the agreement Clay had with the other planters about the complete restriction of all education. I won only because Clay didn't understand—didn't want to understand—the work I was doing. Clay preferred field work. I made him see that as we reclaimed more land, my job was becoming more than one man could handle."*

When the tea tray arrived Elizabeth poured a cup and added a dollop of brandy. She picked up the letter again. *"You have experienced days when death would have been welcomed. You must have felt this way when Clay came to Boston for the children. It must have been even more acute when they were forcibly taken from you in Philadelphia. Aunt Mattie told me of this wretched scene in complete detail."*

Byron Greenleaf knew all the chords. He knew what Clay's final cruelty had done to her—he knew by instinct. He sensed her despair, but he couldn't know the depths of it.

Those memories came crashing back. Her eyes closed. Her nails dug into her palms. In time she relaxed her hands, dried her eyes, and poured another pony of brandy into the teacup.

When she had stopped trembling, she took up the letter again. *"Since you have known this kind of despondency, recall the emptiness it brought to your soul, Elizabeth. If you do that, you will know what my life was like—every day of it—before I found Gordy. I learned to love Gordy.*

"I stayed on the island. I was the clerk, the bookkeeper, the accountant, not because I wanted it to be my life's work; I stayed because I didn't fit with what I perceived to be the moral customs of my class. I was born out of step. Perhaps in another day, in another place, I could have been happy. But we do not choose our time or place. I was safe at Greenleaf. I would not have to face my problems in a world that could not understand them. It was cowardly, but it was necessary—at least I thought so then."

Could Byron have done more? He could have left the island. She did. Yes, but was her daring to protect her daughters? Could she have done it without them? These were questions she couldn't answer. She picked up the page of the letter that had fallen to the floor.

"I wanted to be your friend, Elizabeth, but when you moved too close, I withdrew. I'm not proud of the fear that kept you at arm's length. That must have been difficult to comprehend, but now, I hope, you will grasp it better.

"You must understand why I want an education for Gordy. He must be a free man. He must come back to Georgia to be an inspiration to a people who will begin at the bottom. Few of them have skills that can earn more than a subsistence. Gordy must return to Georgia as a leader.

"And that is why, dear sister-in-law, I am leaving you my share of Greenleaf Plantation. My earthly time is short. I have been to the solicitor and the factor. All arrangements have been made. You will inherit my part of the estate."

For a moment she was unable to breathe.

Her stomach formed a cold and painful knot. "Damn you, Byron Greenleaf, damn you to hell," she whispered as her breath returned. "Damn you! Damn you! Damn you!"

The letter fell from her hands. Her fingers trembled.

She poured a full half-cup of brandy. She did not add tea.

She drank the spirits quickly, coughing as she did so. And then her anger was spent. She was tired. She seemed to shrink back into her chair.

Hours later, as the shadows of the coming night claimed the room, she picked up the scattered pages of the letter, folded them and put them back in the envelope. She looked at the last packet left in the case. This was the bundle that was labeled, *"Clay."*

"Not today," she said aloud. "I can't take any more to-day."

Chapter Three

When Elizabeth stepped into the hall the next morning, the smell of coffee and bacon drew her down the stairwell. Her guest was at the dining room table. "Good morning," she said. "I'm too late to breakfast with you, Gordy, but have another cup of coffee. I have a question or two."

She turned to the maid. "The usual, Margaret, but I prefer the egg soft-boiled today. I didn't sleep well last night. Tell Mr. Conroy I'd like the carriage at nine. I'll go to Cambridge with Gordy this first morning."

She settled herself at the table. "What exactly did Byron tell you about coming to Boston, Gordy? I'm sure you discussed it as you came up the coast from Darien."

"Well, not much, ma'am. Mr. Byron's not well. He said I'd go to school, and that, more than likely, I'd be staying with you."

Staying with me "more than likely," is it? she thought. Byron really was presuming. He may be ill, but he still has the Greenleaf cheek. "I'm sorry to hear of his illness. On the journey, was he in pain? Did you have to help him?"

"No, ma'am, he's never had a lot of pain. He just grows weaker day by day. It's his arms and legs." Elizabeth could see Gordy's concern. "Mr. Byron—he just—" He looked away, blinking his eyes. Then he said: "Yes, ma'am, I had to help him. He said it was so we wouldn't have trouble with the roughnecks on the boat, like I was helping an invalid. That's what he said, but I'm not so sure."

Elizabeth wasn't confident that she was not being used by Byron, so the questions were necessary. "Did he mention Greenleaf—what his plans were for it, now that the fighting is over?"

"No, ma'am. Not the plantation. But we talked about the people. I have a job to do, ma'am, for Mr. Byron, and for the people on Greenleaf Island. I thought you understood that yesterday. If you can't help me, I'll find another way."

"No, Gordy, I really do understand. But I was wondering what is to become of the land.Was that ever discussed?"

"No, ma'am."

She did not continue. All the cards seemed to be face up, but she didn't regret the questions. She knew the Greenleafs.

"Get your coat, Gordy. It'll be fresh out there. In this cold drizzle, the wind off the river cuts right through."

It was afternoon when they returned. Gordy was enrolled at Harvard for the fall session. Tutors would begin at once. It would be a busy summer. There were gaps in his education, but the dean said Byron had done an exceptional job.

Gordy had started the day frightened. At the outset, he had been unsure of his qualifications now that he had to meet formal standards. Elizabeth tried to reassure him. As the day wore on, he became more confident—more aware that the job before him was possible. The first of the tutors could have been postponed until the coming week, but Gordy was anxious to begin. The Latin tutor would be there at nine the following morning.

Elizabeth was pleased. The young man who came back from Cambridge with her was alive and enthusiastic; Gordy was ready for the world. Well, Byron, she thought, we've made a start.

By four o'clock the next day. Elizabeth had taken the last packet from the leather case, the one marked: "*Clay.*" All the memorabilia was on her desk. She looked at it piece by piece. How can a life be reduced to a pitiful pile of rubbish? It was as if Clay had never lived. These do not make suitable ashes, she thought. She touched them. Nothing brought a solid image of Clay. There was a bravery citation from the Confederate States of America for Major Claiborne Greenleaf. It was paper—paper as worthless as Byron's Confederate fiat. She put it aside. The medals were lifeless too, in spite of the bright colors of the ribbons. Why had Byron sent them to her? Was it because they might have been unsafe at Greenleaf House? Yes, she reasoned, they belong to the children. Byron knew I would get them to their rightful place.

There was a pocket knife, a watch chain with an elaborate fob, and three gold rings. There was her wedding certificate and a copy of the divorce decree. The beginning and the ending of a story, she thought. Who would want that? Would the children be interested? Certainly she was not.

There was a copy of the bill of sale for Carlotta, the housekeeper at Greenleaf. "My God," she said aloud. "That, too." It was quickly put aside.

The papers might have meant something to Clay or Byron, but not to Elizabeth. She shuffled through them. Then she put all the loose items in the felt bag Byron had provided. She gathered together all the other packets to be put away. As she picked up the satchel, something slid across the bottom. Some loose piece of this miserable collection has fallen free, she thought. She reached in to find it.

Elizabeth withdrew a painting, a miniature of Clay. As with everything else, there was a note. "*I would gladly have kept this as my own remembrance, but I will have little use of mementos before long. No, dear Elizabeth, I am not being melodramatic. When this dreaded thing began, it wore booties and crept along, but now it wears Mercury's winged shoes. Unless something is found to alter the pace of it, I expect to lose complete use of my limbs. My breathing is labored. I do not mean* to *burden you with my health, but I know your first reaction on seeing this miniature will be to send it back. Don't do it, Elizabeth. Keep it. If you don't want it, keep it for one of the girls. In time you will know which one."*

Damn you, Byron Greenleaf. You write your riddles, you bait me, you tempt me with your plans for Greenleaf Island. You make me recall the school that Clay wouldn't let me start. You fire the imagination of the frustrated teacher I have managed to bury. You take unfair advantage.

Then, with typical Greenleaf highhandedness, you say I "will know" which daughter deserves to have the miniature. Will I? Am I to be the judge?

Along with trying to put the onus of the future of the island and its several hundred souls squarely on my back, along with seeing to the education of Gordy, you now saddle me with what can be a very personal and painful decision. You tell me I "will know" which of my daughters should have this little painting. Byron, you do me no favors.

Should she keep the letter? Or might it cause sorrow to one or both of the girls? Byron must have suffered on the journey from Greenleaf Island to Philadelphia, but he must have felt it was important to get this black case to her, just as he felt it was important to get Gordy out of the South.

Whatever her feelings, she felt sure Byron believed the contents of the case were important. At his request, Gordy hand-carried it to Boston.

She could not destroy anything at the moment. These are the kinds of decisions that should not be made when angry she reminded herself, and she was furious. Her body was rigid with rage.

As she began to relax she took the first real look at the miniature Byron had sent. Her anger faded. She saw a delicately crafted image that took her breath away. It was Clay, not as she remembered him when she ran away, and not as he had looked when they had fought so bitterly in the courts for custody of the children. It was Clay as she had first seen him in her father's study so long ago.

How well she remembered. Afternoons had always been the busiest times for her father. Those were the hours when his parishioners were apt to come for counsel, or when he made his calls.

"Afternoons," her father said, "are for the parish. If you need to talk to me, morning is the proper time."

It was ten o'clock on that July morning in 1843 when she first met Clay. It was already warm. All the windows were open in the narrow three-story brownstone where she and her father lived. The curtains barely moved with the breeze. New York City was in for another hot day. If her mother had been alive, they might have spent the warm part of the summer in Montauk, but Papa did not want her so far away without proper supervision. It was silly of him. She was almost eighteen and quite capable of taking care of herself.

Emma Lauterlein had advised her to ignore his ill humor. "Your papa is just old-fashioned, as mine is sometimes."

"Old-fashioned," Elizabeth laughed. "He's antediluvian. You can't tease my papa like yours, Emma. Your daddy doesn't have a congregation. Papa says it's the burden he bears for the Lord. He's a grouch. The congregation is his excuse."

She rapped on the door and then entered the study as she always did. She was startled to find a young man across the desk from the Reverend Mr. Medlock. Both men looked up.

"Oh, Papa, I'm sorry. I didn't realize you had someone with you." My goodness, she thought as she looked quickly away, he is dazzling. Blue eyes, dark hair, and he stands a head and shoulders taller than Papa.

"It's all right, my child. Our business was over." Papa was using his 'rectory' voice. "Mr. Greenleaf," he said, "may I present my daughter. Elizabeth, this is Claiborne Greenleaf from Philadelphia. Clay is staying with the William Custers. You know the Custers."

"Yes, Papa." Then, with the slightest hint of a curtsy, she said, "I'm pleased to meet you, Mr. Greenleaf."

"It's my pleasure, Miss Medlock. You are a neighbor of my Uncle William and Aunt Lavinia. Perhaps we'll meet again."

"I think we will, Mr. Greenleaf," she replied. "I've been invited to a party there tomorrow night. Candida said it was to introduce her cousin, but it appears that we won't really need an introduction, will we?"

Her little flirtation was brusquely interrupted. "You needed something, Elizabeth? Can it wait?"

"Yes, Papa. I apologize for the intrusion." She turned to Clay. "I do hope you enjoy your stay in our city, Mr. Greenleaf. If I may be excused, Papa."

Elizabeth rushed to the parlor. She heard the sounds of Clay's departure. Then she heard their goodbyes at the entry. From behind the curtain she watched Clay walk away. What a noble bearing. Ten feet beyond her window he turned, glanced back and threw her a little salute.

How dare he? What arrogance! How could he assume she was behind the curtains? Claiborne Greenleaf was quite the handsomest thing she had ever seen, but she intended to avoid him in the future. He can be dangerous, she thought. He might not be controllable. It's easier to cope with tame boys, the kind I know.

"Elizabeth!" The Reverend Mr. Medlock was angry. "Elizabeth, I want to talk to you."

She went to his study. "Sit down," he said. "I have a few observations to make."

"Yes, Papa."

"Your behavior with Mr. Greenleaf is unacceptable."

"Yes, Papa."

"Can't you say anything but 'Yes, Papa'?"

"You have nothing to worry about with Mr. Greenleaf, Papa. I'll be courteous to him, but that's all I intend to be."

"I didn't get that impression."

"Well, Papa, you have it now. He is a visitor who will soon be leaving. I'll go to the Custers' party, but I will be giving Mr. Greenleaf plenty of pasture."

Chapter Four

"Papa, please ask Mr. Hodges to stay late today so I can be taken to the Custers' party in the carriage."

"I will do nothing of the sort, Elizabeth. The congregation pays Hodges little enough. I will not presume upon his time."

"But, Papa—"

"No 'But Papas,' Elizabeth. The Custers live only five doors from us. You can walk to the party."

"But, my dress, Papa."

"I'll hear no more of it, Elizabeth!" He was firm."When the time comes, I will walk to the Custers with you. I can assure you, your dress will be none the worse for it."

"Everyone else will be arriving by carriage."

"Everyone else does not live as close as you, Elizabeth. One more word and you won't be going to the party at all."

"Papa—"

"Elizabeth." The word thundered down the hallway. She heard a stirring in the pantry. Someone had been listening. Papa's refusal would become household gossip. She was aware that being the pastor's daughter did not compare with being one of the Custers, or one of the Billinghams, or a Chase, but Elizabeth did not want to think she was asked to the party only because she was the pastor's daughter, nor did she want to arrive like a poor relation. That's how it might sound if gossip spread from kitchen to kitchen.

The afternoon was interminable. She had her clothes laid out well before noon, even though she had changed her mind three times. The Custers' party had been the topic of conversation for weeks. Elizabeth had been bored by Candida's constant reference to "Cousin Clay," but now she had seen him. Handsome, she thought, but more than a little presumptuous. It was an attitude, an assured air. She hadn't forgotten the arrogance of that little knowing salute from the street, as though he knew she was standing just behind those curtains.

The party was not to begin until eight-thirty, but Candida had sent word for her friend to come early. Elizabeth was relieved. This would spare her the embarrassment of arriving on foot when all the other girls were coming in proper carriages.

If Mama were only here now, she thought, I'd be going in the carriage, but since her death Papa has become mean and penny-pinching.

The income from her mother's trust had ceased. Mrs. Medlock's death had made a difference at the manse. Fortunately, Elizabeth's mother had had enough money in her own right to leave a small trust for her husband, and an even smaller trust for Elizabeth, but, because of the terms of Elizabeth's great grandfather's will, the real source of their income had been diverted after her mother's death to other members of Grandfather Burnside's living heirs.

The church owned the manse and arranged for Mr. Hodges and a carriage, so Papa could carry on his pastoral duties. It was up to Papa to pay for his own servants and all other costs. The address was good, but the house was a narrow building between much larger, much grander homes. The manse was little wider than a room plus the hall and stairway. The first floor amounted to only a comfortable parlor in the front and Papa's office in the back. Both of these rooms were large. The ground floor was Papa's, because of his constant stream of visitors. All cooking was done below the street level. The dining room and the other three floors were serviced by a dumbwaiter.

It saved many trips up and down the stairs for the servants and for Elizabeth, although it did not eliminate what she considered to be a thousand miles of climbing every day.

"When you live in a vertical house," Elizabeth told her father, "you develop strong legs."

"Strong limbs, Elizabeth. Horses have legs, tables have legs—"

"I know, Papa. I know. You develop strong limbs."

She hated their house. It was dreary. Squeezed between the larger houses, it had no side windows. The only light was from either the front or the back, or from the gas lights which Papa did not allow in the daytime. The walls were dingy, and the woodwork ornate and dark. At almost eighteen, Elizabeth could not wait until she was married and had a suitable home of her own.

There was a sharp knock at her door. Are you ready, Elizabeth? It's after seven."

"In a minute, Papa. I'll be ready in a minute."

"All day to get ready, and she's not ready yet. Just like her mother." She could hear his discontent as he walked down the hall. She slipped on her shoes and adjusted her hair. "Ready, Papa. I'll meet you downstairs."

When they arrived, every light in the Custer house was ablaze. Unlike the manse, this was a well-proportioned brownstone with broad oak doors. There was a small foyer before you entered the wide reception room on the ground level. The floors were marble. A graceful stairway curved to the right. The kind of house I want, Elizabeth thought. I wonder if Clay's home in Philadelphia is as grand?

"Miss Candida is in her bedroom, Miss Elizabeth."

"Thank you, Grayson. I know the way."

She found Candida Custer in a stew, "Oh, I'm so glad you're here, Elizabeth. That stupid Marie had to re-press mother's gown, and I'm without any help at all. Will you hook up the back of this dress, please? Isn't it lovely. It's new. I had it made especially for this party."

It was lovely. White lace. "Yes, Candy, it's beautiful. Breathe out. These hooks and eyes are hard to handle without space to work." When the last of the hooks had been inserted she said, "All right, Candida Custer, let me look at you. You'll be the prettiest one there."

"No. I won't. Clay will. Just you wait, Elizabeth. He's just the handsomest, he's just the tallest, the most dashing—I'm sorry we're cousins."

Elizabeth did not mention that she had met Clay when he was in her father's office. "Cousins marry cousins, Candy. It's been done."

"Not by the Custers. Daddy would never allow that, but, oh, wait till you see him. You won't believe it, you won't. I hope you marry him, Elizabeth. Then we'd be kin. You'll be my cousin, too."

"Marry him? Don't be silly, Candy. I wouldn't have a chance. He's probably engaged. One of those Philadelphia girls probably has him in tow."

"No, they've not. He's available, Elizabeth. Did you think I wouldn't have had mother check with Aunt Matilda? He's ours for now. He'll be visiting here for at least a month, and I think you should have him. You must set your sights on him right away. All these New York girls will be trying." Candida took her hand. "But you have the edge, Elizabeth. You live just down the street. You can visit here every day while he's here. He won't know what hit him."

"Candida, you're shameful."

"I'm resourceful." She glanced at Elizabeth's reflection in the mirror. "And you're my friend, my best friend. Why can't we be cousins?"

Elizabeth could see him clearly as she moved down the reception line toward the guest of honor. In evening wear he was even more handsome than he was in her father's study. She could see his glance stray in her direction—even when he was shaking hands with one of the other guests—but she was careful not to let him catch her as she watched.

At one point their eyes met. There was a hint of a smile on his face. He seemed to be saying, "I know you've been watching me, and this time I caught you." He winked at her. Everyone in the room must have seen it. She quickly glanced away, stumbling on the words as she talked to one of Mr. Custer's maiden aunts who was a part of the receiving line. He winked at me! How dare he!

As the line moved along, she dreaded the moment that was finally at hand. "Elizabeth," Mrs. Custer said, "it's so nice of you to come to meet a part of the Philadelphia branch of our family. Clay, may I present Elizabeth Medlock? Elizabeth is our pastor's daughter and a favorite in the Custer household. Elizabeth, this is our nephew, my brother's son, Claiborne Greenleaf."

His reply was quick."We've met, haven't we, Miss Medlock? We are well on our way to becoming old friends."

"You've met? How nice."

Elizabeth's face was flaming. "Mr. Greenleaf was visiting the manse today, Mrs. Custer. I didn't know Papa had a guest, and I just charged right into his study." She turned slightly toward Clay, looking only at his shirt studs as she spoke. "It's my pleasure to meet you again, Mr. Greenleaf, under more formal conditions. I hope you'll enjoy your stay in our city."

"We'll meet again, Miss Medlock. And I hope you'll save one waltz for me." He was smiling again, that arrogant and knowing smile. He angered and disturbed her, but there was a fascination, too. It was like playing with matches when she was a little girl, hiding behind the stove in the kitchen. Each time one of the sulfurous matches was struck, she had an inner excitement unlike anything she had ever experienced. The match incident came to an abrupt end when cook smelled the sulfur and quickly found its source.

This incident, too, was finally over. She moved into the ornate ballroom that occupied almost all of the third floor of the Custer home. She was happy to allow herself to blend into the crowd.

Later she had found a quiet place away from the mass of humanity that filled the ballroom. She had managed to elude Claiborne Greenleaf as he moved among the guests. Soon she could find an excuse to leave the party without appearing rude.

The orchestra began again. She felt a hand touching her arm from behind. "It's one of the new waltzes of young Mr. Strauss. Is it the one you saved for me?"

She was startled by Clay's touch. "Well, is it? You seem to have no partner for this one."

What could she say? She couldn't let him see the effect he was having on her. She turned toward him, smiling, "Yes, Mr. Greenleaf, this is your dance." And then, to be certain he was unaware of any of the intimidation she felt in his presence, she took his hand and led him to the dance floor, just as she would have done with Bobby Fleming, or Henry Wilson, or the Brocksmith boy.

They danced smoothly together. Claiborne Greenleaf was as confident on the dance floor as he was in all other aspects of his life, but Elizabeth did not find him intimidating here. She knew the steps and she loved to dance, particularly when the music had the lilt of Strauss. Their movements were as fluid as the melody itself. She was lost in the moment. It was the only time since she had left Candida Custer's bedroom that she was completely without self-consciousness.

The next song was also a waltz. He didn't ask. He simply took her in his arms and swept her back onto the floor. She was disturbed by his aggressiveness, but the music calmed her as they made those giant looping swirls to its cadence. It was the soft lights and the music. This was the kind of enchantment that can come only to someone who revels in the rapture brought about by her own body moving in time with a lilting melody and a strong rhythm.

Then something happened. She was once again keenly aware of her surroundings and of Clay. She was no longer lost in the music. Something was different; something was wrong. The lilt of Strauss was still there, Clay was moving with her to the beat of the waltz, but there was a subtle change. His left hand held her hand lightly, their bodies were decorously apart. It was the proper position for this more intimate dance that was now so popular. But she was not under the spell of the music.

Then it happened again. This time she knew what had brought her back to earth. Clay's thumb had edged toward her bosom, it was stroking her bosom. On the dance floor, before a roomful of people, this bold, arrogant oaf was making an advance that she could not permit.

The thumb continued to move. It was as though her silence had given him consent. Making a scene was out of the question, but she had to bring the situation to an abrupt end without making all of the City of New York aware of her defilement by this ungallant bore from Philadelphia.

She was afraid her embarrassment might be apparent to everyone. She knew her face must be flaming.

The heat of the room was oppressive—the milling dancers, the warmth of the night. It was then she realized that heat was the key. She brought the handkerchief to her brow. "Mr. Greenleaf," she said in a clearly audible voice, "I do think I must find a place to sit. I'm feeling faint."

He said the only thing a gentleman could say in such a circumstance, "Of course, my dear Miss Medlock, of course." He led the way through the dancers as she dabbed at her face with the bit of lace in her hand.

At the side of the room, near the open double glass doors, he found two chairs. "There is a breeze here, or perhaps you'd prefer to go out on the terrace?"

"No, Mr. Greenleaf," she answered. "This will do nicely. I need to sit until I have recovered." She touched his sleeve.

"And will you sit, too, Mr. Greenleaf?" There was a smile on her face. Her tone belied the rage inside.

He sat on the small gilt chair beside her. Her smile was in place and the level of her voice was conversational. "We have had our first and our last dance, Mr. Greenleaf. I am sure you understand my meaning."

"But, Miss Medlock—"

"I'm not through, Mr. Greenleaf. There will be no discussion of what just occurred. But there will be no opportunity for it to ever happen again. The Custers are friends—Candida is my best friend—so I will be in and out of the house as has always been the case, but I can assure you I will not be here when you are. I will expect you, as a gentleman to abide by these conditions."

"Miss Medlock, I'm sorry if I offended you—"

"You did."

"Men and women, Miss Medlock, do accidentally touch each other—" He hesitated and then said, "Sometimes it is even done on purpose. I only—"

"Don't lecture me on manners or morals. Stay out of my company, as I will stay out of yours." She smiled at him as she stood. "I'm feeling better now, Mr. Greenleaf." She was obviously speaking for the people in her vicinity. "Thank you for being so helpful when I felt faint. If you will excuse me, I'd like to say good night to my hostess."

She walked through the ballroom, smiling and nodding to the other guests as she made her way toward the door.

Chapter Five

It was three o'clock the next afternoon when Elizabeth returned to the manse. She had spent the morning with a children's bible class. After lunch, she had shopped. As she opened the door she heard: "Elizabeth? Is that you?"

"Yes, Papa."

"Come to the study, please. I want to see you."

As she entered the room she said, "I'm surprised to see you, Papa. You're usually not at home in the afternoons."

"Sit down, Elizabeth. I have something to discuss with you." She sank into the leather chair opposite his desk. She thought Papa used the desk as a protective barrier when he talked to her. Their conversations, even when she was a little girl, had always been in the study, and always with him behind that expanse of oak, looking at her from over the top of his spectacles.

"I had a visitor this morning, Elizabeth. Young Mr. Greenleaf came to see me. He is quite a capable young man, with a good head on his shoulders, and while the rest of the world seems to be coming apart at the seams, he still has the good manners to call on his elders."

"I don't understand this, Papa. You don't usually discuss your business with me—"

"Well, this is not entirely my business, Elizabeth. It concerns you, too. But it is my responsibility to see you are watched over now that your mother is gone."

She just said, "Yes, Papa." When he started stroking his chin at the beginning of a conversation she knew he would get to his point only when he had laid what he called "the proper predicate." He was laying the predicate now.

"Clay tells me he has been living in Philadelphia with a maiden aunt, a sister to Lavinia Custer—Lavinia is a Greenleaf, you know. The family has holdings in the South, south of Savannah—large holdings. From what he tells me, they have several thousands of acres under cultivation, and several thousands more in raw land. Some of it, he says, they will still have to reclaim from the sea someday. Well, perhaps not from the sea itself, but from the marshes and deltas."

When Papa got to going like this, when he reared back in his chair, he could really drone on and on. She interrupted. "That's all very interesting, Papa, but Mr. Greenleaf's business interests are of no concern to me."

"Perhaps they are, my girl. You may figure into this."

"You're talking in riddles, Papa. I know you well enough to know that there is more you want to say. I also know that you are probably anxious to go calling on the sick as you usually do of an afternoon. I have things that must be done, too. There is a literary tea this afternoon. I must straighten my hair before I leave. So, Papa, can we have this talk later? I'm sure what Mr. Greenleaf owns and what he does is very interesting, but I'm the person doing the book review this afternoon. I'll be leading the discussion."

"You won't be going to a literary tea, Elizabeth."

"Papa!"

"You can send Hodges around with a note. I've made other plans for you, but let me hasten to assure you, my child, I was unaware of your tea when I spoke for you."

"I'll send Hodges with a note apologizing for not being at your appointment, Papa. Mine was the prior engagement."

"Elizabeth! I don't like your tone. You're being disrespectful and I will not tolerate it."

"I'm sorry, Papa."

He sat up straighter, shoulders back. She had seen this look on his face before. Whatever Papa had planned for her was to be the order of the day, that much was clear. In the end, she would, as he suggested, send a note of apology.

The Reverend Mr. Medlock pulled a large gold watch from his waistcoat, snapped the case open and peered at it. "Very well, Elizabeth, we can have the discussion later. But in the meantime, there is a certain minimum that must be said. I will be brief."

"I truly am sorry, Papa. I didn't mean to offend you."

"Tut, child. We will say no more of it, at least for now. I must tell you, however, that Mr. Greenleaf will be here at four-thirty. You will be going with him to another of his cousins in Gramercy Park where you will be taking tea."

"Papa! You did this!"

"I have given Mr. Greenleaf permission to call on you, Elizabeth. Now, quite evidently, you don't have the time or the inclination to hear my reasons, but the die is cast. You will be ready when he arrives. You are excused, Elizabeth. Go upstairs and do whatever it is you wanted to do to your hair, and you can prepare the note for Hodges to deliver."

"But, Papa—"

"You are excused, Elizabeth."

She tried to reduce the puffiness around her eyes by bathing them in a basin of cold water. The time she had been lying across her bed crying had done irreparable damage. She looked in the mirror. Puffy, splotchy and red. She had less than ten minutes before Clay Greenleaf was due.

She hated them both, but she hated Clay more. The trickery of it was all too apparent, especially after his behavior last night at the party. He had wasted no time in playing on her father's love of decorum to come to see him, formally requesting the privilege of calling on the daughter of the household.

"He's a bastard," she said aloud, "a bastard, a bastard, a bastard." She loved the sound of the word. Through the years, she had thought a great many bad words, but she never allowed herself to say them. But this time she said the forbidden word aloud, and it had a ring to it.

She heard the doorbell. Nan can answer it, she thought. Let him wait. If it were up to me, he'd wait forever.

She glanced in the mirror again. The face looked passable. The cool water had done it, but she dawdled as she dressed and ran the comb through her hair. This was something worked out between Papa and Clay. They could both wait.

She was more than a quarter of an hour late when she came down the stairs. It's a good thing Papa is gone, she thought. He would not approve.

"Miss Medford," Clay said as she came into his view. "I'm so sorry. I seem to have arrived a little early."

"No, Mr. Greenleaf, I'm late. But since this is an engagement not of my making, my own plans have been sent askew. I'm sure you understand."

"You've made your point, Miss Medford."

The atmosphere in the carriage was cool, although the afternoon was warm. The conversation was polite but stilted, and contained no more words than necessary, especially Elizabeth's part of it. In time, his attempts faded away.

One hour later they were on the way back to the manse. Elizabeth was lost in the rhythm of the horses' hooves. She was quite content to say nothing.

"Could we have a truce, Miss Medford?" he finally asked.

"Do you consider this a war, Mr. Greenleaf?"

"I'm sure you think I did wrong when I went directly to your father about calling on you, Miss Medford. But I'm equally sure I would never have had his permission if he had suspected I'd talked to you first. He would have been wary of me. Your father is old-fashioned."

"My father is from another century, Mr. Greenleaf. But I do not appreciate the fact that the two of you discussed my future as though I were not a part of it. That is despicable. While there is blame enough for you both, you truly deserve my scorn, Mr. Greenleaf, because you knew very well how hopeless the situation was between us after last night. It was a clever maneuver to go directly to Father, knowing that he would be impressed by your apparent suitability as a gentleman caller. You are devious, Mr. Greenleaf, that is clear, but you've made a tactical mistake. There will be no courtship."

He shifted his position. "My apologies, Miss Medford. You're quite right. I did try to slide past you. I knew I could impress him easier than you. The gambit failed."

"I'm glad you understand, Mr. Greenleaf. Perhaps there is a gentleman hiding under that roguish exterior."

"Then I'm forgiven?"

"Since this will be our last encounter, Mr. Greenleaf, and since you understand fully that I was not delighted with your gambit, as you call it, you are forgiven. When I say goodbye to you at the door, that will be the end of it."

She thought she saw that irritating hint of a smile on his face, but upon closer inspection it wasn't there. Then he spoke. "Do you think we can do it that way? What would your father think if I never called again? He might believe I had made improper advances, or that you had been rude to me. I did talk to him. I asked for his permission to call. If it should stop, there would have to be some sort of explanation."

She said nothing. "I'm only thinking of you, my dear Miss Medford. I agree with you. Because of my clumsiness, both last night and today, I've made even a friendship between us impossible, but I don't want to add to your woes."

He was right about Papa. Explanations would be required. She certainly would not tell him about Clay's behavior on the dance floor, and she didn't want to appear to be defying her father. If Papa agreed that Clay might call on her, he had given his word. Papa considered his word his bond. If she didn't see Clay, at least occasionally, there would be a need, indeed a necessity, for an explanation.

"As you always seem to do, Mr. Greenleaf, you have it all carefully planned. What is your recommendation?"

"Well, it seems to me, we are going to have to continue seeing each other. Remember, Miss Medford, I'm only here on a holiday before sailing to England. Our deception will be short-lived."

She looked directly in his face. He is such a charlatan, she thought, but he is also right. Papa would not settle for any kind of flimsy explanation.

"Given the circumstances, won't this be a difficult thing for us, Mr. Greenleaf, even if it's only for a short time?"

"We are both capable people," he said. "Of course, we will each have to give quarter from time to time, but we can do it. I know the low esteem you hold me in, Miss Medford, both for last night and for the maneuver with your father this morning, but my motives are pure now, I assure you. The only thing I want you to do is forgive me for the heartache I've caused. We will carry this off, and no one need ever be hurt by it.

"However, Miss Medford, if you can come up with a better plan, be assured that I will do my part—anything you suggest—because I truly do understand the burden, the hardship, I've brought upon you."

"You do the contrite act very well, Mr. Greenleaf."

"I'm sincere, Miss Medford."

"Oh, yes."

"Do you have a better idea?"

"No."

"Then, before we get back to your doorstep, what will it be? Shall we have lunch at the Cadbury House? That's a public place, but away from your friends. It would be safe from prying ears. You could be yourself. You would not have to pretend you like me, or even respect me."

"All right, Mr. Greenleaf. The Cadbury House for lunch. But," she paused, "we won't have to see each other every day, will we?"

"We will make it look right, that's all."

The carriage pulled up in front of the manse. Clay saw her to the door. "I'll be by for you at one, Miss Medlock."

And that is the way it began.

Elizabeth found Clay to be as good as his word. He was a gentleman at all times. There were picnics, lunches, boat rides in the park, an excursion up the Hudson; and there were dances, teas and parties.

In time, another element crept into the relationship, one Elizabeth had not planned. She found she looked forward to Clay's arrival each day. She had developed a new respect for him. There was more than just the look of a gentleman about Claiborne Greenleaf; he proved his mettle when he made a pact with her and kept it. There was no attempt at hand-holding and no unnecessary touching. But there was something new for Elizabeth. She was not aware of it at first, but she realized one day that she was excited by the pressure of his fingers as he helped her into the carriage and by his light touch on her arm as they crossed the city streets. If Clay felt the same kind of excitement, he did not show it. His face was always happy, but that is all she could see.

Early in the third week of their "arrangement" Elizabeth felt it was time for some changes. She was certain that Clay, because of her past behavior, would never suggest changes, so she would have to do it.

When he arrived to take her to still another afternoon tea at his cousin's in Gramercy Park, she met him at the door. "Come in for a few minutes, please, Clay. I want to talk to you."

In the parlor he produced a package he had been keeping out of sight. "I have something for you, young lady, something you've been wanting." He handed her a parcel.

"Oh, Clay, what is it? May I open it now?"

"Of course open it now. You could have done it in the carriage. But since you want to talk, let's take the time. We'll be late for the tea at Cousin Martha's. By now, she must be getting used to that. Isn't that how we started this little truce, being late to Cousin Martha's tea?"

"Let's not talk of that day, Clay." She removed the blue ribbon that held the wrappings, smoothed out the tissue and then snatched the book to her bosom. "Oh, Clay. Thank you, thank you. You can't know how I've wanted a copy of the new Tennyson. Our bookseller said he wouldn't have a copy of '*Morte d'Arthur*' until December. How did you do it?"

"Friends in England, my dear. I asked; they provided."

"I do thank you. It was such a thoughtful thing to do."

"I'm not the beast you first painted me to be."

"No, Clay, you're not. That's what I wanted to talk to you about. I don't know when we did it, it just seemed to happen naturally, but we finally managed to drop the Mr. Greenleaf-Miss Medford aspect of our friendship. You are not all I first thought you to be, although you do have an arrogance that is annoying."

"Arrogance?"

"Yes, arrogance, but forget that for now. I have something to say and you are making it difficult for me."

"I'm sorry, Elizabeth. Please continue."

"My suggestion is that we try to be a little more natural with each other. I promise you, if you should brush my hand in helping me with my wrap, I will not consider it a breach of our own special rules, or of etiquette."

As she spoke, she watched him. There was no sign of his knowing smirk. She saw the genuine smile of a happy man. He looked upward. "We are grateful, Lord, for small favors—"

"No blasphemy—this is Papa's house."

"None intended. I am grateful. I've done my best. It hasn't been easy."

"Then it's agreed." She hesitated, smiled and said, "If this change had been effected when you gave me the book, I would have kissed you."

"I'll antedate it if you will."

"Clay!"

"I mean it."

She stood on her tiptoes. He offered his lips, but she kissed his cheek instead. "And now, Clay, we'd better get on our way to Martha's." She took his hand and led him toward the large front door.

In the days and nights that followed, Clay and Elizabeth were seldom out of each other's sight. The new turn in the relationship was not lost on their friends. One day Candida Custer boldly said, "You have completely stolen our cousin, haven't you?" Elizabeth smiled, but said nothing. Clay had proposed and she knew she would marry him. She also knew Clay did not want a word of their intentions to become public until he had had a chance to formally ask for her hand.

On this point, Clay was as traditional as her father, so she kept the secret.

Chapter Six

Elizabeth made a point of being out on the morning Clay called on the Reverend Mr. Medlock to formally ask for her hand in marriage. When she opened the heavy front door, she heard her father bellowing. "Elizabeth, is that you?"

"Yes, Papa."

"Come to the study, please. I need to talk to you."

"In a minute, Papa."

"Now, Elizabeth! I have a busy afternoon. When I summon you, don't dally."

She put her parcels on the table in the foyer and went back to the study. "I'm sorry, Papa. My arms were filled with packages."

"Sit down, Elizabeth. I have something serious to talk to you about, and I want your full attention."

He leaned back in his chair. He always tried to appear sure of himself. He said it helped to build the confidence of his flock. It was apparent to her that he was not in full control. He tugged and scratched at his ear. "Where have you been? Nobody knew where you had gone?"

"Shopping, Papa. I went with Candida."

"I hope you weren't spending too freely, Elizabeth. We are budgeted. We have to be. You know that."

"I know, Papa. Candida did most of the buying."

"We'll have more expenses soon. That's what I wanted to talk to you about, Elizabeth."

She knew what was coming, but she dared not show it.

"You're not being very clear, Papa," she said. "You always talk in riddles when you're not sure of what you have to say."

"In time, Elizabeth." His pale blue eyes bore into hers. He was watching for any reaction. "Young Mr. Greenleaf called on me this morning. Did you know he was coming?"

"I don't keep up with your business affairs, Papa. I know when he's coming to pick me up; that's because it is always prearranged." It was not the answer to his question, but it seemed to satisfy him.

"He called on me this morning, Elizabeth, to ask for your hand in marriage. You two have been together more than a little recently so I'm sure this is not a total surprise."

"No, Papa, it isn't. I've grown very fond of Clay."

"A direct answer. I don't always appreciate your bluntness, Elizabeth, but this time I do. It makes me feel less guilty when I tell you I have given my permission for your marriage. He is of good family. He will make you a fine husband." His eyes strayed to the rose garden at the back of the house; it had been Minerva Medlock's pride. "Since your mother's passing I have no one to counsel with on matters of this sort. I'm not always sure I'm doing the right thing. "

"You've done the right thing, Papa."

"But this presents two problems, and I am truly not sure how to handle either of them."

"Problems, Papa?"

"Yes. He wants to publish the banns and to have the ceremony within the month, an incredibly short period of time. He must be in England next month. He thinks the journey could be a honeymoon."

"Yes, Papa."

"Such a short time."

"It can be done, Papa."

"It can, but it will set tongues wagging."

"It may, Papa, but the tongues will stop after they've counted to nine, just as they always do."

"Elizabeth!"

"It's what you implied, Papa. I just put words to it."

"Elizabeth!" He glowered at her and then said, "That's not the only problem. There's the cost of a proper marriage. I have some put by, but not enough, I'm afraid."

"What about Grandfather Burnside? He arranged with Mother to pay for my wedding years ago."

"No."

"But it has always been the understanding. Mother knew it; so did you."

"It was your grandfather's way of reminding your mother that she had driven her sheep to a poor market when she married me. I agreed to it when she was alive, because it made her happy. I will have no part of it now."

"Papa, you're being unreasonable—"

"That's enough, Elizabeth!"

"—unreasonable and vain. Vanity is a sin, Papa."

"You have your sins confused, Elizabeth. Perhaps I haven't taught you as well as I should have. I am being proud. Pride may be a sin. Pride, however, is not vanity."

"You're right, Papa, as you usually are, but it's pride, foolish pride. Your enmity toward grandfather, and his toward you, has caused many a heartache. Mother wept over it. When does it end? Can you teach forgiveness when you don't have it in your own heart?"

"Elizabeth! You've said enough."

"No, Papa, I haven't said enough. As you point out, Clay Greenleaf is of good family and will make a good husband. I see no reason why I can't have a socially correct wedding."

The Reverend Mr. Medlock turned red from the edge of his collar to his thinning hair. Elizabeth was defying him. He mopped at his face with a giant handkerchief. She could see determination in every line on his face. She waited. At last he let the air out of his bursting lungs. Quietly he said, "I will not take a penny from my esteemed father-in-law."

"As you wish, Papa, but have you the right to ask me to refuse the money for a proper wedding? Is this a father's prerogative? Grandfather Burnside may mean nothing to you, for whatever foolish reason, but he is my blood kin. He should have some rights here. So should I."

Her father looked away. She knew how long he could nurse a hurt and carry a grudge, but this was a point she could not afford to lose. Vanity may not be a sin, she thought, but I cannot hold my head up if I don't have the wedding Mother would have seen to if she had been alive.

Her father said nothing. He was slumped in his chair, absently picking at the hem of his handkerchief. She pressed her point. "Do I talk to Grandfather, or do you, Papa?"

As she watched, his shoulders squared and the florid color left his face. From an old man who appeared beaten, the Reverend Mr. Medlock arose. He made the room his again. "Your grandfather and I will work out the details of the wedding. You will stay out of it. Your grandmother will help you with the selection of your dress, but other than that, you will stay out of the details. Is that perfectly clear, Elizabeth?" His voice thundered the last sentence. It was very clear. She had won and she had lost.

"Yes, Papa."

"You are excused."

From the moment the banns were posted, Elizabeth's life became a merry-go-round of activity. There was one party or luncheon right after the other; there were fittings, showers, and, finally, rehearsals. She had only minimal conversation with her father.

Three days before the ceremony, Miss Matilda Greenleaf, Clay's Aunt Mattie, arrived from Philadelphia. She took a suite in Cadbury House.

The evening before her first meeting with Miss Greenleaf, Elizabeth saw Clay at a dinner. It was just the two of them in the sun room of the Custer house. Candida made the arrangements.

"If you don't meet with him now and then, Elizabeth, you'll forget the man you're marrying," she said. "I'll have it all ready—cold lobster on a warm evening."

When the serving people had withdrawn, Clay took her in his arms. This time she had no objection to his caresses. The past weeks had been exhausting and now she found comfort in his embrace.

"Oh, Clay," she said, "it's been a madhouse. I never have any time to see you, to really talk to you."

"It will all be over in a few days, my dear. But why complain? You wanted a large wedding. By cutting the time, I had hoped we could eliminate some of the social activities. But, the large wedding, wasn't that your wish?"

"No."

He lifted her chin to look directly in her eyes. "Well, yes, I suppose it was," she said. "But I'm not sure whether girls really want a large wedding or whether we're taught to want one. It's all we hear about, and, in time, it's all we talk about."

"Well," Clay said, "it's nearly over. In another three days we'll be at sea—just the two of us. That's what I'm looking forward to."

"Clay, that kind of talk."

"You know I'm right."

"I don't either. You men!"

"You women! When I held you, when you trembled, were you trying to tell me you were cold? On this hot afternoon? You are human, Elizabeth, just as I am. I've been keenly aware of it from the beginning and so have you. When you're married and more honest, you'll admit I'm right."

This turn in the conversation was not one that Elizabeth cared to pursue.

"We'd better eat, Clay. Cold lobster won't stay cold in this summer heat."

"My vote is to forget the lobster."

"Your vote is canceled."

When they had eaten, Clay said, "Aunt Mattie has arrived. She wants to see you tomorrow morning at ten."

"Oh, Clay, I can't. Can we make it some other time? I have a fitting at ten."

"Aunt Mattie wants to see you tomorrow at ten."

"I can't, Clay. Let me get my book. We'll find a time when I can meet her, and I do want to meet her."

"I'll pick you up at nine-thirty, Elizabeth. Wear something plain, please, and hold your tongue. Aunt Mattie doesn't like forward girls."

"Clay—"

"At nine-thirty, Elizabeth. Be ready. Now I must meet with your father and grandfather."

Clay and Elizabeth were shown into the suite at two minutes of ten. Matilda Greenleaf was a small, thin woman. A bird, Elizabeth thought, but not a helpless wren. She saw sharp, dark-brown, almost black eyes, that seemed to scamper everywhere at one time.

Miss Greenleaf sat in a high-backed chair with crimson velvet upholstery and golden arms and legs. Enthroned, Elizabeth thought, everything but the coronet.

After Clay made the introductions, Matilda Greenleaf said, "You may go, Clay. I'm sure you have better things to do. Come back at eleven to take Miss Medlock home."

Matilda Greenleaf's presence dominated Clay and the room. He left without a word. Elizabeth was surprised. She knew Clay loved this tiny lady from the way he had always spoken of her, but now one more thing was clear: Aunt Mattie was special, even more special than his brother Byron, who, by all accounts, was his closest blood kin.

"Please sit down, Miss Medford—across from me if you don't mind. I want to be able to see you. Coffee or tea?"

"Coffee, please, with a little cream."

As Miss Greenleaf handed the cup to Elizabeth she spoke. "Such a short engagement. Is that usual in New York?"

"It was Clay's idea. I declare, it will be the death of us all before it's over. He wanted our honeymoon to be his trip to England. I'm sure you are aware of the journey, Miss Greenleaf, since it has to do with family business."

"Yes," Matilda Greenleaf said, "but it seems to me a wedding could have followed that. Late summer is a hot and inconvenient time. Many people will be away from the city trying to escape the heat. It seems such a shame."

"Yes, ma'am."

"And that's the only reason, Clay's impetuousness." It was a statement but Miss Greenleaf's eyes made it a probe. Elizabeth was aware of the nature of it.

"Surely you don't think I can speak for Clay."

Those black eyes never left Elizabeth's face. She heard Matilda Greenleaf say, "I meant no offense, Miss Medford. I know my nephew. He can be so rash, so impulsive. He's never content with waiting for anything."

"Yes, Miss Greenleaf, I'm aware of those qualities in Clay, but I've managed to keep them under full control. Is that the question you are asking?"

Matilda Greenleaf held her with those sharp black eyes for what seemed to be minutes, and then she said, "I wasn't aware I had asked a question, Miss Medford. But since you've been so frank with me by volunteering information, let me return the consideration. I am very close to my nephew. I know he has difficulties keeping his high spirits under control, so I am not surprised when he comes to me with a problem that has arisen as a result of his indiscretions."

"If you don't mind, Miss Greenleaf, I'd rather not discuss Clay."

"But you are planning to marry him, my dear."

"His past is past, Miss Greenleaf."

Matilda Greenleaf made a ritual of refilling her cup. "The past is not past, Miss Medford; it is prologue. We are the sum of our yesterdays. Clay is my nephew and I love him, but there has always been more than ample passion in the Greenleaf men. Like his father, Clay has kept the cup of life full to overflowing, even when he was just a boy. You are going to marry him, my dear. You should be aware of what you are letting yourself in for."

"This is not the kind of conversation I expected, Miss Greenleaf," Elizabeth said with as much dignity as she could muster. "I thought you would want to know about my family."

"I know all about your family, Miss Medlock. You forget that Lavinia Custer is my sister. Your background was never a question, although you won't be bringing a great deal to the marriage other than that."

Elizabeth felt the blood rush to her face. She was surprised when she felt compelled to defend her father. "There is more to a person than his money, Miss Greenleaf. My father is a man of the cloth, not a man of mammon."

Once again Matilda Greenleaf pierced Elizabeth with obsidian eyes. "So," she said, "you have spirit. You will need it, my dear. Clay will not tame easily—if he tames at all." Elizabeth wanted to look away, but Matilda Greenleaf's gaze was stronger. She is having fun, Elizabeth thought. This is giving her some kind of inner joy.

"Are you asking me not to marry your nephew, Miss Greenleaf, or are you trying to frighten me so much that I will reconsider it?"

"You should be aware of all the circumstances, Miss Medlock. You should know that Clay can be a dissolute young man." Miss Greenleaf refilled their cups. "And, Miss Medlock, there is a second point I must make: You should be fully aware that our money comes from slavery, from plantation lands in the South. Slavery, I am told, is a subject your father has shown displeasure with in his sermons. If you become a part of our family, perhaps his tone will change."

"My father will speak his mind, Miss Greenleaf. He is a man of the Lord. If he had had another allegiance, I'm sure he could have acquired sufficient wealth to merit your admiration."

Matilda Greenleaf closed her eyes and stroked her temples with slender fingers. When she spoke again it was barely audible. "I did not mean to malign your father, my child. I simply want you to know what you're getting into. Think it over carefully. It may be difficult to undo all that has been done this past month—to make all the apologies, to return the gifts—but it's a minor consideration when you put it beside the hell of a bad marriage."

Elizabeth looked at those trembling hands, the pale skin tinged with blue veins. This tiny woman was not an ogre. She was a loving aunt out to protect her nephew. Elizabeth wondered if her own nerves were showing the strain.

"I'm sorry, Miss Greenleaf. I hope you'll forgive my argumentative tone. I'm sure you didn't mean any of your remarks the way I seemed to have heard them. It's just that I have become so very tired."

"Of course you're forgiven, my dear. The customs surrounding marriage can be barbaric, and you've had them all thrust into just a few short weeks. I did not mean to harass you; I meant only to ask you if you were fully aware of the life you will be going into."

"Thank you, Miss Greenleaf. Yes, I know life will be different, but I love Clay. I want to be accepted by his family. He is your beloved nephew. I hope that one day you will be able to think of me as a newly acquired niece."

"We'll talk no more about it, Miss Medlock. But you will think about it, won't you? My nephew is a man of passion and excess. And, of course, there is the problem of slavery and how you will adjust to it. Remember, my dear, there's no shame in calling off a marriage; there is only shame in going into one that becomes intolerable."

Miss Greenleaf busied herself with the tea tray. When Elizabeth spoke her tone was soft, but her voice remained strong. She knew what her plans were and those plans included Clay.

"I will think of everything you said, Miss Greenleaf, but, right now, I believe, without any doubt, that on the day after tomorrow I'll become Clay's wife."

Chapter Seven

Elizabeth was fortunate to have Candida to remind her of appointments during the two days preceding the wedding. For her part, Candida was already calling Elizabeth "cousin." It was, "Cousin Elizabeth, stop fidgeting while I lace this corset or we shall never arrive at Fiona's tea," or, "Dear cousin, your last fitting is this afternoon. Let's try to be on time. Mrs. Blodgett is the best dressmaker in town, and she is becoming quite vexed with you and your lateness."

However involved she was, Elizabeth couldn't help thinking of the warnings that Matilda Greenleaf had taken pains to plant. She had not intended to give credence to anything detrimental, but the words stayed with her. That Miss Greenleaf had called Clay "rash and impulsive" meant little. Such things could be said of any young man, but there were other words that stayed in her mind: "He has difficulties keeping his high spirits under control." And what did Matilda Greenleaf mean by, "problems that had arisen as a result of his indiscretions," or by, "the more than ample passions in the Greenleaf men"? She had also said that Clay had "kept the cup of life full to overflowing, even when he was just a boy."

These thoughts played games in her mind. At times it was hide-and-seek, and then tag or hopscotch. But they were not carefree, childhood games. Miss Greenleaf's words stayed—she remembered them clearly. It might have been easier if she could have forgotten them, but they were indelible. And then she remembered the final words: "You should be aware of what you are letting yourself in for."

Were these the words of a kindly woman giving advice to a young girl, or the words of a wicked old lady who wanted to control her charming nephew? From what Elizabeth had seen, Clay's father's sister was a powerful influence.

It would have been hard enough for Elizabeth to deal with the new perceptions of Clay, but there was the second thought: What about slavery? Ownership of one person by another was an abomination to Elizabeth. Her father's sermons were discounted; daughters have a way of taking little credence in parental ideas. Elizabeth was no exception. The anti-slavery speakers at the church may have added to her horror, but her real feelings sprang from deep within. It was difficult enough to continue to say "yes, Papa" until she married and left his domination; it was worse to think of what life would be like to have nothing but bondage for an endless future. How would you feel if you were bought or sold? Could you live with the idea of being treated as another asset, no more than a mule, and, perhaps, less than a good riding horse?

If only mother were still alive, she thought. I can't talk to Candida; she is Clay's cousin.

There had been only one opportunity to talk to Papa, an afternoon when she had a two-hour period between social activities. She tried to rest. Thoughts bounced off the sides of her brain. Rest would not come. She put on her dressing gown and tiptoed down to her father's study. She opened the door quietly and peeked in. He was sitting there drowsing.

"Papa? Are you asleep?"

"No, Elizabeth. I'm just taking this tranquil moment the good Lord has provided. You may be enjoying all this premarriage nonsense, but I'm not. My own duties have been given short shrift. I'm tired of it all."

"May I come in and talk to you, Papa?"

"Of course, my child. Come in."

As she sat, her dressing gown fell to one side. Her calf was exposed. "Elizabeth," he said sternly, "mind your robe. You're being indecent."

"I'm sorry, Papa. It was only my leg."

"Limb, Elizabeth. Chairs have legs, pianos have legs, animals have legs; people have limbs."

The moment for talking passed in that quick exchange. How could she have thought she might discuss her fears with her father? His compassion belonged to his parishioners. For his frightened daughter he had only the standard lecture, his ideas on body parts that must never be mentioned.

"Now," he said as he rubbed his glasses with his linen handkerchief, "what did you want to talk about?"

"It was nothing, Papa."

"Nothing? You came down here for nothing?"

"I'm sorry. Maybe I'm nervous about the wedding, Papa."

"A natural reaction, I'm told. I wish your mother were here. All of this on my shoulders. Life can be unfair."

It certainly can, she thought.

"Go back upstairs, Elizabeth. Lie down. Put a cool cloth across your forehead. You have a bride's jitters. That's all it is."

She said, "Yes, Papa," as a dutiful daughter should, but this time she was careful with the folds of her robe. As she climbed the stairs twin thoughts nagged at her. She wanted to be married, but was she ready for the man Matilda Greenleaf described? Secondly, could she live among people, could she be served by people, who were chattel?

The day of the wedding arrived. Elizabeth was up early. She saw the sun rim the silhouettes of the buildings across the way, and she watched as the night disappeared down the alleyways and into the crevices of the city. The sun shown on the raindrops clinging to the leaves outside the casement, and it was reflected in the golden puddles in the street. There had been a heavy rain during the night, and now the city was renewed; the dusts of yesterday, with all its problems, had been washed away.

She opened the windows. The fresh breeze smelled like the air she remembered when she and her mother had gone to Montauk Point in years gone by. What a wonderful day. This is an augury, she thought. My wedding day! The beginning of my life with Clay.

The storm had broken the summer heat the city had experienced for ten days. As it swept out to sea, it seemed to drag a pocket of Canadian air behind it. It was cool on this late August morning; the air had the first hint of fall. She considered this another portent, another good omen.

Yesterday the trunks for her journey had been packed and sent to the *Savannah*, the ship that was to take them to England. Candida had helped her to pack her trousseau, and suitable traveling clothes for the following day.

"I couldn't have done this without you, Candida. My mind has grown mushy. I just don't think of the things that must be done. With you it is just one, two, three."

"Nonsense, Cousin Elizabeth. You could have done it all, but it has been such fun for me. The idea of a holiday in England, two wonderful months—"

"Not two months," Elizabeth said. "Clay said we'll only have about six weeks there. Remember, we will be at sea for such a long time."

"No matter. You'll be gone on a honeymoon of at least two full months. Picking out the clothing you'll need, thinking of the places you'll go and the things you'll see, seems to excite me more than it does you."

"No, Candy, it's that whole idea of marriage that has made my brain go mushy. I can't do anything right. I can't even think straight."

"I want you to lean on me, Cousin Elizabeth, but I'm smart enough to know that if I weren't here, you would have packed just as well. You just wouldn't have had anyone to giggle with."

"Would I have remembered that my wedding dress would have had to be taken care of until my return? No, dear Candida. You thought of that. And I am so grateful to you. You are a dear, sweet friend, and I shall always be grateful. I'm a mush-brain, I tell you."

"I'm more than a friend, Elizabeth. I will, by this time tomorrow, become your cousin, and don't you forget that. I know I never will."

Elizabeth closed the lid of the portmanteau. She looked at her Cousin Candida. Tears formed in both their eyes. As they embraced, the tears flowed more freely. Were these tears of joy, or tears of exhaustion? They clung to each other sobbing, knowing somehow that what had been would be no more.

That was yesterday. The newly minted day outside her window was real. It was important: it was her wedding day.

Elizabeth opened her windows to their full extent. The cool morning air came sweeping in. It was refreshing. Even in the city, it smelled of newly mown hay and woodlands, The breeze was invigorating.

But, beyond the exciting emotions the breeze evoked in her mind, she could feel a chill. The wind coming in the window was cold.

Chapter Eight

Five weeks had passed since her wedding day. Elizabeth was in Cornwall, near the village of Tintagel, staying with her Great Uncle Roderick. Clay was visiting the textile mills many miles to the north. She resented being left with a great uncle she had never seen before, but Clay was firm. "You knew in advance that this was a business trip, Elizabeth. You planned to meet with your kin while you were in England, and I can't leave you alone in London. Now straighten up."

"I could go with you," she protested.

"You could not. The coast of Cornwall will be a healthy and safe place for you. I will hear no more from you."

"But, Clay—"

"No more, Elizabeth! As your father said, you're a most ungrateful girl. It's not everyone who would be lucky enough to have a cousin volunteer to come to London to accompany her back to Cornwall."

That was true. Two cousins had come to fetch her, Cousin Percy and Cousin George. With Clay's schedule, she had seen nothing of England since her arrival. The opportunity to follow the Thames as it wended its way west, the sight of the villages in Surrey, Hampshire and Dorset as the carriage headed for Devon, was an experience she cherished.

Her mother had often spoken of the hills of Devon and the coast of Cornwall, but Elizabeth had not been able to form the pictures in her mind. When her mother had said, "The hills of

Devon are a green unlike anything else in the world," she had marked it down as "mother's childhood memories, exaggerated by time and homesickness," but, as she watched the hills unfold outside, she knew it was she who had been in error. The incredibly green hills, the rolling pastures and fields—even the hedgerows—were so immaculate and so beautiful that they might have been a part of an imaginary world, not a part of the world she had left in grimy London.

Two days after arriving at her uncle's home, Elizabeth and her Cousin Nora walked toward the coast with a picnic hamper. "I'll show you my favorite place on earth," Nora said. "Others may know of it, but I pretend they don't. There's a cove, and, hidden down between the rocks, there's a place to picnic, or to lie on your back and watch the clouds pass over. My own secret grotto. Do you think all that sounds silly, Cousin? Am I more than a little daft?"

"You're not daft for that reason, Nora. Everyone needs a private place. I'm pleased you thought enough of me to invite me to yours, and I thank you."

"You'll thank me more when you see it. It's a place where the little people come on moonlit nights to dance across the rocks, and to pick wild flowers to throw in the sea."

"You are a romantic, Nora. You sound like my mother."

"How old was she when she left for the New World?"

"Eleven, I believe."

"She might have known my secret place."

"I suppose that's possible."

"Of course it is. I found it when I was nine."

They could smell the sea before it came in sight, and as they topped a tor, there it was, acres of glittering diamonds reaching to infinity, and below, down a fairly steep precipice the sea crashed in, lathering each rock with foam.

"Move carefully behind the gorse, Cousin Elizabeth. Mind! It could stick you. Its spines protect the path to my secret place. Robert the Bruce had a spider spin a web across the cave he was hiding in, and the enemy passed by without knowing he was there. Gorse is my spider. It hides my path."

Nora's secret place was a spit of land almost surrounded by rock—a place that truly might have belonged to the little people. There was an emerald green sward that sloped off to where the sea came in between protecting boulders forming a private bathing pool. There were places in full sunlight, and places where the overhanging rocks created cool shade. It was a peaceful spot where the quiet was broken only by the sea lapping at the stones of the bathing pool. In the distance Elizabeth could hear the crash of the surf as it pounded the unprotected shoreline.

"Thank you for bringing me, Nora. It is a special place. I'm grateful to you for permitting me to come."

"I knew you'd like it. I've been planning to bring you here. When George and Percy first brought you in, I knew you had been touched by the little people, just as I am."

"Oh, but we don't have little people in our country, Nora, especially not in the City of New York."

You do, Cousin Elizabeth. They are everywhere. They just don't show themselves unless they're wanted."

"Well, if you say it's true—"

"It is true, and you've been touched by them."

"How could you know that?"

"By the look in your eye. You are here, but, at the same time, you are far away. You left me as you stepped from behind the tower rock back there. It was the first time you saw the grotto I share with them. You knew it was special."

"Well, yes, it was breathtaking. For that moment I was with my mother. I wanted to ask if she had ever known such a place when she lived in Cornwall. We all have those moments when we are here and not here, all at the same time."

"All of us, Cousin Elizabeth, or some of us?"

"We all do. We suppress them—we may call them flights of fancy—but they are there even if dim or fragmentary."

"But are you ready to do battle when you see injustice? You do have those feelings, dear Cousin, or do I just imagine that, as well? The slavery in your country, do you think that is right?"

"There was once slavery here, too, Nora. It's a scourge that has been all over the world."

"Here? In England?"

"Yes, here. But it was banished long ago."

"Do you approve of slavery in your country?"

"Oh, no, Nora. I object to bondage. My father says it is wrong in the sight of God. On that one point we agree."

"You don't always agree with your father?"

"No. Do you?"

"No, but I never let him know. Father has little tolerance for objection."

"Fathers are like that."

"Are you glad to be married, so you can do everything you want to do without your father's objection? I will be. I'm not old enough to be married, but one day I will be."

"How old are you, Nora?"

"Fifteen and four months."

"About three years younger than I am, but they pass quickly. Since I'm an older married woman, perhaps I can tell you a few things you will need to know. You believe you'll be able to do anything you want to do once you're married. That, Nora, is simply not the case—at least, I've not found it to be so. Marriage can be a change for the better if you are lucky, as I have been, but you cannot do as you please, however desirable that may sound."

"But you came to see us. You were free to do it."

"True and not true, Nora. It is true I wanted to come to Cornwall to meet all of you, because I was curious about you, as you must have been about me before my arrival. But, dear Cousin, there was another reason. I came because Clay insisted that I be here while he was tending to the business of the estate.

He said I would be safer with my family than I would have been in the mill towns where he has gone."

"It was Cousin Clay's idea, not yours?"

"Well, not quite. I wanted to come later, when Clay could be with me. You'll meet him, of course, when he comes to fetch me, but I wanted him with me during all of my visit. Clay decided I should come here at this time, just as my father might have done. There is a difference, but it is slight. My point is, Nora dear, once you are married, there will still be someone who makes decisions."

"Then I shall never marry."

"Of course you will. I don't regret it for a moment. Clay is a handsome and wonderful man. You'll like him."

"But he has his way. He decides. You have no rights."

"Perhaps I'm not saying it well, Nora. You have rights. I'm sure your husband will listen to your wishes, just as Clay listens to mine, but in the end, he will decide."

"Then I'll never marry. I'll be like Madame George Sand. I'll write books, wear trousers, and decide my own fate."

"Nora, Nora, how you talk."

"I mean it."

"You'd better not let your father hear that."

"Oh, I'll be careful, but when I'm grown, when I come into the money from grandfather, I will be my own boss."

"In three years, or less, you will fall deeply in love with a young man, just as I did. You are at a rebellious age. So was I at fifteen, but you change when you fall in love."

"You don't regret marriage, even when you have just changed one master for another?"

"I don't agree with the premise of your question, Nora. Clay is not my master. He's my husband. A woman's place is at her husband's side. The Good Book says that. It says, 'Whither thou goest, I will go; thy people shall be my people.' What do you think that means, Nora?"

"And you don't regret your marriage?"

"Of course not, silly. I love Clay."

"What is getting married like? Were there many parties?"

"Too many. It must have been a beautiful wedding, but by then, I was too tired, too confused, to appreciate it."

"And your father gave you away?"

"Happily, I think. It has not been easy for him since mother's passing. I was rebellious, just as you are now."

"Tell me about the honeymoon, Cousin Elizabeth."

"Do you mean the journey to England? Oh, that was tedious. It took weeks, and I was sick most of the time. It was glorious the first day. The sea was calm. That was lovely. But the second day dawned darkly, and, for me, the trip followed the same dark pattern."

"You must have been delighted to see England?"

"Oh, I was. Clay says I'm a very poor sailor."

"No regrets?"

"None."

"Not even about what mother calls the carnal part of marriage? She's talked to me, and it quite frightens me out of my wits. That may be another reason for becoming the English version of Madame George Sand."

"But, dear Nora, George Sand has her Chopin. That is her choice. She is, as you say, independent. If she didn't want him with her, she would send him away. It's not unpleasant to have someone love you, Nora, or to hold you and caress and kiss you. I don't know what your mother told you, but the custom of marrying does not endure because it's abhorrent."

"I think it endures because it's a convenient way of making family alliances," Nora said quietly. "I think it's a way to maintain an orderly flow to money and property."

"You don't strike me as cynical, Nora. We need to talk more, but, at the moment, I'm starving. We walked miles over the moor. You brought me in behind your gorse screen and down to your secret place. Let's open our picnic basket. After we have eaten, I want to know more of this idea of yours."

They climbed down from the large flat boulder that had been their roost, and retrieved the basket. There was cold chicken, a slab of a pale yellow cheese, a loaf of crusty bread and a bottle of wine.

"Are you permitted wine, Nora?"

"There's milk there, too, Cousin, but I am permitted wine, on occasion, ever since my fifteenth birthday. This should be such an occasion, don't you think? It's the first time we have had a chance to really talk since you got here."

"Then we'll share. I'll have your milk with my bread and cheese, and you can have my wine with the chicken."

After the picnic basket was opened there was only the shriek of a distant sea bird and the water nipping gently against the rocks. They had both become quiet.

When their simple meal was over Elizabeth said, "All right, Nora, let me hear more of your theory of marriage. Is it yours, or is this a shared notion among your friends?"

"It's mine. But friends are a part of it."

"I'm not sure I follow you, Nora."

"A friend—she is a little older—is now engaged to be married to Bobby Wickingham. It's an arranged marriage, and certainly not the exception. I think all marriages are bargained down to the last ha'penny. This one is a business arrangement between their fathers. It's not a love match."

"You're sure of that?"

"Yes, fairly sure."

"Because you have an interest in Bobby Wickingham?" Nora's face reddened. "Does he also have an interest in you?"

"Well, I think so."

"Do you secretly meet?"

"Oh, no, Cousin Elizabeth. It's not like that. But I know. It's the way he looks at me when we pass."

"It's you he wants, not this other girl?"

"You do think I'm daft, don't you?"

"I said you were a romantic. I don't take that back."

"You think it's only in my mind, don't you?"

"I would never say that, Nora. I would never belittle your honest emotions. Who am I to say? My own experience is just as silly. I knew it was Clay the moment I saw him in my father's study, and he knew, too. But, to be honest, there have been other moments that seemed to be almost as vital to me. However fleeting and however one-sided these little loves may have been, I cannot say they were any less real. If you are daft, then perhaps I am, too."

"It's just as I said. You've been touched by them."

"Enough talk of the little people, Nora. We have been idle all morning. Papa had an expression about idle hands."

"Your father used an expression that fathers seem to pass around," Nora said. "I have a better one: 'Idle hands don't get dirty; idle hands don't break nails; idle hands are never chapped.'"

"I think I like all three of yours better, Nora."

"My father has two versions of his catechism. He likes to say, 'For Satan finds some mischief still for idle hands to do,' and he also says, 'Idle hands do the work of the devil.' Which did your father use?"

"The last one sounds like my father's version, but we've been here a long time. We should make our way back. Your mother is having a tea this afternoon. As the guest of honor, I must be there, and as the daughter of the household, you'd better be there. So, dear Cousin, let's pick up all the signs that say we've violated this sacred place, let's repack our basket, and let's leave the grotto to the little people. If there is a moon tonight, perhaps, as you suggested, they will dance across the tops of the rocks and throw wild flowers into the sea."

"I hate to leave."

"So do I, Nora, but life is not without duties, is it? On your feet. Let's leave the land of the little people. It's time to return to the real world, just over the moor."

Chapter Nine

They did not return to New York on the *Savannah*. Clay was late in coming to fetch her from Cornwall. Because of the rigors of an Atlantic crossing, all his reasons for the trip to England had to be accomplished. The likelihood of returning to England anytime soon was beyond comprehension. He stayed until all he had come to do had been brought to a conclusion. It took longer than he expected.

In London, Clay had told Elizabeth he would arrive at her uncle's on October 7 or 8. It would allow him time for a short visit with her family before the four-day journey to London to board the *Savannah* for the return trip.

October 8 passed with no sign of Clay. Three days later Elizabeth was frantic. "You're working yourself up, Elizabeth." Uncle Roderick said. "I know Clay's plans, but with the exigencies of travel it's rarely possible to maintain a schedule. You're worrying without cause."

"'The exigencies of travel,' dear Uncle? Did you not mean the 'dangers of travel'?"

Elizabeth watched. Indeed, he was like her own father, as Nora had said. This was her mother's uncle, but the reaction to a female talking back was a mirror of the Reverend Mr. Medlock. Uncle Roderick's face reddened. He reached for his glasses. When the lenses were carefully wiped, when his anger at the affrontive behavior of this snip of a girl had been brought under control, he spoke: "If I had meant dangers, Elizabeth, that is what I would have said. Travel is a fluid thing. A man must be able to decide the need for personal protection, or for a change in plans, and then react quickly. Had you been traveling alone I might well have used the word 'danger.' It is dangerous for a woman, or even a brace of them, to be traveling without a man along. That's why I sent Percy and George to fetch you from London. But Clay will have no problem. I understand he has interests in a part of your own country that is said to be still half wild. The South is said to be primitive, to say the least."

"But, Uncle, you sent both Percy and George to London. Did you not think the journey safer with the two of them?"

Elizabeth had become an irritation to Uncle Roderick. She was impertinent. Why would her father permit such latitude, even to a motherless child? He held his tongue. Soon her own husband would take her away. Poor bugger. She needs to be flogged. She will be happy to see Clay and so will I, he thought. Such an example of womanhood won't do in my house. Nora has already shown a kind of spirit that will have to be quelled or she will never make a man a good wife.

"Tut, my child," he said, hiding the anger he felt, "I could have sent either Percy or George. They are experienced travelers. Either would have been up to the task, wouldn't you, boys? I sent both because they've been too spirited lately. I thought the journey might tone them down a bit."

He changed the subject abruptly. "Have you seen the gray mare, Percy? Evans says she is having trouble foaling?"

"No, father, I haven't. Evans didn't mention it."

"Come then, let's go have a look. Come, George. We will leave the ladies to their sewing."

It was another full week before Clay arrived. Because of the delays, he wanted to leave for London the following morning, but Elizabeth was in no condition to travel. She had been so worried she could not eat. Aunt Esther had put her to bed two days before Clay's arrival.

"You're not helping yourself, my child. You must eat; you must do all you can to conserve your health. He will be here, bold as can be, never conceding that he has near driven you mad; and when he does come, it will not be with so much as an apology. You mind my words. They're all alike."

Nora brought cups of hot soup and herbal tea. "But you must drink it, Elizabeth dear. What good will you be to Cousin Clay? You are as weak as a new-born kitten."

When Clay arrived he was shown to her room at once. He looked weary from the journey, but it was clear that he was not happy to see Elizabeth in bed.

When they were alone he said, "You will get up, Elizabeth. I have arranged for my bath water. When I return, you will be dressed, and we will go downstairs for dinner."

"Clay, I can't. I'm too weak to stand alone."

"You are weak from not eating and from lying abed. If you can't stand alone, you will stand with my support. You will be going downstairs, my dear, and you will eat."

He opened the grip, selected clean linen and let himself out of the bedroom.

"Without so much as an apology," her aunt had said. How right she was. Clay was more concerned with getting to the port than he was with her frail health.

When he returned, Clay helped her dress. She clung to his arm in the hallway. At the top of the stairs Elizabeth felt a wave of nausea. Her eyes blurred. She tightened her grip on Clay's arm, and then the moment was over. As they descended the stairs, Uncle Roderick, passing through the foyer, stopped and waited. "You look lovely, Elizabeth. It is quite amazing to me how women seem to recover when their men are on hand. You should have been back several days earlier, Clay." He turned to Elizabeth. "In that rich color, you look like a violet in its full glory. You were a faded rose before Clay's return.

"Come with me. A glass of sherry will put the color back in your cheeks, Elizabeth, and it will wash the dust of the roads from Clay's throat. Traveling in such a dry season can parch a man. It takes a glass of sherry to revive him."

Uncle Roderick led the way to his library. They were joined by the two boys, and by Nora and her mother who appeared as if on cue, as though they had been waiting in an alcove. When he is around, she thought, they both change. They fade. Nora's exuberance is dampened, and Aunt Esther waits to see which way he moves so she can please him.

During dinner the waves of nausea she had been feeling continued. There were occasions when Elizabeth's eyes lost their focus, but each time the moment passed. She managed to eat, because Clay's eyes were on her at all times. If she did not eat, he would be angry. Elizabeth wanted to avoid a scene on this first night.

By the next morning it was apparent to Clay that leaving was impossible. He had Elizabeth awake as the sky was breaking out the new day, but when he asked her to fetch his boots, she had another dizzy spell, falling forward on the carpet as she bent to reach for them.

He was on his feet in an instant. He picked her up and carried her back to the bed. It was a very gentle, very solicitous Clay that was speaking to her as she felt the room taking shape once again. He looked very concerned. "Elizabeth," he said, "you're not—"

"No, Clay."

"You're sure?"

"Quite sure. I'll be all right."

"You'll have breakfast here in the room. Since you are not with child, then it's just weakness from not eating. We can remedy that problem. I'll see that you get a proper breakfast of hot gruel to line the stomach. Later in the morning you'll have beef broth. By noonday, you'll eat again. And I plan to get you outside in the fresh air. An animal wants exercise when it's weak. The same will do you good."

He was back in thirty minutes with steaming oatmeal, a slab of bread hot from the oven, jam, a piece of cheese and a glass of milk.

"Today is baking day," he said.

"I smell it."

"I've talked to the cook. The broth will be ready by ten. Come, my dear, I'll help you. Prop yourself up and together we will eat. I've managed some for myself, too. After last night, I could use a little rebuilding."

With Clay's help, Elizabeth walked in the garden and as far as the barns. She was tired, but the dizziness returned only momentarily. By tea time she had eaten breakfast, lunch, and three bowls of beef broth, always accompanied by a twist of the freshly made bread she had had for breakfast.

Three days later, on October 18, as the barnyard cocks announced the coming of a new day, Clay and Elizabeth left for Plymouth, a journey that would take a full day. Elizabeth had recovered, but her strength was limited.

The plans had been changed. When it was clear they could not make the journey back to London in time for the sailing of the *Savannah,* Uncle Roderick had suggested going first to Plymouth or Torbay to find a suitable sailing.

"If both attempts fail, Clay, not a great deal of time will be lost. You can go on to London. But if you can arrange for passage in either place, you will have saved yourself three days. At this time of year, the sea can be cold and treacherous. Your trunks can be sent along after you. We have business in London that must be done before winter sets in so the boys and I can see to the shipping of those things. Where did you leave them?"

"The trunks are with Robert Graeham, a solicitor we've used. I'll leave the address with you."

"Splendid. Put a letter in the post letting us know if you managed to obtain passage. Good fortune may be with you in

Plymouth or Torbay. We pray that it will be. The trunks may be long in coming, but you may be assured that we will see to them. Won't we boys?"

They said their goodbyes on a cold October morning. Their breaths turned to vapor, plain to be seen. Aunt Esther pulled her shawl closer about her thin shoulders.

Elizabeth leaned out the window to wave her last goodbye to her English cousins. Nora rushed forward. She handed her cousin a single smooth stone. "I wanted you to have something to remember me by, dear Elizabeth. I could think of nothing I had that you might want. Yesterday I walked back to the sea and found this."

"That's not a proper gift, you dunce," Uncle Roderick bellowed into the early morning stillness. "A rock? I do hope you're not insulted by this crazy girl, Elizabeth."

"Oh, no, Uncle. It's a very proper gift. I want to remember the coast of Cornwall forever, just as my mother did. Thank you, Nora. It's a most thoughtful gift. Now I'll always have with me a part of England and a part of you. Thank you."

The coach rolled slowly over the cobbles. To Plymouth, to Torbay or London? Elizabeth rubbed the smooth stone in her hand. Tears rolled down her cheeks. Was she crying for Nora, the new Madame George Sand? Was she crying for her mother, who would never again stand on the cliffs of Cornwall and look at the sea?

Or was she crying for herself?

Chapter Ten

They were two days out of Plymouth. Elizabeth found a protected place on the deck. It was October, but the sun was out and the sea was calm. What was it her uncle had said? "The sea, this time of year, can be cold and treacherous." You are wrong about that, dear Uncle, just as you are so pig-headedly wrong about many things. My stay with you was not long, but I soon learned that you were a man of one opinion.

"Ah, there you are," Clay said as he walked up to her. "I've been all over the ship looking for you. It's a fine day, and I'm sure the cabin was confining."

"I brought my mending out. I can see better here. That cubicle is dreadful. I didn't like the look of this boat when I first saw it. It's worse when you are on it."

Clay sat flat on the deck. His body leaned against the bulkhead. "One day you'll find something that suits you exactly, Elizabeth. I hope I'm there to witness it."

"I'm not complaining, Clay—"

"You're not?

"Well, yes, I suppose I am, but this boat is dirty."

"The *Savannah* is one of the latest motor vessels on the seas, remember that. This one may not be grand, but we were lucky to book passage on it."

"This one must have been a slave ship."

"It may have been, Elizabeth dear, but don't think a slave ever occupied your quarters. Slaves were kept in the hold.

Slaves were cargo. The more you could bring at one time, the more profit you made. You may not like the cabin, but it's much too good for slaves. And, my dear, it's a cut above some you'll experience as you travel south."

He watched her as he spoke. He knew: Before the journey from Philadelphia to Greenleaf Plantation, Elizabeth had to learn. The South is not all magnolias and sea grass.

"You mean we get stowed in the hold? We are cargo?"

"That may be putting it too strongly, my dear, but, yes, we are cargo. Coastal vessels haul merchandise and they take passengers, too. Passengers pay. In that sense we are cargo. You may find some of the coastal boats are more like slave ships than this one, Elizabeth. On some there are two saloons, two large rooms. One is for men and one for women. Only a few have cabins."

"Oh, no! Public rooms?"

"Don't carry on so, Elizabeth. Some passengers may be from New York or Baltimore and the journey could take several days, but most of the people using those coastal vessels are going shorter distances—just from one city to another, or from one of the islands to Savannah or Brunswick. You are making it sound perfectly dreadful, and it isn't."

"You'll be in one cabin and I'll be in another? You don't call that dreadful? There will be children, and vomit, and didies. Anyone can be rubbing shoulders with you. You don't call that dreadful? I don't understand you, Clay."

"Elizabeth, get this in your head. The rest of our vast country is not like New York and Boston. As your uncle said, some of it is quite primitive. We have two comfortable houses at Greenleaf, but they do not compare with Aunt Mattie's house in Philadelphia, or my aunt and uncle's house down the street from where you lived with your father. The newer parts of our land have few homes that would compare with those in the older cities, or in England. As we build in the South, we are not concerned with trying to outshine our neighbor; we are concerned with reclaiming the land, with putting it under cultivation. That costs a great deal of money. When we earn money, we put it back to earn more. We must take care of our borrowed obligations. One day, perhaps, we will be able to have the time and money to build fine homes, but for now, my dear, you'll see only a few of them, and they will be on the more established plantations."

Elizabeth's mending lay in her lap. She did not like what she heard. "Well," she said, picking up her needle, "that won't concern us. We'll be living in Philadelphia."

"We won't be permanently in Philadelphia, my dear. We will live at the plantation. However, it was my intention to leave you in Philadelphia with Aunt Mattie until Spring. That way, when you come down to Greenleaf it will be in good weather. You will have time to adjust before the journey begins. Aunt Mattie has made the trips dozens of times. She will be with you in those 'public rooms.' You will come to no harm as you rub shoulders with who knows what."

"Leave me with Aunt Mattie, Clay? In her home? Why can't I stay in our own home until you return?"

"Our home will be at Greenleaf Plantation, Elizabeth. When we're in Philadelphia, we will stay with Aunt Mattie. It's a large house. We can have private quarters. It would be foolish to have two homes. The cost of maintaining a place for only a few months of the year would be dear indeed."

"Oh, no, Clay! Not in her house."

"I don't understand you, Elizabeth. It will be easier for you. You won't have the problem of setting up a household. Any girl should be glad to escape such a chore, especially when she's a bride of only two months."

Tears formed in her eyes. "If I can't go with you, why can't I stay at Papa's until you come back to fetch me?"

"Stay with your father, Elizabeth? I had the distinct impression that you were happy to get away. Am I wrong?"

"No, you're not wrong. But which will be worse for me,

Papa or your aunt? She doesn't like me, Clay. You don't know this, but when we had our private talk—the first time I ever met her—she tried to get me to call off the wedding. She didn't want you to marry me, Clay."

"She was testing you, Elizabeth. She wanted to be sure you were ready for marriage. She doesn't dislike you. She did say you might be too young. When I see this cascade of tears, I wonder if she were not right."

"She dislikes me, Clay."

"Complete nonsense. Elizabeth, you're my wife. Start behaving like it. Perhaps we should have had this talk earlier. There are things you must understand. One of them is that Aunt Mattie is a permanent part of Greenleaf Plantation. She doesn't own it; she doesn't even own the house in Philadelphia. Byron and I own that, too. But she has a strong financial interest—she has a controlling financial interest." He got to his feet, brushed the rear of his trousers and said, "Come along, Elizabeth. The deck is not the place for a private conversation."

He walked to the cabin, not waiting for Elizabeth to get to her feet. She gathered her sewing together and followed.

"Close the door behind you, my dear, and put the mending down." He hesitated, unsure of where to begin. "Let me try to explain the complicated way my father arranged to have his sister, my Aunt Mattie, taken care of by Byron and me. Understand, we neither one object to this arrangement. We love Aunt Mattie. We believe our father was right in the way he protected her during her lifetime. She was his only unmarried sister. The way he passed the real property on was very proper. It's wrong to break up large holdings. When it's done, they tend to fragment and soon there is nothing."

"But if you and Byron own it, Clay—"

"We own it, Elizabeth—" He rubbed the back of his neck and then continued. "It's not a simple arrangement. Perhaps I won't be able to explain it clearly. The land is ours, but it's in a kind of trust. So long as Aunt Mattie lives, it's encumbered.

She is to have two-thirds of the earnings of the estate, and she is to have full use of the Philadelphia house. Two-thirds of the earnings is a sizable amount, Elizabeth. That leaves one-third to be split between Byron and me."

"Then we're not wealthy?"

"Did I say we were? The fact is, Elizabeth, Byron is able to live on his income. His wants are simple. He rarely leaves Greenleaf. But my desires have always been more complex. My income has never been sufficient. Since my father's death, Aunt Mattie has been generous with me."

"You are indebted to her?"

"No, not indebted. I don't actually borrow."

Tears formed in her eyes. "We are her dependents?"

"I wouldn't phrase it that way, Elizabeth."

"There's no other way, Clay. She has control. Until you—until we can get ourselves on our own feet we are chattels to the dollar—to her dollar. We are in the same position as your slaves, Clay. We are dependent on your Aunt Mattie. She seemed so sure of herself when she tried to dissuade me from marrying you. Now I know why."

"Aunt Mattie does not dislike you, Elizabeth. Get that idea out of your head. She doesn't know you, so how could she dislike you?"

"I believe I should speak plainly, Clay. There's no other way. I may know little of the world, but I do know women. I'm also sure I know them better than you, even though your aunt was quite clear—when she was trying to dissuade me from marrying you—that you had had more than ample experience with a variety of women. She did not call you a rake. She is much too genteel for that, but she managed to make her point."

"You're being ridiculous, Elizabeth. Perhaps what you're telling me is that you don't like her."

"How could that be, Clay? As you say, I don't know her."

"That's enough, Elizabeth. I don't like your tone."

"Then don't tell me she doesn't dislike me."

"Elizabeth! That will be quite enough. Your father said you were 'outspoken,' but that hardly covers insolence. Your uncle was more direct. He thought you needed a good caning."

"I don't think you'd do that, Clay, not on this ship. It's too small. The uproar couldn't be confined. You may want to cane me, but you won't. I know I irritate you when I persist in saying your Aunt Mattie doesn't like me, but she has spoken for herself, and no amount of caning will alter that. You're afraid I might offend Madame Pursestrings. You don't want me to upset the cider barrel, do you?"

His eyes lost their smile. They were bits of cold blue ice in a colorless putty face.

"I'll be out for a while, Elizabeth. When I return I'd better find the girl I married. I won't tolerate a shrew." He let himself out of the stateroom. The door closed quietly, too quietly.

When he returned three hours later he was reeling drunk. The odor of grog preceded him. He had vomited on himself, or someone had. The stench was overpowering.

Elizabeth's first thought was to leave him in his own squalor, but where could she go? The men she had known in her lifetime, Clay included, were prone to giving vent to their spleen when things were not to their liking; but women, living in a man's world through the centuries, had developed a more practical approach.

This stinky, smelly, vile piece of humanity would be spending the night in the cabin with her. So, with a sigh, she began to undress him, to bathe the spittle from his chin, and the below-deck filth from his body.

When that distasteful job was done, Elizabeth went on deck. She found a bucket in the storehouse, located the water supply and began the unpleasant task of sponging off his clothing.

As she worked, a tipsy deckhand strolled by. "He's sick, is he, Missus?" he said with a smile.

"I'm sorry, Elizabeth," she heard Clay say. He touched her shoulder. "I'm sorry. That was something you didn't deserve, but you have a way of stirring the fire with your words—you persist. You seem to delight in taunts."

It was early morning. She could see his face in the gray light of dawn. He did look contrite.

"It's a strange kind of apology, Clay. You say you're sorry, but you also say your behavior is my fault. Is it? You say I taunt you. At the risk of taunting you further, I must point out that your behavior, your self-control—or the lack of it—is something your wife does not mete out. If she did, she would not have had the pleasure of washing the stink off your body and the vomit off your clothes. I'll take my blame, but you must take yours. You are responsible for your own actions. If you can muster the courage for a dollop of introspection, dear husband, try doing it with a measure of honesty."

"I am sorry, Elizabeth. We must live with what is. There are things that we neither one can change. Aunt Mattie is one of them."

"I've been thinking, too, Clay. I'll do my best to live peacefully with her. You love her and I know you love me. Yours is not an enviable position. We will both try."

"Thank you, Elizabeth."

"If we can have a bedroom and a sitting room, then I should have a place that I can be myself."

"I'll see to it, I promise you."

She moved closer to him, her head on the curve of his shoulder. He stroked her hair. All the tension that was between them slipped away.

"And, Elizabeth, I think we should talk about one more thing. I know how you feel about slavery, but, believe me, you're wrong. I've read the tracts—I've heard the speakers. Forget all that. What they say is the purest tripe, as you'll see when you get there."

"Do you own the slaves? Can you buy them and sell them?"

"Yes, that part is true."

"Then it's not the purest tripe, is it? If you say the abolitionists are exaggerating, then should you be doing the same thing? Your statement, too, is an exaggeration."

"We treat our people well on Greenleaf."

"They are never mistreated, never flogged?"

"When it's required, yes."

"And who decides?"

"We discipline only when we must. When you have upwards of four hundred workers, you must maintain control."

"I have a hard time with the idea of bondage, Clay."

"I know, Elizabeth, but the system we have at Greenleaf is the only system that will work. Don't judge until you are there. They're happy; they're people who are taken care of. Without our help, they couldn't take care of themselves."

"Don't exaggerate, Clay, don't mesmerize me with words. I'll keep an open mind. I don't know anything firsthand, so I promise you I will wait before making judgments."

"One point must be crystal clear, Elizabeth: Whatever your personal feeling may be, slavery is a situation exactly like Aunt Mattie—it's something that exists. It's a fact. It's something you will have to live with. Perhaps you can even bring improvements to it. Maybe there are ways of doing more for our people than we're doing. All of us, every plantation owner I know, would be interested in that. Happy workers produce more. We're interested in—indeed we must have, with our debts—a great deal of production. We must produce quantities of cotton and rice or the whole thing will grind to a stop. What I'm trying to say, my dear, is that we are genuinely interested in the welfare of our people, contrary to what those abolitionists may say."

"I'll try, Clay. I really will. I'd like to see the profits soar so we could live on our part of the income, just as Byron is able to do on his. I have a small stipend from my mother's estate. That could go into the pool—"

"Your income, Elizabeth, whatever it is, will not be used by me. Your mother left it to you. It will remain yours. You may use it as you wish."

"But I could buy things for the house, extra china or silver. You wouldn't object to that, would you?"

If such things are required, and if Byron says we cannot afford them when you think you need them, you may spend your own money for such extras. But those purchases, those items of jewelry and china, or whatever it may be, will be yours and yours alone. You are my wife, and I will tend to your needs."

"If that is your wish, Clay."

"It is."

"Are there more things I must understand, or is that it?"

"That's it." He sighed. "I knew slavery was a problem for you, but now it's Aunt Mattie. We've resolved both."

"I have one more thing. It's been teasing at my mind."

"Let's get it out, get them all resolved."

"It seemed strange to me that your closest relative, your brother, did not attend our wedding."

"In time, my dear, you will get to know Byron. He is the most intelligent, the most caring, the most loyal brother a man could ever want. But Byron is an enigma in many ways. I grew up with him, but I don't understand him. He rarely leaves Greenleaf, by his own choice. He is content with his books and his writing. I don't know what he writes. He has never offered it to me to read, and I've never asked. We are different people, my brother and I, and we have the good sense to respect the differences rather than pick at them."

"You said he rarely leaves Greenleaf. Wouldn't his brother's marriage be sufficient reason?"

"If it had been, he would have been there. It's a choice Byron had the right to make. He had trouble with an overseer leaving in mid-season. Byron stayed in Georgia for the good of the estate. I respect his right to make the choice."

"An enigma he remains. You have not resolved anything in my mind. Perhaps I'll have to get to know him myself."

"Byron does not lend himself to simple explanation."

"I'm looking forward to meeting him."

"He is as shy as a deer, Elizabeth. I want you to be friends, but find your way with care, just as he will."

"I promise."

"Is everything now resolved?"

"I think it is—even your clothing, I should imagine. After I sponged them off, I hung them on the deck to air."

Clay slid an arm under her body. His fingers inched toward her breast "You wench. You had to bring that up again?"

"You're tickling me, Clay."

"That was my intention, my love."

"Is that all you think of?"

"You are my wife, Elizabeth. A husband has rights."

"And a wife has—"

"A wife is a wife."

Chapter Eleven

It was a cold, wet, and dreary day when Elizabeth and Clay arrived at 12 Haverford Place in Philadelphia. At three in the afternoon the dark clouds were already ushering in nightfall. Coal smoke from the chimneys drifted downward, and there was an acrid smell of sulfur. Lights were on in Miss Matilda Greenleaf's four-story brownstone, but it was too early for the street lamps. The word "gloom" came to Elizabeth's mind. A pall hung over the city, or was it her dread of the coming months? She glanced at Clay. He was irritated, but not from the gloom.

"You'd think someone would be watching for us, wouldn't you? Damn that George. He should be taking care of this for Aunt Mattie. He's been around so long he thinks he's the master of the house." As he spoke, the front door opened. A black man appeared.

"There's someone coming out now, Clay, someone to fetch us through this downpour. Is that George?"

"Yes, damn his black soul. Late as usual. I don't know why Aunt Mattie puts up with him, but she hangs on to George. He keeps tabs on the others. It's his only value."

George, at the door, glanced about, as though his gaze would slow the rain. When that failed to happen, he opened a large, black umbrella and walked around the pools of water standing on the cobbles as he came toward the carriage.

"Look at that," Clay said. "He steps as daintily as a dancer, lest he get wet. Well, I can handle that."

In time George was there. He opened the carriage door and said, "Welcome home, Mr. Clay, and you, too, Missus. We've been watching for you for Miss Mattie."

Clay stepped under the umbrella. As he did so, he pulled it out of George's hand. "Come, my dear. I'll get you safely inside," he said. "See to the luggage, George."

Near the steps, Elizabeth looked back at George, his livery dripping water. He had not expected Clay's abrupt action. He was still standing motionless.

"Clay," she said, "how could you? You left that poor old man standing in the pouring rain. He could have made two trips and we would all have stayed dry."

"I will not tolerate insolence, Elizabeth."

"He wasn't insolent."

"You'll learn, Elizabeth. They dare not be openly insolent, but they have subtle ways. I put a stop to it. He won't try anything like that again."

As they neared the door, it swung open. They were out of the weather. A young black girl spoke. "Miss Mattie is expecting you in the sittin' room, Mr. Clay. We glad to have you home. You, too, Miss Elizabeth."

Matilda Greenleaf's private sitting room was through the first door at the top of the stairs. It was a decided change from the weather outside. There was a coal fire in the grate, and the room was oppressively hot. Elizabeth glanced about.

Overcrowded, she thought to herself. Too much furniture, too little floor space and cluttered with every memento she's ever acquired in her lifetime.

There were matching settees on either side of the fireplace. Aunt Mattie faced the door. Her eyes lighted up at the sight of Clay. "Darling boy," she said. "I'm so glad you're here. We've had such miserable weather. I worried about you being at sea. A crossing can be so dangerous."

"We had a pleasant journey, Aunt Mattie. Elizabeth was ill on the way over. It was rough then, but now, when you would be expecting bad weather to set in, it was really quite nice. Wasn't it, Elizabeth?"

"Very nice, Miss Greenleaf, just as Clay says."

"Come in and sit down. I ordered the hot tea as soon as I heard the carriage. It's so dank out there. I'm sure you both must be chilled to the bone. You sit here, Elizabeth, with me. Clay can sit across from us, and we can both have the pleasure of looking at him."

"Thank you, Miss Greenleaf," Elizabeth said quietly.

"Well, Elizabeth, now that we're some kind of kin, I don't think you should call me Miss Greenleaf. Of course, Aunt Mattie wouldn't be right, either—that's reserved for the boys. So what will it be? Mattie sounds a little too familiar, considering the differences in our ages."

Elizabeth said nothing, but she was wary.

"How shall we do this, Clay?" Matilda Greenleaf continued. "I really don't like being called Matilda, even by my friends. It really is a dilemma. If you had not married, darling boy, this question would not have arisen."

"But I have married, Aunt Mattie. We'll just have to find an answer to your unsurmountable problem."

"I really do like to have you home, Clay. You always make me laugh. But, my boy, back to the question. What will Elizabeth call me?" She stirred her tea. "Perhaps Miss Mattie would be the best choice; that way we could avoid both Matilda and Aunt Mattie. How does that sound to you, Clay? Will it be Miss Mattie?"

"Sounds fine to me."

"It'll be Miss Mattie, Elizabeth. Clay has chosen."

The tea was without further incident. Aunt Mattie asked about the business in England. Later, a dried George, in fresh livery, appeared at the door. "Your luggage is in your rooms, Mr. Clay. There are fires in both grates. It is warm enough for you to go up whenever you wish."

Aunt Matilda took charge. "All right, you two, run along. The train from New York always leaves you dirty. I hate those ugly, smoke-belching things. It's all stink, stench and cinders, isn't it? And they clang so, don't they? But there's time to wash up. Clay knows, my dear, but perhaps he forgot to mention it, we dress for dinner at Greenleaf House—here or at the Plantation. You do have something suitable?"

"We almost didn't, Aunt Mattie," Clay said with a laugh. "The trunks are still in England. Our travel plans had to be changed. The trunks will come later. We were limited on the ship. As a matter of fact, Elizabeth had to sponge off one of my suits, didn't you, dear?" The smile at the corner of his mouth told her he was enjoying his private joke. "But after we got to New York, we were able to buy more. If I'm to judge from the bills, I'd say Elizabeth has something suitable, wouldn't you, my dear?"

"Yes, Clay, we can both manage."

"Dinner is at 7:30 sharp. Please be on time. You know how I am about that, don't you, Clay?"

Two bedrooms had been prepared for their arrival. One had been Clay's personal domain for years. His presence was evident throughout the room. The other one was more sterile. It showed no evidence of habitation.

Clay smiled. "This will have to change. I won't be sleeping alone. Aunt Mattie's ideas of decorum are not mine. Tomorrow we'll turn that one into a sitting room. We will sleep here. It's been my room for so long I couldn't be at home anywhere else."

"Her idea of decorum, Clay? I'm not so sure."

"Elizabeth, you said you'd try. It won't be long."

"I said I would, Clay, and I meant it. As far as 'Miss Mattie' is concerned, neither you nor she will see anything. But surely when we are alone I can talk to you? Surely you can see that what I said about her not liking me is not just in my imagination. We may become friends, your aunt and I, but, for now, there's a rift. I'm sure you saw it."

"Saw what, Elizabeth? We had the briefest time together. It was cordial. What are you talking about?"

Elizabeth turned and looked him squarely in the eye. "You mean that, don't you? You simply didn't hear the undercurrents, did you? Oh, Clay. . ."

"Elizabeth, Elizabeth, you baffle me. Not a cross word was spoken. Her welcome to you was not as warm, perhaps, but isn't that to be expected? I'm her nephew. She's known me all my life. You're a new niece. It would be unnatural to expect her to love you as she does me. She will, my dear. Give her time. She must get to know you first."

I do know her, Elizabeth thought, I know her better than you do, although you've known her longer. This just can't go on.

She said, "We need to have another talk, Clay. The first serious talk was because you felt it was needed. You said I had to understand a few things. You were right. This time you need to understand a few things. I don't expect you to turn against your aunt, but I do expect you to understand that your wife is not being unreasonable when she complains to you—in private—that she's being subtly mistreated."

"Mistreated? Elizabeth, my dear, you are fanciful. I certainly saw no mistreatment. None."

"Clay, please listen to me. When we came in the house, you mistreated George. You forcibly took the umbrella. You left him standing in the pouring rain. When I asked, you said he was being insolent. You said the servants could not be openly insolent, but they had 'developed subtle ways.' Those were your exact words Clay, 'subtle ways.'"

"Yes, my dear, I said exactly that. In time, as you live with them, you'll see I'm right."

"Whether you're right or wrong, there is a parallel here. If you can see the one kind of subtle behavior, perhaps you can see the other. I do not know what men do among themselves, but women, through the centuries, have developed this same kind of subtle behavior. The surface can appear as serene as a millpond on the hottest day in August, but underneath that exterior there are currents."

"I don't do well with parables, Elizabeth. If you have something of substance to say, then spit it out."

"All right, I will. The question of what I should call your Aunt Mattie now that we are 'some kind of kin' is an example. We're not 'some kind of kin.' I'm her niece by law, her nephew's wife. I'm not something impossible to define. She wanted me to know that I married you, but the relationship did not extend to her. It was subtle, but clear."

"Oh, Elizabeth, how silly."

"You can see George's insolence, Clay, and yet you can't see hers?" She searched his face for understanding. "No, you can't. All right. I'll grant that you didn't see it. I'll even say that I could have been too sensitive, but, all in the same breath, she got to the question of what I should call her. This time it's not a case of my sensitivity. She was direct, and she had the gall to make it all appear to be your idea. Surely you saw that?"

"I haven't the first idea of what you are talking about, Elizabeth. It was a natural question, and I have no quarrel with how it was resolved."

"It couldn't be Matilda, she doesn't like the name; Mattie seemed inappropriate, since I was so much younger; Miss Greenleaf wouldn't do, since I was 'some kind of kin.' She finally settled on Miss Mattie, and then she maneuvered you so that in the end she said, 'Clay has made the choice for us.' That was her choice, Clay; can't you see that?"

Clay sighed. It was as though he were speaking to a difficult child. "What difference does it make who decided? What's wrong with calling her Miss Mattie?"

"That's what the servants call her! You don't see anything wrong with permitting me—forcing me, really, since she made it appear that you had made the choice—to use the same form of address the servants are using?"

"No, I don't."

"Oh, Clay..."

"Elizabeth, my dear, it's a common expression in our part of the South. There are many older women, women I know too well to call by their husband's name. I'll say Miss Lucy, or Miss Ella, or whatever the case may be. Yes, Miss Lucy's or Miss Ella's servants will use the same words, but that does not put me in any lesser position. You simply don't understand the custom; Aunt Mattie does. No slight was intended. She would not stoop to pettiness."

Clay considered the conversation over. He began to remove his tie and shirt. "I suppose there's water in the pitcher. I see Clarisse has put fresh towels by the basin. I'm going to wash off this grime, and then I intend to lie down before it's time to dress for dinner."

Dress for dinner. The words brought to mind more of what dear "Miss Mattie" had said. She watched Clay soap his face with a cloth, running it behind his ears, and then over his neck and torso. Unconcerned, she thought. That big dolt can't see how adroit she is with the tip of her stiletto. She could hear the words again: "We dress for dinner at Greenleaf House, here or at the plantation. You do have something suitable?" It was meant to make her feel like a poor pastor's daughter. The cut was too subtle for Clay, but Matilda Greenleaf had made her point to Elizabeth.

When Clay finished, he headed for the bed. "Take the trousers off, Clay. Don't wrinkle them." As he removed his trousers, she said, "What are you wearing tonight?"

"I think the gray I bought in New York."

"Oh, the pearl gray. I'll wear something new, too."

"I want you to wear the violet, Elizabeth. The dress you wore at your uncle's the first night I was there."

"No, Clay, please."

"The violet one, Elizabeth. You had to be made to face the world then, and you managed. The same thing is true again.

You're going to live with what is, with what exists, my dear, and that includes Aunt Mattie."

He pulled a pillow toward his head. "You will wear the violet dress, Elizabeth. You may think it a hair shirt—perhaps it is—but you will wear it."

"Please, Clay," she began, but when she glanced at him, sprawled on the bed, his eyes were closed.

The subject was closed.

Chapter Twelve

The next day dawned crisp and cold. The wind chased the remaining scud across the sky. Clay was out of bed early. "Come on. Up. On the ready. There is no time to tarry. I've let the fire die down too much. I'll try to revive it. Aunt Mattie takes her breakfast early, and she likes company with it."

Elizabeth hated to leave the bed. The feather tick was so soft, so warm. As she moved, it made a special pocket for her. Great puffs of it rose up the sides of her shoulders and legs to protect her from the cold.

"Get cracking, Elizabeth, you'll freeze to death in that nightdress. I've nothing but a few embers to work with, and they're at the bottom of the grate. When you're dressed, I'll call for Clarisse. These ashes should be removed so the fire can be roaring before we come back up."

"It's too cold. I'd rather get back in bed."

"So would I, my dear. I'd warm you, in a hurry."

"Clay, watch those remarks. One day you'll say something in front of your aunt. It will embarrass you."

"It may embarrass you, my dear; it won't embarrass me. We have a special relationship. I don't pretend with her. She knows most of my past foibles."

"So she told me."

"Let's don't start that."

"Have you a preference for my dress this morning, dear? The violet one, or did I pass the test last night?"

"Sarcasm doesn't become a lady, Elizabeth."

"Pushing his will to the limit doesn't become a gentleman, either, Clay."

"You said you'd try, Elizabeth. Keep your word."

"Yes, dear husband, I'll keep my word."

"Then watch your tone. It has an edge to it. If you are very, very good, by nightfall you'll have a sitting room right next door."

At breakfast with Aunt Mattie that morning the conversation was more of a duet than a trio, but, Elizabeth had to admit, there was a good deal of family and farm business that needed to be talked about. It was a hearty breakfast. The bacon had an aroma that remained in the air even after the last rasher was gone.

Long before nightfall Clay had assembled a very comfortable sitting room. The red Persian carpet set the mood of the room. There were two matching settees, a tea table, and, best of all, near the windows, a magnificent mahogany desk. It was warm and friendly. Clay's choices had been perfect, but it was the rug that firmly established the warmth of the room.

When the servants were gone, Elizabeth kissed him and said, "You are such a lot of surprises, Clay. The room is exactly right. I'm so happy when I'm in it. You shall be the first to have tea with me. I'll ring for Clarisse."

After tea, Clay said, "This room is yours, my dear. For you, it's exactly right. My room is next door. Come, let me show you the charms of my special room."

She looked at her handsome husband. She watched the smile forming at the corners of his mouth. "You are a debauchee," she said.

"Come on, wench. It's two hours before dinner. I have a great billowy feather mattress. I'll show you how to destroy the smoothness of the counterpane."

Breakfasts were always with Aunt Mattie. Elizabeth was not specifically barred from the conversations, but she would not have been missed. A unique bond existed between Clay and his aunt. New brides tend to have a special set of jealousies, but, strangely, she felt no resentment.

Matilda Greenleaf was sixty-seven years old, but when she was with Clay, she seemed to shed the years. Elizabeth knew his aunt brought a steadying influence to Clay. He was not all banter. He could talk about the plantation, the overseers, Byron, the factors, with precision and clarity. Another thing Elizabeth realized as she listened was that his Aunt Mattie had a head on her shoulders. She understood the work and the finances of Greenleaf Plantation. She did not own it, but she was a strong part of it. She understood the plantation and the two boys. She knew their strengths and their weaknesses. As the days passed, Elizabeth learned to credit the intelligence and the power of Matilda Greenleaf.

After the morning meal, Elizabeth had time for personal correspondence and for writing in her journal.

She was required to meet all of Matilda Greenleaf's friends as they came to call, or came to tea, but she was not a part of all of the social activities of the household. Miss Mattie's friends, even the youngest of them, were at least a generation older.

Life settled into a routine. Elizabeth was able to tolerate Miss Mattie, even when the stiletto found the tiny slits in her armor. Miss Mattie could mask her cuts. They were never apparent to Clay. But when she was alone with Elizabeth, Matilda Greenleaf was more direct. Even so, Elizabeth had promised to try to keep peace and she kept her promise. It had become a matter of personal honor.

The routine permitted Elizabeth to take lunch in her room or with Clay, but dinners and breakfasts were with the lady of the house. Matilda Greenleaf's presence permeated every corner of that residence except for Clay's room and the red-carpeted room next to it. Living in Aunt Mattie's house was not easy, but Elizabeth had the intelligence to bide her time. One day she would have a home of her own, but it could never be this one. It belonged to Miss Mattie. It always would.

In less than a month the routine was disturbed by a letter from Byron. Clay had known the overseer for the rice island was to going to leave. His plan was to return to the plantation in early March to find another man for the job. Now the situation at the island had changed. The letter said that Jonathan Rigby had accelerated his plans. He had managed to find suitable land thirty miles upriver from Greenleaf Plantation, and it was his desire to leave to begin the work of clearing and putting his own holdings in order.

At dinner Clay said, "I think I should leave at once. It's unreasonable of Rigby to change his plans, but that isn't the point now, is it? We have a problem and it must be confronted. The sooner I arrive, the better it will be."

"But, Clay," Aunt Mattie said, "it's Christmas! Stay until the first of the year, stay for the holidays."

"Christmas doesn't mean much to me, Aunt Mattie. Rigby has convinced me there's no St. Nicholas here or at Greenleaf Island."

"Christmas means a lot to me, Clay Greenleaf, and it does to Elizabeth. Doesn't it, dear?"

She was being used, that was clear enough. But the unexpected bad news made Elizabeth realize she had not planned for the future. She had been writing letters and thank-you notes when she should have been conditioning Clay. She knew it was his plan to leave her in Philadelphia until May when she could come to Greenleaf Plantation with Aunt Mattie, but that was not her plan. When Clay left for Greenleaf Island, she wanted to be with him. So far, she had done nothing to convince him they should go together. Her failure to act had created an immediate problem. If she asked to go with him, he would refuse. Damn it all, she thought, why haven't I been working on this?

"Elizabeth, dear," Aunt Mattie said, "Where is your mind? You seem lost, staring into the fire like that."

"I'm sorry, Miss Mattie. I didn't hear you. I'm so upset by this news."

"So am I, dear, and I don't think you want Clay to start south before Christmas now, do you?"

"Oh, no—no, of course I don't." Such a delay might do it, she thought. It would give me time.

"You see, Clay, you simply can't go. The women in your life refuse to let you ruin their Christmas."

Clay appeared to be lost in his own personal turmoil, and then he spoke, "Well, I have some things I should do here and Byron sent along a list of items he wants from Philadelphia. I could buy them, see to their packing, and then leave later I suppose. But it would have to be as soon after Christmas as I could make arrangements."

"Clay Greenleaf, you stop that at once! What difference will a week make to this man? You will stay for Christmas, and you will stay for a New Year's ball I have planned, and then, after that, you can start south."

She turned to Elizabeth. "I hope you have some influence over this headstrong colt, dear. I don't. He hasn't thought it through. Rigby will wait. He agreed to stay until Spring and if he doesn't, withhold his pay! We have—the plantation has—some rights, too."

"I'll look into it, Aunt Mattie. I'll see what I can do. But this letter, this rush, makes it doubly difficult for me. I must go to Weldon. I have business there so only part of this journey will be by boat. Weldon is in rugged country, pines and scrub. So, it will have to be by train from Portsmouth to Weldon."

"Then you'll stay until the first of the year?"

"We'll see, Aunt Mattie. I'll look into it."

"Dear boy, you have made an old lady and a young girl very happy. The ball was planned so Elizabeth can meet girls of her own age."

The ball, Elizabeth thought, was planned on the spur of the moment in that keen mind of yours, but, whatever the reason for it, Miss Mattie, it will give me time to make my arrangements to go with him.

Clay was gone a large part of the days that followed. He purchased the things on Byron's list and he made a list of his own. He knew it could be a long time before he got back to Philadelphia. All the items on both lists were available through the factor, but the cost would be dear and the interest high. Where possible, as his father had done, Clay made every effort to make all the major purchases in Philadelphia.

When he was in the house, Elizabeth took pains not to be petulant about the things that annoyed her, not his shortcomings nor Aunt Mattie's. She was the soul of tact to his aunt. To Clay she was the courtesan that all men hope to marry. She had to be someone Clay could not think of leaving behind. Elizabeth had to watch her outspoken tongue.

She had to be sure her treatment of Miss Mattie did not appear artful, and she had to be careful not to let her romantic aggressions appear to be anything but pure passion he had inspired.

After romantic interludes, Clay had a tendency to want to lie abed, dreaming, dozing, almost in a world of his own making. In those moments, Elizabeth slipped quietly out of bed to punch up the fire and to take special care with her hair. When Clay came dreamily back to the world they shared, the room was warm and his wife looked radiant. This was one of the several ways she had devised to make herself indispensable to him.

As instructed, Clarisse advised Elizabeth each time Clay returned from his business. Whatever she was doing was put aside. She helped him off with his boots; she got fresh, dry clothing when he came in from the snow; she had hot tea ready with a measure of rum in it.

Elizabeth managed to bring all those changes into being with subtlety. Nothing appeared to be different, but changes were being made on a continuing basis.

It was contrived; she had to make Clay want her to be with him at all times. She must not be left behind. As she played the part, she found she enjoyed it. Clay was always a sensual animal and his erotic games increased with her participation. Her honeymoon, she decided, had not started on the wedding night, or on the day they sailed for England. It started with the arrival of the letter from Byron.

On Christmas Eve Matilda Greenleaf had a small party. The guests included two young couples of Clay's and Elizabeth's age, three more who were only a few years older, and three individuals of her own age, two gentlemen and a lady. It was a lovely dinner party for sixteen.

The last guest had said good night. At the end of a successful evening, the three of them were gathered in Aunt Mattie's private sitting room. The conversation drifted to Clay's journey. "I shall hate to see you leave, dear boy, but I know you must. I'm so much healthier when you're here. I'll not be happy, nor will Elizabeth, until the boat sails in the Spring and we'll be joining you at Greenleaf."

"I shall hate to see you leave," Aunt Mattie had said.

That statement jolted Elizabeth into gritty reality. She had almost forgotten that inevitable turn in their lives Clay's leaving could make. She had not broached the subject of going south with him, but Miss Mattie's statement brought instant panic. She had to act.

She heard the talk continue, but it was background. She did not hear the words. Her mind was racing. Each fresh approach to the problem she considered was found to be defective, or ineffective, and it was tossed aside.

"Elizabeth, my dear, where have you been? We were talking to you. I thought you were listening; you appeared to be, but your mind was elsewhere."

"I'm sorry, Clay. I was elsewhere. I was, at least in my mind, enjoying the lovely party tonight turned out to be. It takes a special talent to entertain well, Miss Mattie."

"Nonsense, girl. The trick to it is to invite people who are different, decidedly different. That way they will have something to offer each other. If you invite the same old people, they will have heard the same old things a thousand times before, and you have an insufferable party. Remember, dear, keep variety in your parties, and they will always turn out well."

"I will remember."

"Now, Clay," Aunt Mattie continued, "take this child to bed. She's tired. The party has been too much for her. Young people seem to need more sleep. Go up to bed, both of you. I'll stay here and watch the embers die."

As Elizabeth lay back on the bed, as the feather mattress oozed around her weary body, she reached for Clay's hand. She liked to touch him, or she liked to have him touch her. Going to sleep is an indefensible attitude, a time when you are vulnerable. With Clay next to her, his hand in hers or on her body, she was unafraid.

"Clay, are you still awake?"

"Yes, my dear. Drowsy, but still awake."

"When are we leaving for Greenleaf, Clay? Have you been able to make the arrangements?"

He hesitated before replying. "Did I hear you say 'we,' Elizabeth? 'When are we leaving?'"

"I want to go, Clay. I want to be with you. Four months alone is just too much."

"Elizabeth, Elizabeth, you know why I have to go. I don't want to be away from you any more than you want to be away from me. Our love grows. It's stronger now than it was when we married. It has the strength to bear up under hardship."

"You have to go, Clay, and I understand the necessity, but why can't we go together? Must I stay behind?"

"It's winter, Elizabeth. Travel is hard enough at best. In winter it's worse." He cleared his throat. "It's out of the question."

Elizabeth was quiet. She had heard Papa use the same tone. It was final. She had lost.

Tears poured down her cheeks. She made no sound. At last, one large involuntary sob racked her body, and then another and another.

"Elizabeth. What is it, my dear? What have I said?"

"You're leaving."

"I must, my dear, I must."

She pulled his arm next to her body and clung to it. "Oh, Clay, I can't stay here. I can't, I just can't."

"It's Aunt Mattie again. I thought that situation was getting better. I thought—"

"It's not Aunt Mattie. It's you."

"Me?"

"I don't want to be away from you, Clay—now or ever."

He was quiet. Finally he said, "You love me that much, Elizabeth? You would willingly go through the hardships winter travel will surely entail, just to be with me?"

He pulled her to him, his hand soothed her brow and stroked her closed, wet eyelids. "Oh, my dear, I wish I could take you. I want to be with you as much as you want to be with me. You must know that."

"Then take me with you, Clay. With you, I can endure whatever it is. Take me with you, Clay, please, please."

There was silence. Did he intend to reply? She heard him sigh. It was painful to hear. It told all of his misgivings. Then he said, "All right, Elizabeth. We'll go together. It's a foolish thing, but I'm as bad as you are. I want you with me. Heaven help me for being weak."

She snuggled closer, her head on his shoulder. "Oh, thank you, Clay. I'll be no trouble. I'll never complain. As we go south, the weather will be better, won't it?"

"Let's not talk about it, Elizabeth. I've said you can go. Now, no more talk. Let me have silence while I worry about the consequences of what I've done."

He kissed her lightly. "Go to sleep, my dear, but tomorrow, not one word of this to Aunt Mattie. She'll be sure I've lost my mind. In time, I'll think of a way to tell her of our plans, but let's not mention it now."

Chapter Thirteen

When the day arrived, Elizabeth was out of bed early. She was anxious to leave for Darien, but when she glanced out of the window, she was not so sure. The sky was overcast and the wind whipped debris up and down Haverford Place. She was seized by a chill, but she put on her robe, poked at the fire and soon had it blazing. What a lovely thing a fireplace is, she thought, even if it is only a coal grate and not a proper wood fire.

She kissed Clay awake. "Come on, love," she said. "It's morning. Today we take leave of this gray-looking city. We go south, where the sun is a constant companion."

He turned over. "No, Clay. As you so often say to me,'Up, my dear, on the ready.'"

"Go away, Elizabeth. The household is still asleep."

"No, dear husband. I've already heard noises from the kitchen. Even without opening the door, I can smell ham. Get up and wash the sleep from your eyes. Cold water will do wonders."

That was how the day began. After breakfast, after the dray was loaded, after their personal things were in the hack, after the tears of Matilda Greenleaf were shed as she watched them drive away, Elizabeth leaned back on the worn green velvet of the upholstery with a sigh. It was real. They were heading south. She didn't know how long the journey would take;

she didn't care. Soon she would have a house of her own. She would be in charge. It was the end of a dream.

The slow hack seemed to creep over the cobbles. For the first time, Elizabeth was aware of the bitter cold. It found its way through the cracks in the carriage. The soiled lap robe provided little protection from the bite of winter. She slipped off her shoes and tucked her feet under her.

"I'm cold."

"I remind you, my dear, you elected to travel south in the middle of winter. What did you say? 'I'll be no trouble. I'll not complain.' Well, Elizabeth, it's time to show it. Or, we can turn back and I'll go on alone as planned."

Elizabeth said nothing. "Don't sulk," Clay continued. "It's cold, but the train will have heat."

At their destination, Elizabeth's feet were numb. The attractive leather shoes she wore to complement her traveling suit and coat were no match for the winter. Clay left her on one of the hard benches inside the ticket office while he found the station master.

At last the train came in. Her feet had gone through several stages of recovery as life came back to them, and now the tingling was almost gone. She walked about the ticket office to get the blood circulating in her toes.

"Come, Elizabeth. Let's be among the first. I'd like to see that we find seats near the stove. It's clear to me that those shoes are not warm enough for this journey. We'll see what we can find, either in Baltimore or Portsmouth."

As they stepped into the railway carriage, a wave of heat and the smell of too much humanity made her wince. Elizabeth had been on other trains. She knew public conveyances could be untidy, but this one was filthy. Clay pulled her steadily toward a pair of seats he had seen.

When their grips were stowed, Elizabeth looked around. The seats were in groups of two facing each other. Across from Elizabeth and Clay was a woman and her three children. The woman wore brogans and a cloth coat that had seen too many winters. She clutched one of her brood to her breast as she fed it. The oldest, the boy, stared at her boldly; the girl, with hair streaming in all directions, a finger in her mouth, looked at the floor, while sneaking glances at Elizabeth on the sly.

The train started with a series of shudders and then began to move. Thank God, Elizabeth thought, I can't get to Wilmington soon enough. This car is awful.

As Elizabeth looked around, her disdain grew. More green velvet, even dirtier than in the hack. The seats were spotted with old food, grease marks, and evidence that someone had rested muddy boots on them on more than one occasion. Puffs of acrid smoke escaped from the pot-bellied stove in the center of the car. Up and down the length of it she could see baskets of food being opened. She smelled pickles, onions, boiled egg and nervous people.

"Your thoughts are showing, my dear. We'll find better conditions; we'll find worse. 'What is to be, will be.' That bit of wisdom is from the Good Book, I believe. Brace up."

"I'll manage."

"I'm sure you will, Elizabeth."

The train rolled on toward Wilmington, wheels clicking and with a mournful whistle sounding before each crossing.

The passenger car from Wilmington to Havre de Grace was cleaner and carried fewer people, but even so, Elizabeth found that she could maintain her own balance better if she concentrated on the countryside.

At times the engine would come to a lurching stop, the cars banging down the line, and then it would move forward again at a slow speed. The roadbed was either under construction, or being extensively repaired. Workmen waited as the train passed.

"We are a growing country, my dear, we build as we go."

"Don't make fun, Clay."

"I'm not sure it's a joke, Elizabeth. There's one place, farther down—" He stopped. "Well, you can see it for yourself."

"Worse than this?"

"Well—" Then he said, "You'll see."

"Don't play games, Clay."

"Be patient. You'll see it. It's before we get to Baltimore. That's all I'll tell you now. Later I won't really need to explain."

She continued to tease him, but he merely smiled.

Fifteen minutes later she grabbed his hand. "Oh, my God," she said. "Clay, I can't believe it. I can see the engine on a curve ahead. It's crossing the water and there's no bridge. I mean it, Clay, Lean over and look out there." The engine and several of the first cars were slowly crossing the water on tracks that seemed to be laid directly on pilings and little more. There were no sides to be seen, no bottom. "Clay, I'm afraid. We could fall into the water."

"I've been over it, my dear. It didn't collapse. It looks a fright, but I'm sure it's safe. Let me warn you, Elizabeth, when we're out there on those pilings, don't look out the window. I did. It's unnerving."

"I'd like to get out."

"Close your eyes. Lean back and relax. I'll tell you when we're on the other side. And why worry about it? There's a good side to it: Most of the bridges are better."

When they were actually out on the pilings, her heart almost stopped. Although Clay had cautioned her, indeed had warned her not to, Elizabeth looked out. She knew they would surely fall into those swirling muddy waters. At that moment, she almost wished she were back in Philadelphia.

Elizabeth did not look out again. With eyes straight ahead, nothing bothered her. She found refuge within herself. The children still played in the aisles; the smells were there; the potbellied stove still belched its gases; and the dreary day still forced its cold breath through the cracks. She didn't see it; she didn't feel it.

Clay understood, If she had looked—and he was sure she had—it would have appeared that the train was suspended in mid-air over those roiling brown waters. He had seen it several months before. He said nothing. He let her suffer. Finally, when he grew afraid that her fear had tripped something in her mind he said, "Are you all right, Elizabeth?"

There was a long wait. Then she spoke. He had to strain to hear her say, "I'm fine, thank you, just fine."

"You're sure?"

This time the voice was stronger. "Quite sure."

Much better, he thought. "Lot's wife was told not to look back, too, Elizabeth."

She did not reply.

In time they were in Baltimore, a forlorn city that appeared to be huddled along the waterfront, with grimy buildings clustered together, protecting and sustaining each other.

It was the first time she ventured a glance out the window since the incident at the bridge. Oh, dear, she thought. How can the men who plan railroads find the worst way into each city? The dead weeds of winter, the dirt and debris, are even uglier than Philadelphia.

As they neared the station, the train didn't seem sure of what it was supposed to do. It came to a stop. It backed up. It moved forward again. There was a constant lurch and a banging of cars. "Let's get our things together, my dear."

"I can't stand on my feet, Clay. Not with that mad man jerking us all directions. Must we rush?"

"There are only so many hacks, Elizabeth. We must move or we won't get one."

"You're irritated."

"Travel is never easy. If you make the best of it, you have to move. If you don't, you'll be left waiting. Now, on your feet. Hold to the seat if you must. You take the small case, and I'll get the two grips. Mind, don't leave your coat. It'll be as cold as a stepmother's heart out there."

The train came to a jolting stop, wheels locked on steel, making a piercing noise. She dropped the case to the seat. "That tears at my nerves."

"Damn your nerves. Move, or we'll be sucking hind tit."

She was behind him. "No need for vulgarity, Clay."

"It takes it sometimes, my dear, just to get your attention."

The next leg of their journey was by boat from Baltimore, down the length of Chesapeake Bay, through Hampton Roads, and then to Portsmouth, Virginia. While Clay went to check on the crated freight and their trunks, Elizabeth tried to make their cabin habitable.

It was small, with two berths, an upper and a lower. Even with the ladder, Elizabeth wondered if she could get into it. And if she could, what if she forgot where she was during the night? She could fall to her death. There were no facilities for washing—no pitcher and basin, no soaps, no towels. She was relieved to find clean linens on the beds, but the floors had not been swept. There were lint balls in the corners.

Clay returned. "Everything has been stowed below. This boat will take everything on to Darien, and Byron can collect them. I've posted a letter. He'll know what to expect."

"There's no pitcher and wash basin, Clay. Is there someone we could ask about this?"

"No, not on this boat, Elizabeth. They tried it. They had too much breakage. They only have the public rooms."

"Public rooms? And I had hoped to get some of the grime of that train washed away."

"What would stop you, my dear? I intend to wash up."

"But, Clay, public rooms!"

"We're traveling, Elizabeth. Stop being a millstone. There is no Clarisse here to heat water. Once and for all, you're going to have to live with what you have. You said you could endure hardships if I were with you. You said you wouldn't complain. That's all I've heard since we left Philadelphia."

"You're not being fair."

"The hell I'm not," he snapped. "Live up to your bargain, Elizabeth. I'm getting damned sick and tired of hearing you. Take a bath or stay dirty. It's up to you. But, whatever accommodations we may find on the rest of this trip, you will bathe or not bathe in what is available. No amount of your whining will change it."

"Are you through?"

"No, I'm not. Understand this, Elizabeth, and mark it well, in Portsmouth, we'll be back on a train and it won't be of the quality we've had from Philadelphia."

"Quality? Do you call those moving pig pens quality?"

"I simply want you to comprehend what we are facing. We'll be going from Portsmouth to Suffolk,Virginia, and from there to Weldon in the Carolinas. Rugged country. The best of the railroad's equipment will not be used on those barren stretches of scrub pine. I've never been to Weldon, but we *are* going there. Remember, my dear, you insisted on coming with me. So, for the last time, Elizabeth, I don't want to hear another word from you on your real or imagined discomforts. Not one word. You will live with what you find."

Clay stormed out of the cabin.

Chapter Fourteen

Elizabeth lay across the berth weeping. What a lot she had been given. She was a poor parson's daughter, married to an unfeeling clod. Little Cousin Nora was right. She was no more to Clay than a slave, a chattel. She was a handmaiden, a possession, just as all wives are. She was someone to pick up soiled linen wherever he took them off, someone to help with his boots.

He was handsome enough, but that rubs thin when you discover he has the same mean streak that all men hide until they're married.

The world belongs to men, she thought. If I had the income, I'd be another George Sand, just as Cousin Nora plans to do. Elizabeth knew her mother's trust was simply not sufficient for independence, not even in a garret.

She lay there indulging herself in misery. She played every scene that would allow her to be the martyr. What if she left Clay at the next port? The misery the thought conjured up was so vivid she was frightened by it.

Finally, she tired of the self-pity. There is always a bottom to the well of tears and the last time she lowered the bucket, it came back empty. There were no more tears. Now, she knew the truth: She was nothing. Nothing.

Elizabeth was worn out and dirty. She no longer cared what happened to her. A bitter review of the men in her life gave her a momentary lift, but it, too, lost its spark. How long can you revile Uncle Roderick, or Papa, or the vapid boys she had known in New York? How long can you spend loathing your own unfeeling husband?

She looked around the cabin on this none-too-clean coastal steamer. She smelled the sea water and floating garbage. She smelled the irrepressible odor of hot tar coming from dockside. The odors gave her a sense of her own reality. These smells, this dingy cabin, the lint balls in the corners, were real. Your situation, my girl, is real, too. You are here. This is now. You are in this, she thought, and it will be what you make of it—no more and no less.

Clay is not likely to change. The world belongs to men. It belongs to Clay. Power goes with ownership. He can be anything, do anything, and get away with it. You must conform, or get out and make your own life, in whatever way you can.

Elizabeth hated conforming, but she knew she could. She had done it for six weeks with Miss Mattie. She had done it with Clay. She was with him. It was proof she could do it. She would conform, even if it scraped away at her own person, even if it eroded the Elizabeth she knew.

Her mother used to say, "When all else fails, use your common sense, girl." Mother was right. It was a time for common sense.

She unpacked the grip, chose her prettiest nightgown and laid it on the bed. Then she collected what she would need for a bath, and went to the public room.

There were three private cubicles, with a matron in charge. Warm water was provided, and there was a small tub. If she were to make the best of what she had, the time to start was now. She began to undress. There was no soap. She knocked on the door. "There is no soap in here," she said. "Could you hand me some?"

"We don't furnish soap."

"I didn't know. I'll ask my husband to buy some, but I need a bath now. We came in on the filthiest train you can imagine. Don't you have any soap, even for such emergencies?"

There was a grunt outside. "Oh, please look around in the closets. I'll be glad to pay for it."

There was a knock on the door. The matron handed her a sliver of soap. "Here's a piece I found. Someone left it. It should do, my lady."

"My lady?" What had she said that might have offended the older woman? She could recall nothing. "Thank you," Elizabeth said. "I'm sure it will."

The soap had been on the floor. It was dirty, hair was stuck in it, and it had been stepped on. Nevertheless, she thought to herself, this is the reality of the moment, and I must live with it. She picked the strands of hair out of the soap, and washed off the dirt. She had to use the remainder carefully.

At the end of her bath, she looked for a towel. The only thing she could see was a used towel left by a former occupant. Elizabeth put it on the floor to keep down puddles, stepped to the door and knocked again. "I hate to bother you, but I don't have a towel. Could you hand me one, please?"

"There's one in there, my lady."

"Not a clean one. This one has been used."

"It's only been used once. You can make-do."

There was a finality to the statement. One more reality, Elizabeth thought. She picked up the towel, shook it, and began to wipe away the water from her body.

Back in the cabin, she brushed her hair. She could think of nothing that could have offended the matron. Had her unspent anger with Clay been in her voice? She wasn't sure.

She slipped a nightgown over her head and imagined what Clay would be like when he finally came back. She remembered the other shipboard argument when he came reeling back to the cabin. "Drunk, I'm sure," she mumbled aloud. As though he had been summoned by her remark, Clay stepped back inside.

"I see you've managed to bathe."

"Yes, thank you," she replied, "and from the shine on your face, so have you." He was not drunk. Thank God, she thought. The freshly scrubbed face was undeniably handsome.

"My body is clean, even if my clothes are not."

"I've unpacked the grip. Clean clothes will be no problem."

She hesitated, and then decided to say something that needed to be said. "I don't want to make a long thing out of this, Clay, but I am sorry about my behavior. I promise you, I'll not complain for the rest of the journey."

"Your apology is accepted, my love—if mine is. You were a nag, it's true, but I was short. Our first day of travel did not go well. We'll forget it. Let's pile into bed and hold each other close until morning. That's the way to ensure a better tomorrow."

"The berth is too small."

"We'll make room, my love. I don't intend to use that upper, and I don't think you could manage."

He pulled her to him. "I like the smell of you after a bath, Elizabeth." He kissed her lightly, and then he slapped her playfully on the bottom. "All right, now, into bed, and mind you, slide over to make room for your husband."

When she became aware of the world again, it was morning. Sunlight streamed in. There was the sound of a chugging motor, and the ship seemed to tremble. She stirred. Clay was awake with her first movement.

"It's late," he said. "It must be after eight. We were supposed to sail at eight." He was out of bed in a trice. He stood nude, as he looked out the small window.

"Put clothes on, Clay. You're not a pretty sight."

"I thought I was," he replied. "But all the same, I will dress. It may be bright and sunny, but this cabin is cold. Roll out, Elizabeth. Let's try to find a heated room on this ark, and there must be someplace to eat, too." She stayed in bed, with the bed clothing pulled up to her chin. "Up, my dear. On the ready. We've a nice day ahead of us."

After breakfast they found the two heated rooms for passengers: one for men and one for women. Elizabeth said nothing, but she gripped his hand a little tighter. He was aware of her wariness. "We'll go back to our cabin, my dear," he said. "We'll find our warmest clothes, and then we can stay out on deck, watching the shoreline pass."

"Thank you, Clay. I'd like that. Maybe later, after lunch, I'll work up the courage for that all-women room. I think it's barbaric that we can't stay together."

"It's one of those things to endure, Elizabeth."

"I know, Clay. I'll manage when the time comes, but this morning let's stay on deck to watch the bare shores of Maryland hurry by. It was thoughtful of you to suggest it."

As the hours passed, the sun warmed the earth, reflected from the pilot house windows, and outlined the stack. It glistened on the decks. The drab coastal vessel was not so bad. Yesterday was a trial. This new day brought only good.

The fresh air was more to Elizabeth's liking than the faint smell that permeated the cabin, so they stayed on deck. It was dark before the captain turned westward into Hampton Roads. They could see lights on either side of the vessel, and ahead, in the distance, lights of Portsmouth.

"The captain told me of a hotel near the railway station, Elizabeth. You should repack. We'll be late arriving—"

"And you want to get off quickly, among the first."

"Absolutely right. You'll be a traveler yet, my dear."

"I've a persistent teacher."

"And tomorrow we will find you some decent shoes. Then it's back to the trains for our overland journey to Weldon. Those slippers may be fine for Philadelphia or New York, but they won't keep your feet warm on a train. My boots will take care of me. We need to find something suitable for you."

"Not boots, surely?"

"Why not?"

"We'll see what they have, Clay. We'll check the stores in Portsmouth."

"There's been a change in you, my dear. Yesterday you would have said firmly, 'I won't wear boots.'"

"That was yesterday."

Chapter Fifteen

In the hotel room the following morning, Clay was up first. He sat on the bed beside her, put his hand gently on her forehead and said, "Up, my darling—"

"Not 'on the ready' so soon, Clay?" she asked, her voice still husky with sleep. "It can't be morning?"

"Oh, but it is. We have a train to catch and shopping to do. You need warm shoes before we leave Portsmouth."

Elizabeth turned toward him. She took his hand and held it to her breast. "Let's buy soap, too, Clay. There was none on the boat, at least not in the ladies' bath. I don't want that again."

She told him of her encounter with the matron. He thought the story was funny, especially the "my lady" part. "You can sound a little high-handed, Elizabeth. It was that grand manner of yours that first attracted me to you."

"Is that why you made me aware that you knew I was behind the curtains, with that cute little salute of yours?"

"I was never really sure you were there, my darling, but now I am." As he talked he got the corners of the coverlets in his hand, and then, with a yank, he pulled them off the bed. "Now, look at you! Half naked, lying there, trying to destroy the morals of an innocent young man."

"Give me back my blankets. I'm cold."

"You're not cold. You're just trying to stay in bed. Get up. Let's have another glorious day." As he spoke he grabbed an ankle and pulled her to the edge of the bed.

"Clay! Stop it. You're exposing me."

"True, true. I see a lot of leg under the muslin."

She laughed, remembering her father, and then, imitating his voice, she said, "Not leg, my son. Dogs have legs, horses have legs, pianos have legs; people have limbs." Then, in her own voice, she said,"That's what Papa always said to me."

"So I've heard, my dear, but they look like legs to me." He reached out his hands to help her rise. "No more nonsense. We have things to do."

After breakfast they found the largest store in Portsmouth. Clay said he wanted a warm, serviceable shoe for Elizabeth, but everything the man brought was no more practical than the shoes she wore.

"Look," Clay said, "It's winter. We're leaving this morning for Weldon. Then to the coast at Wilmington. I'm told the rail lines are not completed. My wife may be walking in mud to get from the train to the carriage. These slippers you're showing us simply will not do. Do you have boots?"

"Boots?"

"Yes, boots. Boots, like I'm wearing."

"No, sir. The ladies of Portsmouth do not wear boots."

Elizabeth was amused by Clay's frustration.

"Well, then," Clay asked, "what about a small man's boot? What do you have that will fit my wife?"

"Nothing, sir, not in a man's boot."

"Do you carry clothing for boys?" Clay persisted. "Surely you have boots, small boots, for boys."

The store owner sighed. "We have boy's clothing, but not boots. As you know, sir, boots are expensive. Around here, we have no call for boots—not for boys. They are just too dear to be scuffed around as boys will do. Most of the boys in these parts wear brogans, except for church, of course."

"Is that it, brogans?"

"I'm afraid so, sir. That would be about it."

"Bring them out, in my wife's size."

The store owner went to the back of the store. When she was sure he was out of sight Elizabeth said, "You're not serious, Clay. First boots, and now brogans? I'd rather have cold feet."

"Your feet are not cold now, my dear. You can be brave. I'll look at the shoes. If they're suitable, I'll buy them."

"You'll also wear them," she said quietly. She could see the man coming with several pairs in his hands.

"Let's try these. They look about the right size." Elizabeth allowed her foot to slide in the ugly work shoe. "Where is your toe, madam? Are these too short?"

"No," she replied, "the length is right."

"We'll take a pair, but one size larger. I also want four pairs of heavy stockings. There needs to be room inside the shoe for more than one pair of the woolen stockings."

The store owner looked at Elizabeth and then Clay. "Are you sure, sir? One size larger and four pairs of stockings?"

"Quite sure. Wrap them, please."

When they were on the street Elizabeth spoke. "Have you lost your mind, Clay? Brogans? Clodhoppers? They look like river barges. Do you expect me to wear them?"

"No, my dear," Clay replied, "I do not—not in your present state of mind. I'll pack them in my grip. When you think you might wear them, you may ask for them. In the meantime, I'll keep them."

"But, Clay—"

"That will be the end of it, Elizabeth. We will not discuss it. When you think you can use them, let me know. And now, my dear, let's shop for you. We need to find some sweet smelling and very mild soap."

They boarded the train on a cold winter's day, with high clouds stretching across the sky: blonde hair with a curl at the end. After several asthmatic wheezes, the train jerked its way out of the yard at Portsmouth. They were ready for the next part of the journey. The train was dirtier, older and more decrepit. On that point Clay was absolutely right.

As they headed for Suffolk, the land on either side of the train was swampy and dismal. The roadbed appeared to be the only thing above the black and turgid water of the backwater bog stretching through the trees into infinity. Why would people choose to live here? she wondered. And yet, at each spit of land that raised its head above the inky water, there were houses.

The land at Suffolk was higher. The town was a cut above the hovels she had seen in the swamps, but even so, it was dirty and unattractive. Farther away, she could see several handsome homes and a structure that could have been a court house, but the view from the coach window was so forlorn, she was eager to have the train in motion again.

In answer to her silent prayer, the engine puffed steam, and they were once again moving. Some parts of the roadbed looked fairly substantial, but there were parts of it that would surely disappear with the next flooding rain.

Elizabeth knew Clay was watching her. He expected another complaint, but she was determined to meet each new situation as it arose. She said nothing. Instead, she called his attention to the water lilies and to a pair of birds with snow-white plumage, but she said nothing about the train, the dirt, the smelly stove in the middle of the car, or the downright dangerous conditions she could see outside her window.

It was nearly six and already dark when they crossed the Roanoke River into Weldon. She was aware of the river only by reflections on it. She was glad it was dark. She was certain it was one of those bridges that were little more than tracks on top of pilings. She had seen two of them during the day, two small ones.

In Weldon, Clay took her to what was called The Inn. It was a grand name for an unpainted, weathered, wooden, three-story structure that served as a boarding house for the railroad men and also accommodated transients. Elizabeth was in their room when a black man came to light the fire in the fireplace. Was he a slave? She had seen several men and women in Portsmouth that might have been slaves, but she was not sure. She wanted to talk, to find out if he was unhappy with his lot, but she wasn't sure where to begin.

"Oh, thank you," she said, trying to open a conversation. "It is chilly in here. A fire will be very nice." The man said nothing. He continued blowing on the embers he had created, trying to breathe life into the fire. At last it caught. Elizabeth tried again. "Do you work here?"

"Yes, Missus."

"Have you been here long?"

"Yes, Missus." The pine knot was in flames. Satisfied, he moved it under the logs.

"Do you live here at The Inn?"

"Yes, Missus, behind it." He gave the fire another punch and left the room. She wasn't sure. Was he a slave or wasn't he? He didn't look bedeviled or mistreated.

Clay had come to Weldon to see a Mr. Bazemore, a man who said he had a better way to remove seeds from cotton. As soon as they got to town, Clay went to find Bazemore to see when they could discuss the invention. He was back within fifteen minutes. "I found him. I'll talk to him after we eat." he said. "If you need to pretty-up, Elizabeth, do it now. The meal will be served as soon as everyone gets downstairs." A bell sounded below. "That's the call to supper."

The dining room of The Inn was large. Food was already on the long table, and one of the men—one who had been on the coach with Clay and Elizabeth—was serving himself. A stern looking woman at the end of the table knocked sharply with a serving spoon. "In this house, sir, we say the blessing," she said. The offender said nothing. "Please sit, all of you," she continued. "I'll say the blessing and then you can get on with it. But, I declare, I don't know what is happening to manners. No one can be that hungry."

The hungry man who had reached for a chicken leg was in Elizabeth's line of sight. He grew smaller with every reference to his transgression, but he was not to be let alone. Elizabeth's head was bowed. She heard the woman begin, "Our dear Heavenly Father. . ." As the blessing droned on, it was clear that the woman of the house was an expert on sin. Within the body of her prayer, the hungry man's sin was cited, clearly and concisely. The sinner, it seemed, had to endure some of his suffering while he was still on earth.

Elizabeth did not enjoy the meal. The soup had been watered when the kitchen was informed of the extra passengers who would be staying. The fried chicken was scarce, and the ham, at least to her taste, was tainted. There was a platter of a kind of corncake, a hoecake, fried on top of the stove. Pools of grease formed at the bottom of the platter. It might nourish her body, but would do nothing for her soul.

After supper, Clay went to see Mr. Bazemore. Elizabeth joined the other ladies in the parlor, but the conversation revolved around quilt patterns and crochet stitches, so she excused herself at the first opportunity. In the hallway she encountered the same black man who had lighted her fire. She asked him if she could have some warm water and more firewood.

An hour and a half later Clay returned. "The Bazemore thing is a good idea, but it needs work. He'll send me a working model before the end of Spring."

He reached up to unknot his tie. "And, Elizabeth, one more thing. I talked to the men at the station. They don't know when the train will be in. When it arrives, they want to continue without delay. It could come in during the night. If it does, we'll be awakened. It's on the ready for both of us."

The tie came off, the shirt was opened at the neck. He paused, hunting for the right words. "There is still one more thing I should mention. I don't want to frighten you, but from here to the coast at Wilmington, the roadbed is not completed. We'll go as far as we can with a work train. That's all it will be, a work train. It doesn't pretend to be a passenger train. There will be one passenger coach. The rest will be camp cars for the men or cars for the tracks and timbers. Now, my dear, I mention this so you'll not be disturbed by it. It could be rather less than we have had in the way of accommodations. The workmen will be cautioned that there are ladies on board, but, even so, you may hear some rough language.

"There will be other women in the coach?"

"Yes, there will be other women."

"I'll manage."

"I'd hoped you'd say that, my dear."

He glanced at the bed. For the first time he saw what she had carefully arranged. There was Elizabeth lying in bed surrounded by clean white linen, her hair loose on the pillow, and her skin glowing in the lamplight.

He walked to the edge of the bed, leaned over and kissed her. "What a lovely scene," he said. "Being married to me is good for you, Elizabeth. You've grown more beautiful."

"And you take full credit?"

"Without question, my dear. I married a mousy parson's daughter. And now what lies in my bed? A radiant woman, eager for her husband's caress."

"Your pride continues to astonish me. You see a woman who has brushed the dirt and cinders from her hair, a woman who has scrubbed the soot off her face, and in the effort brought a little color to her cheeks, and you think it's because you decided to return from your night's prowling. It's more than pride; it's arrogance."

"A little arrogance never hurt, either, Elizabeth. A man's passion is an ephemeral thing. Who's to say what brings about the proper mix?"

"You seem to have discovered the secret."

"Did you force yourself to go to the public bath, my dear? Does mingling with 'who knows what sort' come easier the second time?"

"You don't like my sharp tongue; Clay, I don't like your sarcasm. No, I did not go to the public bath. Since I had soap, I turned the lamp low and washed here in the room."

"Without shades at the windows? You undressed?"

"I did not undress. I removed some things I washed up as far as possible and down as far as possible."

"And, my dear, did you wash possible?"

"I hate it when you're vulgar, Clay."

"Do you, indeed?"

"Yes, I do. You enjoy twisting things into something they were never meant to be, and you do it with a leer."

"Sorry if I offended you, my darling, but, so you'll know, I intend to shuck all my clothes and I'll wash everything that's possible—I'll do so, that is, if there is water here."

"*La bonne femme* has arranged for an extra bucket of hot water. It's near the fire to stay warm. It's for you."

"You took a bath, you put scent in your hair, you arranged for hot water for me, and now you pretend this is all accidental? Come on, Elizabeth. I'm your husband."

"Is that more of your arrogance?"

"No, my dear, it's my honesty. It's a pity you don't have more of it. I watched you as I took off my clothes, as I bathed. You enjoyed every minute of it. And, my dear, so did I. Women may like to be admired, but they don't have a corner on that market. I saw admiration, and I loved it."

He walked to the bureau where the oil light was placed. "And now, Elizabeth, I'll blow out the light. When I walk back to the bed, you will hold the covers back for me."

"Clay, your nightshirt."

"There will be no nightshirt."

Chapter Sixteen

Elizabeth could hear two sets of footsteps coming down the long, second-story hall, and the sharp rap on each door. "Clay," she said softly, shaking his shoulder, "do you still remember what you said about being 'on the ready'? Up, my darling. It's dark as a raven's wing out there, and cold, too." She shook him again. "Come on, Clay, out of bed."

"What time is it?"

"I don't know. Far from daylight."

In fifteen minutes they were following a man with a railroad lantern toward the station. The street mud had frozen, so the earth crunched beneath their feet. The cold bit at her skin. She wished she had not washed her face. It was beginning to feel tight and sensitive.

There was no fire in the passenger car.

"Stone cold," one of the men said as he opened the door of the pot bellied stove. "Ain't been a fire in there for days."

The men began to look for fuel. There was none in the car. "No planning, none at all," Clay muttered aloud as he left the car. "What in the hell were they thinking? No fire, no wood, no coal."

In a few minutes he was back with an armload of wood. "There's more near the station," he said. "A couple of you men get wood, and there's coal there, too."

Two hours later, with both wood and coal onboard, with a fire warming the interior of the coach, the train still had not moved. There was the hiss of escaping steam from time to time, but nothing happened.

"I'm going to find out what's going on."

"No, Clay, you could be left in Weldon."

"But, damn it, it's nearly daylight. They routed us out of bed in a hurry and we haven't moved."

"When you travel, Clay, you must be able to adjust to the conditions you find."

"That tongue is getting sharp again, Elizabeth."

"What's sauce for the goose is sauce for the gander."

"I'm going to find out what's wrong."

"No, please. You're going to stay right here."

There was a loud hiss of steam, the engine groaned as if in pain, but there was an arthritic forward movement. It was followed by another one, and another, until at last the coaches were jerked into a taut line. They were moving slowly forward. In the east a cold dawn was breaking, outlining the edges of the trees on the other side of Roanoke River.

From time to time the train stopped to leave supplies, but never for long. There was steady southward movement.

Six hours later, after passing through endless miles of piney woods, through areas where farms had been carved out of flat wilderness, after passing over many streams and creeks, after edging their way through swamps and bogs, the train slowed, puffed a couple of times and stopped completely. This was the end of the line.

The engineer walked back to their car. "Hey, in there," he shouted. "This is as far as the track goes. Everybody out. You'll be taking horse-drawn coaches from here."

Clay was at the door of the passenger car in a bound. "Where are the coaches? I don't see any."

"Don't know, mister. That ain't my concern. I was told to get you here. I done that. My job is through."

"We'll keep the ladies in here until the coaches arrive. It's too cold for them to stand around out there."

"Can't do that, Mister. I've got to move back a mile or two. That's where we're working. Can't waste time here."

"But you can't expect the ladies to stay outside. It's colder now than it was early this morning."

"It may be, but I got work to do. I want you out." And then he shouted, "Come on, now, everybody out."

"You're being unreasonable. We are your passengers."

"This is a work train, Mister. It ain't no passenger train. I told'em I didn't want no puling passengers, but they done it anyway."

"We won't move. My wife is not coming out of this car." Clay's statement was firm. The engineer looked him full in the face for the first time.

The two men eyed each other.

"I'll tell you what, Mister," the trainman finally said,"We'll make a good fire with some of them logs over there. When we have something to keep the ladies warm, you'll all get out, bag and baggage. How about that?"

"When are the coaches due?"

"I don't know. That's the yard's work, not mine. I'll get the boys to build a fire. You take care of the rest. But get this in your head, Mister, I'm moving this train back, with all of you in it or out of it."

Thirty minutes later the fire was blazing. Clay saw to the unloading of the passengers and the baggage, and the train moved back up the track. With one of the other men, he walked down the strip of log-covered roadway that would bring the coaches, but they heard nothing and saw nothing.

"This is a fine state of affairs," Clay said. "I told my wife there would be hardships, but I didn't expect anything like this."

"Didn't you know the line wasn't through to Wilmington?"

"Yes," Clay replied,"but coaches were supposed to be here to take us to the other end of the line, the one coming north from Wilmington."

"It's a bad situation."

"It'll be worse if some fool failed to line up those coaches," Clay said. "Come on. We'd better walk back. Mrs. Greenleaf will worry if I'm gone too long."

It was another hour and a half before the coaches arrived. Everyone was irritable. The fire, so cheery at the beginning, was now a source of additional rancor. You could warm your front, but your back got cold. Elizabeth made no complaint. She wished she had eaten her unappetizing supper. They had been herded to the train without breakfast. It was now nearly seven hours later. She was starving. How she longed for one of those greasy-looking hoecakes.

You could hear them long before you could see the six coaches, each drawn by four horses. When everyone was loaded and the baggage tied down, the journey began. Elizabeth could feel the hard boards of the thinly padded seat. There was no heat, but there were lap robes.

The road itself, she could see, was a series of logs, laid side by side over oozing black mud that seeped through the cracks. As the coach was pulled along, they would lurch forward and then be thrown backward. She felt momentary spasms of nausea, but the effort it took to hold on to anything you could grasp inside the coach took so much of her energies that the nausea was forgotten.

It was over a mile before they reached high ground. In the sandy ruts, the movement inside the coach subsided. Elizabeth leaned back. "Thank God," she said. "That was intolerable. Pray the rest of the way will be like this."

"I'm afraid, my dear, there will be more low spots."

"How many miles of this, Clay?"

"I don't know. The driver said they're taking us to Stantonsborough. That's all he knows."

From a relatively smooth road, they were back again on a roadbed of logs. The coach wheels creaked, the springs cried out in pain, but the horses moved relentlessly on. "Watch your wicked tongue, Elizabeth. Now see what you've done. We're back on the logs again." There were three more hours of this kind of travel.

Some of the road was almost good, some of it was tolerable, but most of it was bad, with mud holes and roots that brought single or multiple jolts. The worst parts of it were those log roads laid through the mires and swamps.

The coach came to a stop. The coachman opened the door for them. Clay helped Elizabeth out.

"This is it. Stantonsborough. Was the road too rough for you, Missus?"

"It was, sir. I hope I never have a ride like it again."

Clay turned to the driver. "You say this is Stantonsborough? Or is this just where we'll be staying?"

"This is it, sir. This is Stantonsborough."

Elizabeth looked around. There was no town, not even a village. There was no inn. She saw one lone two-story house, with a large barn and outbuildings.

A man walked up. "I'm Stanton," he said. "You'll be staying here for the night. I reckon you might want to wash up before you eat. You ladies go to the house. My wife will take care of you. You men come on this way. You can wash up at the barn."

Elizabeth went with the other ladies to the house. Mrs. Stanton showed them to a room, a part of the porch that had been roughly closed in. It had a shelf along one side, with a series of pitchers and tin basins. This was as near to a public bath as the house afforded. She had promised Clay she would manage—whatever the situation—so she said, "Come on, ladies, let's get some of the train's cinders washed away."

"No soap," someone said, "and the water's cold."

"I have soap," Elizabeth said. "We can each use it." She opened her case and took out her sweet smelling soap. "You be the first, Mrs. Hutchins. You have three children to look after."

"No towels," someone said. "Maybe we weren't expected."

"I'll ask for towels," Elizabeth said.

As she opened the door, Mrs. Stanton was standing there with a towel in her hand. She had been eavesdropping.

"Oh, thank you, Mrs. Stanton," Elizabeth said, as she took the towel. "We'll need several. There are eight of us."

"You'll have to share. I ain't got a lot of towels."

Elizabeth waited at the door. Mrs. Stanton brought back one more towel. "We will pass the towels, ladies."

When they were clean, the ladies went to the sparsely furnished parlor. It had bare floors and no curtains, but there was a fire in the fireplace and the room was warm. This is better than the coach, Elizabeth thought, and I can smell food. Thank heaven for the food.

As the men came from the barn, she could hear one of them curse. Someone quieted him. The accommodations at the barn must have been more primitive than we had, Elizabeth thought. It serves Clay right. He brought me out here on this wild search for a new kind of cotton gin. He could have checked the details beforehand and saved this dismal trip.

As the front door swung open, Mrs. Stanton appeared at the door of the parlor. "All right, ladies," she said, "let's meet the men in the dining room so the blessing can be said."

The meal was substantial, but not appetizing. There were three large pones of corn bread, a thin soup made of turnips, potatoes and dried corn, and a large dish of green beans unlike any Elizabeth had ever seen.

Clay sat on one side of Elizabeth, Mrs. Hutchins on the other. Elizabeth asked about the beans. "They are tasty enough," Elizabeth said, "but they seem tough. Where did she get green beans at this time of year?"

"They're dried," Mrs. Hutchins said. "I dry beans this way, too. You string them on cotton thread with a little air space between and hang them outside. When they get dry, they keep. To use them, you wash and soak them. These might not have been soaked long enough, but they're nourishing. My George likes them better than beans fresh from the garden, but most folks don't. They're best cooked with fresh pork, but salt side will do. We call them leather britches, but whatever they get called, it's just another chore to be done before winter sets in." Mrs. Hutchins looked at Elizabeth with an air of speculation, almost as though they hadn't been traveling together all day. "You must be a real city girl, Miz Greenleaf. I thought everybody knowed about dried green beans."

"I've a lot to learn, Mrs. Hutchins."

Elizabeth realized for the first time that food had to be harvested and stored when it was available. "And the potatoes, Mrs. Hutchins, are they dried, too?"

"No, darlin', you bury potatoes in a straw-lined pit, or in a cave with layers of straw in between. If you keep them cool and dry, they'll keep until spring."

"And the turnips?"

"The same."

"Oh, dear, so many things to—"

"You'll learn, Miz Greenleaf, if you need to. And you may not have to. George tells me you're going to a very large holding in Georgia, one with lots of help."

"I will learn. I want to do my part. If I'm to run Clay's house, I must know about all these things."

There was no fireplace in their room that night and it was cold. Clay brought two hot, cloth-wrapped bricks for their feet. The bedding was like ice. They huddled together. Chills wracked their bodies.

When they finally stopped shivering, Elizabeth said, "So this is Stantonsborough."

"It's as much a surprise to me as it is to you, my dear. I thought we'd find a town. But this," he hesitated, "this is just a dream of the railroad—a dream that someday a town will appear and there will be commerce."

"Whatever it is," Elizabeth said, "I'm glad we had a place to stop. My bones were aching, and, I declare, I must be black and blue all over. How much more of this, Clay?"

"At least another day. The driver doesn't know any more than that. He lives in Waynesborough. We change horses there and that's where we'll spend the night, he says."

"Waynesborough? Another mythical town?"

Clay laughed. "You are perceptive, my dear. That's exactly what Waynesborough is. I asked our driver. He said there are eight houses in the area, but not at Waynesborough. They're to the west, nearer the river. The drivers live there. They'll take us to what is called Waynesborough, take care of the horses, and then be on their way home."

"I wish we were on our way home, too."

"We are, my dear, but we're going the long way 'round."

"But after tomorrow we'll be back at the train?"

"Yes, Elizabeth. The driver says the next day we'll come to where the line comes north from Wilmington. We'll be back on the train at least."

The last two words had an ominous ring to them. Had he simply said "back on the train," she would have been happy, but she heard two extra words. "What do you mean, Clay? You said 'back on the train, at least.' What are you not saying?"

"I said more than I meant to say."

"What is it? What's wrong?"

"I shouldn't have startled you, Elizabeth. It may be nothing at all. It's just that one of the drivers heard there was a bridge out north of Wilmington. It's being repaired, of course, and it will probably be ready for us by the time we get there. I shouldn't have mentioned it."

"A bridge out?"

"There's been some flooding."

"I'm afraid of those bridges."

"Now, Elizabeth, don't be foolish. This may be just a rumor. I wish I'd never mentioned it."

"Clay, there are children—"

"Get hold of yourself, Elizabeth. Don't get hysterical. It's only a rumor." She started to cry. "Elizabeth," his tone was stern, his meaning clear, "you'll not mention one word of this. I can cope with your hysteria, but I won't let you spread this to the other women."

"It's the only fair thing, Clay. They must be told."

"Not a word, Elizabeth. Not one word. If you so much as hint at it, I'll do what your uncle says you sorely need: I'll take a cane to you."'

"You wouldn't."

"Don't put it to a test, Elizabeth."

Chapter Seventeen

By ten the next morning the carriages were well on the way down the road. During the night the low clouds of a few days earlier had moved back to the north. It was warmer and wetter.When the rain wasn't falling, there was mist.

"Look at it," Elizabeth said."Why can't it just rain and get it over? Heavy mist is unnatural. It's a wet shroud."

"Elizabeth," Clay said,"The day is dreary enough."

"I don't care. It's true, Clay Greenleaf. This day started out wrong. It's a shroud. It's an omen."

"Elizabeth!" There was an edge to his voice.

Mr. Hutchins had been temporarily shifted to their coach. One of his three children had become ill during the night so more space was needed in the Hutchins carriage. Elizabeth turned to him. "It's an omen, isn't it, Mr. Hutchins? First your child gets sick during the night and then this drizzle."

Mr. Hutchins, a red-faced man in his mid-thirties, smiled, but said nothing. Elizabeth persisted. "That boy was perfectly healthy. I helped with him while Mrs. Hutchins washed the other two. Why, he was the picture of health. And then to just get sick, with no reason—"

"Elizabeth. That's enough. Mr. Hutchins doesn't care to hear your far-fetched ideas. Let's have no more of it."

Once again, they were back on log roads. The jolting was more severe than it had been the day before. Elizabeth didn't like what she could see outside the window. They were in a bog, an extensive swamp. "The logs are covered with water and mud, Clay. How can the driver know where the road is? If we slide off the edge, we'll all die here in this mire, with snakes, and lizards, and leeches." She released her grasp on the framework of the carriage. She clung to Clay with both hands. "I'm scared, Clay. We're all going to die."

Tears streamed down her face, her skin was white and she seemed not to be breathing. What a fool he had been to bring her. Aunt Mattie had been opposed to it from the outset.

In order to hold and comfort Elizabeth, Clay loosened his grip on the side of the carriage. As he did so, the rear wheel of the carriage slipped off the log roadway. They were thrown violently into a corner of the carriage. She fainted.

When Elizabeth became aware of the canted carriage and the shouts going on outside, Mrs. Hutchins was with her. Clay and Mr. Hutchins were gone. As Mrs. Hutchins bathed her face with a wet handkerchief, she kept repeating, "You'll be all right, darlin', you'll be all right."

"Clay," she said, "where is Clay?"

"He's fine, Miz Greenleaf. He's helping the other men. They have to pry that wheel up. It would be better if we got out while they work. Are you able to stand? Can you do it?"

What must Clay think of her? Elizabeth said she could cope, but she had failed. She straightened her shoulders. "I'm fine, Mrs. Hutchins. If we ought to be outside while they lift the carriage, we'll be outside."

"Don't try to get out by yourself, child. That side's too high. The other wheel's buried in mud. I'll get help." Mrs. Hutchins stuck her head out the window and called, "Come here, George. Come over here and help us down."

Mr. Hutchins had not been far away. When she found the step with her foot he said, "All right, now, Miz Greenleaf, when you feel my hands on your waist, just ease back." His fingers were too high, but eventually they found her waist and she was lifted to the ground. She should have been grateful for his help, but she couldn't bring herself to thank him She was glad to have his hands off her body. As quickly as she had her footing, she walked back to a dry spot on the road. She was joined by Mrs. Hutchins. "I'm glad you're feeling better, child. I didn't want to be in the carriage when they tried to lift it, beating those horses and all."

Elizabeth watched the men fit the pine pole under the carriage. On a signal from the driver, the men pulled down on the end of the pole causing the other end of the fulcrum to rise. As this was done, the driver, shouting and cursing, lashed at the horses with a whip. After a momentary hesitation, the carriage lurched forward onto the log roadway.

In another five minutes everyone was back in the carriages. The caravan moved forward. Clay's boots were covered with a thin, drying layer of mud and his trousers were wet to the knees. The swamp water, stained the color of strong tea, was clearly evident on his trousers.

Within half an hour they stopped again. A man from the lead carriage shouted, "You'll have to get out here folks. The bridge over the Neuse was damaged in the last rain. It's safe enough, I reckon, but we ain't goin' to take no chances. We'll walk across the bridge in groups of four or five, and then when everyone's on the other side, the boys will bring the coaches over, one by one. So get out here folks, and start walking toward the river."

Clay helped Elizabeth down. She chose her way carefully, trying to do no more damage to her shoes than she already had.

The wind had shifted and had a bite to it. It got colder as the sky cleared. Elizabeth's feet were wet and so cold walking was difficult, but she said nothing. It would give Clay too much satisfaction. His comments about her shoes and his purchase of the brogans was still a bright memory.

Elizabeth, Clay and Mr. Hutchins stood at the end of the bridge waiting to walk across. At last their turn came. As they moved away from the protection of the trees, the winds grew more intense. With the sun out, she thought, how could it get colder? But minute by minute the temperature dropped.

"Watch it, Elizabeth. Be careful. We don't want to have to fish you out of that cold water." Clay gripped her arm firmly. "Would you mind, Hutchins? Elizabeth doesn't seem too sure of her footing. Would you take her other arm?"

Elizabeth felt more secure, even though Mr. Hutchins' hand pushed against her ribcage. She would have asked him to remove it, but she could see the muddy waters below. Making a scene would anger Clay, since he had asked Hutchins to assist. Even with support, her cold feet were not functioning well. Out in the middle of the Neuse, away from the shore, the wind seemed to sing its icy blast.

As they neared land on the other side, she heard the first of the carriages being brought on the bridge. Thank God, she thought. I'll welcome the carriage—hard seats and all—and I'll ask Clay for the shoes. I cannot let my feet get worse, not when it's only a matter of pride.

Because of the sudden change in temperature, the ladies were permitted to get into the coaches as they arrived. Elizabeth was helped into the second arrival, because Mrs. Hutchins saw her pain. She was no more than ten years older than Elizabeth, but she was a full-figured woman with a motherly air.

When they had crowded in the carriage Mrs. Hutchins said, "Take off your shoes, Miz Greenleaf, and slide your feet behind me. You're chilled. I'm warm enough, I'm used to this weather, but I know what frozen feet can be."

Elizabeth hesitated.

"Come on now, Miz Greenleaf. Don't worry about custom. You've got to warm those feet. You need to put on warmer shoes. You have other shoes, don't you?"

Elizabeth blushed."Well, yes, Mrs. Hutchins, I do. A day or two ago, in Portsmouth, Clay bought me a pair brogans and several pairs of woolen stockings. I wouldn't wear them, but now— Well, it's time to swallow my pride, isn't it?"

"Pride ain't much good for cold feet, Miz Greenleaf;" Mrs. Hutchins said. "It ain't much good for anything else, either."

Their carriage arrived and Clay came to fetch her. "Her feet are in bad shape, Mr. Greenleaf," Mrs. Hutchins said. "We can't get these wet slippers back on her. You'd better carry her to your coach. She's just a slip of a girl anyway."

With Clay carrying her, they were the object of everyone's attention. "A pretty spectacle, Elizabeth. All because of those stupid shoes of yours."

"I'm sorry, Clay. It's an embarrassment for you."

"It's worse. It shows I have a stupid wife. There's no room for stupidity out in the country, Elizabeth. That's where you'll be living. It's over an hour by boat from Greenleaf to Darien. It's time you begin to face the facts."

"I'll wear the brogans, Clay, and the stockings."

"You don't have brogans, Elizabeth."

"The brogans are in your grip, Clay. We bought them in Portsmouth."

"I bought them, Elizabeth. They're in your size, but it is I who have a pair of brogans and four pairs of stockings."

"But Clay—"

"If you'd like to wear my shoes, dear wife, you may ask to do so. If I'm so inclined, I'll permit it. But you didn't want them; you didn't buy them. You have no brogans."

"You want to humiliate me."

"Call it what you will, Elizabeth. You were too good for brogans. Now you'll have to ask the owner for permission."

"You are insufferable. I hate you, Clay."

"Whatever you say, my dear," he said, swinging the carriage door open. "I think you can make it now. Reach up. Help pull yourself inside out of the cold wind."

He turned to walk back toward a cluster of men at the center of the caravan. He meant it. The shoulders were pulled back, his head was erect. It was her pride that had caused the problem in the first place; it was now his pride that kept the flame ignited. Elizabeth knew she had to make the first move. "Clay—"

He stopped, but he didn't turn back. "Clay, may I wear your brogans? My feet are like ice. And I'd like two pairs of your stockings, too. Please, Clay, I'm frozen."

He turned. She saw that wry smile."Of course you may, my dear. They're in my grip. Help yourself. I'll be back before we're ready to move on."

After two more hours of rough road, the six carriages once again came to a halt. This was another of what the driver called a "public stop," although there were no public facilities. It was high ground and heavily wooded.

She could hear the man from the lead carriage as he shouted. "We'll be here for about ten minutes. Women to the left and men to the right. This is the last stop before we get to Waynesborough."

Mr. Hutchins was out of the carriage first. Clay followed and helped Elizabeth. The brogans were not pretty, but, with the stockings, they were warm. Her feet still tingled from the cold, but the shoes were functional.

The men drifted into the woods on the right-hand side of the road, and the women on the left-hand side. This was another part of the trip that Elizabeth hated.

There had been a series of such stops. None of them had been easy for Elizabeth. Some of the ladies seemed comfortable with their traveling companions. They could take care of these absolutions in the company of each other. Elizabeth could not. She hated it. There was something intrinsically undignified about hoisting your skirts and tugging down your undergarments. This hammock was better by far than some of the stops. There were more evergreens, so there were fewer bare branches. Some of the previous so-called "public stops" were almost impossible for her.

With her skirts drawn into a wad and lifted to safety, with her undergarments pulled out of the way, Elizabeth had just completed relieving herself when she heard something—a noise she had not made. She looked up. It was Mr. Hutchins. That silly, smiling red face. Elizabeth was stunned. Movement was temporarily impossible. He continued to stare. He licked his fat, red lips, and then, with no effort to hurry, he disappeared quietly through the woods.

As she walked back, she was joined by Mrs. Hutchins. What do I do? she wondered. Should I tell on him? What would it do to the only friend I've had made on this horrid journey? Should I say nothing at all to her? And the other thought: Should I tell Clay? The man deserved a thrashing, but was the hurt it might cause his wife worth it?

They walked together in silence."You're quiet, Miz Greenleaf. Are the feet still bothering you?"

"No, Mrs. Hutchins," she answered, choosing words carefully, "I'm fine now. My feet are finally warm. I didn't think I'd ever want to wear these ugly shoes, but now I can't imagine life without them."

"I hope George is no bother in your carriage Miz Greenleaf. That boy of mine is still not feeling too good."

If she were going to expose Hutchins, and God knows she should, this was the time, but when she looked into the open and trusting face, she couldn't bring herself to say a word.

"There's room in our carriage, Mrs. Hutchins. We could take one of the girls, too, if it would help."

"Oh, no, Miz Greenleaf. The girls are no trouble. I just hated to bother you and Mr. Greenleaf, since you two are practically newlyweds."

As she walked up to the carriage, Mr. Hutchins said, "Can I help you up, Miz Greenleaf?" He looked at her boldly.

"No, Mr. Hutchins. Clay will give me the help I need."

"You're sure of that?"

"Quite sure."

Clay joined them. "I offered your wife my help, Mr. Greenleaf, but she wanted to wait on you."

"Very kind of you, Mr. Hutchins."

Then, humming to himself, Mr. Hutchins turned from them slightly, looking out over the hammock. "This is a nice rise of land here. I walked around a bit. Seen some real pretty scenery, I did."

He smiled as he turned back toward them. "We'd better be loading. Looks like we're ready to move on."

Chapter Eighteen

Waynesborough was another version of Stantonsborough, but the accommodations made it a much nicer experience. As Clay had been told, there was no village. There was a lone farm house, a barn, slave quarters and a variety of unpainted outbuildings.

For Elizabeth, it had been a dreadful day. She was distraught by the wet shoes and frozen feet, the humiliating episode over the brogans, and worse, the degrading experience with Mr. Hutchins. Her head throbbed from the sum of it. She had a headache powder in her case. She would take it and go to bed.

Mrs. Bledsoe met the carriages with her husband. The men went to the barn and the women to a public room with ample towels and a large kettle of water, steaming on a wood-burning stove. The house was scrupulously clean and the smells were delightful.

"If you ladies are hungry, or if the children are, I can furnish freshly baked bread and butter with a glass of milk. I'm afraid that's the best I can do, but I wouldn't want you to eat more than that. I do have a nice supper planned."

All of the children and some of the women followed her to the kitchen. Elizabeth couldn't eat. She was too upset from the day's events. She found the headache powder and took it with a glass of water.

Elizabeth was in the parlor when she heard footsteps on the porch. I hope it's Clay, she thought, I'll tell him I need to lie down for an hour. She heard boots crossing the hall. She turned, expecting Clay. It was Mr. Hutchins.

"Oh," she said, "I thought it was Clay." She felt short of breath. He said nothing. Without making a move to depart, Mr. Hutchins looked at her from head to toe and licked those silly fat lips. "If you're looking for Mrs. Hutchins, sir," she continued, the words rushing out, "she's in the kitchen with the other ladies and the children."

He said nothing. He scratched his crotch. "Mr. Hutchins, either go outside or go to the kitchen. I have not created a scene—because of your wife—but if you don't get out of this room at once, you can be sure that I will."

She heard a door open. He turned. "Oh, Martha, there you are. I was just asking Miz Greenleaf where you were."

"I'm going to put Billy to bed, George," she replied. "You mind the two girls while I get him settled. They're in the kitchen eating bread and milk. Maybe you'd want some, too. I won't be long with Billy."

With a final leer, he moved toward the kitchen.

As Mrs. Hutchins and Billy started up the stairs, Clay arrived. "If you're feeling up to it, Elizabeth, I could rent a horse and buggy from Mr. Bledsoe. We could ride down to the river, or, have you had too much riding today."

The pleasant feelings she was beginning to have about this nice, clean house were ruined by Mr. Hutchins. She welcomed the chance to be alone with Clay. "I think I'd like that. Could we ride down to where the coach drivers live? What we've seen of the Carolinas so far hasn't been what I imagined the South to be."

"The South has many faces, Elizabeth. And, since roads are few, the river will be our destination. I'm glad you want to go. I'd hoped you'd say yes." He turned. "Get your things and come along. I'll see about the buggy."

The countryside on the way to the river was the nicest thing she had seen since leaving England. It was not as green as Devon and Cornwall, not so well tended or civilized, but it had a wild kind of beauty. The road followed a ridge to a bluff overlooking the Neuse. There on a rise of land was a cluster of houses with well-tended yards.

Two of the coachmen came out to greet them. "We don't have many callers," one of them said. "We're the only folks who live around here for miles, us and the Bledsoes. In one way or another, we're all kissin' kin, ain't we, Charlie?" Charlie grunted. "But why don't you all get out and sit a spell? My wife can fix some sassafras tea."

"No," Clay said, "thank you just the same, but we'd better drive on back. It gets dark quickly in winter, and I wouldn't want to miss Mrs. Bledsoe's fresh-baked bread. I could smell it as I walked through the house."

He pulled the horse around and they began the return trip. On the way to the river, Elizabeth knew there was something on Clay's mind. She wondered if he knew about the Hutchins' incidents.

Finally he spoke. "You've had a bad day, Elizabeth. I know I didn't make it any easier. I want to apologize for my part in it."

"You have nothing to apologize for, Clay."

"Yes, I do. I should have offered those shoes. I knew your feet were wet—and cold. I knew you'd be reluctant to ask. You see, my dear, in the short time we've been married, I've learned something about that silly pride of yours."

"My pride, Clay? Was it only my pride?"

"Let's not argue, Elizabeth. I'm sorry. I can't say more than that. Let that be the end of it."

She was furious. "Let that be the end of it." How often she had heard that phrase? To her it said, "I've had my say, Elizabeth, and I don't want to hear you. Shut up. Don't annoy me." Fortunately, her anger passed. He had apologized. He moved closer to her in the buggy and put his arm around her shoulders. She relaxed against him.

"I'm glad you bought the brogans, Clay. It's nice to have warm, dry feet once again. They want a little for style, but, with the woolen stockings, they're wonderful."

They rode in silence. He tied the reins to the buckboard and allowed the horse to meander along. He took her hand in his. There was a wintertime Carolina sunset. The sky was brilliant red, like a forest fire behind the distant pines.

"Beautiful," she said.

"So are you."

"Clay, be serious."

"I am. A beautiful clear night. I have plans for it."

"And tomorrow?"

"Tomorrow will be better, I promise you."

"And warmer?"

"Yes, and warmer. We get cold this far south, but it doesn't last. I think we've seen the worst of it."

"I've been wondering, Clay. Our last stop was called Stantonsborough, because the man's name was Stanton. This one is called Waynesborough, but the man's name is Bledsoe."

Clay laughed. "His name is Wayne Bledsoe."

"Well, I'm glad to know. Even if it's not a proper town, I wouldn't want it called Bledsoeborough."

He picked up the reins. "We'd better move. When the sun drops, it gets dark before you know it. Besides, I still remember the good smells from that kitchen."

They were ready by sunup. After a hearty breakfast, the journey toward the terminus of the rail line began. Elizabeth and Clay were in their carriage without Mr. Hutchins. Billy Hutchins had improved. It was a good omen. In this area, the land was higher and there were fewer log roads.

At one o'clock, the six coaches came to a stop.

"What is it, Elizabeth? Why are we stopping?"

"I'm not sure. I can see that here are fifteen or twenty people up ahead, standing around a fire."

"Let's find out what's happening." Clay helped her out of the carriage, and they joined the others. As they neared the fire, they could see the rail line. "Oh, dear," Elizabeth said, "this is the end of the track, but there's no train."

Clay asked a driver, "When is the train due?"

"There ain't been much passenger service on these tracks. It's due when it's here, I reckon. Sometimes it's settin' here when we git here and sometimes it ain't."

"It might be a cold wait."

"Yes, sir, Mr. Greenleaf, it might. Ain't no tellin'. But it'll be here 'fore too long. These people from out here in the woods, they ain't seen no trains before. When it's time for one, they come over to watch it come in."

"But it will be here today?"

"Yes, sir, I think it will. Far as I know, it will."

"But you're not sure."

"No, sir, not real sure. I done told you about that bridge down yonder. We've had some bad rains."

"It may be out?"

"That's what I hear'd. Don't know—not for sure."

Elizabeth had been listening. "But what about us, sir? What are we supposed to do?"

"The train will come, ma'am. It just ain't here now."

"Do we get back in the carriages? It's still chilly."

"No, ma'am, can't do that, neither. We've got to get back 'fore dark. Hit'll be a hard ride at best. Ain't no place to stay out at night, not in weather like this."

"And leave us here?"

"The train'll come, ma'am. It always has."

"But, sir, I heard what you said about the bridge."

"Just talk, ma'am. No one knows, not first-hand."

"But, sir, are you planning on leaving us here?"

"Well, we ain't got no choice, ma'am. We need to unload and start back. The train could take an hour or two, and then we'd be left without a hope of getting back home."

"*If* the train comes," Elizabeth persisted. "It may not."

"We done this before, ma'am. The train always comes."

"But, sir—"

"Beggin' your pardon, Miz Greenleaf, but I must help with the unloading." He tugged at his hat and was gone.

The baggage was unloaded and stacked on a small flat car that stood at the end of the tracks. The carriages were turned around and they clattered off toward Waynesborough.

"Clay—"

"The train will be here soon, Elizabeth. Have faith. For a parson's daughter, you have a short supply of faith."

But the train was not there "soon." The first hour of waiting had passed quickly. The local people joined the travelers in discussions about the train's imminent arrival, the crops, the weather, but in the second hour those conversations slowed. By the third hour, with no sight or sound of the train, Clay began to consider their plight. He approached one of the white men milling about the fire. "Has the train been this late before, sir?"

"Nope."

"Do you think it will come before long?"

"Cain't say. Always has."

"Have you heard anything about a bridge being out down below here, down toward Wilmington?"

"I hear'd about high waters. They was talk about a railroad bridge, but they's talk all the time."

"But, you don't really know about the bridge?"

"Nope." He stamped his feet because of the cold. "I got a piece to go," he said. "Reckon I won't wait on that train."

"Before you leave," Clay said, "is there a farmstead around here, one near enough to the the railroad track so we can watch for the train?" The man made no reply. "We'd need a place large enough that we could spend the night there if we had to. We have to get our women and children to some kind of shelter."

"Nope."

"What about your house? We could sleep on the floor."

"My house— Hit's in the woods. Hit's a mile or more, maybe closer to two."

"But there must be some farmhouse near here."

"Well, yes, there's one. Duncan Sanders lives on the railroad—about a mile from here, I reckon, maybe a little less. Hit's a big house. Maybe he could take you in."

"How do we get there? It will be dark in another hour."

"Just walk down the track there. Hit ain't all that fur. Hit'll be the only house you'll see. Hit's back from the track, maybe a hundred foot. You cain't miss it."

Clay told the men about the Sanders farmhouse. The local people, black and white, listened, but offered no help.

"Can the women walk that far?" one man asked.

"We can't leave the baggage here," another one said.

"Each man is responsible for his wife and kids, and for his own baggage," Clay said. "Take what you can and leave the rest. If we had a horse, we could try to pull that baggage car down the tracks, but we don't. It'll be dark soon."

There was a lot of grumbling, most of it mumbled, and then Mr. Hutchins said, "That's easy for you to say, Greenleaf. You've only got a wife and a couple of grips. But what about me? I've got a wife and three kids, and I've got two trunks and three grips. We're moving to Wilmington. That's all I own. I can't leave it out here."

"I'm sorry, Mr. Hutchins. I see your problem, but what do we do? The main thing is to find shelter. The baggage is a consideration, but it must be secondary. Take what you can; leave the rest. It'll be safe until morning, or until the train gets here."

"That's horseshit!"

"Mr. Hutchins," Clay said firmly, "there are ladies present. That kind of language will not be tolerated."

To that point, the local people had quietly listened.

Then a large black man said, "That car rolls."

"I know it does," Clay replied. "But it needs to be pulled and the train's not here."

"It can be pulled or it can be pushed. It rolls."

"I doubt we could budge it. Those wheels weigh a ton."

"It's heavy," the black man persisted, "but, get it moving and it ain't so hard. I think I could do it by myself."

Clay took another look at the black man. He was tall, and with a powerful build. "Could you? Or are you bragging? What's you name, boy?"

"They call me Hector."

"Well, Hector, if you can push that car down the track, I'd pay you well. Is there anyone who wants to help Hector?"

Four other black men, without saying a word, moved over to stand by Hector.

"That may not be enough, what about you men?" Clay turned to the the white men.

"You sound like you're from the South," one of them said.

"I am," Clay replied. "From Georgia."

"Then you know that ain't white man's work. That's nigger work. Don't go tryin' to low-rate us."

"Don't you worry none, Cap'n," Hector said. "You got all the men you need. Get your women and chil'ren on the cart—they's room there. You gentlemen can walk behind."

After the women were loaded, the five black men put their shoulders to the rear of the baggage cart. They heaved forward, but there was no movement. On the second effort, the wheels moved slightly. The black men continued to strain, back muscles bulging. The wheels moved. Slowly the forward roll of the wheels gained momentum. Soon they were moving at a pace that required the men behind to step lively to keep up.

It took twenty minutes to get to the Sanders homestead. The black men knew where they were headed. As they came to the grove of trees that sheltered the house, the forward movement ceased. "That's it, Cap'n. That's where Mr. Duncan Sanders lives. See it over there, in the trees?"

Clay looked. The house had never been painted. In the gathering twilight, the weathered wood blended in with the bark and branches of the bare trees. As Clay squinted, he could make out the angles of a house.

"Wait here, all of you," he said. "I'll go see about accommodations. If we all go, Sanders might turn us away."

A black girl opened the door to his knock. "I'm looking for Mr. Duncan Sanders," Clay said. "Is he home?"

"Who's at the door, Tassy?" a voice roared from the back of the house. "I don't want none of them no good niggers coming 'round here sniffin' at the ground like a no good hound. I say, Tassy, who's there?"

Tassy looked scared

"My name is Greenleaf, Mr. Sanders, Clay Greenleaf," Clay called out. "I'm one of the people waiting for the train to Wilmington."

As a large shadow filled the dark hallway, Tassy slipped by and moved toward the back of the house. Clay could see Sanders more clearly as he came toward the door.

"You're right," Mr. Sanders said, running his fingers through uncombed hair, "that train ain't come by yet." He looked out the door at Clay. "Who'd you say you was?"

"My name is Clay Greenleaf, sir. There are twenty-two of us waiting for the train to Wilmington. We need a place to stay until it gets here. There are women and children. They can't stay out in the cold now that night is almost upon us."

"Twenty-two? I ain't got room for twenty-two . Ain't even that many chairs in the house."

"Look, Mr. Sanders, we're not looking for fine living; we're looking for shelter. We can't let those people stay outside much longer. The sun's down; it's getting cold."

Sanders looked Clay over carefully. "I guess you'll be wanting something to eat, too. It'll be a dollar a head. If that's too much, find another place."

"That'll be fine, sir. I'll go get them."

"I don't know what we can find to eat, but we'll try," Sanders said. He turned back into the house."Tassy! Tassy, get your black ass in here. There's work to be done."

Clay went back to give the others the good news. As he drew near, Mr. Hutchins was standing in front of where Elizabeth sat in the coach. "Come on, Miz Greenleaf. We ain't got all day."

"No, Mr. Hutchins. Clay will be along in a minute."

"I'll help you down. Don't be afraid."

"Help the others, Mr. Hutchins."

"I'm back, my dear," Clay said emerging from the shadows. "I'll lift you down. Thank you, Hutchins, for your concern."

As Clay lifted her, she said, "He makes my skin crawl."

"He was only trying to help."

"Well, I don't want his help."

"You're being unreasonable, Elizabeth. Now, go along with the other ladies, I've got to pay these boys."

It was seven before the food was prepared. In the hallway, before the meal was served, Clay counted out twenty-two dollars and handed it to Mr. Sanders.

Sanders was right. There were not enough chairs. The children sat on the floor. With benches from the back porch, the adults found a place to sit. They were grateful. It was *indoors,* and it was warm.

At nine o'clock Clay asked, "What is the latest you have seen the train come in, Mr. Sanders?"

"It ain't never been this late, not that I recall. There was talk of bridge trouble. Maybe that's why they're late."

"Yes, we heard a rumor about the bridge. What if the train doesn't come in tonight? Could you put us up?"

"This house ain't that big, you can see that."

"But you wouldn't ask us to leave," Clay persisted. "You could find some place for us."

"On pallets, maybe. I'm not sure of that either. Wait a minute." Mr. Sanders yelled, "Hey, Tassy, come in here."

She came to the door. "How many could we sleep, girl, counting pallets on the floor? How much bedding have we got?" Tassy's eyes rolled back in her head. She looked around the room. Was she counting as she looked at them one by one? Elizabeth was not sure. Her eyes told nothing.

"We'll do what we can," Mr. Saunders said. "You, Tassy, get a couple of women and set to making up beds and pallets. Use the big room upstairs for the women and the one downstairs for the men. I wonder if we have enough bedding. Go on now, Tassy, get at it."

He stood up. "I need to see you in the hall, Mr. Greenleaf. We have some business to talk over."

In the hall Sanders asked for three dollars a head for the lodging, and that included any part of the night, even if the train should come in. Clay paid for all the passengers. He told Sanders he thought the price was dear, but Sanders was firm. "Go elsewhere, Mr. Greenleaf. I'm being accommodatin' or you wouldn't be in here at all."

Most of the men elected to sleep in their clothes, but the women, with corsets and stays, wanted out of them. The arrangements Mr. Sanders provided, pallets on a bare floor, would not bring rest, so the women decided there was no reason to also be uncomfortable.

Before going to bed, most of the ladies had gone to the privy behind the house. Elizabeth did not want to ask someone to go with her and she was afraid to go alone. In the early hours of the morning she was in pain. I must go, she thought, I really have no choice. I'll move quietly and perhaps I will disturb no one. She put on her dressing gown and went downstairs and out the kitchen door. She stood on the porch, letting her eyes grow accustomed to the night. Gradually, she could see the pathway and the privy at the end of it.

As she stepped off the porch she saw him, standing beside a cedar tree. In the light of a thin sliver of moon, she could see his face. It was Mr. Hutchins.

My God, she thought. I must go, but I dare not. What should I do? It took only a moment to know that inside the house was safer than the outside, so she let herself back in. She knew the answer. She knew what to do.

She found the bed by the light of the fire. "Mrs. Hutchins," she whispered, touching her on the shoulder, "I must go out to the toilet. I'm afraid to go. Will you go with me?"

Mothers wake up quickly. Mrs. Hutchins was awake at the first touch. "Of course, child, I'll go. When I was your age I would have been afraid, too. I'll be right with you. Let me find a wrap."

Chapter Nineteen

The night passed for Elizabeth without further incident. If Mr. Hutchins still lurked outside, the presence of Mrs. Hutchins made the walk down the path to the privy perfectly safe. When she was back in the big room the women shared, Elizabeth settled herself on the pallet. With the pain in her belly gone, the fire's flickering shadows on the ceiling lulled her into a deep and restful sleep.

The clatter of the other women and children awakened her the following morning. Mrs. Hutchins said, "You're finally awake, child. I thought we'd have to leave you here."

"Oh, the train is here?"

"No, Miz Greenleaf, more's the pity. It's just that I thought you'd sleep forever. The noise didn't seem to bother you. You were sleeping the sleep of the innocent."

The word "innocent" brought the memories back. Elizabeth remembered Mr. Hutchins' leering face. Once again she considered telling Clay, or Mrs. Hutchins, but she did not have the courage.

"Come along, Miz Greenleaf," Mrs. Hutchins continued, "get dressed for breakfast. I can smell ham frying."

There was an ample breakfast of ham and redeye gravy, coarse corn grits, scrambled eggs, stewed dried apples, and biscuits. The black serving girls' dresses were washed and ironed, a contrast to the wrinkled look of the guests.

Elizabeth looked at the grits. "What is this?"

"Where did you find this little girl, Mr. Greenleaf?" Mrs. Hutchins asked. "You've got trouble on your hands, taking her into the deep South with so little knowledge."

Clay laughed. "I've had trouble for some time now, Mrs. Hutchins. Not knowing about grits is only part of it."

Everyone at the table began chuckling.

"Laugh, all of you, but how can I learn if you poke fun at me. You call it grits, Clay. But what is it? I won't know unless someone tells me."

"Grits is ground dried corn, my dear," Clay said.

"Corn meal?"

"Well, no." He hesitated. "Maybe it is both yes and no. Corn meal isn't as fine. Corn meal is often coarser, and is used for making bread. Grits get boiled, a kind of gruel, and it's eaten with eggs or gravy."

He looked around the table. "Can anybody do better? I've eaten grits all my life. I never thought I'd have to explain them."

As the laughter subsided, Elizabeth gave the grits a tentative poke, and then she tried a bite. "Not much flavor."

"Lots of nourishment, but not much flavor. Right you are, my dear. Now try some dipped in your redeye gravy. I guess this Yankee girl will have to learn to eat grits."

It was a long day. The train did not arrive. No one wandered too far from the house. There was no way of knowing when the train might come.

Elizabeth tried to stay with Clay. She could not give Mr. Hutchins another opportunity to scare the wits out of her. When Clay was somewhere else, Elizabeth sought the protection of Mrs. Hutchins. There would be no lustful behavior while Mrs. Hutchins was near.

Mr. Sanders continued to collect a dollar a head for each meal served. Because Elizabeth was at Clay's side, she became aware of the cash transactions between her husband and the host. "Why are you paying all of it, Clay?"

"Well, my dear, I brought them here, so I paid. I thought it would be one meal and maybe the night, but you see what it's turned into. Our visit will be his best cash crop this year."

"They can't think he's doing this for nothing."

"I don't know what the others think, Elizabeth, but I would be embarrassed to bring it up now. I'll pay Sanders. I can afford it, and I'm sure some of them can't."

"You should tell them, Clay. Explain what Sanders wants for meals and lodging. It shouldn't be our expense."

"It's not *our* expense, my dear; it's my expense. It's not from your mother's trust. What I spend is from my pocket. How I spend it is my business."

What he said was gently spoken. He was not chastising her. It was a simple matter of logic. He was spending his own money and, therefore, with his money, he would be the determining factor, both now, and in the future.

Elizabeth was hurt and then angry, but she said nothing. Her mind, however, was a frenzied whirlwind.

As she grew calmer, she clung to one idea: He will change; our love is strong enough, and, in time, we will share responsibilities. She assured herself that being married was new to Clay. It would take time to adjust. She kept thinking: He will change. I know it. He will change.

It was eight o'clock at night before the train arrived. They could hear it before they could see it. With the first sounds, each man began to bring his baggage to the track.

The engine came to a stop within a few feet of the baggage car Clay had commandeered. The engineer rammed his head out. "Who in hell's name moved that cross tie car."

"I did," Clay replied.

"That's railroad property, Mister. You can get yourself in trouble—fast."

"I'm not afraid of the railroad. I fully intend to go to the office in Wilmington. What happened to us is beyond the pale.

We were left out here to fend for ourselves for a day and a half. How dare you criticize us for moving your flat car?"

"I want your name, Mister," the engineer said. "I'll be making a report, you can put money on that. Because of you, it will take us extra time to get the supplies and the men to the end of the line. You had no right to touch railroad property and I intend to make trouble for you."

"Do what you have to do, my friend. If I had to do it over, I wouldn't hesitate a second. Add that to your report."

By nine o'clock, the train began the return trip to Wilmington. It was another dirty passenger coach, but Elizabeth didn't complain. The stove still belched puffs of smoke and sulfur, but the steady click of the wheels on the tracks said "Wilmington, Wilmington, Wilmington."

At last weariness claimed her. She drifted off to sleep. When she awakened, all of her bones ached. In the East, she could see signs of the coming day. Her movement awakened Clay.

"We're moving faster now. We must be near Wilmington where the roadbed is better," Clay whispered.

"I hope so," she said quietly. "What time is it?"

"Ten minutes to five."

"Eight hours!"

"Would you prefer a rutted road and a carriage?"

She put her hand over his mouth. "No more of that, but I do have another problem. I'm hungry."

"We'll find something in Wilmington," he said.

In another half an hour the train began to slow. The change in the rhythm awakened the rest of the passengers. It was still dark when they made their way into the station.

Clay went to ask where they might stay until he could make the necessary arrangements for the next boat to Charleston. "We just got in from Weldon," he said.

"I know."

"Where we might find lodging and breakfast?"

"Miz Middleton has a boarding house, turn left in front of the station. She might have room for you."

"It's dark out there. Could you have someone show us the way with a lantern.We have women and children in our group."

"Ain't nobody here but me. I have to mind the station. You could wait here or you could take a lantern. I'll send for it later."

Clay led the way with the lantern. It was easy to recognize Middleton's boarding house. Lights were on in the kitchen and the rest of the ground floor.

Inside there was a porter and a woman. "Are you Mrs. Middleton?"

"I am, sir."

"We need lodging, madam, and we are all hungry. Could we—"

"The dining room is not open for another hour, sir. You may all sit outside on the porch until then."

"But it's still quite cold out there, Mrs. Middleton. Couldn't we wait in the dining room?"

"You'd be in the way of the help, sir. We're trying to get things ready for breakfast."

"We'd stay out of the way. If we could have tea—"

"That's quite out of the question. We open at seven."

"But, Mrs. Middleton, as you can see, we have women and children in our group. It's cold outside."

Mrs. Middleton looked at them. They were a sight: rumpled clothing, hair standing on end from a night on the train, sleep-filled eyes. "Well, the women and children can find places in this room, but you men must go outside. You'll hear the bell. Until you do, we won't be serving the public."

This had been a trip filled with boorish people. Very quietly Elizabeth whispered, "Is this Southern hospitality?"

"I heard you, madam," Mrs. Middleton said. "You can wait inside or outside, but don't tell me how to run my house."

"My wife meant no harm, Mrs. Middleton—"

"Your wife? This woman is your wife? I can hear the South in your voice, sir, but I can hear only criticism in hers. We don't need any additional help from the North. We can run our own lives in our own way, and we intend to do it."

"Mrs. Middleton, my wife has no interest in politics. She's new to the South, so she's formed no opinions. I think you misunderstood her."

But, this exchange was more than Elizabeth could take. First, the insolence of the woman and then Clay's pandering and making excuses.

"Mrs. Middleton didn't misunderstand me, Clay," Elizabeth said firmly. "I can tell you, I would hate to be a black in this woman's kitchen. I now begin to understand what Mr. William Lloyd Garrison has been writing about."

"Elizabeth!"

Mrs. Middleton looked her over slowly and then turned to Clay. "You have my sympathy, sir. I hope you can teach her to keep her mouth shut, but it's too late for that here. I'm sorry, but your wife is not welcome. However, there's another public house nearby. It's on this street, in the next block. Maybe you'd better take this follower of Mr. Garrison there. She will not be a guest here."

Mrs. Middleton turned from them abruptly. "You other ladies, take your children and find places to sit. You men, go on outside. We'll ring the bell when service begins."

Clay took her arm. "Come on Elizabeth, you've done it now." He guided her to where they had left the grips.

Away from the others he turned to her. "That was uncalled for Elizabeth. You're going to have to control that tongue of yours. You are the wife of a Georgia planter. We own slaves, many of them. Get that through your head."

He picked up the grips. "Let's find the other public house before word of your behavior spreads."

Chapter Twenty

Elizabeth and Clay, in fresh, clean clothing, boarded the *General Oglethorpe* late on the same afternoon they arrived in Wilmington. The paint on the hull was a gleaming white, and the decks were clean.

Elizabeth joined Clay at the railing. Her impression of Wilmington in the early hours of the morning was that it looked squalid, but it was now washed in late afternoon sun. If she had not been asked to leave the town's leading public house, and if she had been able to get a cup of hot tea after the train ride from the Sanders farm, she might have considered it picturesque and not without a measure of charm. But these things had happened. Wilmington was not on her list of Southern cities to revisit.

She let her mind recount the past hours. It had been a full day. They unpacked and took turns going to the public room of the boardinghouse for a bath. Clay was first. While he was there, Elizabeth laid out fresh clothing for the two of them, and re-packed their bags.

When she returned, Clay was in a playful mood. "Come here, my dear. Let me smell a clean woman for a change."

"Clay Greenleaf, you spend the better part of your life being randy. Be sensible."

"We'll be sensible later. It's time to play now."

"Let me ask you something. Then, depending on your answer and your own good conscience, we'll play." She put her fingers under his chin and lifted his head. She wanted to see his eyes when he answered. “Do you have the arrangements made for a boat to Darien?”

“I have tentative arrangements, made in Philadelphia.”

“And we’ve had delays, haven’t we? Your arrangements are less than tentative now, aren’t they, Love?”

“You don’t have time for me, is that it? I expected you to say tired from the journey, or you had the vapors, or a headache. It isn’t like you to be practical.”

“Let’s just say that this time I’m being sensible. Let’s arrange for our passage, and then—if we have the time—we’ll come back to our room and tarry.”

“You’re assuming we’ll be leaving today,” he said.

“I hope so. But if not, we’ll have time for tarrying. It’s sensible to see to the travel plans, isn’t it?”

“I’m not sure I like it when you use your head. I like a pliable, moldable, warm, loving flibbertigibbet.”

“You took me for better or for worse, remember?”

“It should’ve been even-handed. I should get as much of the better as I do of the worse.” He laughed at his own joke. “But this time, I’ll make the effort, just for you. We’ll both be sensible. Come, my dear. Put on your dress, and we’ll go find the steamship line.”

At last, their travel to Darien was assured. The first leg was to be on the *General Oglethorpe* from Wilmington to Charleston. There would be a two-day delay in Charleston because the *Kenneth Cooper*, the coastal steamer to Savannah, had sustained minor damage on the previous trip. It was in dry dock.

On the street Elizabeth said, “Another delay. We began this journey under a bad star.”

“One of your omens, Elizabeth? At least we’re not out in the Carolina woods waiting for a train.”

“But, Clay, here it is again, a boat damaged on the same run that we’ll be making aboard it.”

He sighed. "You and your omens. Maybe it's a good omen and we can enjoy the delay. We'll be in Charleston for two days, my dear. I can show you the city."

"If it's like Wilmington, I'll forget the grand tour."

"It's not like Wilmington, but I dare say you'd not have found Wilmington so distasteful under better circumstances. Charleston is Charleston. It's not like New York, or Boston, or London. Charleston dares to be itself. I think you'll find, my dear, when you have had time to savor the South, that it's made up of eccentrics who will not fit a mold. Charleston has its full share of eccentrics, and so the city is unique. It refuses to be compared to anywhere else on earth."

Elizabeth joined Clay on deck as they arrived in Charleston. At mid-morning the warm sunshine highlighted the distinctive architecture of the city. She liked Charleston at once. There was a permanence here. This was not a series of makeshift buildings. This was a city that knew it had a place in the world. There was pride here. The buildings along the waterfront were built to last. Some of them, governmental buildings she imagined, with rich external decorations, with columns and curlicues, with cherubs and friezes.

As they grew nearer, she could see the houses, built along noble lines, but each dared to be different. It seemed to her that each householder must be determined to express his own standards, his own individuality. This city was unlike any she had ever seen. Nothing here seemed new or transplanted. The roots went back into time.

"You like Charleston. I can see it on your face."

"Oh, yes. I haven't even put a foot on shore, and I already know I like it."

In the cab she kept thinking: Charleston, Charleston, Charleston, I thought I'd never see you. You are civilized. You are what I had lost all hope of ever seeing again. Her eyes swept in every detail. After the piney woods and the bumpy log roads, after the mud and the comfort stops in the woods, it was wonderful to see Charleston, a charming, bustling, cultured Southern city.

The hotel was an old building, one that had its place along the waterfront for years. It was a dowager, a grand dame. It faced the Promenade across a wide street. They were shown to a suite with a large sitting room, a smaller bedroom and a room where they both could bathe in privacy.

When they were alone he said, "Will this do, Elizabeth, or would you prefer the floor at the Sanders farm?"

"Oh, Clay, it's heaven. I'd almost given up hope of seeing anything civilized again."

"The South is largely unsettled, my dear, but we are gentlemen and ladies, and we know how to live. Savannah is not as large as Charleston, but you'll find it both civilized and charming. Darien is smaller, but we're not without our people of distinction."

As she passed him with an armload of dresses, he pulled her close. "I've been thinking of this for eighteen hours. Drop those dresses, wench, and attend to your husband."

"Clay! Those dresses are a sight now. Just look at the wrinkles. I need to hang them."

"Hang them! That's what I say, my dear, hang them! Who gives a damn about them? Let them stay on the floor. This time I don't have to go book passage. We're going to be sensible, my love, but we'll do it my way this time."

"But, Clay, my dresses—"

"Damn your dresses! That can be taken care of. Later a maid can press your precious dresses, but right now, you have a precious husband who wasn't happy last night sleeping on a boat, in a room with forty snoring men. Where is your sense of priority, my dear?"

"We can get all the things pressed? And maybe—"

"Elizabeth! Not another word about laundry." He kicked her dresses aside, picked her up and carried her to the bed. The dress she had on had a lace collar and a series of small covered buttons running down the front. He tried to undo the buttons, but his fingers were no match for them.

By this time she was laughing at him. He was so clumsy and so intent. "Let me, Clay. I'll hang the dress."

"My God, she's back to housekeeping again—"

"I don't want to ruin it and I could feel the buttons giving." She was out of his arms, out of the bed and out of the dress in one continuous movement.

Clay watched. How can they do it? A woman will fight like a tigress to keep every button fastened, and then, in a trice, change her mind, and the dress falls to the floor like an autumn leaf. What made the difference? What had he said, or done? The answer to that question would make life simpler.

Clay was up and dressed. As he adjusted his tie he said, "Your Uncle Roderick showed me a piece of equipment, Elizabeth, one we could use at Greenleaf. I want the factors to see if they can order it. But, my dear, I'll be back to take you for a late lunch." He was at the door of the suite. "I'll have a maid sent up. I don't want a worry in your mind as we drive around the city, I want to really show you Charleston. I want you to learn to love the South as I do, and so far, we've been off to a bad start, haven't we?"

"Portsmouth had possibilities. At least the ladies there don't wear boots."

"I know one who borrowed a pair of men's brogans."

"Don't remind me."

"But you haven't been enchanted with the South."

"Some tastes have to be acquired."

"We'll start today, with Charleston."

They took lunch at the hotel. Afterwards, in a hired rig, Clay drove through the main streets of the city, into the business district, and later past rows of grand homes. They went down a street facing a lovely little park. Elizabeth was enchanted with the iron grillwork that enclosed the grounds, and the polished brass on each of the massive front doors. "This is truly a beautiful street," she said. "I think it's nicer than any we've seen."

"I saved it until last. It's the grandest street in Charleston. I've kept a secret from you since I returned, but now the time is near, so I'll tell you. See that house down there, the yellow one, trimmed in white?"

"With the fence that looks like spears turned on end?"

"Yes. It belongs to Stoppard Carruthers. He is Greenleaf's factor here in Charleston. You'll be taking tea there today, at four. Fifteen minutes from now."

"Oh, Clay, no. You haven't done that to me?"

"What's the matter, Elizabeth? I thought you'd be pleased. I thought you'd want to meet some of the ladies."

Elizabeth fought back the tears. "I would, Clay, but not in these circumstances."

"What's wrong with the circumstances? I told Carruthers you were with me, he sent a note to his wife, and that's all there is to it. Why are you carrying on so?"

"I'm not dressed for it, Clay. I dressed to go for a ride with you, not for a tea, especially with women I don't even know. How could you do this?"

Clay was exasperated. "Hell, Elizabeth, you're not being presented to the queen. This is a tea, a simple afternoon tea. You look fine in what you're wearing."

But Elizabeth was in tears. "I can't go. I won't go. You can send a note. Tell them I've taken ill."

"You will go, Elizabeth. I'll give you five minutes to start acting like an adult. At the end of that time, I'll take you to No. 7, where you will take tea. Is that clear?"

Tears were rolling down her cheeks. "You'll just take me there and dump me. You don't care how I feel. You don't care that I'm not properly dressed, that my eyes are puffy, that I look like a frump."

"You have five minutes, Elizabeth. If your eyes are puffy, it's because you brought it about. But, my dear, you are going to the tea. Carruthers was kind enough to see you were invited, and you will not embarrass me."

"It's always you, and how you feel."

"I will not be embarrassed."

"Oh, it's you, only you. You'd be embarrassed. You're a beast, a thoughtless, cruel, uncaring—"

"Let that be the end of it, Elizabeth. I'll listen to no more. Now dry your eyes. You're going to a tea."

She was furious. "Let that be the end of it, let that be the end of it," she said. "I hate that expression—"

"Elizabeth!" They were already creating a spectacle. People were beginning to stare. Her tears subsided. It was over. She had to go to the tea. "Are my eyes puffy?"

"Yes, they are, just a little, but you look lovely, Elizabeth. They will all love you, just as I do."

"I need to bathe them in cold water. When I cry, my eyes always get puffy." She looked around. "Wait," she said, getting out of the rig, "there's a fountain. The water should be cold." She ran across the green. She dipped her handkerchief and held it to her eyes. She dipped it again and again, and then she came back to the buggy. "How do they look? The water was quite cold. They feel better to me. But, tell me, how do they look, Clay?"

"They look fine, Elizabeth, just fine."

"You're not going to take me up there and dump me, Clay. That would be so mortifying."

"No, my dear, I'll take you to the door. I'll ask for Mrs. Carruthers and I'll wait. I will introduce you properly. Will that make it better for you?"

"Yes, Clay, and I thank you."

They drove slowly back to No. 7. Clay climbed the wide, curving steps to the front door with her. His hand was firmly on her arm. They stopped on the landing. Clay bent down and kissed her lightly on the cheek. "It will work out fine, Elizabeth. They'll love you here in Charleston, just as I do."

And then he lifted the polished brass knocker and brought it firmly down.

Chapter Twenty-One

Mrs. Carruthers was enough like Elizabeth's own mother to be a sister. The resemblance unnerved her. She saw the same high forehead, delicate but definite brows, and white hair parted in the middle and caught at the back in a wide bun.

When Clay was gone Elizabeth said, "Before we go in, I'd like to apologize. I must have appeared gauche when Clay introduced us, but seeing you for the first time was a shock to me. You're so like my late mother. I was tongue-tied."

"What a nice compliment. What was her family name? Perhaps—distantly, at least—we're related."

"She was a Burnside."

"No, that's not a name in my lineage, but it is a nice compliment all the same. Come, Mrs. Greenleaf, I want you to meet the others. I didn't invite many." They entered a large, friendly room facing the street. There were three other ladies, and a blazing fire in the hearth. As the doors slid open, all eyes were on Elizabeth.

"Ladies," Mrs. Carruthers said, "may I present our special guest today, Mrs. Clay Greenleaf." Nobody moved. It was as though a photographer had carefully placed each of them in her own special position for a daguerreotype. "The lady in blue is Mrs. Ewell," Mrs. Carruthers continued. "Behind her is Miss Blanton, and, just across from Miss Blanton, is Miss Lacy."

With those words the picture became animated. The ladies mumbled polite responses, and Mrs. Carruthers pulled

Elizabeth forward by her fingertips. "You will sit here, please, Mrs. Greenleaf." There was a settee on one side of the fireplace, two matching chairs on the other, with the tea service in between. The tall winged chair Elizabeth was led to was at the end. Mrs. Carruthers sat beside Miss Lacy.

"Ladies, shall I pour?" It was a question directed at no one, and one that required no answer. "Our guest will be served first. How do you take your tea, my dear?"

"No sugar or cream, please. I'm a purist."

"As is Mrs. Ewell. And I will serve her next."

The only noises in the room were the sounds of china being touched by silver. The silence bothered Elizabeth. She spoke. "Mr. Greenleaf has been showing me your city, Mrs. Carruthers. This is a lovely street. It is quite the loveliest I've seen, in a city of handsome homes."

Miss Lacy spoke first. "We saw you as you passed. You went all the way to the end of the street before returning, or did you go farther? It seemed a long time."

Had they seen her arguing with Clay? Was it apparent from inside the house? She had been furious with him. Making an arrangement without discussing it with her! It was the kind of thing Papa always did. The room faced the street, with tall windows, almost from the ceiling to the floor. The view they had had of the street must have been clear. "Yes, we did go all the way to the end. Each house is so beautiful. I wanted to see them all. My husband has been such a dear. He has taken me to many parts of the city."

"And do you like Charleston?" Mrs. Ewell asked.

"Oh, yes, I truly do. It must be the loveliest city in the South."

"You might get another opinion in Savannah, my child, but here, we're inclined to agree with you."

The conversation dwindled. Elizabeth was wary, partially because she didn't know them and partially because of the way Miss Lacy had made a point of the time required for their drive to the end of the street. After an eternity, Miss Lacy spoke again. "We understand you've been married only a short time, Mrs. Greenleaf. How long have you known Clay?"

Clay? Had Miss Lacy known Clay? Was she one of his previous friends, one of the people Aunt Mattie had alluded to? Elizabeth kept her voice under control. "I met him only this past summer, Miss Lacy. It was a whirlwind courtship."

"It must have been," Miss Lacy replied."He left us in June, and when we see him again, it's with a new bride."

"Pay no attention to Georganne Lacy, Mrs. Greenleaf. All of our young ladies considered Clay one of the most eligible bachelors in the South," Mrs. Carruthers said. "Our supply of bachelors here in Charleston is limited. The girls hate to see one of them taken, especially one as handsome as Clay. He had to work at staying single, I can tell you."

Elizabeth was now in control of her emotions. She sipped her tea and then said, "I'm so grateful he worked at it, Mrs. Carruthers; otherwise, I could not have married him."

"You've been to England, I understand. Oh, how I envy you," Mrs. Ewell said. "I'd like to go back, but I dread it. I shall probably never make it. How was the crossing?"

"Going over was dreadful, at least for me. But we returned much later in the year—in October when the weather can be treacherous—and it was fine."

"You give me courage, my dear. Perhaps I shall try it one day. My mother is frail, my brother tells me, but still able to get about. I pray to see her again, and I'd like to see Sussex. Charleston is now my home, but, oh, how I would love to see Grinstead again—even the name has a ring to it. And, I would like to visit my cousins in Eastbourne.

"You're becoming nostalgic again, Grace."

"Yes, yes, I suppose I am, but. oh, my dears, when I think of England—"

"You're a Northern girl, aren't you, Mrs. Greenleaf? From Boston, is it?"

"No, I'm from New York. I suppose I'd be called a Yankee. Or are Yankees only from New England?"

"You're a Yankee," Miss Lacy said. "If you're not from the South, you're a Yankee."

"Girls," Mrs. Carruthers said quickly, "you are making Yankee sound like a bad word. It isn't, my dear, it's just a way of saying where you're from. Southerners take a great deal of pride in the South, even those who were transplanted here, as I was. You will put down roots, as we have."

"I have a great deal to learn," Elizabeth replied. "On this journey, I encountered grits for the first time."

"Did you like them?" Miss Blanton asked.

"Well, yes and no," Elizabeth replied. "They are rather bland, but Mr. Greenleaf thinks that's an asset. They can take on the flavor of whatever they are cooked or served with. At any rate, I will learn to cook and serve them."

"You intend to cook? Greenleaf is a large estate."

"But I want to learn to cook, Miss Blanton."

"Not me, not while we have blacks. It must be a hot, sticky job, especially in summer. I know the North is opposed to slavery, but you had servants, didn't you?"

"I must have expressed myself poorly," Elizabeth said. "I want to learn to cook so I can prepare special things for my husband, things that he especially likes. I suppose you could call it an act of love."

"I don't think love need extend that far."

"Newly married women have romantic ideas," Mrs. Carruthers said. "I had some of the same thoughts. But I soon forgot about cooking, even special things for Stoppard. It's a full-time job just attending to the staff. It's a romantic notion, Clara Alice. You'll have some of your own one day. Love does make us do strange things."

"Perhaps it will, but I doubt it," Miss Blanton said. "I like the South as it is. It can be tediously hot in summer, but it has many advantages. Servants are just one of them."

"After New York, it will take adjustments on your part to get used to plantation life, won't it, Mrs. Greenleaf?" Miss Lacy asked. "Won't you miss the social activities of the city? Greenleaf Plantation, I'm told, is quite remote."

"There will be adjustments," Elizabeth replied. "The state of being married is, in itself, an adjustment. There will be others. Being a planter's wife may not be easy, but it wasn't all that easy being a minister's daughter, either."

"Yes, I had forgotten you were a minister's daughter," Miss Lacy said. "Your father, I presume, is an abolitionist? I'm sure a Northern preacher, one from Boston, would be."

"My father is opposed to slavery, yes, but I would not call him an abolitionist."

"He's not opposed to it on Biblical grounds, surely, for even the Bible gives it at least tacit approval."

"We've never specifically discussed slavery," Elizabeth said, "but I know from his sermons and from his general demeanor that he is opposed to bondage of any kind."

"But he does speak against slavery in his sermons?"

"Well, yes, he has. His sermons reflect his views."

"Then he's an abolitionist, isn't he?"

"No," Elizabeth said firmly. "He does not advocate, so he is not an abolitionist. Mr. Garrison is an abolitionist."

"That's not the word I hear used for William Lloyd Garrison—that's not even one of several words used, but they're never voiced in polite company."

"I'm sure Mr. Garrison is called many things in the South," Elizabeth said. "But he is an abolitionist. My father is just someone who opposes slavery in all its forms."

"And preaches about it—about the evils of it."

"Well, yes," Elizabeth said.

"Then he's an abolitionist. Perhaps not as rabid as Garrison, but he's an abolitionist all the same. And you, Mrs. Greenleaf, have you forsaken your father's ideas? An acorn does not fall far from the oak, I'm told. You're in the South. If you believe as your father does, you will—as you suggested earlier—have many adjustments to make."

"You press the point, Miss Lacy, and since you do, since you want an expression of my beliefs, I'll tell you that I do not think any person should ever be chattel to another."

The exchange between Elizabeth and Georganne Lacy started without rancor, but it was now beyond anything the hostess had bargained for when she chose her guests for the tea.

"Ladies," Mrs. Carruthers said. "Teatime is not the time for such a conversation. If the people in the North fully understood the nature of our economy, I'm certain they would also understand the need for slavery."

There was a telling period of silence. Finally, Mrs. Ewell spoke. "Did you get to Sussex, Mrs. Greenleaf?"

"We were in London, Mrs. Ewell," Elizabeth replied, "and then I went on to Cornwall where I have an uncle. I stayed there while Clay was in the North of England on business. I'm sorry to say I did not get to Sussex, but you sound as enthusiastic about it as my mother always was about Cornwall. Her enthusiasm was justified, and I'm sure yours is, too."

"Your husband has come to fetch you, Mrs. Greenleaf," Miss Blanton said. "I can see him tethering the horse."

"I'll see you to the door, Mrs. Greenleaf."

"Ladies," Elizabeth said, "I enjoyed taking tea with you. My father always said that we learn from our experiences, or we are obliged to repeat them. I hope I've learned something today. Good afternoon to you."

When they were alone in the entry, Mrs. Carruthers said, "I apologize for Georganne, Mrs. Greenleaf. She is upset, as many of us are, about the tensions between the North and the South. She tends to speak without thinking. I do hope you'll forgive her."

"I'll forgive her if you'll forgive me, Mrs. Carruthers. As our hostess, you didn't deserve either of us."

"You are forgiven, my dear. I believe you were goaded by Georganne; you had to say something in defense of your father. Think no more about it."

She opened the door. "We saw you, Clay, and I do want to thank you for bringing this lovely child around to see us." She turned to Elizabeth. "You must visit us again, my dear, any time you are in Charleston. And, please, Mrs. Greenleaf, don't be disturbed by Georganne Lacy; she means well, she's just too outspoken."

"Thank you again, Mrs. Carruthers. You not only look like my mother, you are as gracious as she was."

As they walked down the steps toward the buggy, Clay said, "What is this about Georganne Lacy?"

"It was nothing, Clay."

"If it were nothing, Elizabeth, I'd have heard nothing."

"Really, Clay, I can't imagine you having an interest in teatime conversations. It's not like you. Or, are you interested because it involves Georganne Lacy?"

"You're avoiding my question, Elizabeth. If it's nothing, as you say it is, then it will be forgotten. But, for now, tell me about it. I'll decide."

"You sound like Papa."

"Elizabeth, the more you delay your answer, the more dire it sounds. What was this thing with Miss Lacy?"

"How well do you know her, Clay?"

"Elizabeth!"

"Are you avoiding a question, too, Clay? As you said, the more you delay the answer, the more dire it sounds."

"Elizabeth, I will not tolerate this. You will answer my question, and you will do so now. You are being disobedient, and I will not tolerate it. Now, a straight answer, please: What is this about Georganne Lacy?"

Elizabeth was silent. She was angry, she was jealous and she was hurt. Tears formed. "I'm waiting, my dear," Clay said. "I've only so much patience. Don't push it too far." He took the buggy whip from its holder. Did he mean to use it? She couldn't be sure, but she knew his temper.

Finally she spoke. "She pushed and pushed for my views on slavery, that's all. She called Papa an abolitionist."

"So," he said, "you've done that again?"

"I'm sorry, Clay. She pushed me, she goaded me. Papa is not an abolitionist, you know that."

"He's not an activist, if that's what you mean, but he wouldn't find a happy congregation if he were a pastor anywhere in the South. You won't find it easy, either, if you persist in voicing your views."

They rode on in silence. Clay's anger had been vented, the danger was past. He looked worried. "Elizabeth, I don't know how to say this, but you'd better learn quickly—and well before we get to Greenleaf. You must keep your mouth shut. What you said at that tea will be repeated, and no doubt, in time, it will find its way to Greenleaf." He paused. "But if you have not made a complete ass of yourself, it will pass. It will just be a rumor, a bit of gossip. If, however, you make your views on slavery known in Darien, I can't imagine all the ramifications."

"I can't help how I feel, Clay," she said quietly.

"No, you can't. But you can keep your mouth shut. You don't have to say what you think to make it valid."

"I'm sorry, Clay."

"I don't want you sorry, Elizabeth, I want you silent. Do you understand that? Silent."

"But when I'm asked a direct question, I have to say something."

"You can say, 'I have no interest in politics; I have enough problems running my home.'"

"Then I'll sound vapid and boring."

"You'd better practice being vapid and boring. Abolitionist ideas are not popular here."

"I'll try."

"You will do better than try, my dear. You will remain silent. Is that clear?" She said nothing. "Is that perfectly clear, Elizabeth?"

"Yes, Clay."

Chapter Twenty-Two

There was no further discussion of Mrs. Carruther's tea or Miss Lacy, but Elizabeth could plainly see that Clay was still nettled by what she had said about slavery. For her part, she could not forget the intimate way Georganne had said Clay's name.

Nor, could Elizabeth forget that Clay had made a point of not answering her question about the earlier relationship she was certain Clay had had with Miss Lacey.

If Clay were as much a roué as his aunt had implied, she must be sure to accompany him whenever he went to Charleston. Old habits die slowly.

But, this was a new day. Charleston was behind them They were on board the *Kenneth Cooper* on the way to Savannah.

"You've forgotten your hat, my dear. On deck you'll need something to keep the sun off your face."

"I left it in the saloon. This is a glorious day."

"Get your hat, Elizabeth. You're in country where importance is given to being white. We expect our ladies to have skin as soft and white as a magnolia blossom."

"But, Clay, the sun gives me a glow."

"Get your glow in some other way, my dear. You can enjoy the outdoors, but only when your skin is protected. Get your hat and gloves."

"We're in the South, Clay. The wind may be fresh, but I certainly don't need gloves."

"You haven't heard a thing I said." He took her hand and tugged at it, turning her toward him. "Now sit still, Elizabeth—listen to what I'm saying—and do not interrupt. In the South, we expect our women to be white—as white as it is possible to be. Which means that when you go abroad, you will wear suitable clothing to protect your skin from the sun. Your dresses will have long sleeves, you will wear gloves, and you will never venture forth, even a short distance, without a sun hat and a parasol. Have I made myself clear?"

"If I go for a walk—if I go to pick some flowers for the table—I must wear long sleeves, gloves and a hat? Is that what you are saying? Or are you saying that if I go to Darien or to Savannah I should be thus attired?"

He sighed. "Aunt Mattie was right. I should have found a Southern girl."

"Aunt Mattie again."

"Yes, Aunt Mattie. What she said is true. I must teach you everything. I have to explain about keeping your skin pure. I have to explain our food to you—" He hesitated. "I struggle with you, Elizabeth, I argue, I preach. You must keep your ideas about how we treat our people to yourself."

"By 'our people,' Clay, do you mean our kin, or is this just a way of avoiding the word 'slave'?"

"I'll not tolerate insolence, Elizabeth." She could hear anger and she realized for the first time that Clay's voice always had anger just below the sound of it. Most of the time it could not be heard, but it was there. When he spoke again, his voice was low but firm. "I'm being patient."

"I'm sorry, Clay, but you were avoiding the word, weren't you?" She was pushing him, but she had to know. "Go ahead. You can say 'slave'. You won't upset me."

He took her chin between his thumb and forefinger, forcing her head around so that she was looking directly in his eyes. Then, as though he were speaking to a difficult child, he said, "Stay with the subject, Elizabeth. Listen to what I say. Listen to it well. I want you to protect yourself from the sun every time you are out in it—every single time—however short the period. Is that clear?"

"There will be no short-sleeved dresses?"

"For indoors, yes. They may be worn at night, or when you are inside the house. If you choose to go out, you will change clothes if necessary. Have I made that point clear?"

"Yes."

"Run along and find your hat and your gloves."

Elizabeth saw her first cotton gin on Edisto Island. It was not in operation, but she was fascinated. When she tried to remove the seed by hand, she was even more impressed with the usefulness of such a simple mechanism. She also saw slaves, field hands, for the first time. She had seen servants in houses along the way, and in the inns and hotels, but to see a hundred men at work in a field brought reality to the lectures she had heard. She looked, but she saw no whips.

As the boat moved through the channels, there were beautiful homes in the distance. One house sat on a rise of land facing the channel. It was surrounded by large and sprawling trees with branches that seemed to be reaching outward instead of upward. Two black men were working in the garden, and there was a lady in a large hat. She must be a Southern girl, Elizabeth thought, she has her delicate skin properly protected.

"It's a handsome place, isn't it?" Clay asked. "It belongs to one of the several branches of Hamiltons who live along this coast. They're kin to those down our way."

"It's beautiful. I wish Uncle Roderick could see it. He said again and again that the South was a primitive place."

"And he was right. Parts of it are. Need I remind you of what you've seen in the past week?"

"But not where we're going to live?"

"Oh, no, not Greenleaf."

"Is our house that grand?"

"No. The main house at Greenleaf is comfortable, but not as ostentatious—not many are. Father didn't build for show. Our money went back into the land. That was father's credo, and it's mine. We have a large area under cultivation, counting both the rice and the cotton, but we own much more that has not been reclaimed. Our money has gone back into the source of it—either in reclaiming land, or in buying or the breeding of our people."

"Breeding? You make 'your people' sound like livestock. Are you establishing bloodlines, Clay?"

He looked her squarely in the face. "You're trying to anger me, Elizabeth. Your tongue is too often dipped in acid. But I won't rise to your bait, I won't dignify your effort. Instead, I'll give you another lesson in being a planter's wife, so listen well. As you say, we do attempt to establish bloodlines, although I doubt that any planter I know thinks of it in exactly that way. Nonetheless, that's what we are doing. When we have a strapping buck, we will use him to sire offspring, and we also take care to choose suitable, big-boned women. Such a combination will, more often than not, throw fine children."

"It *is* breeding."

"Oh, yes, my dear, it's breeding. It's commerce. I don't deny that. It's done with purpose. You have better people to work your lands, and you have marketable people for sale or trade. Some plantations are better known for the quality of the people they produce than for cotton. We don't take it that far at Greenleaf. Byron objects to restricted breeding. But as I see it, we have too many yard children."

"But there is selective breeding, even at Greenleaf?"

"Yes. There should be more. But Byron is against it. He has romantic ideas—Byron is a dreamer, a poet, his sensibilities are much too tender for a man in a man's world."

"Byron sounds like someone I'm going to like."

"Yes, you probably will."

"And you'll be jealous."

"No, not of Byron."

"Because he's your brother?"

"No, just because he's Byron. You'll see."

When the Hamilton plantation was well out of sight, the *Kenneth Cooper* moved from a restricted channel to open waters.

"My only worry is that you might be lonely at Greenleaf." Clay said. "That's why I hope you'll like Byron and that you'll become his friend. You have a lot in common."

"Like what?"

"Well, music, for one thing. And he reads. There is always something in the mail for Byron. He's been a constant reader as long as I can remember. He has quite a library."

"What does he read? What kinds of things?"

"Anything and everything."

"Will he be living with us?"

"No, not at the main house. Byron lives at Wolf Head."

"Strange."

"Not when you know Byron. He always liked that finger of high land, even as a boy. It faces the marshes. It's a lonely place, but it suits him. He's built there—the offices for the estate, and his own personal quarters."

"And he lives alone?"

"Well, not exactly alone. Wolf Quarter, is nearby. He has women to cook and clean for him and there's Gordy."

"Who is Gordy?"

Clay looked at the distant horizon. He was such a long time in answering that Elizabeth turned to look directly at him. The expression in his eyes disturbed her. Clay always seemed so happy, but she could see melancholy now. His bright blue eyes were clouded. "Are you all right, Clay?" She touched his arm.

"I'm fine," he said, "just fine."

"But you don't want to talk about Byron anymore—or Gordy?"

"Let's wait until you meet him, Elizabeth. I love my brother, and I hope you will. I love him, but I don't understand him."

"So, for now, we'll drop it right there."

"Thank you, my dear," he said quietly. "There are times when I don't really care for your perception, but this is not one of them." He turned and walked away.

Chapter Twenty-Three

The following morning the *Kenneth Cooper* drew closer to the Port of Savannah. Elizabeth had been on deck since breakfast. She wore the most severely tailored dress in her grip. She wanted to be able to move about freely. It had long sleeves to protect her from the sun, and, as Clay had instructed, she wore gloves and carried a parasol. A very proper Southern lady, she thought to herself, he cannot object to any of this. She was wrong.

"I haven't seen that dress before, have I?"

"It's one of the new ones. I got it in New York."

"You look more like a boy in a skirt."

"It's a new style, Clay. Candida helped me choose it."

"Then Candida has no more sense than you have. You may wear it today. We'll be rushed in Savannah. I'm told the *Altamaha* should be sailing at nine tonight, ten at the latest. You can tag along or rest in the room."

"We'll leave by ten, and you're going to take a room?"

"You need to rest, my dear. This journey has not been easy. And I have plans for this afternoon. Fortunately, I don't have all that many errands." Then his eyes seemed to skip across the grassy marsh at the side of the *Kenneth Cooper*. "It's beginning to look like home."

"Like home, Clay? You were born in Philadelphia."

"Only because father sent mother there. Byron was actually born on Greenleaf Island with just a midwife in attendance.

But make no mistake about it, my dear, we're both Georgia boys—we're Southerners. It's more than a location; it's a way of life. I can't explain it. You have it or you don't; you live it or you don't. Georgia is a state of mind, my dear. But I can tell you one thing, if it ever comes to it, I'll fight for that state of mind."

He had started out softly, but at the end of his speech his voice had hardened and grown louder. Two gentlemen, walking along the deck, drew abreast as he made his final statement. One of them spoke, without breaking stride,"Well said, Greenleaf. We'd have less of a problem in Washington if we had a few like you there."

Neither Clay nor Elizabeth said a word. Both were lost in personal thoughts. Elizabeth was acutely aware that she did not share Clay's feelings, either for the land they were to live on or the slavery that supported it. She could only hope she could bring about changes. There were things she could do. She could start a school and a hospital. She could make life better for the people at Greenleaf. Clay could not oppose that. He had said a happy people work better. If he meant it—if he really meant it—she could begin her work as soon as they arrived.

"We'll be in Savannah in another hour," Clay said, breaking the silence. "It's a city on the move. I told Hutchins that if things didn't work out for him in Wilmington, he could come down here and stay with us until he decided on Darien or Savannah."

"Stay with us? Oh, Clay, you didn't."

"Of course I did. Why not? We have the room, and I could be helpful to him. We could use another general store in Darien. There's only one worth anything. I told him to come to Darien if he didn't like Wilmington." He turned toward her. "I thought you got on well with Martha Hutchins, Elizabeth, or were my eyes deceiving me?"

"I do. Martha was helpful to me and I genuinely liked her, but he—he was another thing. He—" A chill ran from the top of her head to the tips of her toes. "I don't like him, Clay. He gives me the creeps. Those fat lips—"

"Fat lips? You hate a man because of his appearance? Come on, Elizabeth. You're being a real ninny again."

"I hope he never comes."

"He may not. I made the offer, that's all. He may be happy in Wilmington. But I don't understand you, Elizabeth. You're being completely unreasonable. Fat lips, indeed!"

"You're defending him, Clay. You don't even know him."

"Neither do you," he said. Elizabeth looked away, out across the undulating reeds and grasses toward a nearby hammock covered with stunted pines and palmettos. She tried to blot out his words, but Clay continued. "He's not someone I would want as a boon companion, but there's nothing wrong with him." He waited for a reply. Elizabeth said nothing. "He's just someone trying to make a living for his family. You have to admire that. If I can help him, I will."

"I hope it never happens," she said at last.

"So do I, since you've made him into a villain." His eyes were directly on her. "But if he does come to Greenleaf, you will be civil. Do you understand that? I will not be embarrassed by you."

She was angry. Maybe she sometimes acted like a ninny, but he was forever treating her like one. This time she was not being a ninny. She had reason to avoid George Hutchins.

Clay continued. "You women! You never use your heads. You carry on without reason—stupid, senseless emotion."

Just like Papa, she thought, condescension.

"Right now, this thing about Hutchins—" Clay tried to reason with her once again. "Can't you see, it's as silly as your baseless feud with Aunt Mattie?"

"Don't start that again, Clay, please."

"But it's the same—"

"I have good reason for disliking George Hutchins. I don't want to hurt him. I just want to avoid him."

"Good reason? What is it, Elizabeth? What has this monster done?" She made no reply. "Speak up, Elizabeth." She pressed her lips together. Clay waited. "Just as I thought. Nothing. Whim. Female craziness."

It was too much. Her fear was not "female craziness," and it was time Clay acknowledged it. "We left George Hutchins at Wilmington," she said, "and I had hoped to forget him. But you push the point, Clay, so I'm going to tell you the whole story." She began with Hutchins' first overture. She told Clay about the occurence at the "public" stop, and she told him of how she was forced to get Mrs. Hutchins to accompany her to the outhouse at the Sanders farm. He was silent through it all.

"And that's it? That's the whole thing?"

"Would you have preferred rape? What's the matter with you, Clay? I didn't mention it then, because I was afraid of what you might do. I think I may have over-estimated my husband's protection."

"Watch your tone, Elizabeth. It's been a tiring trip for me, too. I will not put up with impertinence."

"I received insulting treatment from a stranger, and now you discount it completely. What else can I think?"

"That will be the end of it, Elizabeth!"

"You're angry? And what about me? I'm the one who has the reason to be furious. You listen to me and then you discount what I say completely and then call me a dunce."

"Oh, indeed you are. I don't know what it is about chaste women. They hang on to their virtue with such tenacity that they go soft in the head. Such a silly story. All imagination. He leered at you and licked his lips, did he? He touched your breast with his thumb?"

"Yes, he did. Just as you did. Don't tell me that was in my imagination."

"No, my dear, that was not your imagination. But this new story, this wild thing with George Hutchins. How can I believe it? He has a woman with more breast in one teat than you have with both. You're talking nonsense. If Hutchins had been on the women's side of the road, don't you think someone would have seen him either coming or going? Don't you think he would have run into at least one woman who would have screamed? Why didn't you scream?"

"Because of Martha Hutchins and the children."

"Because he wasn't there. That's the real reason. No, my dear, it just doesn't ring true. I don't think you're fabricating this whole story. Because of our marriage, because of our intimacies, I think I've aroused passions you didn't know were there. You're now having erratic, even erotic, thoughts. The virginity that we keep on striving for in our females can warp a girl's brain. The blacks have it all over us. Their lives are more natural; their matings are in keeping with what nature intended."

Tears streamed down her face. She was no longer angry. She was empty of feelings. "You don't believe me."

"I believe you. You're saying what you think happened, but I don't think it did. You're overwrought. The past six months haven't been easy and this trip has been a nightmare. Society is wrong, completely wrong, to expect a girl to go from a virgin to a wanton after a short religious ceremony. It has upset many a girl, and I think it upset you."

The silence between them was formidable. He looked out across the reeds in one direction and she looked in another. Finally, she spoke: "How far are we from Savannah, Clay? How long will it be?"

"About an hour, my dear, perhaps a little less."

"Then, if you'll excuse me, Clay, I think I'll lie down. I did not sleep well last night."

From the time they hired the rig in Savannah until they stopped for lunch it was confusion. They crisscrossed the city, they doubled back, and then went forward. Clay had a list of things he wanted to accomplish, purchases he needed to make for the estate, and people he had to see. This time she saw the back alleys of the town, some of the grand houses, and, of course, the commercial section.

As she waited in the rig, she realized that this was the South she had been looking for. This was the antithesis of winter in Philadelphia. Here it was, a day in mid-January, but it was spring in every way. She could close her eyes and smell lilacs, she could see tulips, she could feel the warm breeze toying with the lace at her neck.

When Clay got back from one of the riverfront warehouses, he found Elizabeth with her eyes closed. "Sorry to awaken you, my dear. I think I must have worn you out with all this."

"No, Clay," she said, "I wasn't napping. I was daydreaming. This is the South I hoped I'd find: the charm of this town, the warm breeze and such a gentle sun."

He took her hand. "Gentle sun, is it? Mark this well, young lady, there is more to the South than magnolias and cape jasmine. We don't think the South is paradise, but it's as close as we'll find in this life. The South is home." He said the word again. It was almost inaudible. When he spoke once more, the words were directed inward. "After you've lived here, no matter how far you wander, you will always, at least in your mind, come home. You'll come home even when you remember the dog days of August when the heat wants to smother you. Georgia may not mean much to the world, but Georgia is everything to a Georgian. One day, Elizabeth, you will be a Georgian."

"You love it."

"Yes, ma'am, I do. And so will you."

After lunch he said, "I have a few more errands, Elizabeth. You can stay in the room this time. I may be a while at the bank. You stay here and rest. When I get back, you might not find time for resting."

"You always leer so."

"I'm an earthy man, my dear. You knew that when you first discovered I had an errant thumb."

"Clay!"

"Get your rest. And when you are looking to our clothing, be sure you do what needs to be done to the pink dress. I want you to be wearing it tomorrow when we arrive in Darien."

"The pink one, with the lace collar and long sleeves?"

"Yes. It makes your skin look pure and white. I want Darien to see the new Mrs. Greenleaf looking lovelier than any woman within a hundred miles."

"If Clay Greenleaf had bought a new riding horse, he'd want it curried, so everyone would know that Greenleaf knew horseflesh."

"If that's the comparison you wish to make, my dear."

"Well, it's not. But isn't that what you're saying?"

"Here's that damnable female mind again. It has no logic. If I say how I want you to look, I'm parading my own good taste, as though I had made a good bargain in choosing you. But if I had said nothing, you would have spent hours selecting the right dress, and primping, so you could present your best face to Darien. What's the difference?"

She hesitated. "I suppose there's really no difference, but when you say it aloud, when you tell me what to wear, how you want me to look, it's different."

"There's no reason, no sanity, no common sense to that, Elizabeth. You're simply being perverse."

"I don't know why you can't see it my way sometimes."

"I could do it only if I threw logic to the winds, my dear. You're a female. Accordingly, you know as much about logic as a nigger knows about Judgment Day. The female mind is not meant to deal with the complex aspects of life. That's why civilization is as it is. You have your men to protect you, to think for you. That's the pattern of life, both by law and by the hand of God."

"You don't believe that? You don't think men and women have different brains?"

He took a closer look at her. She had surprised him. "Of

course I do, Elizabeth. And that's as it should be. A woman's mind is very good, as long as it's utilized for its purpose. Women can drive themselves crazy—they can literally go beyond—if they try to exceed the limits of their capability. That's the reason women should not be over-educated. A man runs a risk, a terrible risk, when he permits such a thing."

Elizabeth couldn't believe his words. They were insane. He couldn't mean it.

"You have a fine mind, my dear. You know how to be a proper wife and to make a man feel capable of meeting the world on its own terms. That's a valuable attribute. In time you will know—because you are a woman—how to bring children into the world and to mold them as they grow. That's the female mind. It's not something that a man can do. You know how to set a table, how to run a household, how to cook, sew and mend. There are thousands of things your brain is capable of, but it's not the brain of a man, that much was clearly established long before either of us came into this life."

"You sound even more stupid than Papa—"

"You are overwrought, Elizabeth!"

"No, I'm not."

"That will be the end of it, Elizabeth! I mean it!"

There was a pause. As he spoke, his voice lost some of the sharp edge, but he was firm. "You will wear the pink dress."

He picked up his jacket and satchel. "I'll be back in an hour, perhaps a little more. See that you get yourself calmed down before I return."

Chapter Twenty-Four

Elizabeth kept the pink dress on a clothes rack after the maid had cleaned and pressed it. She did the same to Clay's linen shirt with the fluting down the front. That shirt, his dark coat, the maroon tie, and pearl gray trousers would make suitable attire for his homecoming.

If he wanted to dress for the few townspeople who might be on the docks in Darien, why not go along with it? It could do no harm.

When he returned, Clay was full of vitality and excited about being close to home. Elizabeth intended to harbor resentment for his continued reference to her minimal brain power, but she was unable to maintain the pose.

After she managed to get settled on Greenleaf Island, after she had had time to organize a school and change what Clay called "the infirmary" into a proper hospital, Elizabeth was sure he would see she was an intelligent woman.

The *Altamaha* was smaller and dirtier than the *Kenneth Cooper* or the *General Oglethorpe*, but Elizabeth was more forgiving. She should have been restless the night before arriving at her new home for the first time, but the noise of the boat and the poor accommodations did not disturb her.

She was wide awake as the first traces of the sun etched through the nighttime sky. She made her way to the women's public room for her morning's absolutions. It was an act of purification. She eliminated the past, and, as she bathed in the limited way possible, she washed away yesterday and all other yesterdays.

This was the beginning of something new. Today she would meet Byron. She would see the marshes surrounding Greenleaf Island; perhaps she'd know why they occupied Clay's mind so thoroughly.

Today she would become mistress of a plantation.

They were near his home. From the deck she saw a mysterious but beautiful place he loved so much. Patches of fog clung to the water's surface. It made rivulets of white that skittered off in the distance; it followed unseen currents to unknown places. The fog hung like a fragile veil on the island hammocks in the distance. All around her were gently moving reeds. It was a sea of reeds broken only by a hammock, and another and another, each more distant, each more hidden in the fog. As the boat lumbered through this pristine place, it disturbed the wildlife. Birds complained about its noisy passage. Its wake caused the shoreline palmettos to object to such a rude intrusion.

She wore the pink dress, of course, but because of the morning chill, she had elected to pull a mauve shawl about her shoulders. She walked to the other side of the vessel. Surely it could not be as strangely beautiful. But it was. There were miles of reeds, broken occasionally by a wider bay, or another channel to the sea, and by an unending collection of large and small island hammocks, dotted with palms, pines and withered and dwarfed vegetation. As the boat moved through the sea of reeds, she saw trees on the larger spits of land. They were the kind of oaks that she had seen on the Hamilton Plantation, strange trees that tended to lift their gnarled branches constantly outward instead of upward. They looked old and arthritic.

In that early morning hour, when the sky was mother of pearl, the Witch of the Sea Marsh captured her heart. For the first time, Elizabeth could understand Clay's rapture when he spoke of Greenleaf. He never had the words for it. But how could he? It was primal, it was something you could see, you could feel, but you could never explain. The rapture defied logic. On this first day of her new life, Elizabeth was under the spell of the sea islands of Georgia. It was a moment suspended. She could not comprehend it, but she could feel it in a haunting, piercing, crucifying way.

The passengers and crew began to stir. With the noise, the Witch of the Sea Marsh went back to her island, where the fog hung low over the water, allowing the oaks to rise from a white blanket at their feet. She was gone, the witch was gone, the moment was gone. It was as though it had never been. Elizabeth thought of Cousin Nora in far-off Cornwall. "It's the little people," she would have said, "they are everywhere."

As Elizabeth walked back to their side of the boat, she caught a glimpse of herself reflected in the pilothouse windows. Clay was right about the pink, she thought. Damn him. He has such stupid ideas about so many things, and yet he manages to be right too many times.

She could smell bacon; she could see people and hear them. The sun appeared from behind night's barrier and it lifted her spirits further. "It will be a perfect day," she said aloud.

"Do you talk to yourself often, Elizabeth? My father's aunt did. She was daft," Clay said as he came to her side.

"I think I am daft, or I have been. I've been out here since early morning. For the first time, Clay, I understand how you feel about the marshes. Now, I begin to know how you feel about Greenleaf. I can't explain it, and I know you can't, but, after this morning, I—"

"Wait until you see Greenleaf."

"It can't be better."

"It is." He stopped. "No, it may not be better. It's much like this. Maybe it's my own bias. Maybe it's because there I know all the secret spots. Maybe I, like my brother Byron, have private places. Maybe, because of my personal feelings about the land, I only think Greenleaf is better."

"You're not always that honest."

"You shared a private moment with me, Elizabeth. You couldn't say it in words, but you found the—" He stopped. He touched her arm and she turned toward him. She loved him more at that instant than through all the months of their marriage. "I'm not sure how to say this, Elizabeth," he continued slowly. "It sounds so stupid. But I know you experienced the marshes, the sea islands of Georgia, and the memory—hell, it's more than a memory—the experience will be with you as long as you live." He lifted her hand to his lips and kissed it.

"Where are the gloves?"

"I came on deck before the sun was over the rim of the world. After breakfast, I'll wear the gloves."

After breakfast they watched the channels grow wider. At times Elizabeth felt they were truly at sea. It was a perfect day. The winter sun was warm and the breeze was gentle. It was January but there was a hint of Spring in the air. What must it be like at the manse? Papa would be grumpy. He always was when he had to have fires all over the house. She could see it in her mind. A gray winter's day, with gray light coming through the windows, a feeble light, unable to find the corners of the room. Papa would be at his desk, squinting, but still working without a light.

As Clay spoke she returned to the warm January day and the sea. "Watch the sun, my dear. You're not using that parasol. The last thing a Southern girl wants is freckles."

She raised the pink parasol. "I was thinking about what a gray day it must be in New York. January is so dreary."

"You're far from New York, my dear. You have to contend with a Georgia sun from now on."

"How far are we from Darien, Clay? We must be close."

He looked around, sighting islands and markers. "I know this area well, Elizabeth. We should see Darien in about fifteen minutes." He took her gloved hand. "Shall we walk toward the front? We can find shade there."

She put her hand on his arm as they made their way forward. "One more thing, Elizabeth." He paused for a moment. "Don't expect too much from Darien." There was another pause as if he were unable to find words for what he was thinking. "I love Darien. It's my hometown. But it's no great shakes by other standards. It's not Savannah, or Charleston. It's just a nice town, with nice people and nice churches. It's provincial and hidebound and gossipy, but it's where I grew up. It's home to me."

"If you love it so much, I will."

"Maybe I said it poorly, my dear. I don't know that I love Darien because of what it is, or because of what it is to me. There's a difference. I don't expect you to love it. In time, you'll make up your own mind about it. Darien will be a part of your life, though, whatever you think. It's where the doctor lives, it's where we shop, where we bank and where we go to church. All the plantations are entities, each trying to be a self-sufficient unit, but Darien is the lodestone."

As the *Altamaha* rounded a bend, Darien came into view. Clay was right. It was not as grand as Charleston—it could not be compared with Charleston in any way. She saw a clutch of houses at the water's edge, a mixture of old and new, a melange of architectural styles. Some of the buildings were painted, and some had never seen paint. She saw a waterfront: a series of pilings, docks and jetties. She could feel a change in atmosphere. It was not what she could see, but what she could smell that formed her first impression of Darien. She smelled the sea and the damp ocean grasses that had washed to the shore. There was the smell of fish, of tar and pine smoke, the smell of iodine, and the smell of people. There is a fresh smell where the sea meets the land on its own terms, but when the sea meets the land and man is also present, you can get smells that are not so pure. That was Darien.

But the biggest surprise was not the town—not how it looked or how it smelled. The biggest surprise was the activity that had been generated by the arrival of the *Altamaha*. The docks were alive with people, and the bay was full of boats of every imaginable kind.

"The people—" she said. "Why so many people?"

"The arrival of the *Altamaha*, or any coastal boat, is an event, Elizabeth. You saw it at every stop we made."

"Nothing like this. This is wild. Everyone for miles around must be here."

Clay laughed. "No, not quite. Most of the people you see are blacks. They're from Greenleaf. I don't always get this much attention when I return, but this is special. Today my bride is with me. Byron must have made a holiday of it."

As the *Altamaha* blew the whistle, a cheer went up from the people at dockside and from those bobbing on the water in boats. There were shouts, grunts, whistles and laughter. There was singing, a lone voice and then a chorus.

"It's pandemonium."

"It's the welcome you deserve, my dear. I don't think you will forget your first visit to Darien."

"How could I? Oh, Clay—" There were tears in her eyes.

"Get hold of yourself, my dear. No one wants to see a weeping girl. Smile. Wave to them. They want to see the new mistress of Greenleaf and they deserve to."

Clay led her to the railing. "Wave, Elizabeth. It's what they expect. It's what they came to see." She raised her hand. Another cheer tore at her ears. She was laughing, she was crying, and she was holding Clay's hand with an iron grip.

"Oh, Clay, I didn't know it would be like this."

"I tried to tell you, Elizabeth, but you are so caught up in your own ideas that you have rarely been open to reality."

"They seem so happy."

"And you expected the downtrodden. You expected an overseer with a whip in his hand." She glanced at him. She saw that wry smile, that irritating, I-told-you-so smile. "Sorry to disappoint you my dear."

As the *Altamaha* nudged the pilings, Elizabeth said, "Do you see Byron, Clay?"

"No. I guess he decided not to come to Darien."

Elizabeth was disappointed. "Oh."

"Don't judge, my dear. Byron doesn't like crowds."

"I had hoped—"

"I told you, Elizabeth, Byron is as shy as a deer. Wait until you know him, then you'll understand."

"Byron seems to require a lot of forgiving."

"Yes, I suppose he does, but when you know Byron, it's easy to forgive him. He answers to his own gods, just as you answer to yours and I answer to mine. He doesn't fit a pattern, but he's a good man, an honest man, and he's my only brother. I love him, even if I don't understand him. Wait until you have a chance to know him, Elizabeth."

The engines stopped. Lines were thrown to the docking crew. There was a new clarity to what she could hear. She had become so accustomed to the noise of the chugging, puffing *Altamaha* that the lack of those noises was disconcerting. Now she could hear individual voices in the crowd. "Welcome home," "Me so glad you home, Mistah Clay," "Oh, skin-so-white Missus, you look so fine," "You come home, you come home, you come home," "Lordy, we need you back Mistah Clay."

At last the *Altamaha* was secured and the ramp was lowered. As they made their way through the crowds, she could hear shouts, she could hear bits of conversation, she could feel timid fingers touch her dress as she passed by. "My, my, ain't she a purty one," "Oh, Missus, you is lily white, lily white," "All pink and white—ain't that sump'n."

"Clay!" He could hear fear in her voice.

"Stay with me, Elizabeth. Smile. No one means you harm." He glanced at her. "I said smile, Elizabeth." His voice was firm. He lifted her arm, he made her wave at the crowd. There was another cheer and laughter and applause.

Farther down the dock they came to the boat that would take them to Greenleaf Island. The man waiting for them wore a white suit and a wide-brimmed hat. As Elizabeth came near, he removed the hat. "Welcome to Darien, Mrs. Greenleaf," he said. He turned to Clay. "I had hoped you'd get here sooner, Clay. I have a lot I'd like to get done this Spring."

"I got here as soon as I could, Rigby. Your change in plans didn't help, either."

There was irritation in Rigby's voice. "I couldn't let the opportunity I have upriver pass. You don't get a chance like this everyday."

"No matter, Rigby. I'm here now. We'll talk about it later. In the meantime, I don't think you have been properly introduced to my wife. Elizabeth, this is our very best overseer, the one we are losing to his own plantation. This is Jonathan Rigby."

She was the center of attention, not only to the three involved in the introduction, but to the crowds that had moved along behind them as they walked down the dock. It was disconcerting to have so many eyes on her. In response to the introduction, she was only able to say, quietly, "Mr. Rigby."

She saw bold features and bold eyes. Rigby was not handsome, not in the way Clay was, but the self-confidence that surrounded him gave the illusion of a handsome, commanding, dominating man. He lifted her gloved hand to his lips. "It's my pleasure, Mrs. Greenleaf. Since I'm still an employee, let me bid you welcome to Greenleaf Plantation."

"Thank you, Mr. Rigby," she finally managed to say.

"You'll have to excuse her, Rigby," Clay said, "she was not expecting this kind of welcome. I should have warned her. I half suspected Byron would do something like this—he's always looking for an excuse to give the people a holiday."

"It's not a busy time. It won't create a problem. We talked about it. I was in favor of it."

"Come, my dear," Clay said. "Let me help you aboard. We still have a distance to go. We'll be expected for lunch."

"Yes," Rigby said. "Carlotta has planned an elaborate lunch for the new bride."

Carlotta, Elizabeth thought. Where have I heard that name? Clay must have mentioned it, but who is she, how does she fit in this puzzling day?

Their arrival at Darien, the crowds, the noise, the confusion, was too much for Elizabeth. She could not grasp it all. And now Carlotta. Who was Carlotta? Her mind was in turmoil. She tried, but she was unable to bring reason to it.

And to add to the rest of it, she knew that Carlotta had prepared a special luncheon.

Was Carlotta a cousin there especially for her arrival?

To forget someone she should know would be upsetting enough, but this day offered a variety of fresh challenges. First there was the welcoming committee, at least two hundred strong. Then there was Clay, asking her to smile and wave, like a princess at a garden party. It was overwhelming.

And, as a final thing to shatter a day that had begun so brightly, there was this man Rigby. When she thought of him a shiver ran down her spine. Why? Why should he cause her a moment's trouble? He was an employee who would soon be gone; that's what Clay had said. He said Rigby was anxious to leave, to move upriver.

Clay was onboard their boat. His hand was extended. "I'm speaking to you, my dear. Give me your hand."

Chapter Twenty-Five

It was a lumbering, clumsy boat, but it was utilitarian. Their luggage and the purchases Clay had made along the way had been loaded onto this slow-moving vessel of uncertain age. It was called the *Mary Ann,* in honor of Clay's mother.

As they took leave of the harbor at Darien, the smaller vessels loaded with blacks from Greenleaf were soon left in the distance. Elizabeth could still hear the singing. Sometimes it was a mournful song and at other times it was a chant everyone knew. The voices and the rhythm seemed to permeate the reeds that surrounded the *Mary Ann.*

Thirty minutes later, after many a twist in the waterway, they turned into a smaller stream. She could see elongated, tall mounds ahead. As they grew closer, she saw they were earthen dikes with sluice gates. There were people all along the top of the dikes. Once again there was the confusion of the waving, cheering, singing and shouting. As they drew closer to the dikes, Elizabeth could see the colors of the dresses and headbands. They were in their Sunday best. They had been given a holiday; they were in holiday spirits.

"More of the welcoming committee."

"The boats couldn't hold them all," Clay said. "Those on the dikes are only a part of it. They'll be at the house, too."

Elizabeth took his hand. "It's overwhelming. I didn't expect anything like this. I'm glad it's taking so long to get to the house. I need time."

"You'll manage," Clay said. "I should have warned you. Your problem in Darien was, at least partially, my fault."

The *Mary Ann,* fired by a wood burning boiler, moved slowly and noisily along scattering birds and the wildlife of the marshes as it moved relentlessly forward.

Rigby had boarded with them, but, once on the vessel, he had made his way toward the steaming, clattering, hissing engine where he saw to the firing of it.

"Where's the house, Clay?"

"Look ahead and to the right. Do you see those oaks—the trees with branches extending above the dikes? That's the island's only high land. That's where the house is built."

"I see the trees, but I can't see a house."

"Keep looking. It will be coming into view."

There was a gentle bend in the river. The *Mary Ann* was heading toward land.

"Oh, I think I see something. It's a large barn with a steep pointed roof. It's quite tall."

"You're looking at your home, my dear." He was silent for a few seconds. He wanted her to understand what he had said, and then he continued: "No, it's not the main house of Greenleaf Plantation. It's for the overseer on the rice island, but it's where you'll be living."

"I'm sorry, Clay. I seem to say the wrong thing all too often. I shouldn't have called it a barn."

"Well," Clay replied, "maybe I owe you another apology. I simply didn't think of how this house might look to someone seeing it for the first time. I never thought of how it might appear to you." It would be easy for Elizabeth to say the wrong thing again, so she said nothing.

The house was a crushing disappointment. As they drew nearer she could see the unpainted, weathered siding. It was a large, square building, with four steeply pitched sides that made up the shingled and weathered roof. Even in the sunlight, it was gloomy.

"My father designed the house.You'll find it practical, considering the weather during the growing season. Blacks can take the heat of course, but not the overseer. Father made a house that breathes. You'll see what I mean when you get there. It's really quite a marvel."

Clay looked at the house with something that seemed akin to reverence. She could see that structure meant something to him. My God, she thought, what can I say? It's a miserable place. It's not a dwelling; it's a nightmare.

The gray building stood on tall piers. At the second level, there was a veranda on all sides. Part of the ground level was enclosed with a filigree of brickwork. The rest was open. Chickens picked at the earth under the house. A fat pig ran across the yard. It was a yard; it could not be called a lawn. There wasn't a single blade of grass. From the docks to the house, she saw bare earth, as gray as the house itself. This was something his father had designed? Designed? It looked haphazard; it looked thrown together. She felt ill.

"His ideas, the engineering that went into it—" Clay seemed lost in his own thoughts. "Well, you'll see. Wonderful innovations, and he wasn't an engineer. He just used his common sense. Heat rises, everyone knows that, but father put it to work for him. He had many new ideas for a house and he used them all. The result is that this is a comfortable house, even in August."

The dock, like the house, looked thrown together. Further conversation was impossible because of the crowd at dockside. At close range, the colors were vivid—a startling contrast to the old gray house. She saw bright oranges, reds, violets, purples, magentas; every color, every hue. They rivaled the sun for brilliance.

This time Elizabeth knew her role. She took Clay's arm and moved to the railing. She raised her handkerchief. There was a cheer from the crowd along the shoreline. This is what they had come to see. "Well done, my dear, well done. You'll become a Southern lady in spite of yourself."

"Don't laugh at me, Clay."

"I'm not laughing. You handled it well." They walked down the rough ramp that rested on the dock.

Clay led her through the crowd. It was a repetition of the docks at Darien, but she was ready for it. She smiled. She was spoken to, welcomed, and touched. She said thank you again and again. Elizabeth held tightly to Clay's hand as he moved toward the house. She could see it more clearly now. The stairway leading to the veranda was elegant, a startling contrast to the house. It rose from two sides, curving up to a common center on a level with the veranda.

She didn't have to be told the man at the top of the stairs was Byron. He looked like Clay. His hair was brown instead of black, but his eyes were the same clear blue. He was smaller, more diffident, kinder looking. Clay had an arrogant demeanor, a self-confident, defiant look. There was none of that in Byron.

He came forward, extending his arms to her. "Elizabeth, welcome to Greenleaf. I'm Clay's brother, Byron."

"I know," she said. "I could have met you on the streets of Savannah or Charleston and I would have known." She walked into his embrace. "Thank you, Byron. I seem to have been welcomed all morning long, but yours is the one I most wanted. Clay loves you very much."

"I hope he does," Byron said. "He and Aunt Mattie are all the family I have left." He held her hands in his, looking at her. "And now you are here." Yes, she thought again, pink was the right choice. "But come on in," Byron said. "I must mind my manners. I've kept you standing in the hot sun. It was thoughtless of me."

The double, leaded-glass front doors were as much of a contrast to the house as the wide curved stairway from the ground to the veranda. The unpainted, weathered building had entry doors with crystal inserts. The incongruity of it startled her. This was the first of the surprises. Beyond the entry was one very large room. It served for living, lounging and dining.

It was expensively and comfortably furnished, but it had no ceiling. When you glanced up, up to that towering peak, you could see the skeleton of the house. There were two large skylights on the north slope of the roof. The large room was flooded with natural light. There were doors leading off on all sides. Clay was watching her.

"Those are the bedrooms, my dear, or the private rooms. Later I'll show you the other things father devised. It really is something special. Father wanted the main house to be built the same, but mother would have no part of it."

"You're surprised by it," Byron said. "I can understand that, but, really, for our weather, it's most practical. Low vents to allow the cooler air in, and nature takes the hotter inside air right out the vents at the top. It may not be needed at this time of year, but it's heaven-sent in summer."

"Time for a tour of the house and father's engineering later. I'm starving now," Clay said. "I can see a loaded serving table over there."

He walked toward a tall, slender and graceful, yellow-skinned Negro woman who stood near the table. "Carlotta," he said, "you have outdone yourself. The meal was prepared especially for me, I can tell. All my favorite things."

"Welcome home, Mistah Clay," she said. The voice had a lilt to it, a melody. It was low and warm and musical.

So that is Carlotta, Elizabeth thought. Now, I remember. Clay had said Carlotta was the housekeeper, in charge of all the house blacks, and that she was scrupulously clean. "She keeps the house niggers in firm control." Yes, she knew who Carlotta was; she had simply forgotten the name.

"Come, my dear. I want you to meet Carlotta. I've told you about her. She runs the house. She'll be a great help to you."

Elizabeth looked into amber eyes under arched eyebrows, the eyes of a tigress. She saw a noble head. "Carlotta," she said, "Mr. Greenleaf has spoken often of you."

"Thank you, Missus." The voice was soft. The jungle eyes missed nothing. I hope, Elizabeth thought, all my buttons are buttoned.

"Come on, everyone. Let's eat," Clay said. "It's well past noon and I can't wait for some of this fried chicken. Yankees don't know how—and never will know how—to fry chicken. I've been away too long. Come, Elizabeth."

Clay and Byron spent the afternoon showing Elizabeth about—not just the house, but they went for a short ride along the top of one of the wide dikes that enclosed the rice fields. They rode far enough for Clay and Byron to try to explain how rice was grown.

"The harvest is over," Clay said. "It's time to make certain the fields are ready for planting in the Spring. I know how, of course, but I want time to go over it with Rigby before he goes upriver."

"We turn the fields by hand," Byron said. "Some planters use a plow, but we do it the old way. You can keep the grade better by hand. Without good drainage, production goes down."

Elizabeth was astounded. "By hand? One shovelful at a time? When you could use a plow?"

"It's to keep the grade, the slope, my dear," Clay said quickly. "It's a sensible thing. It takes more time and labor, but we've found it to be the right way. We have the people here, plenty of them, so we just put them to work."

Elizabeth looked unconvinced.

"He's right, Elizabeth," Byron said. "It takes a series of flows—that's when we flood the fields—to bring in a rice crop. We have to let the water in to sprout the rice, and then we drain it. We do it again in about three weeks to kill weeds and grass, and then we drain it again. There are three flows in all. Each time you must drain the water off completely, or you have damaged a part of your crop. It's essential that the grade is maintained—"

"Enough of this, Byron. Elizabeth has no interest in rice or how we flood the ponds. She's going to have enough to do to keep the house in order."

"I thought she'd like to know what keeps you away for so many hours each day."

"I am interested, Clay."

"Well, I think it's wasted effort. You'll never oversee the rice fields, my dear. If you really want to give her lessons, Byron, tell her how to handle the blacks she'll have under her control. I've tried to talk to her, but she doesn't listen."

"She'll have no trouble," Byron said. "Carlotta will keep them in line. In fact, with Carlotta, you're going to have time on your hands, Elizabeth. Carlotta is a wonder."

Both of the Greenleaf men seemed content to have Elizabeth do nothing. It was their idea that Southern ladies should be like the lilies of the field,"...they toil not, neither do they spin." That was not her plan. She would be mistress of Greenleaf in the fullest sense of the word. She intended to make a difference in the lives of the people who cheered as she came into the harbor that same morning. Her lips were pressed together. She needed to stake her own territory; she needed to make them aware that she was a person who could bring change. Carlotta might be helpful, but running the household would be Elizabeth's province.

"I think, gentlemen, that you both need to know that I'm quite capable of running a household. I did it for my father, and I can do it here. I'm sure Carlotta is the paragon of all virtues; I'm sure she has done an admirable job of running both this and the main house, and that she will continue to do so, but you also must know that I am ready to take my rightful stand at my husband's side."

"Hear, hear," Byron said.

"Hold on, Byron. She's a headstrong, Yankee hellion. She's listened to too many talks given by the likes of that idiotic fool Garrison. I've warned her that she's now living in the South, and that Georgians, as we always have, intend to keep on running things here. I warned her, but I didn't stop her. She got us into trouble in Wilmington and she caused a minor furor in Charleston. Don't encourage her, please."

"I thought we'd buried that, Clay. However, this may be the South, and you Georgians may be proud, and you may be determined to run things as you have in the past, but that doesn't mean there can be only one opinion."

"Now, Byron, you see what I mean?"

"But she has a valid point, Clay. There are many opinions, even here in the South. They may not always be voiced, but they exist. We have abolitionists here. You know that."

"Damned few."

"You're right. But, other opinions do exist."

"Don't encourage her, Byron, please. We have to live with our neighbors. Elizabeth must learn that. If she continues to say the things she said on our journey to Greenleaf, I'll be unable to take her to that new church in Darien, if we ever get it built. What is the news there, Byron? I could see no activity from dockside."

"I went to the last meeting, as you asked, Clay. St. Andrew's will be finished this year. You may not have seen it, but it's under construction. I've seen the plans. It will be a fine church, with the first bell tower in Darien."

"Good. It's been a time in coming. But, as Elizabeth's Uncle Roderick said to me, 'the Southern part of those colonies you live in are backward.'"

"Did he say that, Clay?"

"Well, my dear, perhaps not those exact words, but he said it all the same. England has been civilized since the Romans—at least they like to think so—but we've only recently hacked a place for ourselves in this part of the world."

Clay looked out across the endless acres of rice fields. "Look at that. We didn't have the benefit of the Romans building roads for us. We had to do it. This was all done in one generation. When father first came, this was all marsh. Oh, there may have been an abandoned midden or an Indian burial mound on that rise of land where the house stands, but most of it was hammock and marsh, a virtual sea of reeds. But now—" His arm made a wide sweep. "Well, you see it. Land, firmly under control, producing rice instead of reeds. I'm proud of it."

"We have reason to be proud, Clay," Byron said quietly, "but, to be completely honest, we've not made it all it can be—not until we've made a life for all the people here. There is work to be done, work that should be done if we are proper stewards to this great land we have."

"Not another lecture, Byron. We're riddled with debts, but yet we manage to provide a life here for several hundred people. They have no worries. We do. We give them food and shelter. When that's done, there's damned little left."

"Then these aren't slaves at all," Elizabeth said. "This is just Aunt Mattie and the two Greenleaf boys taking care of the downtrodden. This, truly, is *noblesse oblige*. I've read about it; I've just never seen it before."

Clay was capable of quick fury. She heard it now. "Elizabeth! That will be the end of it."

She was silent. She had embarrassed Clay in front of his only brother. She must learn to control the tongue that had managed to get her into trouble all her life. She should not have spoken her mind in front of Byron. She had no intention of saying those words, but they were in her mind and they just tumbled out. She waited for Clay to speak.

"It's time to start back," Clay said when the red left his face. "I need to talk to Rigby. If you will, Byron, spend the night. I want Rigby to stay longer than he means to, and I may have to bribe him a little."

"If you need me, Clay."

"Thank you, Byron. Please stay."

Chapter Twenty-Six

Clay was sullen on the ride back. He found Rigby, and the three men set off to see a field where a major repair was needed on an intake gate.

Later, Elizabeth was excluded from the conversation at supper. She wondered if the slight were deliberate, but she couldn't be sure. The men talked of last season's crops and how they had been plagued with freshets. Rains at the wrong time can make rice plants weaker. Fast removal is essential. The past season, she heard from both Byron and Rigby, had been rampant with rain and threats of rain.

At one time or another, both Rigby and Byron tried to bring Elizabeth into the conversation. Their attempts were blunted when Clay brought in more technical aspects of the gates and the flows, or the mechanical details of the tidal mill that was used to polish rice before it went to market.

Elizabeth ate quietly. When she felt she could be excused without appearing to be offended by Clay's slight, she found a lamp, a book and went to their bedroom. The book did not hold her attention. She knew Clay was angry. She wondered what course his anger would take.

She lay on the bed looking upward. There was no ceiling to this room. What had Clay said? "Those are the bedrooms, my dear, or the more private rooms." Private? These are private rooms? Clay you are as mad as your dear father. When Clay got into the "feather tick," as he called it, he tended to be rollicking, verbal, and noisy. These were not rooms for that, especially when she learned there was to be a servant in the house at all hours of the night. The situation was even worse because Rigby would share the house until his departure—in these rooms, without ceilings, without the first trace of privacy.

The bedroom did not inspire confidence. As she put on her nightgown and pinned up her hair, she glanced around. Anyone could stand on a chair and look over the tops of the walls. Clay's mother was right in refusing to have the main house built in the same manner.

She slid between the clean white sheets. There was a faint, pleasant, spicy aroma. Was it something in the water, or had they been ironed and then put away in a chest with a sachet bag? She couldn't be sure. Carlotta, she thought. Carlotta just might be everything the two Greenleaf brothers thought her to be. Perhaps Carlotta would be her first friend at Greenleaf Plantation.

Elizabeth must have been asleep briefly, because she didn't know the three men were gone, but she heard them coming back to the house long before the doors were flung open. All three had been drinking. The din hushed as the door was opened. It was replaced by the kind of noise that only the inebriated can make. Voices were exaggerated whispers. There were shushing sounds. The scrape of their boots was louder, and when furniture was bumped, she could hear muffled curses.

"Gentlemen," Clay said, "we will keep our voices down. My wife has had a difficult day. I know she's tired." She heard a series of agreeing mumbles. "I'll look in on her," he said. "No doubt she's asleep, but we'll be sure." She heard his boots. The last thing she wanted was this smelly bull coming to bed with her, not in this open-topped room.

When he opened the door, her eyes were closed. He stepped backwards. She could hear his footsteps recede. "She's sound asleep. The day has been too much for her," he said. No, Lord,

Elizabeth thought, I'm not asleep, but I wish I were. She could visualize them. Three drunken, bumbling, sodden pains in the arse. She listened as they continued making fools of themselves.

"I'm glad you agreed to stay over another month, Rigby. There's a lot that must be done before planting." She heard Rigby grunt. Stay over another month? Is that what she had heard? Live with Rigby under the same roof for another month? Oh, how dreadful, how dreadful. She might keep Clay quiet during his nocturnal games on one or two occasions, but for a month? Clay was both lusty and noisy. She heard Clay continue, his voice mellowed by the rum, "The weather we've had this past year has played havoc with all the gates. You see to the preparing of the land, Rigby, and I'll see to the gates. In a month, it will all be ready."

"I tell you, you don't need me," she heard Rigby say. "You can handle it. I'd like to be on my way."

"No," Clay replied. "A deal's a deal. You said you'd stay, didn't he, Byron? Sure, I can do it by myself, but I want you to stay, Rigby. Besides, you want Robert, and the only way I'm going to let you have him is if you stay."

"I'll buy him from you."

"No, I'll give him to you, but only if you stay."

Here it is, Elizabeth thought, on my first day at Greenleaf. I knew it would happen. A man is being bartered. He has no choice. He's being sold, or traded, or whatever it might be. Clay calls the blacks "my people," but that's little consolation when they're being thrust into a new life somewhere upriver. I don't know Robert, she thought, and yet my heart bleeds for him. I wonder if he knows he's being traded? I'm sure he doesn't.

She heard Rigby again. "From what Byron says, Clay, your wife's a Yankee who doesn't hold with owning slaves."

She heard Clay refill his glass. "Yes, my wife's from the North, Rigby. She's not acquainted with our way. She doesn't know that the South has to depend on a large labor supply. She'll learn. We have to have people for the work that must be done.

The whites won't work in the fields. There's only one way to do it. She'll learn; she'll adjust."

"But she's against slavery, isn't she?"

"She thinks she is. She thinks we flog them, whip them, mistreat them."

"And that happens," Byron said.

"We beat them when they need it; we beat our dogs when they need it. It's the same kind of thing. If you've got an old dog that won't mind," Clay said, "you don't have a dog at all. He's worthless. It's the same damned thing, Byron, you know that. We have to have discipline."

"They are people, Clay. They're not dogs."

"You keep out of this, Byron," Clay said. "There's not a man or woman here who could take care of himself for a month. They can do simple jobs, but they're sorely lacking in intelligence. We help them. We need to help them. When a planter buys a slave, he takes on a duty. He knows they're essentially stupid, so it's his responsibility to look after that man or woman. It's an obligation."

"Is it, Clay? Or are you protecting an investment?"

"It's both," Rigby said. "You know that, Byron. I side with Clay. Yankees would do well to mind their own business. You can't grow cotton or rice without people, lots of people. I don't know why in the hell the abolitionists can't get that through their heads. Slaves are as necessary to us as the factory workers are to the owners up there. It's the same thing." She heard the bottle touch glasses. They were drunk and getting drunker.

"I was at Couper's a week or so ago," Rigby continued. "There was this man there, from Boston he was, and he brought this whole thing up, as they always do. I said, 'Burn your factories, and we'll free our slaves.' I stopped his tirade with that. I said, 'You need your slave labor; we need ours. There's not a tuppence of difference.'"

Clay laughed. "What did he say to that?"

"He said, 'It's not the same thing at all. You are exploiting people,' and I said 'Maybe you don't really want to talk about exploiting, Mr. Greene. You forget, I've been up your way a time or two. I've even been to your fair city, I've been to Boston. I've seen the people you have in those factories. I've seen how they work—children, too. Let me tell you, those conditions are a damned sight worse than working in the fields under clean skies.'"

"Did that shut him up?" Clay asked.

"It might have," Rigby answered, "but I was having so much fun then I didn't stop. I said, 'What do you factory owners do, Mr. Greene, when the working season is over, when you don't have anything for those workers to do?' He said, 'Well, we close the plant, that's what we do.' And I said, 'You close the plant. What do they live on, Mr. Greene?' He said, 'Well, they better have something put by for a rainy day. We can't pay them unless they work.' So then I gave it to him, I hit him hard. I said, 'Well, that's the big difference, Mr. Greene. We have fallow times on the plantation, we have times when there is virtually nothing for our people to do, and we have bad years when we don't make a ha'penny for our efforts, but we still feed them, we clothe them, we house them. We look after them, Mr. Greene. Don't you talk to me about exploiting people.'"

"I wish I had been there. What did Couper say?"

"Well, I think I embarrassed him. Greene was a guest there. Couper tried to steer the conversation away from the subject, but I'd have none of it. Those fellows come down here, noses in the air, and they offer a lot of advice they wouldn't consider taking if they were planters. Hell, Clay, most of our large landowners are not from the South. We do what we must do to grub a living from the soil, and we damned sure don't go up there writing in their newspapers, speaking against their way of making a living and writing tracts. I'm tired of it. There's been talk of getting the hell out of the Union, and I, for one, am all for it."

"Well," Clay said. "I don't know about that. I don't think that will be necessary. There may be talk, but that's all it is. If they don't get our cotton, the mills will close. There's a lot of people up there who understand, people who know perfectly well what makes the wheels turn. They may be afraid to stand up to Garrison and his kind, but they understand our problems. They are not opposed to our way. Cotton makes jobs, jobs make money, and they want money, just as we do. One hand washes the other."

"I think we're headed for trouble," Rigby said.

"It won't ever happen, Rigby. They need us; we don't need them. We can always sell more to England. We don't need the Yankees, but they sure as blazes need us."

"I think we should get the hell out."

"Maybe some day. If it gets worse, then I'd be for getting out. But that day is not now."

"There's been talk of using force against us."

"Just talk, Rigby. Believe me, they'll never try that. And besides, who'd do the fighting for them? Hell, man, the best officers are from the South. Do you want names?"

"No need, Clay. I know who they are, same as you do."

"It's a Southern tradition, Rigby. You become a planter or you go in the army. Rankling aside, it's still a nation of laws. And we have the laws on our side. The Constitution gives at least tacit approval to slavery, the way I read it. Nobody's going to take away our freedom. Forget Garrison and his ilk. That's talk, nothing more."

"Right now it's only talk, Clay, but they're fomenting trouble, you mark my words. The day will come—"

"Pour yourself another drink, Rigby. Pour me one, too. Those Yankee windbags will finally get tired of it." In the still of the night she could even hear the rum as it gurgled from the upturned bottle. These rooms, she thought, not a modicum of privacy in the entire house. Clay continued, "There are sound financial reasons for slavery. That's a fact. There's been slaves in one part of the world or another throughout history and that's another fact. Slavery is even recorded in the Scriptures. There's right on the slavery question, but the right is on our side. I tell you, there's a lot of wind through the pines—in Washington and in the North—but that's all it is."

Byron had been quiet. "It could be more than talk," he said. "The talk could grow—"

"Mind your ledgers, Byron. What do you know of it? You never leave Greenleaf. I'm out and around. I'm in the North, and I tell you both it will come to naught."

"I read. 'The pen is mightier than the sword.'"

"A platitude, Byron, nothing more. You take the pen and I'll take the sword. When I meet you on the field of honor, your best effort might gouge out my eye; I would cut you into mince."

She heard the scraping of chairs. "One more, gentlemen, one more short one. Tomorrow will be a full day. I want to get as much out of my trade for Robert as I can. And, you, Byron, you must be on your way back to the counting house. With a crop like the last one, you'd better do some fancy counting or our creditors will descend on us."

The talk had stopped. She could hear footsteps moving off in three different directions. Clay's boots, beating the pattern of a drunken dance, moved toward her door.

He carried a lamp. Oh, she thought, the smell of him! The cloying scent of the liquor, the aroma of the bay rum he splashed on his face after shaving, and the stench of stagnant perspiration. He blew out the lamp and shucked his clothes and stepped on the crumpled heap at his feet.

Elizabeth, on the edge of the bed, took little space, but it did not work. Clay's first desire had been to convince Rigby to stay; it was time for his second desire.

"Move over here, woman; your man has come to bed." She feigned sleep. "Move over here, I said." He was getting louder. Elizabeth moved toward him. The smells were overpowering. He pulled her closer, the stubble of beard scratched her shoulder as he slobbered on her neck. His hands were all over her. There was nothing gentle in his manner or in his voice. Liquor had not dampened Clay's desire, it had only loosened his tongue.

He was talking out loud. He described what he was doing and what he intended to do in graphic detail. His voice echoed up the sides of the steep ceiling. She tried to quiet him. She whispered, stroked his back, hoping to sooth him into a more silent kind of ardor.

"Oh, you're not so cold anymore? You like it, don't you, Lizzie?" She put her fingers over his lips. "Get your hand away from my face. You're smothering me." She removed her hand. "That's better, that's one hell of a lot better."

"Oh, Clay," she said, shamed as she had never been.

"Oh, Clay; oh, Clay. That's all? Say you like it, Elizabeth. I know you do." He thrust himself forward. He hurt her, but she did not whimper. Tears streamed down her face. "Say you like it, Elizabeth!" He was loud and threatening. "Did you hear me?" His hands were rough. He gave her breast a vicious pinch, a twisting, downward tug. She suppressed a scream of pain. "Say it, woman. Say it!"

"I like it," she whispered.

"Say it louder, Elizabeth. I can't hear you." The hand on her breast increased the pressure.

"I like it."

"Louder."

"I like it."

And then it was over. With a groan of pleasure, with a series of gradually fading thrusts, he collapsed, licking at her face and moaning.

She had been humiliated. Neither Byron nor Rigby could see her, but the picture must have been crystal clear.

Clay rolled over. His snores were immediate. She was not able to find sleep. There were no tears. The time for crying was past.

She tried to find excuses for him. It was the liquor; it was his fear of trying to handle the rice island alone for the first time; it was the rigors of the journey that had finally ended on this fateful night.

The excuses dimmed; the pain stayed.

Something had changed. She still loved the man she had married, but she could never forget tonight.

The day was done The tide had gone out, and there had been a shift in the sands.

Chapter Twenty-Seven

Clay was up at the first light of day. Elizabeth pretended to be asleep. He dressed and closed the bedroom door. The rest of it was as clear as if she were in the room. With the first sounds from the bedrooms, Carlotta came into the central room for breakfast orders. Father Greenleaf's house was an echo chamber.

Even though there was little conversation, she heard it all. The night's drinking—or Clay's manhandling of her—had left the three men speaking in grunts. Her face flamed with the memory of Clay's behavior.

Carlotta's voice sounded alive; the men's grunts did not. "You need coffee, Mistah Clay—you all need coffee."

Elizabeth stayed in bed with her eyes closed. In time, Clay and Rigby left together talking of the day's work. Byron went out shortly thereafter. She was grateful. They were gone. Later today she would have to face Rigby, but, fortunately, Byron would go back to the main island.

She put on her dressing gown and made her way to the central room. There was no one to be seen. She walked to the back door. The kitchen was separated from the house by a walkway. She could hear voices and laughter from there.

As she opened the kitchen door, the activity stopped. She was first to speak. "Good morning."

"Good morning, Missus," Carlotta said. "Are you ready for breakfast? Jude has fresh biscuits ready for the oven."

"No, thank you, Carlotta, I'd like to bathe first. Could you have someone fetch some warm water, please?"

"Yes, Missus." Carlotta said. "We will have to heat it. Would you like coffee or tea while you wait?"

"Tea would be wonderful this chilly morning. Would you send it to my bedroom, please? I'll lay out my clothes."

"Tess can help you with that, Missus. Mistah Clay told Tess to be with you all the time. She is to run and fetch for you." As Carlotta spoke she swept a hand towards a small black girl who was half hidden behind the stove.

"That won't be necessary. I can lay out my clothes." The moment Elizabeth spoke she knew she had made a mistake. Tess, who had looked bright-eyed but shy, was now staring at the floor. Elizabeth had hurt this little girl's pride. A job had been assigned to her, an important job, and now she was not considered worthy of it. Elizabeth spoke quickly, hoping to make amends.

"Have your breakfast now, Tess, a big one. We have a busy day ahead of us."

It helped. The sag of the shoulders was less pronounced, but Tess was still not sure. "There is so much you'll have to show me, Tess. I don't know my way around. I will depend on you." She looked at Elizabeth, but not directly. "I'd like to see the hospital today. Do you know where it is?"

Then Tess looked directly at her. There was no understanding in her eyes. Elizxabeth saw fear. She spoke, "There is a hospital on the rice island, isn't there?" And then Elizabeth remembered, Clay called it the infirmary. "The infirmary?"

"Oh, yes, Missus, I know where it is." Tess was smiling.

"Good. When I've eaten, we'll go to the infirmary." Elizabeth turned to Carlotta. She wanted all the eyes in the room to be taken off this poor little frightened girl. "For breakfast, Carlotta, could I have grits and one egg?"

"Yes, Missus. When you are dressed and ready for it, send Tess." She turned toward the little girl behind the wood stove.

"Now, Tess, girl, you go with Miz Greenleaf and you do what she says. If she don't need you, stay out of the way; if she need you, you better be there, you hear?"

"Yes," Tess said almost inaudibly.

"Speak up, girl. You hear what I say?"

"Yes, I do," Tess said more loudly. "I hear."

Elizabeth could hear authority in Carlotta's voice. A point was being made. It was one Elizabeth did not miss.

"When the tea is ready, Tess," Elizabeth said, "fetch it to my bedroom, please. We can see to the breakfast later."

By the time she had bathed, dressed and eaten, the sun was well up in a clear blue sky. Yesterday had been pleasantly warm, but today the air was fresh. As they walked toward the infirmary, Tess lagged behind. "Come and walk with me, Tess. How can you show me the way unless you're with me?" The little girl caught up. "Do you go to school?"

"No, Missus. We got no school."

"Well, maybe we could start one." Tess said nothing. "How far is it to the infirmary?" Tess said nothing. "We need to get along with each other, Tess. We need to talk to each other. How else can you tell me all about Greenleaf?"

"I don't know all about Greenleaf."

"But you know more than I know. When I ask you about something, will you tell me? Or, if you don't know, just say you don't know. Will you do that, Tess?"

"Yes, Missus."

"Now then, how far is it to the infirmary?"

Tess hesitated. "You see where the road stop?"

"Yes, beyond the grove of trees."

"That's where hit turns. We be halfway when we gets there. The infirmary at Mealy Point. I live at Mealy Point."

Father Greenleaf's house, his "marvel," stood on the highest land on the rice island, but there was a curving rim of high land that formed one part of it. On this strip there were many trees: pines, palmettos, magnolias, and, best of all, those twisted, spreading oaks that grew in coastal Georgia. They walked along a shell road that was little wider than a pathway, but it was high and dry, and clear of brush. At times they were under a bower of oak branches that intertwined and, in places, were so thick that the sun could not break through. In each clearing the roadway had been built up so that it safely crossed a fen where reeds, water lilies and fern grew in close proximity. The water in these low spots looked dark, stagnant, stained by rotting vegetation, and unhealthy.

"Oh, dear," Elizabeth said. "These are ugly looking places. Are there snakes in there?"

Tess raised the stick she had been carrying. "I carry this. If one crawls out, Missus, I beat him to death."

"But, there are snakes in there?"

"Yes, Missus. Snakes, and 'gators, and otters. Lots of things live in the woods and in the water. But you got no worry. Tess'll kill anything that crawls up on the road."

"Maybe I should have a walking stick, too."

"No, Missus. That's my job. Ain't nice for you to carry a stick. You carry the parasol; I'll carry the stick. Mistah Clay, he say, 'You take care of her, Tess.' One stick enough. Maybe we don't see none. Most snakes ain't bad no way."

The area was primitive but beautiful. Palmetto fronds glistened in the sunlight, as did the magnolias with their deep green wet-looking leaves. As they passed the bend in the road, Elizabeth could see a cluster of buildings ahead. The bend was more than halfway.

"Is that it, Tess? Is that Mealy Point?"

"Yes'm. That's where I live."

"I don't see the infirmary."

"No'm. Hit sets back from the road."

As they drew near it was clear to Elizabeth that they had already attracted attention. Their voices must have been heard as they walked. All eyes were turned toward the road. There were five or six people there, clustered near the door of the infirmary. It was a tabby building, larger than the one- and two-room houses. The earth surrounding the houses and the infirmary had been scraped clean of all vegetation, just as it was at the drab main house of the rice island. There were no flowers. It was ugly.

No one spoke. They must be waiting for me, Elizabeth thought. "Good morning," she said. "I've come to visit."

They came alive at the sound of her voice. There were smiles and greetings. "Who is in charge of the infirmary?"

"I am, Missus," a large, raw-boned black woman said. "They call me Roselle."

"I'm glad to meet you, Roselle. I'm—"

"We know who you is, Missus. I didn't see you so plain when the boat come in. You even purtier close-by."

What do you say to such outrageous compliments, Elizabeth wondered. There was nothing to indicate deliberate flattery. The faces were open and honest. "Why, thank you, Roselle."

There were five other people there: three pregnant young women, an old man with a cane, and one who had lost a leg.

Roselle followed Elizabeth into the first room. It was a ward with eight beds and seven occupants. The wood floors needed scrubbing. There were no halls. Each room could be reached through an outside door, or you could go from room to room. Roselle kept the infirmary tidy, but not really clean.

"How often does the doctor come from Darien?" she asked.

"'Bout once in six or eight weeks, Missus, unless we sends for him. We mostly do what we can."

"Some of these people look very sick, Roselle."

"They is sick, Missus. If you miss work, you be sick."

At the end of the building were two newer rooms. There were no beds. There were only pallets on earthen floors. Elizabeth said nothing until they were outside. "What about those last two rooms, Roselle. Those are very sick people, and they are on thin pallets—on the ground."

"Yes, Missus. Ain't no hope for them. They's goin' to die, that's sure."

"They need beds. They need a floor in those rooms."

"They goin' to die anyway, Missus. They ain't no hope."

"Did the doctor say that?"

"No, ma'am, he ain't, but I know when they's no hope."

"Where do you keep the medicines, the bandages—all of the supplies? I've seen nothing like that."

"We got a shed. That's where we keep them, Missus."

"Show me, please."

Elizabeth was appalled. The supply shed was in shambles. There was a barrel of rags. They looked clean, but they were not rolled or covered. There were few actual medical supplies, but there were dried herbs that Roselle used.

"How many people help you here, Roselle?"

"One regular, one sometimes. And them here for bornin', unless the pains is started."

"I'll work with you, Roselle. We must make changes here. I know you've done all you can with what you have, but maybe I can prevail upon Mr. Greenleaf to get beds for those back rooms. Even a dying person needs to have some dignity. A pallet on the ground is no more than you'd give a dog."

"Yes, Missus," Roselle said. She didn't expect changes.

Elizabeth wanted to see the conditions inside the houses. She couldn't just walk in. How could she help if she didn't know the problems? Tess solved the problem for her.

"Come with me, Missus. I'll show you my doll."

Tess led her to a house near the road. It was a simple, handmade doll. "The clothes, Tess, who made them for you?"

"I made them, Missus. I can sew for you, too."

"This dress is beautiful. Such fine stitches. You are a very talented girl. Do you know what that word means, Tess?"

"No, Missus."

"It means you have a special skill. Not everyone can sew like this. Did you think of this lovely dress by yourself?"

"Oh, no, Missus. A book Miss Mattie left. I just take something here and something there until she have pretty dresses. She has more." Tess pulled a box from under her bed. It was filled with beautifully made little dresses.

"You have real skill with a needle, Tess." I wonder what I can do for her, Elizabeth thought. I'll find out.

Before she left Elizabeth took a quick look around. There were two rooms, one large and one smaller. The larger one was filled with beds. You could reach from one to another. Seven people slept in this room. There were two double beds and a single. There was also a crib. "What a lovely crib," Elizabeth said.

"My daddy, he made it," Tess said. "It was mine. Now it be Bootie's." She pointed to one of the double beds. "I sleep there, with Laura and Annie. Boston Boy, he's my brother, he sleeps there." She pointed to the single bed.

"Your daddy does lovely work. The crib looks smooth."

"It be smooth. He rub it with sand and then he polish it with the oil from his hands. It take a heap of time, he say. It been through five babies and he keeps right on rubbin' it."

"Well, it's lovely. What does your daddy do?"

"He do what he told."

"He doesn't work with wood?"

"Sometimes he do. He work on the gates, he fix furniture, he work in the fields."

"What is your daddy's name, Tess?"

"He called Reuben."

As Elizabeth took a last look around. She made a mental note to talk to Clay about both Reuben and Tess. People with special talents should be put on jobs where those abilities are utilized. If there is a carpenter's shop, Reuben should be considered for it. Tess is much too talented for simple mending. She should be apprenticed to a dressmaker, Elizabeth thought, if the island has one, and if it doesn't, then I have still another project in front of me.

The walk back to the house seemed much shorter. Tess was more comfortable in Elizabeth's presence. She ran ahead, skipping and singing, and then she would run back to walk for a while at Elizabeth's side. Elizabeth decided she liked the little girl who had been arbitrarily assigned to her. Clay had not consulted her, but he had done well in choosing Tess.

Elizabeth saw a small plot."Who tends the garden?"

"That be Jude. She cook for Mr. Jonathan."

"She's the cook here now?"

"Yes'm. Jude, she do the cooking. Carlotta just see to things when Mr. Clay be here. Carlotta is the head man, the head man." She laughed as she spoke.

"Carlotta is in charge of all the people at the house?"

"Yes'm. She be the head man." She laughed again. It was her joke. She thought it was very funny.

"What is a 'head man,' Tess, other than Carlotta? What does a head man do?"

"He be the man who boss the gang. He get the work done. Mr. Jonathan tell the head man, and the head man, he see the gang do it. Head mans, they's the boss."

"The head man is a foreman?"

"I don't know. Mr. Jonathan jus' say, 'You, Micah, you take your men and fix that ditch,' and that what Micah do."

"I see. Then there's more than one head man?"

"Yes'm. Lots of 'em, and they's Carlotta." She laughed.

"You wouldn't say that to Carlotta, would you, Tess?"

"No, Missus. She'd box my ears good for sure. Carlotta can be—" Tess gave Elizabeth a sidelong glance. Had she said too much? Elizabeth was amused, but she tried to show no sign of it. Tess continued, "Well, she be Carlotta. Like Jude say, 'Anyone can take anything for a time. One day Carlotta will go back to the main house and we have peace again.'"

When the house was in sight, Jonathan Rigby appeared at the side of the road. "Hello," he said. "I could hear you coming." His voice was friendly, but his look was bold. He fell into step beside them and said, "You run along to the house, Tess. I want to talk to Mrs. Greenleaf."

Elizabeth had no desire for a private talk with Rigby, especially in view of the incident with Clay the night before. Jonathan Rigby had a masculine presence that both repelled and attracted her and she did not like her reaction. She didn't trust it. She was afraid of him. Tess started running and skipping toward the house. "Tess, wait a minute. I want you to walk with me."

Tess stopped. "Come back and walk the rest of the way to the house with me," Elizabeth said. Tess turned.

"Tess," Rigby said sternly. "I told you to go to the house. Now you get on your way. I won't say it again." Tess hesitated. Elizabeth could see fear in her eyes. She didn't know which of them to mind.

Elizabeth spoke softly. "You may go, Tess." There was relief in the girl's eyes. She ran to the house. Elizabeth turned to Rigby. "You, sir, are a bastard. You frightened Tess for no reason."

"I may have frightened her, Mrs. Greenleaf, but it was not without reason. At all times, you must make these people aware of who is the boss. That's why I'm good at my job. I always know how far I need to go." His eyes never left her face. He was testing her, too, waiting for her reaction.

"If you always know how far you need to go, Mr. Rigby, then your keen sixth sense must have told you that you have gone too far at this moment."

"Have I? Perhaps not."

"If you are a gentleman, Mr. Rigby, you will excuse yourself and let me finish my walk alone."

"It's a claim I've never made, Mrs. Greenleaf. Manners can cause a gentleman to miss the main chance."

"You are insolent, sir."

"Perhaps I am, Mrs. Greenleaf, but you won't deny you are interested, will you?"

"If you were the last man on earth—"

"That phrase is pretty well worn, isn't it, Elizabeth?"

"Oh, you are a bastard."

"And, my dear, you don't sound like a parson's daughter."

They were nearing the house. Clay came around the corner and joined them. "Well, we are all three here for the noonday meal at the same time. Where's Tess, Elizabeth?"

"I sent her on to the house to hurry up the meal," Rigby said. "And as we walked along, I tried to remind Mrs. Greenleaf how important it is to keep full control over the servants, even the young ones. I was just telling her that the sooner she learns how to deal with our coloreds, the easier it will be for her. I've been explaining that we don't mollycoddle our people here at Greenleaf. I'm not sure I convinced her."

"He's right, Elizabeth."

"In time you see that, Mrs. Greenleaf. Even your husband agrees with the wisdom of what I've been telling you." He was enjoying the word play. He was well aware of the second meaning of his words.

Chapter Twenty-Eight

Elizabeth, Clay and Rigby ate in silence. Rigby made attempts at conversation, but the extent of the chasm between the Greenleafs made it difficult. He knew of Clay's behavior the night before, but he expected them to put a face on it. "Please excuse me," he said. "I need to get back to the job." There was a mumble. He didn't understand the words, but he assumed he had been excused.

"Elizabeth," Clay said, "we need to have another of our little talks. I'll be back later, when I have the work going."

"Not in the house, Clay. What is done or said in one room is heard everywhere. Your father's design might have many advantages, but privacy isn't one of them."

"We'll take a walk, my dear. But, there's no need for you to take a sly poke at father. The house is open so hot air can rise. There's nothing wrong with that."

"Not if we are ladies and gentlemen."

In the afternoon, the several trunks and grips were move to an unused bedroom. Elizabeth and Tess began to unpack. Each item was aired, and then Tess went over it to see if it needed to be mended.

Elizabeth arranged with Carlotta for an ironing board in the kitchen so the clean and mended items could be pressed before they were put away. "I'll have Racy do that," Carlotta said. "Just send them back to the kitchen with Tess, Missus."

"While we're living here, Carlotta, we'll be using three rooms—the bedroom we're in, and our clothes in the other two. As the ironing is done, put Mr. Greenleaf's clothing in the room to the left and mine in the other one." Carlotta nodded. "And please have the beds removed from those two rooms."

"Yes, Missus."

Elizabeth had been looking at the clothing as it was unpacked and sorted. When she turned to face Carlotta, she caught a look of amusement, the briefest hint of a smile in the eyes and around the lips.

"Thank you, Carlotta," she said, dismissing her. But the look bothered her. What had Carlotta been thinking? Did it have anything to do with Clay's behavior last night? Had old Thomas told what he overheard? Was there now talk among the servants? She needed to take charge. "Is there something else, Carlotta?"

"Oh, no, Missus. I was just looking at the blue dress with the lace. It'll look fine on you, with such white skin."

"Oh, that one," Elizabeth said. "It's new. I got it in New York. It is lovely, isn't it?" She kept her eyes on Carlotta. There was nothing. No hint of a smile. Carlotta did not look away. It was the face of a very lovely, dusky-skinned sphinx with yellow eyes. Carlotta touched the blue dress lightly with her finger tips and left the room.

It was a busy afternoon. Tess took the clothing out to hang in the sun. Elizabeth unpacked. After the first group of dresses had been aired, Tess got busy with her needle, and soon there were several garments ready for ironing. "Stay with what you're doing, Tess. I'll take these back to Racy."

"But Missus—"

"Mind what you're doing, Tess. That linen blouse will require a more fragile thread. The cloth is very fine. A coarser thread just won't do. In the meantime, I'll take these to Racy. I want her to be careful with this gray one. The peplum is stiffened with buckram. It will need special care." She left the room before Tess could do any more explaining of what her duties were supposed to be.

She found Racy testing a hot iron with a spittle-wet finger. Tears were streaming down her face.

"You must be Racy," Elizabeth said, and then she noticed the tears. "Are you all right? Is something the matter? What is it?"

Racy put the iron to the cloth and began smoothing out the wrinkles. The tears were still streaming. "Racy," Elizabeth persisted, "what is the matter? Did you burn yourself?"

"I'm Jude, Miz Greenleaf. I'm the cook." Elizabeth turned. Here stood the woman she had barely seen this morning. She was tall, smooth-skinned and beautifully proportioned. She had the dignity of an African princess. "We met this morning."

"Oh, yes, Jude," Elizabeth said. "I apologize. I didn't see you. What's the matter with Racy. She won't speak."

"She got man trouble."

"Man trouble?"

"Her man being traded away."

At that moment, and for the first time since she had listened to the drunken conversation of the night before, Elizabeth remembered that Clay had traded a man named Robert.

"Oh, my God," she whispered.

"You knew?"

"I heard it last night. I didn't know who Robert was, of course. Oh, Racy, I'm so sorry." Racy said nothing. Her sobs were quiet, but they wracked her body.

"Robert be her man; he be daddy to her two children." As Jude spoke a fresh torrent of tears flooded Racy's cheeks.

"Why not a single man? Why Robert if he has a family?"

Jude sighed. "Mistah Clay, he say, 'Robert you is a good man. I hate to see you go. Ain't many like you.' Robert, he say, 'Why can't someone else go with Mr. Jonathan?' but Mistah Clay, he say, 'He want you, Robert. He want a man like you.' So, ain't nothin' anybody can do."

Maybe there is, Elizabeth thought. Clay was not so drunk that he didn't remember last night. He remembered. It was he who suggested their talk. Elizabeth had that card to play. "I make no promises, Racy. I'll do whatever I can."

"Ain' no use," Racy said. "Ain' no use. This be done before." Her sobs tore at Elizabeth's mind.

Jude spoke. Like Carlotta, she was accustomed to giving orders. Before Carlotta came, Jude had been in charge of the house. "Now you hush up, Racy. Hush up now. The Missus say she goin' to talk to Mr. Clay. You let her talk. You pray, girl, you pray good. Hush up now. Get on with your work."

Carlotta came in with two more dresses. "Racy, I told you to dry up. I don't want to have you whupped, but—"

"Whipped?"

"She's been good for nothing all morning," Carlotta said. "If I tell Mr. Jonathan, he have her whupped good. Ain't no sense in the way she's acting."

"I don't blame her, Carlotta." She turned to Racy. "I understand, Racy. I truly do. I'll talk to Mr. Greenleaf."

"Hush, Racy," Carlotta said coldly. "Miz Greenleaf say she will speak to Mistah Clay. Dry up and get on with your work, or I'll talk to Mr. Jonathan about you."

Racy wiped her eyes with the backs of her wrists. "Thank you, Missus, thank you. God bless you," Racy said.

All this while, Elizabeth still held the dress with the difficult peplum. "You could have sent Tess with that dress, Missus," Carlotta said. "That's what Tess is supposed to do, run and fetch."

"I brought the dress because it needs special attention," Elizabeth said. "This peplum is backed with buckram. The iron cannot be too hot or it could be ruined. I wanted Racy to be aware of that before she started."

"Leave it, Missus. I'll see to it." Without question, Elizabeth was being dismissed. This was the servants' part of the house, and, very clearly, Elizabeth felt she was not wanted there.

"Let me see the dress when it's pressed, Carlotta. It's one of my favorites and I want no harm to come to it." Elizabeth walked back to her room with Racy on her mind. The poor young girl. What a day this must be for her.

Clay was back from the fields at three. "Are you ready, Elizabeth? Take gloves, hat and parasol. You'll need them. It's sunny and warmer than it was this morning."

On the veranda, Clay looked out over the marshes. He was happy to be home."Which way, Elizabeth? Along the road towards Mealy Point, or along the dikes?"

"The dikes, Clay, in a direction where there's no one working. We do need to have a private talk."

"Yes, my dear, we do. We can walk toward Silas Gate. There'll be no one near there."

In the first five minutes of their walk, neither spoke. Clay's eyes swept the marshes as though he might never see them again. The day's work had lessened the effects of the grog. Elizabeth's mind was not on the sea of reeds. She was concerned with how they could discuss Clay's behavior the night before without causing a permanent rift. Her humiliation was not something that could be forgotten. This could be a turning point. She wanted it out in the open. There must never be a repetition of such shame again. He had defiled her. She loved him, but she also hated him. Her mind told her she had been abused; she had been denigrated. And in that house, it had been public. Public shame.

"Elizabeth," he said at last, "I'm sorry. I'd give anything if I could undo what I did. Can you forgive me?"

She was a long time in answering. "Not last night. It was too humiliating. Even this morning, I didn't think I could—"

"And now? Can you now?"

"I love you, Clay. But I don't understand you. It is almost impossible for me to even look at Mr. Rigby. You caused that. I wonder what Byron thinks—of me or of you?"

"Rigby will be gone upriver in a month, Elizabeth. Neither of us will ever see him again. Forget Rigby. As for Byron, he knows you were no part of it. He'll never blame you for what I did. He may never truly forgive me, but he knows me, Elizabeth. We're brothers. He has no illusions about me. We each have to forgive the other—Byron and I—for many things. There is a dark side to his character and to mine. Last night only adds one more facet to it."

"Yes, Clay, you have a dark side. I didn't see at first. I saw some of the results of it this afternoon when I took a dress back for Racy to press." She waited. She wondered if he would say anything to defend his trade of Robert. He said nothing. "I found a girl there, Clay, in hysterics. Her sobbing tore at my soul. How could you do this?"

"I wanted Rigby to stay." He said it simply. He expected to get what he wanted. "You must understand, Elizabeth." He hesitated. "None of this is anything I can't do alone. But I want the support of someone who has done the job for years. We've had a bad rice crop this past season. We can't afford another one. The fields must be right. I can't really explain it further, but I want Rigby to stay."

"Enough to trade a man? Enough to break up a family?"

"He's a slave, Elizabeth. I bought him; I can sell him."

"You bought a single man, Clay. He's married and has two children now."

"Married! A voodoo marriage. You have to remember, Elizabeth, this is a sub-species. These are Africans. They're not far removed from the jungle. Robert and Racy are not married like we are. It was a pagan ceremony, some jungle incantation and that's all."

"And our marriage Clay? Was that not incantation, too? Is ours more real just because we were married in my father's church? We went to our own voodoo house and heard our own voodoo incantations."

"Elizabeth!"

"That's my feeling."

"I'm glad your father didn't hear you."

"There's no difference, Clay. If anything, we are less married in the eyes of God. They have children. I feel we're waiting for our bond to be validated; theirs has been."

"I've made a trade."

"Change it."

"I can't do that, Elizabeth."

He had that look again, the look she hated. The discussion was over.

But, it wasn't quite over for Elizabeth. It was time for her to play her only trump card.

"Clay, how do you think I'd feel if *you* were being traded away?

She waited. Clay said nothing.

"Can't you see this from their point of view?"

When Clay didn't reply, she said, "What did Robert say when you told him?"

They walked along in silence. Finally, he spoke. "It was the hardest thing I've ever had to do, Elizabeth. Robert is a good man. That's why Rigby wanted him."

"The hardest thing you have ever done, Clay? Because of the pain you were causing him?" She waited. There was no reply. "Or was it because he's a good man—because there are not many Roberts in the world?"

"Maybe it was some of both—a little of both."

"Talk to Rigby, Clay."

"It won't do any good."

"All things are negotiable, Clay. Rigby wasn't going to stay. He was firm. You negotiated with him, and he's staying. Negotiate again. There are other good men at Greenleaf. There are many people here, and in the cotton fields. You said so. Trade for someone who is not bonded to another. There are good men who are not already fathers."

"I can't do it, Elizabeth. It's my word."

"And I am your wife, Clay. Don't I count? I feel her pain. I'd rather die than lose you; Racy feels the same. She loves Robert, as I love you. Can't you see that?"

They were at Silas Gate. Clay's eyes strayed to the marshes. At last he turned back toward her and groped for her hand. "I'll talk to Rigby, Elizabeth. I'll do what I can."

"Thank you, Clay."

"Now about last night—"

"Last night is over. I'll never mention it again. All I ask is that as long as Rigby is under our roof, as long as you insist upon having a servant in the house, that you keep your ardors quiet. It may be difficult for you, but you must do it. That house was designed to stay cooler in summer, and it may do its job well, but it was not designed for the noisy lover that you are."

"I'll be so quiet that you won't even know I'm there."

She laughed. "Oh, I'll know you're there."

"I'll try, Elizabeth, believe me, I really will. I'll try on both scores. I'll be very quiet in the bedroom, and I will see what I can do about Robert."

"You could solve both problems, Clay. Let Rigby go on upriver. Robert needn't be traded."

"I told you, Elizabeth. I want Rigby to stay."

Oh, if only Clay would let Rigby go now, she thought. What a lot of humiliation it would save her. She tried again.

"I haven't told you this, Clay. I'd hoped it wouldn't be necessary. My hope was that Rigby could go on up the Altamaha river. But, apparently, you need something more."

"No preamble, my dear. If there's more to say, say it."

"When we met you before lunch, Rigby told you he had sent Tess to the house to hurry up lunch. That was a lie. He sent her away, even though I asked her to stay and walk with us. He threatened her, Clay. She was frightened of him. There are beatings here. I know it now. I know it from the look in her eyes, and I know it from listening to the grog-induced conversation you three had last night. Tess was frightened, so I told her she could run on ahead of us."

"She's afraid of disobeying. What's wrong with that?"

"That's not the point I'm trying to make. Rigby sent her ahead so he could make an indecent proposal. I don't know how much last night had to do with it, but he made a cleverly phrased but unmistakable approach."

There was a full minute of silence. Then Clay laughed.

"You don't mean it? Another one! First there was fat and pudgy Mr. Hutchins, and now it's Rigby. Your taste is improving, my dear, but your stories just don't ring true."

"Clay!"

He started laughing again.

"Another one, sniffing the air and chasing you. Did Byron try something, too?"

"You are insufferable."

"Yes, my dear, I am, and at the same time, you are impossible to believe. Every man you meet is trying to bed you? Oh, my God." He was laughing so hard he was bending double. Finally, he laughed himself out.

"Are you through?"

"Quite through. But, my dear, one day a man may really force his attentions on you. With all these stories, who would believe you? It's the fable of the shepherd boy who called wolf when there was no wolf; when the wolf did appear, the lad called, but no one came." He paused. "I don't want to hear any more of these assignation tales. Is that clear?"

She said nothing, but her eyes were brimming with tears. "Now," he continued, "I said I would and I will. I'll do what I can for Robert, and I'll honor your wishes about the bedroom. But please, my dear, please don't tell me any more stories of the men who are after you."

She watched him from the corner of her eye as they walked. For Clay, it was over. That was more than apparent. They had talked about it. They had made an agreement. With Clay it was final. His eyes swept the marshes of Greenleaf. He was happy with what he saw.

Elizabeth said nothing. Once again she had been called a liar. She felt empty. How could she love him? But she did, she knew she did.

The walk back from Silas Gate was quiet.

Chapter Twenty-Nine

The following morning Elizabeth stayed in bed until Rigby and her husband had gone to the fields. He hadn't believed her about Rigby. The memory of his laughter was still there.

As she and Tess set off for the infirmary, Elizabeth went over the day's work in her mind. The first thing needed is a thorough cleaning. Each room must have the floors and walls scrubbed with a solution of lye soap and water.

There was a fire burning out in front of the infirmary. Clustered around it were the old and frail, and those left behind to tend to the ill. Roselle walked forward as they came into sight. "Morning, Missus. We didn't know you was comin' again today."

"I'll be here every day, Roselle. We must do everything we can for the people here at the infirmary." She realized how that might have sounded so she rushed the next thought to remove any unintentional hurt. "There's nothing wrong with what you've been doing, but if we put both our minds to it, we can do even more."

"Yes'm," Roselle replied. Elizabeth had no idea what she was thinking. The face was impassive; the eyes said nothing.

"As long as we have a fire going, Roselle, I think we should wash all the cotton cloth in the barrels back there."

"Hits clean, Missus. Hit's been boiled."

"I'm sure it was clean, Roselle, but the freshly washed cloth just goes in on top. Some of it down near the bottom must have been there for a while. It can't be clean now."

Roselle said nothing.

"We'll get a fire under the pot, and we'll reboil everything. Then we'll strip it and roll it."

Roselle remained silent. Elizabeth found her situation difficult. The burden of the conversation was squarely on her shoulders. She considered dropping the matter. The silence she found in the people there was intimidating, but it was also irritating. She intended to do her part in the marriage, and that meant making the entire plantation function better. The school was one way; the infirmary was another. She must not crumble. Clay had tried to prepare her. He had made it clear. She must be the one in charge or her effectiveness would be over. She mentally squared her shoulders.

"How many women have we here today, Roselle? Can the men help—with the fire under the pot for example?"

"We got seven women, and they's Isaac yonder. He ain't much no more, but he can take some lightwood over there and get a fire going, soon as he fills the pot with water."

Elizabeth was relieved. She had just won a minor victory. But she wasn't sure; was it a victory over herself or over Roselle?

By eleven o'clock, two boilings of white bandage cloth had been washed, rinsed and were blowing on the line. While this was going on, everything had been moved out of one room in the infirmary. Ladies with scrub brushes washed down the walls and bleached the floors.

Eleven o'clock. The morning was nearly gone, and the work was far from over. She had hoped to get all the rooms scrubbed the first day, but it was clear that when you moved the bedridden out, removed the furniture, scrubbed and rinsed, then waited for the floor to dry, it would take at least three hours for each room. It would take a week to get the infirmary thoroughly clean.

"I asked for a job, and I got a job," she muttered.

"What did you say, Missus?" Tess had been standing behind her with a fresh basket of clean cloth.

"Talking to myself, that's all," Elizabeth replied. "We're going to be here all day, Tess. With so many things to do, walking back for lunch is a waste of time. Go back and ask Jude to make a lunch for us. And ask Carlotta to tell Mr. Greenleaf where I am. I wouldn't want him to worry. Tomorrow we'll be smarter. We'll bring our lunch."

"Yes'm." And Tess went skipping off toward the house.

The work went well in the afternoon. Two of the rooms had been scrubbed and dried, and rearranged. The patients were brought back to a clean bed, in a clean room. At three-thirty Clay arrived in a small black buggy drawn by a shining strawberry roan. "How are the tasks coming, my dear? Have we reorganized the infirmary?"

"You drove over to ask that?"

"Oh, you have been working! You're testy."

"There's so much that needs doing."

"Well, it won't be completed today. See that Roselle has it moving, and then you can run away from your job, just as I've done. I want to show you more of the rice island."

"I shouldn't, not this first day."

"What isn't done will wait for tomorrow. A planter's wife must learn to move with the seasons. There is an ebb and flow out here on the marshes. The sooner you begin to live with it, the easier it will be for you."

"But, Clay—"

"No more talk. Get in the buggy, and I'll show you the fields down near the Clary Gate. Maybe we'll ride to the south dike. You can see the main island from there."

"Are we that close to the main island? I thought it was more than an hour away."

"It's closer to two hours by boat, but it's not far from the south end of this island. Maybe it isn't a separate island at all. Father always said it was one mass of land, but there are marshes in between and no waterways. Maybe one day we'll try to put a shell road across the marsh. It was father's dream, but we never got to it; we were always too busy reclaiming more land and planting more cotton or rice." He reached out his hand. "Come on now, Elizabeth, into the buggy, or we won't have time to get as far as the south dike."

Clay drove back toward the house and then turned in a southerly direction. The view was spectacular from the top of the dike. On either side it was stark but compelling. On one side was the recently prepared rice fields, clean of all debris, and on the other, the marshes.

"Use your parasol, my dear. The buggy won't fully protect you from the sun."

She had the parasol with her so constantly these past two days that she was beginning to think it would be impossible to go outside without it. She adjusted it to keep the sun from touching her neck.

"You haven't asked about Racy's man Robert. I thought you'd want to know about that as soon as I drove up."

"I've been thinking of nothing but Robert all morning. That, and how you laughed at me about Rigby."

"One thing at a time, Elizabeth. You have a talent for bringing in three or four subjects, and switching back and forth until I have completely lost the thread. Let's don't do that. Let's talk about Robert."

"One thing at a time, then. What about Robert?"

Clay pulled the buggy into the partial shade of Clary Gate. Was he unsure, or was he playing with her emotions? Finally, he spoke. "Robert will not be going with Rigby."

"Oh, Clay, I do thank you. I know how difficult it was."

"You're damned right it was. I looked like a fool. But I told Rigby it was one of your romantic ideas. It cost me dearly, I can tell you."

"You had to buy Robert back?"

"No, but I had to trade two good men to get out of the bargain. Two damned good men, and he knew the ones to pick."

She could tell he had more to say. She remained silent. With Clay, as with her father, it was the sensible approach.

Finally, he turned toward her, his voice calm. "There will be no more, Elizabeth. This incident with Robert will be the end of it." As he spoke, his voice took on a harder edge. "I don't know how you got yourself involved, but you will never interfere again. You are not to concern yourself with the people at Greenleaf. If you need help, you will ask and help will be assigned, but, neither the welfare nor the tenure of the people here, even the ones working directly for you, will be of any concern to you. Is that perfectly clear?"

What was he asking? She couldn't turn from injustice. In her father's church, she had been told of the sale of slaves, transactions that tore families apart. And now this. She had only been in the South for two days and already she had seen what the trade of Robert had done to Racy. What would it do to their children?

"Did you hear me, Elizabeth?"

"I heard you, Clay. I'm not sure I understood you."

"What I said was clear enough."

"I can't believe you meant it."

"Well, my dear, I did. I chose my words carefully."

"Tess has been 'assigned' to me," she said, "but I'll have no voice in her welfare? Is that what you said?"

"Exactly. We have hundreds of people here. We must maintain the system and strict discipline. Until she is old enough for the fields, Tess is one of the house staff."

Had she heard him clearly? This was using people—blindly, stupidly using people.

"Send Tess to the fields? If you have a system, Clay, it's a stupid system. Tess is talented. She can sew beautifully. She should be apprenticed to a dressmaker, if we have one at Greenleaf, and if we don't, Tess should be trained to be the first. Your system doesn't seem to consider the special abilities your people have."

"Tess works directly for Carlotta, or for Jude when Carlotta is back at the main house. If Tess has talent, Carlotta will see it and direct it."

"Are you abandoning *your* responsibility to these people? The slaves here are at the mercy of the slaves?"

He was angry. "Certainly not. Tess works for Carlotta and Carlotta is, in this instance, the headman. She is responsible to Rigby or the new man, and Rigby is responsible to me. I am the authority."

"Did you know Tess was a capable seamstress? Did you know she has designed and made lovely clothes for a doll. Did your system give you this information?"

"Elizabeth, you are the most argumentative woman in Georgia. We're not talking about Tess. We're talking about discipline. On Greenleaf, discipline is first and foremost. Without it, the system won't work. It's a very basic hierarchy. Each man is assigned to a gang, each gang has a headman. Discipline within the gang is handled by the headman. The headmen are the responsibility of the overseer. We have two overseers at Greenleaf, and they are responsible to me. It's that simple."

"It's that simple," he had said. It was simple all right, but simple with a different shade of meaning. It was stupid.

"And, dear husband, you have a system that can overlook any real ability 'your people' may have. If the headman doesn't know Tess' father, Reuben, is a carpenter, then his talent is lost, and he grubs the fields."

"We know it. It's been brought to Rigby's attention and to mine. Reuben works on maintenance of the gates. He also does whatever needs doing at the house and the barns. We know about Reuben. The system works."

"I chose the wrong word. Reuben is a carpenter, yes, but he's more than that. The man is capable of better than rough work. I saw a cradle he made. Clay, it's beautiful. It's a fine piece of work done with primitive tools. He's an artist in wood. We should have a shop here at Greenleaf. He could make furniture for all the houses. We might even be able to sell some of it. I'm talking about a talent that is not being used, because it's not being recognized."

Elizabeth saw his anger, but those were words that she had to say. She could see the fury her words had evoked. She knew that when Clay got red at the collar, it wasn't long before it spread to his face. She could see the flush rising.

"That will be the end of it, Elizabeth." He turned the horse around.

"I thought we were going to the south dike."

"Sorry, my dear, you don't deserve it. We're going home." His voice was calm. His fury was under control. "But, I do have more to say. I have obliged you with Robert. I've looked like an ass for your sake." He waited for her to fully comprehend the point.

"Elizabeth, that kind of thing will never happen again. Not ever again! So you will not allow yourself to get into such a position with the slaves. I don't know what you said, I don't need to know, but I do know you put yourself in a position that was untenable. I got you out of it. Don't ever do it again."

Clay waited. He wanted Elizabeth to understand his meaning. He continued quietly and deliberately. "So the first point is, stay out of the management of the plantation. You'll have no more to do with the people here than you have to do with rice planting. Is that clear?"

"Yes. But I will be in charge of the infirmary?"

"Yes."

"And the school?"

"There will be no school."

"But, Clay, I thought you said—"

"I let you prattle about the school. I said nothing."

Prattle about the school? Prattle? He knew what the school meant to her. He knew. She could fight back the words.

"You can be a bastard, can't you?"

"I expected you to learn a little something as we came south, but you managed to put your foot in the mud several times. I must conclude that what I said was lost on you."

She held her tongue. This was a time for reason.

"But, Clay, the school— The need is there. If the people at Greenleaf are taught, they'll be able to do more. They will be worth more. If you can't see it from any other point of view, just look at the cash value."

"Do you think the only thing I consider is money?"

"It sometimes sounds that way to me."

"Well, you're wrong, Elizabeth. But, money is important. It has to be. There may be some value in teaching our people to read and cipher. But, my dear, if that value even exists, it is nullified by the dangers it brings. There's been trouble on some of the plantations in Georgia, and it's always sprung from an attempt at educating. An educated black is a dangerous black."

"You believe that?"

"I certainly do. None of us, none of the planters I know—and I know most of them from here to Charleston—will permit any kind of school. We've all agreed on that. We teach them what they need to know to do a job and that's all. No use looking for trouble."

"I can't believe it. I can't believe what I'm hearing."

"Reality will come to you, my dear. In time you'll see the truth in the wisdom we have learned through the years. We have had the experience; you have not. You're mouthing the drivel you've heard at church meetings. It's utter claptrap. This is reality. You're living on a working plantation. The key is discipline."

Elizabeth was losing ground. She must have a chance to show him how it could be done better. Clay would change his mind when he saw the difference she could make.

"But I can continue at the infirmary?"

"Of course, my dear. But," he waited, wanting the point to be clear to her, "you must remember: Roselle does not work for you; she works for Rigby. You may direct the operation there, as long as it does not interfere with his overall job. We will maintain discipline right through the lines."

"Even if it takes beatings."

"We don't do much of that."

"But you do it?"

"We maintain discipline. If a beating is required, the headman will not hesitate, or he won't be the headman for long. All under the supervision of Rigby, of course."

"And of you."

"Yes, of course."

Clay picked up the reins. "You will not interfere again, Elizabeth. Is that clear?"

"Quite clear."

"There will be no more talk of a school."

"There won't be much for me to do."

"Aunt Mattie does needlepoint."

"Then you can be sure I won't."

"So, my dear, that little problem is still with us. You haven't gotten over it."

"Friends are a choice we make, in-laws are not."

Clay picked up the whip. He snapped it once over the head of the roan. He let the tip of it hit the horse on the hindquarters on the second snap. They headed back to the house at what Elizabeth felt was a dangerous speed.

She thought she could see the trace of a smile as he leaned back in the seat. She hoped she was mistaken.

Chapter Thirty

The next day Elizabeth waited for Rigby to leave. As she entered the central room, Carlotta saw her and disappeared toward the kitchen. In a few seconds Tess appeared. "Jude say, what you want for breakfast, Missus?"

"Oh, Tess, good morning. I saw Carlotta as I came in, but she left so quickly—"

"Carlotta come to tell me you up, Missus."

"Oh?" Was it that, or did Carlotta want to avoid talking to her? She was always distant, always slightly aloof. It was almost as though Elizabeth was in some kind of indefinable secondary position. "Well, tell her I'd like a soft-boiled egg, one biscuit and a pot of hot tea."

There was no frost that morning, but it was colder. The wind had the sting of winter even though the sun was out. Elizabeth felt it would be a good day. She had the lunch basket on her arm and a woolen shawl about her shoulders.

Beyond the smokehouse, Racy stepped out of her hiding place. "Oh, Missus," she said, tears streaming down her face, "Thank you. Mistah Clay, he tell Robert yesterday he don't go with Mr. Jonathan. You saved Robert. You done it, and I thank you."

"I did nothing, Racy. I thought Mr. Greenleaf didn't know about the children—your children and Robert's. I mentioned it to him. That's all. I need no thanks."

"You is a white angel, Missus. I done tol' Robert, there ain't many like you. You is blessed."

"Racy, please, no more. If I helped, I'm happy for it. But you make too much of it."

Carlotta stepped from around the corner. "Racy," she said, "what you doing out here, pestering Miz Greenleaf? I done told you not to come bothering her. Don't you have ears? Can't you mind? I told you not to, and you done it anyway. Mr. Jonathan, he tell you, too. You are in trouble, girl, in a heap of trouble."

"It's no bother Carlotta. Racy is emotional. I would have been in her place—or you would have been. Take her back to the kitchen and get her eyes dried, but no more need be made of it. She's overwrought, but is it any wonder?"

"She was told," Carlotta said firmly. "Back to the kitchen, girl. You're in trouble now, deep trouble."

Racy turned toward the house, tears running down her face. Carlotta followed her, a few paces to the rear.

"Oh, my," Elizabeth said. "What have I done now?"

"Racy gonna get a beatin'. Racy in deep, deep trouble," Tess said. "That Carlotta, she riled."

"A beating? Why? Racy has done nothing."

"Carlotta tell her—I hear Carlotta tell her—she say, 'You don't bother the Missus. Mr. Jonathan tell me to tell you and you better mind my words.' Racy, she don't say nothin', but she hear. She know."

"But she doesn't deserve to be beaten. What she did was a natural thing. She certainly does not need to be beaten."

"She gonna get it sure."

As they walked toward Mealy Point, Elizabeth's mind churned. What could she do? This was exactly what Clay had been talking about yesterday. This was discipline. She dared not interfere. This was an instance where an order had been disobeyed—no matter that the incident was minor. Carlotta would demand the beating because her authority had been ignored and Rigby would approve it.

Coming on the heels of Clay's conversation with her yesterday afternoon Elizabeth wondered if the whole incident were contrived. They all knew Racy would try to thank me, she thought. Has Racy been forbidden for a reason? Is this more than a beating for Racy? Is this a test for me? Her mind raced on. If Racy is beaten, as Tess says is sure to happen, and if I beg Clay to stop it, he will refuse. I know that. I can hear him saying it, "Sorry, my dear. This is a matter of discipline. Racy disobeyed; she will be punished."

With all this on her mind, it had seemed a short walk to Mealy Point. "Good morning," she called as they rounded the corner of the infirmary. There was a murmur of greeting. Like yesterday, she thought. I'm a stranger to them. Or is it because I'm a white? Conversation will have to be initiated by me and sustained by me. I must make it happen.

"As soon as we are all warm," she said, "we'll get back to the cleaning. It's so cold, though, I hate to open those windows, and yet the floors will never dry if we don't."

There was no reply. She had expected to hear something. It was clear from the silence, she was not wanted. For her to regain control, she needed a more direct approach.

"Isaac," she said, turning directly to face the old black man, "will you start the fire under the wash pot again? We have most of that job done, but not all of it."

"Yes'm." He ambled off for a piece of lightwood.

"If you'll get the ladies on the scrubbing, Roselle, I'd like to talk to you about the medicines. I know you know where they are, but if you fell ill, no one else could find a thing."

Roselle and four of the women moved toward the infirmary without a word. "Tess, you and this lady can work on the washing. I'll go back to the storeroom. When Roselle is through, ask her to come back there, will you?"

"Yes, Missus," Tess said.

What could she hope to do about the storeroom? Roselle guarded her knowledge of herbs. She answered questions, but never volunteered. She agreed wooden boxes would store the leaves, seeds and roots better.

"When we get the boxes, Roselle, we'll label the outside, showing what it is and what it's to be used for."

"Won't do much good, Missus. Ain't no one can read."

That hadn't occurred to Elizabeth. It pointed up the need for a school, if only for certain people on the plantation. But Clay had put the idea to rest. "We could mark the outside of each box with a picture of the leaf."

"Some be bark, some be roots."

"We can do it, Roselle. We can think of a way of marking each box. You'll help me, won't you?"

"Yes, Missus."

"Maybe we could fasten a leaf or a piece of bark to the outside. How would that be?"

"A dried leaf will fall off."

"Well, we'll try."

All her talks with Roselle ended in a draw, but Roselle was always polite, even when she was a wall of silence. Even so, when the day was over, Elizabeth felt good about her work. There had been progress. The uneasiness she felt when Carlotta confronted Racy earlier in the day had disappeared. She had been so busy she hadn't thought about it.

"You live here, Tess. Stay. I'll walk back alone."

"No, Missus. I best go with you."

"There's no need. It's not far. Clean the house for your mother. She'll be tired after a day in the fields."

"I best go with you, Missus—"

"I'll hear no more about it, Tess. Off with you, now. Head for home." Elizabeth turned to Roselle. "I'll see you in the morning and I'll try to be early." Roselle's face remained impassive. Elizabeth set off toward home.

Beyond where the shell road crossed a finger of marsh was a wooded area. The oaks spread their long arms parallel to the earth to make a bower. It was lovely in the soft light of the dying sun. Elizabeth stopped to look, and then, with the empty lunch basket on her arm, she continued toward the house. As she entered the shaded archway of oaks, Rigby stepped from behind one of the large trees. "Good evening, Mrs. Greenleaf."

Elizabeth was frightened, but tried not to show it. "Good evening, Mr. Rigby. You startled me. I didn't know there was anyone around for miles."

"I've been waiting for you."

"I can't imagine why, Mr. Rigby. I've made every effort to avoid you."

"Yes, you have, Mrs. Greenleaf, and I know why. You don't trust yourself when you are around me, do you?"

"Nonsense, Mr. Rigby. You're an employee who will soon be leaving."

"On the one hand you don't like me, dear Mrs. Greenleaf, but on the other hand you have more than a casual interest. Don't deny it, please. I know women."

"Mr. Rigby, if you were a gentleman, you would stop this disgusting conduct at once. You would apologize for intruding where you are not wanted, and you would leave me alone to continue my walk to the house."

"If I were a gentleman, my dear, you would not be as interested in me as you are."

"Leave me alone, Mr. Rigby. If you don't I shall have to tell my husband of your unwanted attention."

"If you'd been going to tell your husband, my dear lady, you would have done so. The fact is, you don't intend to tell your husband. You are titillated by my attentions far more than you care to admit. The fact is, Elizabeth, you are interested, more than interested, just as I am." He reached for her. She quickly withdrew.

"Keep you hands off me, Jonathan Rigby. One step closer, I'll scream so loud they'll hear me in Darien."

He stepped back one pace. "So," he said with a smile, "perhaps you're not quite ready. Never fear. I have patience.

There's no need to climb the tree; when the nut is ripe, it will fall of its own accord."

He turned and walked back to where he had been hiding. As he withdrew, Elizabeth began to get her breath back. He stopped and faced her again, still smiling,

"I have another way back to the house, my dear. I can keep a secret. When you're more fully aware of that, you'll be more ready for what we both know is inevitable. Good day to you." He tipped his hat, and disappeared into the dense growth behind him.

Elizabeth had been holding her breath through a part of this encounter. Her chest ached as she tried to fill her lungs with air. "Oh, my God," she said aloud. "Oh, my God."

She walked toward the house, slowly at first, and then faster and faster. Her mind moved as fast as her feet. This was Clay's fault. She had told him about Rigby and he didn't believe it. He had laughed at her. He had insulted her. The result was that this swine was certain she had withheld the information because she was interested in a dalliance. What can I do? Her brains were in a fog.

Avoiding him doesn't seem to help. One thing sure, I'll not go anywhere alone. Tess is safer walking back on this road than I am.

She looked at each large tree, half expecting to see him. Why did he pursue her? There must be women in the county who would be happy to have his attentions. Why me? I hate him, hate him!

When she got to the house, Rigby was with Clay down at dockside. The boat from the main island had come over, and they were talking with the people who had brought supplies. She entered the house, past the detached kitchen. There was a difference. The laughter and talk was missing. She could see people inside, but it was quiet. It was too quiet.

Elizabeth went to the bedroom. She patted her hair into place. She looked calm, but she was afraid. She hoped Rigby hadn't seen her fear, but now she was even more disturbed by the pall, the eerie quiet, that hung over the kitchen. She remembered Racy and the threat Carlotta had made. "Racy in deep, deep trouble," Tess had said. "She gonna get it sure."

She heard the dinner bell. Clay knocked and said, "Time for dinner. Come join us so we can say the blessing."

The blessing? If Racy is to be beaten, would they precede dinner with the blessing? What hypocrisy. She knew she had better try to appease Clay, not annoy him. Perhaps she was wrong about Racy. "I'll be there shortly, Clay."

She realized now that the pall hung over the entire house, not just the kitchen. She could feel it at the table, but neither man seemed to notice it. They talked of the day's work.

After they had eaten, while the three of them were still sitting at the table, the dinner bell sounded again. This time it was a series of rings. The clapper hit four times, then there was a pause followed by another four, and another. Twelve in all. The men got to their feet.

"Who's ringing the bell?"

"The bell is used for more than calling us for meals, my dear. It's used in emergencies—a fire would be an example—for calling the men from the fields."

"We have an emergency?"

"They're not all emergencies, my dear. This time the bell was struck four times in a series of three. That denotes punishment for disciplinary reasons. When the bell is sounded for discipline, everyone must be present. The bell was struck twelve times for twelve lashes. If the problem were more serious, it might be repeated twice for twenty-four lashes. It's an easy code once you learn it."

By that time Rigby had left the house, and the staff was either gone or preparing to leave. Elizabeth was stupefied. She knew this could happen, but she kept hoping it would not.

"Come, my dear, on your feet. The bell is for everyone. A breach in discipline is a serious matter. Everyone must be present. Everyone includes you. There are fewer infractions if everybody fully realizes what the results will be."

Elizabeth was numb. Tears streaked down her face. Clay touched her shoulder. "Come, my dear. You must go. You caused the problem. Now you must see it through to the end."

"I'm not going," she said.

"Oh, yes, you are."

"I'm not, Clay. This is barbaric. I refuse to add to that girl's degradation."

"On your feet, Elizabeth." His fingers ground into her shoulder. "Now!"

"I will not go," she said, and as she spoke his hand caught her sharply across the jaw. She cried in pain. Her hand flew to the spot where the mark of his fingers still showed. She couldn't believe he had struck her.

"You bastard."

"You could be joining Racy, Elizabeth. The whip doesn't care if you're black or white and don't you forget it. Discipline is for all the people on the island and that includes you, my dear. On your feet, and I mean now!" His fingers dug into her shoulder. The pain was intense, but she didn't make a sound. She got to her feet. Clay turned and left the room. She followed.

Across the back of the sand-covered yard, over behind one of the barns, was what Elizabeth had assumed was a playing field. Tonight the area was lighted by a large fire. She could see a crowd there—a silent crowd, without voice, without touching, without hope.

She moved toward it as she knew she must.

Racy was in the center, stripped to the waist. Robert was with her, a whip in his hand. Were they going to make Robert beat his own wife? Rigby was a son-of-a-bitch. No one but an inhuman bastard could have conceived anything so cruel. He's leaving Greenleaf, but not soon enough, she thought.

On signal, the beating began. Robert's arm came back and on the forward motion the whip struck Racy across the back. A welt was visible. She stood, head up, waiting for the next lash to fall. His arm came back, and the beating continued.

Elizabeth could not bear it. Each time the lash cut into Racy's flesh, she could feel the searing pain. She backed away from the crowd toward the barn. On the other side of it she was sick. When her supper was lost, when she could only retch bile, when she was so weak she wondered if she could make it back to the house, Elizabeth could still hear the beating continue at a measured pace.

She used the last of her strength to find the haven of her bedroom. She fell across the bed, spent. Clay opened the door.

"I hope, my dear, you realize now what you caused." She said nothing. "You did this to Racy, Elizabeth. You told me you wanted to help me with Greenleaf. Well, my dear, you're off to a poor start. I'll tolerate no more interference. You will not meddle, Elizabeth. Is that understood?"

"Clay, Racy did nothing to deserve that."

"She disobeyed."

"She tried to thank me for Robert—"

"I'm aware of what happened, Elizabeth. Don't bore me with it."

"Rigby's punishment— You could have stopped it."

"Yes, my dear, I could have. But I'll not have discipline go to hell—not for you, nor for anybody else. I will run this place with a firm hand, just as my father did."

"But to have her beaten by Robert, by her husband—"

"A man must control his wife. Robert failed."

"Robert knew nothing about it."

"He will keep her in line from here on, that's sure."

"The beating was—" She turned to look at him squarely. "You could have stopped it, Clay."

"I ordered it, Elizabeth. It wasn't Rigby. I ordered it. A man's woman is his responsibility. He must control her." He waited. He wanted Elizabeth to understand what he had said.

And then he continued, "I ordered it because Racy disobeyed. Racy fully understood the order I sent back through Rigby and Carlotta."

"You?"

"Yes, my dear, me."

He had delivered a message to her—through his actions and through his words. This time he felt certain she understood him. In the future, she would be more careful.

He took off his coat and loosened his tie. As far as he was concerned, the incident was over.

"Now, my dear, into bed with you. I want to practice keeping my ardors quiet. I keep my word, and as I promised, I'll be as quiet as a mouse."

Chapter Thirty-One

Weeks passed. Elizabeth had Tess at her side at all times, but the fear of Rigby kept her on edge. His work in the outer fields had been completed ahead of schedule, so he and his crews were doing work that was closer to the house. Proximity made her fear increase.

It had been Spring-like the day Elizabeth arrived at Darien only a few weeks earlier, but the last days of January and the first week in February were bitter.

Conditions at the infirmary were intolerable, in her opinion. She begged Clay to provide heat for the ill people there. Since the work on the plantation was going well, he agreed to allow a fireplace to be built for every third room. Elizabeth felt it was not sufficient but it was better than no heat at all.

Early in February, the weather turned warm again, and the work on the chimneys came to a stop. "Winter is not over, Clay. We've not seen the last of it. In any case, we'll need heat next year. Please let the men finish those chimneys, if not for the people who are ill, at least for me. I'm there the better part of each day."

"You don't have to go there on cold days."

"Clay!"

"Why did I let you talk me into this, Elizabeth? They're used to cold weather. The whole thing is a needless expense."

"Why not finish the work? With heat, we'll save lives."

"We need the strong, not the weak."

"You need the newborn; you need mothers to produce more children. Look at it as an investment, not a needless cost."

"You're as logical as Byron—and as soft-headed."

The infirmary was more like what she imagined a hospital should be. Two of the fireplaces were functional. By dint of having one room too hot, you could get warmth to the others. She was moving in the right direction. And she had begun to win grudging respect from Roselle. The boxes Reuben made brought order to the supplies. The idea of fastening a leaf or a piece of bark to the outside was successful. Roselle was proud of it. Elizabeth let her take credit for the idea.

The next job was to bring order to the patients. Pregnant women were scattered throughout the building. They had been simply assigned to a vacant bed. Elizabeth and Roselle made the largest room the maternity ward. Then they moved patients around until they had a ward system for the entire infirmary.

With the rearrangement, space was available in some of the rooms. Elizabeth thought the terminal patients should be moved out of the ward with earthen floors. Roselle was against the idea. "Ain' no call to bring them in with well people. They is gone, I tell you. Nothin' can help."

"I'm sure you are right, Roselle, but, even if they are going to die, they need to be able to die with dignity. They need a fire; they need to feel that they are still loved."

"Ain' gonna do no good. They be same as dead."

"What if you were in one of those beds, Roselle? What would you want?" Roselle said nothing. The face, once again, was without expression. "What I'm suggesting is temporary, Roselle. We'll move them out of there only until a floor can be put in and until a fireplace made." Elizabeth managed to get approval, but it was without enthusiasm.

Spring comes early along the southeast coast of Georgia. With the arrival of the warmer weather, Elizabeth began to think of the summer clothing. Since the infirmary was being looked after by Roselle with renewed interest, Elizabeth decided she and Tess could take a day off too see to the washing and airing of summer dresses. They went to the barn and each one brought back an armload from the trunks.

As Elizabeth tried them on, she found she had gained weight. Her breasts were larger, and with some of the dresses there was a tightness at the waist. Tess was busy letting out seams and making adjustments. A favorite dress, the yellow one with a small rounded collar, was so tight in the bust that alteration was impossible. Elizabeth was crestfallen. "Let me think on it, Missus. We find a way to fix it," Tess said.

"While you think, I'll get another armful from the barn."

"I'll go with you, Missus."

"No, Tess, stay with what you're doing. With the amount of alterations that needs doing, you'd better keep busy on it. I'll go get this load. You can go with me for the next."

Elizabeth crossed the sunlit yard to the barn. Inside, she had to wait for her eyes to adjust. Still not seeing well and blinking as she walked, she moved to the trunks.

Rigby grabbed her from behind. She gasped, both from the fright of this sudden occurrence and from the realization of who it was. "I've been waiting. I waited for you to come back without that pickaninny," he said. His face nuzzled her neck. His hands were rough and she could smell tobacco.

She struggled, but Rigby's firm grip pinned her arms to her sides. "Let me go, Mr. Rigby or I'll scream."

"So you want to play innocent before we play house?"

"I told you, Rigby, I warned you. I'll scream, and the whole place will know what a blackguard you are."

"If you didn't scream when I grabbed you, my love, you won't scream now. It's what you've wanted from the beginning. Do you think I didn't see you looking at me? I know when a woman is interested. You're something of a crotch-watcher, aren't you, my dear. You don't look at my face, but you do look, don't you?"

"Let me go at once. I mean it, Rigby."

He laughed. His left arm held her immobile. His right hand worked at the front of her dress. He fumbled at the covered buttons on the high neck. His fingers were close to her mouth. Without thinking, she bit his hand as hard as she could. She wanted to bite to the bone.

He cried out in pain. He was unprepared for the surprise and the ferocity of her attack. The pain was immediate and intense. He threw her aside and clutched his hand. He stared at a bloody thumb. "You bitch," he said, "you'll pay for this and you'll pay dearly."

The barn door swung open. Sunlight spilled in. "Missus, are you in there? The sun's so bright I cain't see you."

"I'm here, Tess," she said firmly. "Wait there. I'll bring these things and walk back with you." She grabbed an armful of dresses and made her way to the door. "Come, Tess. You can tell me about it when we get back to the house."

It took three more days before Elizabeth found the proper time to talk to Clay about the terminal ward. When she broached the subject, Clay was involved in Rigby's departure. "The supply boat is in to take Rigby to Darien. Send Byron a note about the infirmary," he said. "If he approves, I have no objection."

She knew Byron would approve. She rushed to pen her note, but Rigby was unable to get his gear packed in time for the boat to go to Darien and back before nightfall. Clay decided to hold the boat over until morning. There would be one more night with Rigby under their roof.

Elizabeth was unafraid. Rigby was brave enough when she was alone, but the presence of Tess stopped his forceful intimacies. One more night. She would not be alone with him. That would not be difficult if she stayed with Clay, or in the house where there were always servants present.

Because of his delight at having the rice island ready for planting, Clay was generous with whiskey. Rigby encouraged the drinking. By nine o'clock Clay was tipsy; Rigby was not. He had managed to appear to be drinking one for one, but Elizabeth was wary. When she realized what his plan was, she abandoned her idea of going to bed. She was unable to see Rigby dump his liquor, but she managed to spill some of Clay's. "You must be getting tired, my dear. You've spilled my liquor twice. You're tired, or clumsy as a cow."

"Yes, Clay, it was clumsy, but I'm not tired. It's Mr. Rigby's last night at Greenleaf. He's been of immeasurable help to you, both recently and through the years. It's only fitting that we both stay at his party."

"I'm sure he would excuse you, my dear."

"I'm sure he would, dear. He's a Southern gentleman, but I want to stay. We're both grateful for what he's done. I'll stay until the three of us are ready for bed."

The drinking party went on. At midnight she could see the effects of alcohol on Rigby. Since Elizabeth was watching, he was unable to give Clay a drink without taking one himself. There was no dumping, she saw to that. At last the evening came to a close. It was Rigby who spoke. "Dear friends," he said, "the hour is late. I know I'll have a full day tomorrow. It's time for bed."

"The party's over," Clay mumbled.

"Oh, it needn't be," Elizabeth said. "I was going to suggest that we rouse Jude and have her prepare a large platter of ham and eggs. How does that sound?"

"No, dear lady," Rigby said, "don't awaken Jude. I don't want to create a problem on this my last night."

"It's no problem," Elizabeth said. "With food, the party can go until sailing time tomorrow. Thomas can rouse her."

"Grand idea, my dear," Clay muttered with a thick tongue. He scowled at her. "I thought you didn't like Rigby. I was wrong, I guess. You're being hospitable, most hospitable."

"Indeed she is," Rigby said, "but the offer is too generous. I must decline. Really, Clay, I do have a day before me."

"As you wish, Rigby, old friend," Clay said."

At breakfast the next morning Clay looked terrible. Rigby looked a shade better. Both men insisted they wanted only coffee. "What you need," Elizabeth said firmly, "is a pony of whiskey, taken neat, and then a wholesome breakfast. The grog will give you the courage to eat."

"Is this what they did at the parish house?"

"No, Clay. As you know, Papa didn't drink. But it's what happened at Uncle Roderick's on several occasions. My Aunt Esther knew both the poison and the cure." She found the nearly empty whiskey bottle. "I think the recommended dose is two fingers. I'm sure you both know how to pour that, or shall I pour for you?"

Clay had to repeat the cure, but it worked. They both ate an ample breakfast and looked better for the effort.

When breakfast was over, the three of them walked to the dock. The household staff followed. Elizabeth was surprised to see so many gathered for the occasion.

She remembered what Tess had said of Rigby. "He ain' no mean man, my daddy say. He lay it on you when you need it, but he be fair." Perhaps Tess was right.

"I wish you well, Rigby. We hate to see you leave."

"I thank you for your good wishes, Clay. Then he turned to Elizabeth. "We never got to know each other well, ma'am. Perhaps we'll meet later. When I build upriver, maybe you and Mr. Greenleaf will come to enjoy my hospitality."

Indeed we didn't get to know each other well, Elizabeth thought, and we never will. As for your hospitality, I've already had quite enough of that. "Thank you for the invitation, sir," she said. "My husband and I would consider it an honor."

After one last handshake, Rigby boarded the boat. The steam hissed and the boat moved into the channel.

"Well, my dear," Clay said. "I must go to South Gate. Rafe says there's a problem there with the outer canal."

As he left her side, Elizabeth was joined by Tess. The two of them walked back toward the house. The milling crowd at dockside was breaking up. There were jobs to be done. It was another day at Greenleaf Plantation.

As they walked back, Elizabeth spoke. "I know you said Rigby was a fair man, Tess, and maybe a lot of people were sorry to see him go, but I saw Jude crying."

"Mr. Jonathan, he be Gordy's daddy."

"Gordy?"

"Gordy. Jude's boy. He be the brightskin that works for Mr. Byron. You don't know Gordy?"

"I don't think I do, Tess," she said.

Chapter Thirty-Two

It had only been a matter of weeks since their arrival at the rice island, but they were difficult days for Elizabeth. Clay's boorish behavior the first night started the nightmare. Her work with the impassive Roselle had not been as easy, and there was the problem with Rigby. Elizabeth was certain Clay's refusal to believe her was the genesis of her encounter with Rigby in the barn before his departure.

On the first full day after Rigby had gone upriver. Elizabeth was still in bed at eight. Tess was already there. She heard her talking to Carlotta. This damned house, she thought. Father Greenleaf's masterpiece! She could hear every word. Tess was being Tess, with her ten thousand questions. Carlotta told Tess to hold her tongue or she would see that she got a lashing. That stopped Tess instantly.

Elizabeth knew she should get up, but there was an uneasiness in the pit of her stomach. She was not nauseous, but she was close to it. It was as though her stomach was saying to her, "Don't push it, honey. If you do, I'll show you just how upset I can be." She was careful as she arose. The strange feeling in her stomach was still there.

As Elizabeth entered the central room, Tess rushed toward her. "Missus, I thought you might sleep away the whole day."

"Yes, Tess, it's late, even for a sleepyhead."

"What you want for breakfast this morning, Missus?"

"Nothing, Tess. My stomach is a little upset."

"What you need, Missus," Tess said, "is a biscuit in warm milk. That what my mama give me when I is poorly."

"No, Tess. We'll get our lunch basket and go."

"Your belly need something warm in it before you walk out into the cold, Missus. I'll get it. Eat what you can, one spoon at a time." She trotted toward the kitchen.

She brought back a steaming bowl. One of Jude's flaky biscuits had been crumbled in the warm milk. There were flecks floating in the milk. "What's in this Tess."

"Nutmeg, Missus. I done tol' Jude you poorly, and she say, nutmeg's good for a gnawing stomach. She put it in."

Elizabeth tried the first spoonful. It had a pleasant taste. She tried another. When there was no adverse reaction, she continued until the bowl was empty.

"Here's your wrap, Missus. The sun be up, but the night air just hang around like it don't want to go."

"Thank you, Tess. Did you tell Jude about the lunch?"

"Jude, she know you now. She done made lunch."

As Tess said, it was nippy. They walked quickly on that familiar pathway toward Mealy Point.

There was the ever-present fire burning outside the infirmary, and the usual number of people still clustered around it. Roselle was not to be seen.

Elizabeth walked through the wards. This is what an infirmary should be, she thought. There were fires in all the fireplaces, the floors were clean, the chamber pots had been emptied, and the breakfast dishes had been removed.

In the terminal ward she saw something lying on the floor. She stooped to pick it up. The bright daylight of the ward dimmed before her eyes and she lost consciousness.

Tess rushed to her side. When she found Elizabeth's eyes partially closed and unseeing, Tess screamed. An old man in one of the beds grabbed his cane and began beating it against the wall. With Tess' scream and the old man's pounding, the room came alive with noise. It was pandemonium.

Roselle appeared. Her quick black eyes took in the whole scene at a glance. "Quiet!" she said. The noise subsided a little. "I said quiet," she demanded. The room turned silent. Roselle felt for a pulse. She put her hand inside Elizabeth's dress to feel for a heartbeat. "She's alive," she said. "You two," she commanded, "get her to a bed. No, no, not in here This ain' no fit place. Take her to maternity, it be close by."

When they had Elizabeth on a bed with cold compresses on her brow, Roselle turned to Tess. "What happen' in there?"

"Nothing happen'," Tess replied.

"Girl, somethin' happen'. I find the Missus on the floor. Now tell me what happen', Tess?" Tess stared at the floor. "Speak up, girl. How can I help if you don' tell me 'bout it?"

"She stoop down, and she just tumble over real slow."

Reality was coming back to Elizabeth. The details of the room were clearing. "Tess," she said. "Tess, where are you?"

"I be here, Missus." Tess said. "Right here, Missus."

Elizabeth turned. She saw Roselle and the crowd in the room. "What is this? What's this commotion?"

Roselle took charge. "It's all right, Missus. You fainted, that's all. You soon be feelin' better."

"I'm all right." Elizabeth said. She started to get up.

"No'm, you is not all right. Not jes' yet. You lie there. You, Clothilde, make hot tea for the Missus." She turned back to Elizabeth. "You is all right, I feel sure, Missus, but 'till you get strength, you jes' stay there. Color coming back now. You be all right, by and by."

When the tea came, Elizabeth was propped erect with pillows. "Tell me 'bout this, Missus," Roselle said as Elizabeth sipped the tea. "How come you stoop over and fall?"

"I saw something on the floor. I stooped to pick it up, and that's all I remember."

"Tess, what kind a no-good are you?" Roselle said fiercely. "You supposed to fetch for the Missus, that's your job. Ain' you no good for nothing'?"

"Please, Roselle, don't chastise Tess. She did nothing. I stooped and fell. Tess did nothing wrong."

"You been dizzy before, Missus?"

"No, Roselle. I've been fine. I don't understand it."

"She be sick this morning," Tess said.

"What kind of sick you was, Missus?"

Elizabeth wanted to shout at them. "I felt queasy."

"She don' want no breakfast," Tess said.

"Sick in the morning?"

"Now, wait a minute," Elizabeth said. "It was nothing. People faint. It isn't a sign of the end of the world."

"Dr. Barnes, he say, people don't faint for nothing. You better go to Darien, Missus," Roselle said. Elizabeth sipped her tea and said nothing. "You be regular, Missus?"

"Regular?"

"With the periods, Missus. You be regular?"

Elizabeth laughed. "Do you think I'm pregnant?"

"It happens, Missus, it happens. You regular?" Elizabeth didn't reply. "You have to think about it, Missus? You ain't regular, I can tell that."

She had not been, as Roselle phrased it, "regular." Elizabeth had been aware of it, but she blamed it on the rigors of the trip and of the circumstances since her arrival. It didn't concern her. When conditions are upset, the menstrual cycle can be upset. That's all it was.

Those sharp black eyes were fixed on Elizabeth. Roselle made her points and she ticked them off on her short fat fingers: "You ain' been regular, you be sick this morning, and now you faint. That tell me something, Missus. I think you is pregnant. Glory be, I hope you is!"

"Roselle, please. You're imagining things."

"Yes, ma'am; yes, ma'am, I know. You is with child. I'm sure. Mistah Clay best take you to see Dr. Barnes. We gonna have a new white baby at Greenleaf. Glory be! Glory be!"

"Now, Roselle, you don't know that—"

"I know that for sure when you get back from Darien."

Tess spoke: "And I have to let mos' her dresses out, too. She be gettin' bigger."

Roselle took a good look at her. "Yes, indeed. I ain' been seein' it, but you is filling out your dresses, jes' like Tess say. Glory be."

"Roselle, there will be no more talk," Elizabeth said. "Not a word. I'll see the doctor, but not because I think I'm pregnant; I'll go to be sure there's no valid reason for the fainting. But, for now, I'll not hear another word." She turned to the others in the room. "Please," she said, "all of you, promise me you won't say a word. Mr. Greenleaf is so anxious for a child. Let it be true before he hears about it. Please, ladies, promise me that this will be our secret."

"Yes, Missus, I promise. I won't say a word," Roselle said, and there was a murmur from the other ladies present.

"Thank you, ladies. If Dr. Barnes says it's true, I'll tell you. For now, please, not a word."

But how do you stop a wild fire in a brisk wind? Before Elizabeth got home, word had spread. The house people did not look at her directly. They watched her on the sly. They saw the fullness of her breasts, the shape of the hips, the way she walked, and knowing heads nodded in agreement.

Clay was at home, which surprised Elizabeth since she left the infirmary early. "Are you working only a half a day now, my dear?" Clay smiled as he spoke. "Are things going so well that you can lay about like this?"

She wanted to speak to him about going to see Dr. Barnes. How could she do it without causing him undue concern, or without suggesting that she might be pregnant? "Things are going well, thank you; and, yes, I did leave early."

The smile broadened. "Did you have something to do here, my dear, or did your sixth sense tell you I had come home early? Were you drawn here like steel shavings to a magnet?"

"Are you making fun of me?"

"Yes, I am. When are you going to be honest with me?"

"I'm not sure what you mean, Clay."

"Well, to begin with, tell me why you're home early, or, would you rather I tell you why I'm home early?"

"You tell me first."

"All right, my dear. Here it is. I came home early because word came to me in the fields that you had fainted—"

"I asked them to promise—"

"If I may continue, my dear—that you had fainted at the infirmary, that recently you had some of your summer dresses let out, and that you had a familiar sickness this morning and that you had almost refused breakfast."

"Oh, that Roselle. What does a promise mean to her?"

"Roselle said nothing. But, my dear, there was a roomful of wagging tongues. Such good news could not be kept. It went from one to the other, until it reached me in the field."

Tears were running down her cheeks. "It may not be true."

"Such a possibility exists, Elizabeth. But there's the other side of the coin: It may be true, and the possibility was enough for me. I threw down my hoe and came home."

She laughed at his absurdity. "Threw down your hoe?"

"Figuratively, of course. But I am home, as you can see."

"Yes, Clay, you are."

"The boat is due to return here tomorrow. It couldn't be better timed. We'll go to Darien. If you need anything, make a shopping list. But the important thing is, we will pay a call on Dr. Barnes."

Chapter Thirty-Three

The two months that followed Rigby's departure were the happiest of Elizabeth's marriage. The house had no servants at night. Old Thomas was no longer required to "fetch." But it was more than having the house to themselves.

As nearly as Dr. Barnes could determine, Elizabeth was four months pregnant. Even so, Elizabeth felt she was on her honeymoon, and Clay was excited about the prospect of having a son.

As they lay in bed at night he would talk of his boy. Elizabeth reminded him that a son was only one of the possibilities. He didn't hear her. He had romantic ideas of pony carts, and fishing poles, and teaching the boy, from an early age, to manage a plantation.

"If it's a boy, Clay, it'll be a long, long time before he'll need instruction in rice planting."

"Not long, my dear. He'll be with me in the fields from his earliest days. He'll grow up with the feel of this place, just as I did. Father took me everywhere. It was rough and dirty, but I saw it done firsthand. You sometimes wonder why I love this place—"

"No, Clay, I live here now. I understand it."

"In a way you do, but it's more than the strange beauty you see. I'm happy you see and understand that part of it, but it's more than that. These marshes, the rivers, the rich earth, and the sea are as much a part of me as my right arm.

Mother was sent to Philadelphia when I was born, but that was an accident of birth. I'm Greenleaf Plantation and it's me. That was my father's legacy."

"But, Clay, my darling, your son could be a daughter."

"If that be the case, I'll renew my efforts, my dear. The second one will be a son."

"It takes two, Clay. What about saying 'our efforts'?"

"Elizabeth, it's unladylike to talk like that. A woman is meant to be a wife and a companion, but it's unseemly for her to talk in such a coarse manner."

"Don't be silly, Clay. What men and women say or do in private is not what they might do when they are abroad. Why can't I say such a thing when we're alone? And it's true, you know. You won't be having a child without me."

"A man's passions are one thing, Elizabeth; women are not driven by similar feelings."

"Your Aunt Matilda told me you were a man of rather broad tastes, Clay. Experienced, I think she said. It surprises me, at times, how little you know of women."

"And you know so much?"

"I know that much."

"Then why didn't you know you were pregnant? Four months. And yet you had no idea. That's unbelievable."

"There was just too much going on."

"I talked to Roselle." he said. "She said you wouldn't believe her. It seems to me, my dear, you were as unworldly when I married you as I had hoped you'd be. I was hunting for a good girl, and I found one. But to miss four months and think nothing of it? That borders on being stupid, my love."

"Is it any wonder? The unsettled time in Philadelphia, that horrible trip through the Carolinas—"

"A trip you chose to take, that you insisted on taking."

"True and I'm not sorry I did, although I wouldn't like to repeat the experience. But that's the reason I lost sight of my bodily functions. It was a nightmare."

"A good excuse for ignorance."

The rice was planted to coincide with the first high tides in March. Clay's hours were longer. When the planting was completed, the fields were flooded with fresh river water.

On the ninth day after the first flood, Clay had a horse and buggy ready in the early morning. He wanted Elizabeth with him. He wanted her to see the healthy sprouts under the water, and he wanted her to watch the process as the gates were opened at low tide to allow the fields to be drained.

"My son will miss the planting this year, but if you are there, perhaps it will begin his education."

She laughed at his romantic idea. "Are you trying to mark my child with a rice field? I should refuse to go."

"You'll do as your husband says. If little Georgie can't be there in person, you'll be his proxy, my dear."

"Little Georgie?"

"I intend to name him George Edwin Manley Greenleaf, after my father. He'll be the second to bear that name. I hope he turns out to be as good a man as its original owner."

"That's what you intend to do, is it?"

"It's a fine name."

Elizabeth let the subject die.

"And I'm to be Georgie's proxy today, am I? Well, fortunately, I do want to go with you. I want to see the results of all these many weeks of work. Besides, I'm curious to see how you get all that water off the fields."

It was an exciting day for Elizabeth. She saw the tender shoots, thousands upon thousands of them, in every corner of every field now covered with water. She marveled at the ingenious system of ditches and canals that had kept the water over the seeds for sprouting.

It was a miracle of birth, almost as exciting as the miracle she was experiencing. Whether it was the boy Clay wanted, or a girl, she knew it was a robust child.

Clay's work was impressive. And she was even more impressed as she watched the water being drained from the fields, leaving the sprouts to grow strong in the sunlight.

"Well, my dear, what did you think?"

"I'm without words. It's just overwhelming."

As they drove along the dike, Elizabeth's eyes were on the fields, watching the men and women at work, but she was aware that Clay had something else on his mind. He ran a finger around his collar, as though it fit him too tightly, and then in a few seconds he would do it again.

"There's something more on your mind, isn't there, Clay? What is it? Has Byron objected to the extra fireplace I wanted for the terminal ward?"

"Oh, no, my dear. Nothing like that. Byron would have approved that in a trice. I didn't even mention it to him. It's just that I'm not sure how to tell you this, since you seem to take what you do at the infirmary so seriously."

"Do you want me to stop going there? Is it because I'm beginning to get so big?"

"No, my dear. You can still go. I know having something to do is good for you. That's not it."

"Then what?"

"You know that we won't be living here—not later when the summer heat arrives?"

"Yes. You told me."

"Well, we'll be leaving—I don't know when. It depends on how things go, but we'll probably be leaving by the end of April. I realize now how seriously you take what you've been doing with Roselle, and I just wondered, is it—" He stopped. "Do you have what you wanted to get done—is it all—"

She laughed. "You don't know how to say it, do you? You are a strange one, Clay. There are times when you run over me roughshod, and then these times when you're overly concerned. I declare, I can't understand you."

"I want you happy. If it takes work at the infirmary—"

"I am happy, and yes, it does take doing something useful. I want to help, and I think I am. Let me see if I can say what you're having such a problem with, Clay. You want to know if it's going to upset me when we have to go to the main island, is that it?"

"Yes. Can you leave your work with Roselle, knowing it's in good hands, just as I can leave the rice fields, knowing they are in good hands? You see, my dear, those little rice plants you saw today will be left in the sun to grow stronger. In about three weeks, when the tides are right, we'll flood the fields again. The second time will kill any weeds that may also be there. It's a tricky thing. It must be judged exactly right, or you don't kill all the weeds; or worse yet, you let the water stay too long and weaken your crop. I want to be here. I'll be the final judge of when to begin and end the second flow, but once that's over, once the fields are drained, we can go to the main island. What I need to know is, do you have—or will you have—your work to the point where you can be gone all summer? Will the infirmary continue with the improvements you've been making?"

"Yes, Clay. Roselle is now as interested as I am. She is truly a good nurse, even if she seems a little less than caring with people who are in a final illness. I understand her, even if I don't agree. She wants to give her time to the people who have a chance of recovery. Like your men, Roselle can handle the job. I sometimes suspect I'll have nothing to do when we return in the fall. You say a school is out of the question."

"Don't start that, Elizabeth. I don't want an argument. There will be no school."

"Then, Clay, when you're ready to go to the main island, I'll be ready."

Chapter Thirty-Four

The second flow was completed at the end of April. Clay checked the rice fields daily, even hourly, toward the end of the period. Water must not be allowed to weaken his rice plants, but it had to be there long enough to sap the strength of the weeds. It was a delicate balance. It was his crop. He wanted it to be bountiful since it was his first planting without an overseer.

By Dr. Barnes' examination and calculation, Elizabeth was now in her sixth month. She believed it was only the fifth at most. Surely she could not have been so far along and not have been aware of it. Whichever month it was, her shape had changed. Most of her clothes, even with alterations, were too tight for comfort, or impossible to wear.

Elizabeth wanted Tess to become a dressmaker. The opportunity was at hand. Tess was becoming a designer and maker of maternity clothes. It was work she loved. In making her doll clothes, Tess had been forced to make incredibly small stitches and the practice carried over.

The dresses were masterpieces of ingenuity. They were stylish and had clever hidden vents that could be adjusted daily. Tess made use of overblouses and jackets as a part of the complete costume.

Then the day came. In early May they moved to the main island. Elizabeth was sad to leave Clay's father's ingenious house. She hated it at first, but she had grown accustomed to it.

We like the things we have when we are happy, she thought, and I've been happy here since Rigby left. She would have been more reluctant to leave if Clay had made Tess stay.

Before the decision about Tess was finally reached, Elizabeth put Tess to a sewing task, and then made her way to Mealy Point. She had heard Annabelle and Reuben were pleased to see Tess have such an opportunity, but Elizabeth wanted to be sure. Since she was going to become a mother soon, Elizabeth was already filled with ideas of how a mother might feel if her child were being taken from her.

She knocked on the door of the white tabby house. She heard talking within. It was Gullah, a language brought by the slaves. The door swung open. "Annabelle," Elizabeth said, "I'm Elizabeth Greenleaf."

"I know who you is, Missus. Everybody know who you is."

"May I come in? I'd like to talk to you about Tess."

"Yes'm, you come right in. Reuben, on your feet. It's the Missus, come to talk about Tess. She done somethin' bad?"

"No, Annabelle. She is a wonderful, talented girl. It's just that I'd like her to go with us to the main island. She'll be gone until next fall. I couldn't take her until I knew it was all right with you and Reuben."

"Oh, Lordy, yes'm. Hits fine. We'll miss her pesky questions, but she ain' strong, and I been worrin' 'bout when she have to go to the fields."

"She sews beautifully, Annabelle. You taught her well."

"I show her how to sew, but when she fin' how, she take such pains. She sew like she sew; I cain' do it like that. Lordy, no, Missus."

"Is it all right with you, Reuben? You're her father."

"Yes'm. Hit be fine with me. We glad she can sew. Like Annabelle say, she ain' strong enough for no field work."

"I wanted to thank you, Reuben, for the beautiful boxes you made for the hospital supply room. It was exceptional work. When we come back in the fall, I hope to find other jobs for you. As your daughter has, you have a special talent. It should be used."

"We thank you, Missus. It be good for Tess. We thank you, don't we, Gumbo?" Reuben touched Annabelle's shoulder.

"Gumbo?"

"Gumbo. That be okra, Missus. That be a Gullah word. Reuben, he call me that. He say he like gumbo and he like me." Annabelle's musical laugh filled the room.

"Gumbo, is it? Well, let me tell you both, Tess will be safe. We'll be leaving in a few days, but I couldn't take her away without talking to you. Thank you for the help of a wonderful girl. She has been a godsend to me."

"Thank you, Missus," Annabelle said. "She be a good girl. We is obliged to you, ain't we, Reuben?"

"Yes'm, we is, much obliged."

The trip to the main island took over two hours because of the winding river that flowed through the marshes. It would twist and turn, doubling back on itself. "I see why your father wanted to build a shell road across the marshes, Clay," Elizabeth said as she watched the boat come within a few feet of where it had previously been. "From the south dike, it really isn't more than a mile to the main island."

"No, my dear, it's more than a mile. When you're looking across the marshes, especially on a clear afternoon, it can seem quite close. Father never got to the road building, and neither have we. The road would be convenient, but convenience must wait on practicality."

"But couldn't you cut out some of the loops in this river? We've been doubling back and forth."

"It may look easy, but cutting a channel is back-breaking work. Others have tried. This deep channel is natural. Nature takes a dim view of tampering. The Hamiltons tried it, but with each storm the cuts kept filling back in. In time Dan Hamilton decided to use the channel as nature made it."

"Maybe they didn't make them deep enough."

"Man proposes, my dear, God disposes."

"I think I'd try."

"I'm sure you would."

"We're back in open water. Are we getting close, Clay?"

"Yes, my dear. As we pass that point down there to the right, you'll be able to see the house."

"Does it face the sea?"

"The house is well back from the ocean, Elizabeth. We have fierce storms along this coast. A house too close to the water would not last long. We're protected by the dunes, and by a wooded barrier that father always insisted upon maintaining. We'll never get so greedy for cotton land that we will cut those trees and destroy our protective barrier."

"But you can walk to the sea?"

"Oh, yes. It's a quarter of a mile on a shell pathway. But, my dear, don't go beyond the dunes. The sun reflecting on the water can ruin your skin, even with a parasol."

"But I love the sea."

"There will be days when we can go to the beach. I like it best when it turns nasty, when the waves come in with enough passion to sweep the dunes away. They never do, of course. The dunes, like the marshes, have a way of lasting."

Elizabeth watched intently as they rounded the point. There it was ahead, a large two-story house, well back from the docking area. Like the house on the rice island, it was a disappointment. It was large, but without any interesting architectural details. It did not have the grandeur of the houses she had seen with the handsome Greek columns, nor the stately grace of the those in either Savannah or Charleston. Greenleaf Hall was a square, two-story box in need of paint. It had a veranda on the upper and lower floors on three sides, but no other pretensions. There was no ornamentation. It stood in a square of sand, devoid of vegetation. What should have been the garden was the same. She knew the sand yard of the house on the rice island was to keep down work, but she expected a proper lawn and garden at Greenleaf Hall.

"No lawn," she said, almost to herself.

"No, my dear. Father didn't approve. He wanted the grounds to be kept simple. He didn't squander labor. Anything other than a producing garden was wasting work hours. Labor had to produce a return. The land around the house can be kept clear of debris easily by the house people, and when the leaves fall, they can be swept up and burned."

"But your mother—"

"She wanted a lawn and flowers."

"She didn't get them, did she, Clay?"

"We were building Greenleaf, just as we are now."

"Without a lawn. Not even when she grew old and could sit on the veranda and appreciate it."

"Don't be maudlin, Elizabeth. A lawn is simply not a practical idea, not until we have money to throw away on nonsense, and that's certainly not now."

"I feel sorry for your mother."

"Mother was a romantic, just like you. She didn't adapt well. Father said he should have left her in England."

"Left her in England!"

"He would have gone back to see her, of course. She was his wife, but she didn't do well here on these islands."

"What kind of a man was he?"

"Don't disparage. He was a man of courage. What you see here is what he made with his own hands."

"Don't stray from reality, Clay. He may have been brilliant, but he really did very little with his own hands."

"Elizabeth you are being impertinent. If you can't speak well of the dead, don't speak of them at all." He walked away.

As the boat was brought into the dock, Elizabeth saw people there to greet her. How would it look if Clay were not with her? She moved back toward the noisy wood-fired engine where he stood talking to the engineer.

"We are nearly there, Clay. Will you come to help me off, please? I'm not as steady on my feet as I might be, especially when we have been on board for so long."

He turned toward her. He wanted to be sure he had made his point. She saw the smile at the corner of his lips.

"Yes, my dear, I am, as always, ready to assist."

Chapter Thirty-Five

The house was not as bad as it first appeared. It was still a large, ugly box, eight feet above the ground, but the interior was a contrast, reflecting current styles. Heavy double front doors opened into a large hall. Elizabeth thought it must be twenty feet wide, or perhaps more. It went through to the back of the house.

She thought the room unusual but acceptable, especially when she noted the graceful curve of the stairway to the second floor, the ornate cornices at the ceiling, the warm woodwork and the floor of polished pine.

"Your nose was up as we walked to the house, my dear. You looked as if you had sniffed an unwashed armpit."

"Clay, don't be vulgar. Someone may hear you."

"They may have seen you. Your contempt was apparent."

"The house is plain on the outside."

"Father kept the cost down."

"But inside it's quite nice."

"Mother was not a demanding woman. Father would never have put up with that." He paused. He wanted her to fully understand that point. "But," he continued, "she managed. For that reason, the inside is mother's."

"It's lovely." She hesitated. She wanted to know about this wide, long entry. How could she ask, especially since Clay had taken pains to watch her discontent with the outside of

Greenleaf Hall? Was it named because of this room? It was more than an entry; it was truly a long, wide hall.

"But—" He waited.

"But what?"

"Come now, Elizabeth. You have more to say."

"Well, it's this room." She hesitated. "I can see the value of a generous entryway, but this one goes on through to the back of the house. It's as large as a ballroom."

"Very good, Elizabeth. You are astute. It's our ballroom at Greenleaf. And it opens on both ends, another of father's innovations. It's a pleasant place for a ball, even on a warm night. Father wouldn't make a separate ballroom, but he allowed mother to alter this entryway so that it could also be used as a ballroom. We had few occasions for balls."

"But you have used it as a ballroom."

"Oh, yes, from time to time. But, my dear, it's also utilitarian. The servants can get to any room on this floor without passing through a second room. Father's idea."

He took her through the house, even to the warming kitchen in the bricked-in area under the living quarters. Here the ceilings were low, and the floors were earthen. "It's work space for the servants. It's all that's needed."

Everything was brought from the kitchen, a separate building. In this room, under the living quarters, all the dishes were kept hot. There was a narrow stairwell up to the pantry where two men made the food ready for correct and prompt serving. Clay's father would not tolerate long delays between courses, nor would he wait an undue amount of time until all at his table had been served.

As Elizabeth walked through the house, she knew she must become the mistress of Greenleaf Plantation.

She should have done it upon her arrival in January. She had not because of the newness of her position, because of Clay's boorish behavior, and because of Rigby. She had been remiss in not taking charge, but time cannot be unraveled and then rewound. She would begin here and now. She would talk to Carlotta.

Clay had shown her through the house the day before, but as she wandered around by herself after breakfast, she found doors that had not been opened. One of them adjoined the bedroom that she shared with Clay. Theirs was not the largest of the bedrooms, but it had been Clay's from boyhood, and he did not want to move. She had seen the door the day before, but it had not excited her curiosity.

On this first morning at Greenleaf Hall, the slower walk through the house finally brought her back to that closed door. She opened it. It was an unkempt and littered storeroom that smelled stale and dusty. Its contents appeared to be Clay's accumulation of the years of his life: things he couldn't or wouldn't throw away. She looked at the rag-tag collection he had amassed: toys from childhood; boots that were no longer serviceable; guns; fishing gear; three bottles of rum, with the wax seals unbroken. Why? Why hide rum? Was it from a day when his drinking had been discouraged? Here it was, shoved into a darkened corner, half under a painted canvas floor mat, dusty and forgotten.

With lifted skirts she made her way through the debris. There was a fireplace, a small, handsome fireplace, faced with blue and white glazed tiles. This room was a treasure.

She stood in the center of it, surrounded by Clay's special things, she knew she was intruding into a time and space she had not been bidden to enter. She was an interloper. These were private memories, these were things he had hidden away from the eyes of others: the toy drum and the hand puppet were not things Clay had—or would ever have—on display. These things were behind a closed door because he wanted it closed. She saw an old jacket on the back of a worn winged chair. She saw a knife collection on the window ledge. She saw a lace decorated bloomer of white linen. She touched it. Some of the lace had been torn loose. "Oh, my," she said aloud, "I must get out of here."

After her private tour of the house, she stopped in the room where Tess was sewing. "Would you find Carlotta for me, Tess? I'll be in the blue room at the front of the house, and ask cook to make a pot of tea, please. Who is the cook here at Greenleaf, Tess? What is her name?"

"That be Gerda, Missus. Jude, she stay at the rice island. I 'spect she do. She stay there when Mr. Jonathan live there. I don' know what they do now."

"But Gerda is the regular cook here?"

"Yes'm."

Elizabeth waited for Carlotta, dreading the encounter. By taking charge of her own house, it might appear that she was taking authority from Carlotta. How should she do it? Was there an easy way? She decided to ask Carlotta to have the household staff assemble in the large hall. She could meet them all and she could learn what their jobs were. Then, at one time, without any misunderstanding, everyone would clearly be told that Carlotta was fully in charge of the staff, but that she, Elizabeth, would see to the overall planning of the household.

As they assembled, Elizabeth could see a definite order, a ranking, within the line that formed. Carlotta stood at the head of it, of course. Elizabeth felt her stomach tighten. She was unable to shake the unease she felt in all her encounters with Carlotta. The woman had such a positive bearing. As she was doing at this moment, Carlotta did her job well. For Elizabeth, speaking to Carlotta was like speaking to a carved figure. She was always attentive, but her face remained placid, as though she could hear but had no capacity to respond. Carlotta was unfailingly polite but remote.

"This is the staff, Miz Greenleaf," she said. And then she gave their names and the jobs they were expected to do.

When she finished Elizabeth said, "Thank you, Carlotta."

She turned toward the staff. "This has been a bachelor household since my husband's mother died some years ago. You have all done wonderfully well in keeping this house, and the one at the rice island, functioning so well. I thank you, each of you, for all you've done."

Her eyes swept down the line. There wasn't a friendly face except for Tess. They were not unfriendly. Like Carlotta, they were without expression. They listened, but they offered no encouragement.

"For a number of years now," she continued, "Carlotta has been in complete charge of this household and the one at the rice island. But I am the new Mrs. Greenleaf. A woman always feels better when she's making the decisions for her own household, for her own family." Had she said that poorly? She saw and heard nothing, but the atmosphere in the room had been subtly altered. She could feel it. As her eyes swept the room, she saw no changes—not in Carlotta, not in any of them—but something had changed.

She grew more uncomfortable, but she tried again. "Nothing will be different at Greenleaf Hall. Carlotta will be in charge, as she has been. She will be working with me. We'll do our best not to disrupt the harmony you have here. As in the past, you will look to her for direction. I thank you all for being here, and I hope to get to know each of you better as the days pass." She turned more directly to the head of the line. "Thank you, Carlotta. Now, we can all continue with the tasks we have before us."

Carlotta's head turned slightly toward the line. Her eyes closed for a moment, and without a sound from her, they all knew they had been dismissed. Quietly the room emptied.

"Do you have something planned for the midday meal, Missus," Carlotta asked, "or shall I continue?"

"I'll have the menu for tomorrow, Carlotta. Today will be as you planned it. But I'd like for you to show me through the larder. I'll need to know what we have on hand, and what I'll need to ask Mister Byron to order."

"Yes, Missus. And will you want the keys as well?"

"Oh, no, Carlotta. You will keep the keys to the stores, as you always have. It's just that I must make this my home."

Clay arrived home at sunset, his face ruddy from the ride in the open air. He liked what he found in the fields. That much was apparent in his gait as he walked toward the house.

"Supper will be ready as soon as you wash up, Clay. I saw you and Mr. Barnwell ride in. I sent word to the kitchen. Was it a good day? How did you find things?"

"Barnwell and Byron have done a fine job. Last year was a good one for cotton, and they have the fields ready for another good year."

As the soup was served, she spoke. "I, too, have had a good day. I spent it getting acquainted with the house."

"I showed you the house."

"Yes, you did, my darling, but you raced me through it. Today I spent time getting to know it. Your father may have brought his ideas to this house, but so did your mother. I could see her influence as I walked through the rooms."

He hesitated. "Yes," he said, "I wasn't aware of it until yesterday. Always when I thought of Greenleaf—" He stopped. She could feel his parents standing at his shoulder. "All my life I've never thought of Greenleaf without thinking of father, nor have I thought of father without thinking of Greenleaf. It was he who conceived it, who tamed it, who built it. It bears his name; it is him." He was quiet again. She waited. He had more to say, but he wasn't sure how to say it. Finally he spoke: "It was not until yesterday, not until I returned after a long absence—and with another woman at my side—that I was aware of how much of it is my mother."

After the dishes had been removed, when Clay was having strong black coffee with his pecan pie, the conversation drifted back to Greenleaf Hall.

"Yes, the stamp of Mary Ann Greenleaf is here in the house,"' he said, "but you're the mistress now. If you wish to make changes, I'd approve. A woman has a right to make her home a personal thing. I realize that now."

"There are no changes I'd like to make, Clay. I'm content with the home your mother made, but we must have a nursery, and I'd like a room where I could tend to my correspondence." Elizabeth hesitated. She had plans for the little room with the blue and white tile fireplace, but she was not sure how the subject should be broached.

"You got acquainted with the house today, Elizabeth. You must have some idea of what you want to do."

"Not exactly, Clay. Not yet."

"But, my dear, you have your own views."

"Not as concerns Greenleaf. My views will be subservient to yours. I spoke to the upstairs maid—

"Aletta."

"Yes, Aletta. She told me the large room at the front of the house had always been your parents' room, and that the nursery was toward the back of the house. "

"Yes, that's the way it was. The wet nurse took care of the children at the back of the house, so father could sleep undisturbed. It was the small room that adjoins my bedroom. You may not have seen it."

"I saw it." She hesitated. "I opened the door from our room. Clay, it's filled with debris, castaways, trash, worthless-looking things. It needs to be cleaned."

He smiled. "Yes, my dear, but I gave Carlotta instructions not to touch it. Maybe some of it should be thrown out. The value of all treasures, I'm sure, changes as our perception changes."

He was lost in his thoughts. Was he thinking of the knife collection, the drum, or was he, perhaps, thinking of the lace-trimmed bloomers? She did not rush his reverie. It was a personal time. When she saw his memory fade, she spoke.

"You said yesterday you wanted us to stay in your room. Was that a thought of the moment, or—"

"My parents' room is larger, but somehow—"

"Your old room is fine, Clay."

"Thank you, my dear. I'd rather stay there."

"I want the nursery close to our bedroom."

"And to hell with my sleep."

"I dare say you'll survive."

"Yes, my dear, I will, and, as strange as this may sound, I'd like our son to be nearby, too."

"Your son or your daughter."

"Yes."

"So, Clay, if we use your old room, then we will need the room at each side, for the nursery and my writing desk."

"I'll ask Barnwell to send a couple of boys to the house tomorrow. I'll direct them. Some of what you call trash can be thrown away, but there are a few things that I'd prefer to keep. Those items, whatever they are, can go to the attic."

"There's one other thing, Clay. I intend to be the mistress here, so today I called the staff together and let them know that I will be directing the details of our home."

"That's fine, my dear. It's not something I need to concern myself with. That's your job, Just do it."

"Well," she said, "I may have offended Carlotta. She's been in charge for so long she feels it's her house—"

"Nonsense."

"Well, that's the impression I get."

"She's a servant."

"But she's—" Elizabeth wasn't sure how to say it. "She's like a headman. Headmen are important. They are vital to the work of the estate. You've told me that."

"That's true—"

"And Carlotta is a headman, at least here in the house. She's important to me."

"I'm sure of it."

"I believe I may have offended her."

"Then, my dear, if that's the case, you have a problem. Solve it. What has it got to do with me?"

"You could talk to her. You could smooth it over."

"You wanted to be a part of this plantation, Elizabeth. If that's true, then stop whimpering. You seem to have made yourself a problem. Solve it, my dear; don't expect me to do it for you."

Chapter Thirty-Six

Other than the incident with the staff, Elizabeth could think of no reason why Carlotta should resent her, but she was keenly aware that resentment existed. There always seemed to be a constant, subtle struggle between the two of them. The fact that it was not overt did not make it any less real.

Carlotta was in an inferior position, but she was confident of her personal strengths. She knew Elizabeth would never have the whip brought to bear. She had seen Elizabeth's reaction to the lashing administered to Racy. Without the courage for the whip, Elizabeth earned Carlotta's contempt. Had their roles been reversed, Carlotta would have had no compunction about using whatever strengths she had available. Her life was in a rough world where you did what you had to do.

Elizabeth quickly learned to be careful in giving the day's schedule to Carlotta. Her instructions were always carried out to the letter, and that was the problem.

Carlotta's bright mind had no difficulty in remembering the exact words her mistress used. When the day was over, the meals had been prepared and served exactly as the instructions were given, and the work in the household proceeded in the same fixed and precise manner.

On one occasion, the noonday meal consisted only of baked ham and boiled potatoes. There were no other vegetables, no bread or biscuits, no tea or coffee. Clay said, "Are we low in the larder, my dear?"

"I'm planning an elaborate dessert for your supper, Clay. You can manage with this. But the tea has been forgotten—and the biscuits. I'll send Tess to fetch them."

When Clay was gone, Elizabeth sent for Carlotta. "Our dinner was incomplete, Carlotta. Is there a reason for it?"

"You ordered ham and boiled potatoes, Missus."

"But you know that's not a complete meal. Mr. Greenleaf didn't even have his tea; there wasn't a single biscuit on the table. Why didn't you round out the meal, as you have done so nicely in the past?"

Carlotta's gaze was unwavering. "I'm sorry, Missus, but I thought you meant it just like you asked for it. I didn't understand it, but white folks do have strange ways sometimes. You said ham and boiled potatoes."

"That's true, Carlotta, that's what I said. I'll be clearer in the future. What if I made a list of each day's meals? Would you prefer that?"

"I can't read, ma'am. None of us can."

It was a simple statement of fact. Elizabeth's frustration rushed back. They needed a school, but Clay was firm. No school. She couldn't do it now, but, like Mary Ann Greenleaf, she might be able to find a way to go around the stubborn and inflexible Clay.

Carlotta was right about being unable to read. The encounter was a subtle victory for her. Elizabeth needed to take the sting out of it. So she continued, "But a list of the day's menus might still be a good idea. I could read them to you. Having a list will be a help to me, too. With a record of the daily meals, I can bring more variety to Mr. Greenleaf's table. So there's a bright side to it, and I thank you, Carlotta, for helping me think of it." Had she turned the tide in her favor? Carlotta's eyes said nothing.

These small encounters continued. There was one or more of them every day. Elizabeth was sensitive to them. She watched for every minor but irritating incident. Were they only in her imagination? Was she going mad? There were times when she wasn't sure.

One morning Elizabeth decided to go to the kitchen to talk to Gerda about a different way to prepare the rabbit shot earlier that morning.

It would be duck today as scheduled, and rabbit tomorrow. She remembered how wild hare had been prepared at the manse when a parishioner was kind enough to bring in one from the country. Their cook soaked it in wine. Cook said wine made the meat tender and took away the wild taste.

Whether that was true or not, Elizabeth reasoned, wine will add something, a change in flavor. As she rounded the corner she heard Carlotta.

"Don't talk back to me, Gerda."

"But Mistah Clay, he always want cherry sauce with duck. He say duck ain' much without cherry sauce."

"She ain't said cherry sauce; you don't cook cherry sauce. You understand that, Gerda? You hear me?"

"But Mistah Clay—"

"Now you listen to me, and you listen good, Gerda. You do as I say. Plenty of women can cook. You ain't the only one. You get that in your head good. If I say so, you be in the fields tomorrow. I don't want no back talk from you, or you be a field hand again. If you want to keep this nice, easy job, it be what I say, not what you think."

Elizabeth stood quietly listening. It's not my imagination, she thought. This has been going on and it's deliberate. She backed away, turned and went to the house.

After a five-minute wait, Elizabeth went back to the kitchen. She took pains to be heard. She slammed the back door, and she hummed as she walked along the brick pathway. In the kitchen was Carlotta, Gerda and a girl cleaning pots. "Good morning, ladies," she said. "I've come to make a change for dinner today, that is, if it's not too late."

"What change, Missus?"

"If it's not too late, Carlotta, I'd like a rice stuffing in the duck, instead of the cornmeal stuffing we usually had over at the rice island. If you don't know how to do that, Gerda, I can tell you."

"No'm. Ain' no problem. I knows how. The dressing ain' started yet nohow. No problem, Missus."

"And I forgot something else. I don't know where my head's been today. I've been doing everything wrong. Duck always tastes a little flat to me. Do we have cranberries? They could be cooked—a little on the tart side, please—to go along with the duck. Is that possible, Gerda?"

"Yes'm," Gerda replied. "We got some, but Mistah Clay, he ain' much for cranberries. Mr. Byron, he like'm fine, but Mistah Clay, he say they make his mouf pucker."

"I think Mr. Clay prefers cherry sauce, Missus," Carlotta said. "Make the cherry sauce, Gerda."

"Cherry sauce, yes," Elizabeth said. "That would be just fine, Thank you, Carlotta. We've been married almost a year, and I truly don't know all Mr. Greenleaf's tastes. Thank you, both of you, for helping me."

She walked toward the door, and then turned back to the watchful eyes of the three women.

"There is one more thing, Gerda. Not about today's meals, but I thought we might have the rabbit tomorrow. Could you skin it out and soak it overnight in a bottle of wine? That's one of the ways we did it at home, and I think Mr. Greenleaf will like it. Wild game can be strong. Soaking it in wine seems to take that taste away."

"Soak it?"

"Yes, Gerda. Just cut the rabbit into serving pieces, pour wine over it, so that each piece is covered, and then put it in the coolest place we have—"

"Old Mr. Greenleaf's springhouse, that be the place. Yes, yes, that be the place"

"You ladies handle that part of it. After it has been soaked, you just smother fry it as you usually do. That's how our cook used to do it."

When Elizabeth asked to be shown around the infirmary on the Greenleaf Island for the first time, she found the patients had been segregated into wards; bandage materials had been washed, stripped and rolled; the floors had been scrubbed with strong lye soap; and, there was even wooden boxes for the herbs.

She was surprised to see how quickly word had spread.

It was morning in May, but there was still a chill in the air. "How was the winter here, Lulu? Did anyone suffer from the cold? I know you'll not be needing much heat from now into summer, but there will be need of it next winter. Only two of the rooms have any heat. That's all I saw."

"We fine, Missus. The cold don' las'."

"But it does get cold. That's one of the things we'll be working on before next winter gets here."

"You fixin' to go to Philadelphia to have that child, Miss Elizabeth? You ain' stayin' here, is you?"

"I'll go to Darien when the time draws nearer, Lulu, so I'll be closer to Dr. Barnes, but I won't be making that long trip back to Philadelphia. Besides, I'd like to have my child born in Georgia. Why did you ask? Am I that big?"

"No, ma'am, you ain' showin' much, but I jes' thought, Miss Mary Ann, she go back for bornin' Mr. Clay. I was jes' wonderin'. You lookin' mighty fine, Miss Elizabeth. Is you feelin' fine, too?"

Lulu was the first to call her "Miss Elizabeth." Was she finding her way into the hearts of these people? It was a good omen. Elizabeth believed in omens. Papa laughed at them and so did Clay, but what did they know?

Clay came home a little early. He had been to all five slave quarters on the main island.

In each of them, he found the coloreds to be well-housed

by his standards. Barnwell had done a better job than Rigby, but, in truth, Rigby did not have an easy task on the rice island. The land was low over there and the swamps bred thousands of insects. Summers were almost unbearable for a white man.

White people left the rice fields when the summer sun began to bear down. Clay offered suitable housing to Rigby on the main island, but it was declined. Rigby stayed on the rice island winter and summer. Clay presumed it was because of the dalliance Rigby had been having with his cook, Jude. How long had that been? Gordy was her only child, and Gordy was now twelve or thirteen. Rigby had been there at least two years before the birth of Gordy. Clay had expected Rigby to ask for Jude—ask to buy her—when he started upriver, but Rigby said nothing.

Elizabeth met Clay at the door."You're early today."

"Yes. I've finally made a complete inspection. I stopped by to see Byron. He says you've not visited him."

"That's true. I've been meaning to go. I have it all in hand now. I'll walk over to Byron's one day soon."

"You and Tess could ride over in the pony cart."

"I'd rather walk. I'll go tomorrow."

"Byron had a letter from Aunt Mattie."

"How is she?"

"She'll be in Darien the last Friday of this month."

Aunt Mattie. Elizabeth had put that thought completely out of her mind, but here it was. It was Spring. It was time for her annual trip. Damn Aunt Mattie!

"Are you all right, Elizabeth? You seem pale."

"I'm fine, Clay. I just had a momentary pain. I should expect them, but that one surprised me." It's a pain all right, she thought, and his Aunt Mattie is the pain.

"Your time is close. Why not go back to Philadelphia as Aunt Mattie goes? She'll be leaving in about a month.You'd be much nearer first rate medical attention there. Dr. Barnes may not be—"

"Dr. Barnes has delivered hundreds of babies, Clay. Don't be silly. I want the baby born here. I've listened to you this past year, and I think not having been born here in Georgia is the biggest disappointment of your life, I honestly do."

"You're right, my dear," Clay said. "I'll take any river within a day's ride to the Schuylkill or the Delaware."

"Then let's not talk about Philadelphia. Dr. Barnes will be just fine." Even though Elizabeth was not impressed with Darien's only doctor, he was better than going anywhere with Aunt Mattie. Philadelphia was out of the question.

"Whatever you say, my dear." Clay took her hand and led her inside. Elizabeth never loved him more than now. She was making a contribution to the estate. The house was firmly under her control. At times she felt like a little girl playing house, but, no matter, it was real enough to suit her.

The moment was perfect. He was beside her, strong, handsome and in command; she was married, with a home and with a child due during the summer.

The moment was perfect, but the future was not.What had he said? She remembered the words. "...she will be in Darien the last Friday of this month."

Chapter Thirty-Seven

The day Aunt Mattie arrived was another gala. Work was postponed. Every available boat took the field hands to Darien. The slower boats were permitted to leave on the afternoon before her arrival, but Elizabeth and Clay did not leave until seven on Friday.

"We'll have time for you to see Dr. Barnes."

As Elizabeth waited for the doctor, she looked around. What a place! It smelled as though it has been sealed for months. The oiled floors needed a broom. A layer of dust frosted the shelves where his medical books were carelessly shoved into place. The stove needed blacking and the spittoon, spattered with tobacco juice, made her feel ill.

There was no examination. Dr. Barnes asked how she had been feeling. He mumbled, almost to himself, about morning sickness and contractions. He took her pulse and listened with his stethoscope. That was the extent of it.

"You seem fine to me, Mrs. Greenleaf," he said. "It will be a couple more months before your child is born, but you are carrying it well. Clay is lucky to have such a strong, young woman for a wife. You must remember, though, my dear, that Darien is far removed from Greenleaf Island. You must send for me as soon as the contractions start."

"But until I'm sure—"

"You're not to decide. It's your first child, so you may not be the best judge. When the contractions start, send for me.

False labor may occur, but I need to be on hand. If I have to wait, it won't be the first time."

The air smelled fresh and clean when she stepped outside. Her nostrils were delighted to leave the smells of iodoform, carbolic acid and dust. She could see Clay coming down the street. "We have time, my dear. Do you have any shopping?"

"Yes, thank you, Clay. I have a list."

"One more thing, Elizabeth. Remember your promise. You will make the effort to get along with Aunt Mattie."

"Yes, Clay. I said I would and I will."

"It's only a month, my dear."

The arrival of Matilda Greenleaf changed everything at Greenleaf Plantation. The house Elizabeth had finally managed to get firmly under her control became Aunt Mattie's house.

"With the exception of Byron, we will have our breakfasts and suppers together, as we always do at Greenleaf Hall," she announced.

"We need to know what we are each doing with our separate lives. Clay, inform Byron he is expected for supper. It's absurd for him to live in that little tabby cottage. I suppose each of the Greenleafs must forgive the other for these strange twists we all seem to take. But it is silly. We have plenty of room here."

The meals were no longer planned by Elizabeth. The household chores were no longer under her domain. She dutifully had her breakfasts and suppers with Aunt Mattie and Clay, but she took the noonday meal in her office or she ate at Byron's house. Until Aunt Mattie's arrival, Elizabeth had been to Byron's cottage only one time. Now she had little to do, so her visits there became more frequent.

At first Aunt Mattie made an elaborate show of running the household. As days passed, the details were once again left to Carlotta. This subtle shift in authority was not lost on Elizabeth or Carlotta, but it was not acknowledged.

Had Matilda Greenleaf been informed of the slight Carlotta felt when Elizabeth became the mistress of Greenleaf? Had Carlotta, directly or by inference, told her of it? Was this more punishment for having married Clay? Had nothing changed?

Elizabeth remembered their first meeting in New York City shortly before the wedding. The underlying meaning of their conversation had been clear. Clay's aunt did everything possible to frustrate the marriage except forbid it. That, of course, she dared not do. As Miss Mattie herself acknowledged, the Greenleafs were a headstrong lot.

The week after Matilda Greenleaf's arrival, the house was scrubbed and polished. The unused bedrooms were aired, the linens changed, and the windows washed. There was to be a party at Greenleaf Hall. Elizabeth was neither invited nor barred from the party-planning meetings between Matilda Greenleaf and her housekeeper; she was simply ignored.

Elizabeth was certain Aunt Mattie's cut was intentional, and she was equally certain Carlotta was enjoying the secondary position Elizabeth had now been forced to assume.What chewed at Elizabeth's insides was the clever way Carlotta masked her joy as she watched the subtle change in power. But she remembered Clay's words: "It will only be for a month, my dear." What a heart-warming thought.

One day, my dear Carlotta, Elizabeth thought, Matilda Greenleaf will be back in Philadelphia. You will be taking orders from me. What was it she heard Carlotta say to Gerda? "If I say so, you be back in the fields tomorrow." It would not be easy to send Carlotta to the fields, but surely Clay would permit a reassignment of some sort. She would have to approach him carefully. Carlotta seemed to enjoy a unique status. Clay gave her special treatment.

Elizabeth had a twinge of jealousy. Was it only Carlotta's special status? Something more nagged at her. It was not the same as the overt jealousy she felt toward Georganne Lacy.

She knew deep inside that Georganne was someone Clay had known in the past. But this feeling that grew within her was a subtle jealousy that asked questions without answers.

Elizabeth had nothing to do. Her days fell into a pattern. She wrote letters, she did needlework, she read. There were few books at Greenleaf Hall, so she visited Byron where she could borrow from his diverse library.

Since school days, Byron had not traveled far from Greenleaf Island, but he had a vast curiosity about everything beyond its shores. "I have no interest in travel," he said. His words were confusing. How can a person who has no interest in travel have such an avid interest in all one could learn from traveling?

When Elizabeth tried to lift the lid from Byron's personal life, he turned the subject in a new direction. If she persisted, he easily parried her thrust.

One time he had said, "Here, Elizabeth, here's a book I think you'll enjoy. Now, don't be put off by the slow beginning. It's well worth reading. While you are looking at it, I'll check on the supply list Gordy is preparing."

And so it was with Byron. He was good company. He was a warm host. He was, she often thought, the brother she had always hoped to have. But if she crowded him, he was gone.

After Aunt Mattie arrived, Elizabeth was over at Byron's, whether or not she had need of new books. She would take her needlework. With Byron and Gordy, she could work silently or talk. It was the kind of companionship she wished she could have had with Clay, but it was something Clay would not, or could not, permit. With Clay, there was always something that said I am male and you are female; this barrier did not exist with Byron and Gordy. The three of them were just friends, happy in each other's company, without pretense.

Elizabeth told Byron of the school she wanted to start and of Clay's resistance to it. Byron thought the school a good idea but he offered no hope. "Clay has agreed with the other planters. There will be no education for the people. He is supported by Aunt Mattie—she agrees completely. Who knows, Elizabeth? I don't think so, but they may be right. Education could upset the situation here in Georgia. We have our lives invested in this plantation. Father's life, too, went into Greenleaf. Maybe they're right and we're wrong. I would support your idea of a school, but my voice would not be heard, you may be sure."

On a pleasant night in early June, she was lying beside Clay with just a clean sheet pulled over them. Moonlight through the water oak leaves made patterns on the floor, patterns that spilled across their bed.

"What do you think of the party, Clay?"

"It's a good time, my dear, before we all get busy with the cotton. Greenleaf is too quiet for Aunt Mattie."

"I meant the kind of party it is. 'A birthday party, in honor of my late brother.' It's on the invitations."

"Yes, my dear, I know that."

"But it's ghoulish."

"Nonsense. Aunt Mattie does this every year. It's a tribute to my father. It's tradition, Elizabeth. Don't tamper with tradition."

"But, Clay—"

"Any excuse for a party is a good excuse." He turned toward her. His hand caressed the side of her face. "What's got into you, Elizabeth? Why complain? They're doing the work. Aunt Mattie said she didn't want to tax you too much, now that you're getting closer to your time. She also said you were not eating well. That must stop."

"I'm eating, Clay. She has nothing to worry about."

"She worries all the same. She really does like you, Elizabeth. She told me so. And she wants the best for our child. I'm glad she has decided to stay over. It's not something she would do if she had no feeling for you."

"Stay over?" Her heart stopped beating. "For how long?"

"Until after the child comes, of course. You won't have a worry. Aunt Mattie will look after you."

What a turn of events! Elizabeth needed air, but a full breath was impossible. The moment was infinity. Aunt Mattie staying! It couldn't be worse. At last she was able to draw air into her lungs. Life was coming back to her.

"And you thought she didn't like you," Clay said. "You can be such a goose."

And you can be such a fool, she thought.

Chapter Thirty-Eight

Elizabeth, in her eighth month, was not ready for a party, even in the new ball gown Tess had made for the occasion. She was seen, she was introduced, but it was Miss Mattie's evening. As soon as she felt it would not embarrass Clay, she went to her room.

That was not to be. He found her lying on the bed in her chemise, her dress draped over a chair. "What in the hell do you think you're doing, Elizabeth? There's a party going on downstairs. You are the hostess."

"I'm sorry, Clay, I didn't feel well. I stayed as long as I could. When I left, I was sure no one would miss me."

"Well, you were missed. Aunt Mattie looked for you. She wanted you to meet the Hotchkiss girl. She's a Yankee, too. Aunt Mattie thought you might have common interests."

"That was thoughtful of Miss Mattie."

He took her roughly by the shoulder. "There's an edge to your voice I don't like, Elizabeth. I won't have it."

"I'm sorry Clay. I'm not feeling well." She pulled her shoulder away from his grip. "But it seems uncommonly strange to me that she didn't introduce Sally Hotchkiss earlier."

"She's trying to help. You seemed ill at ease."

"I'm pregnant. You don't always feel wonderful."

"Well, you have an obligation, a duty to me. You are the mistress of this house, the official hostess here."

"It's her party, not mine."

"Elizabeth!" His voice was low, as though he felt there could be someone in the hallway. "Get up and dress. I'll go back to our guests. Be downstairs in five minutes—"

"But, Clay, I told you I'm not feeling well—"

He slapped her. It was the reaction of a man who would be obeyed, who would not tolerate delay. Her hand touched her cheek. "You bastard," she said, "you cowardly bastard."

"This is not over, Elizabeth. We'll discuss it later. For now, without another moment's hesitation, get that dress on and get back to the party. I'll wait for you at the bottom of the stairway. Don't make me have to come back up here, Elizabeth, or you'll regret it."

"You wouldn't dare, not with a houseful of people."

"Don't put me to the test. A man has a right to punish his wife if she's disobedient, even with company present. I'll do whatever is necessary, and, I dare say, I'll have approval for my actions. For your sake, I'd like to avoid it." He walked to the door. "I'll wait five minutes."

He meant it. She rinsed her face in cold water. The sting of the slap was gone, the mark of his fingers faded with the cold water, but the inside of her mouth was torn. It continued to react to the acid in her spittle.

As she descended the stairs, he was waiting at the bottom. He smiled and offered his arm. He held her hand as he took her to the rear of the hall where Aunt Mattie was enthroned and holding court.

"Here she is, Aunt Mattie. She'd gone to her room. Momentary nausea. She's fine now, aren't you, my dear?"

"Yes, Clay. I'm fine." The inside of her lip burned, she could feel a pulse in the wound he had created. She hated them both, but there was a smile on her lips. "You wanted me to meet Sally, Miss Mattie, but you're too late. We've already had time for a very nice chat. I had hoped she could come over to visit, but, alas, she must go back to Hartford soon. Nevertheless, it was kind of you to think of me."

"I know it must be lonely for you, Elizabeth," Matilda Greenleaf said. "Perhaps we could have parties more often."

"I don't look like a party giver now, Miss Mattie."

"Nonsense, my dear," the older woman said, "you are quite the most beautiful girl here tonight; isn't she, Clay?"

"She is, Aunt Mattie. She's the one I love." Oh, yes, Elizabeth thought. She's the one you slapped. I still feel the pain of your love.

Elizabeth knew she would always remember the party to honor the late George Greenleaf.

In the days that followed, she and Byron had long discussions about the need for education. They agreed that training would increase the profits of the plantation. As she did, Byron felt that everyone who wanted to learn should be taught to read and cipher. But, he always brought her back to reality.

"One day, dear Elizabeth, we may be able to put our ideas into action, we may have a school here on Greenleaf Island, but for now you must enjoy those ideas only as conjecture; there's no hope that they will come about."

As time passed, she grew so comfortable with Byron that she discussed her fears about the baby. She recited the tales she had heard. He was a calming influence.

"Yes, Elizabeth," he said, "we've all heard such stories, but, my dear, you've heard about all the snakes on this island, too. You walk back and forth to Greenleaf Hall. Have you actually seen any?"

"Tess and I saw a dead one. I do believe they're here."

"I do, too, but those snake stories are exaggerations. So are the numerous stories of childbirth. Dr. Barnes thinks you're doing well. He knows more than the talebearers." Byron's words were reassuring.

When she got home that day, Clay was waiting for her. "We need to talk, Elizabeth. Go to the bedroom and wait." What is this all about, she wondered as she climbed the stairs. Before she could remove her sun hat and gloves, he was in the room.

"You've been spending an inordinate amount of time at Byron's, Elizabeth. It's not wise. You will discontinue the practice."

"Byron is your brother, Clay."

"Byron is a man; you are a woman. You've been going there daily, I'm told. It must cease."

"But, Clay, this is absurd. I'm on the eve of having a child; he's your brother. Do you know what you're saying?"

"I know full well what I'm saying."

"Then, Clay, I may not understand you. Your words say clearly what you think I might be capable of—" She hesitated and then decided she must continue. "But, surely, not Byron—not after the things you said about Byron."

"I said nothing about Byron—"

"Oh, yes you did. You were not very direct—you hinted, you made allusions—but your message was clear. So why, if Byron is really not interested in women, would he be interested in me, pregnant, big as the side of a barn, and walking like a splayed elephant?"

"I said nothing of the sort."

"Yes, Clay, you certainly did."

He hesitated. He had been crowded into a corner. He spoke quietly. "You will stop going to Byron's. We will ask him over from time to time if you like, but these daily visitations will stop."

"Because I may be defiled?"

"Enough, Elizabeth. It will stop."

"Is this what you think, or what she thinks?"

"Who?"

"Don't pretend, Clay. Miss Mattie has been talking. If I'm transparent, so are you, dear husband. She might not understand Byron as well as you do—or maybe she does—but this is her way to continue punishing me for my defiance when I married you." She shrugged her shoulders. "But, what Aunt Mattie wants, she gets, because she is the money lender, isn't she?"

"Elizabeth! Shut your smart mouth. Not another word." He had a crop in his hand. It wasn't raised, but she saw a movement.

"What will Byron think?"

"I'll talk to Byron."

Toward the middle of July, the humidity seemed to hang suspended in the air. Elizabeth was bored with needlepoint and reading. There were no walks to Byron's. The summer sun was doing its miracle in the cotton fields, so Clay worked harder. He was irritable. Elizabeth was happy to see him gone for long hours.

She had not forgotten his cruel slap so she was delighted that he demanded less attention at night. His touch was not what it had once been. It could have been because of her size. In her mind there was a common denominator between his touch and his slap. Was he ashamed of the slap or was he tired of her?

On this July morning her back ached. The load she was carrying in front was just too much for the muscles in the back. By ten o'clock she was having irregular pains. She had not begun to time them. She had had these pains before and they went away but they seemed a little more persistent. She wished Dr. Barnes were nearer.

Within a half an hour the pains grew more intense. She sent for Tess. "You're the one I depend on, Tess. You're my rock in the storm. I'm not sure I need Dr. Barnes, but, on the off-chance, send someone to the fields for Mr. Greenleaf, and while that's being done, ask Hiram to fire the boilers on the *Mary Ann*. It's probably false labor, but—"

"Oh, Missus, I'm scared."

"Now, Tess, no nonsense. Get someone on the way to the fields and then find Hiram. Now, scoot." Elizabeth saw fear in Tess' eyes. She could hear her bare feet on the stairway.

The first floor came to life. There was a burst of noise from every room. This is silly, Elizabeth thought. Two simple jobs and the entire house comes apart at the seams.

The floor maid knocked. Elizabeth saw another frightened girl. "What is it, Aletta? Ready to make up the bed?"

"Yes'm, I can. I was in Miss Mattie's room. Carlotta made me get out. Miss Mattie, she takin' on. She hear'd you done started having pains, and, Miss Mattie, she jes' go to pieces. Carlotta, she with her. Miss Mattie on the bed."

Elizabeth smiled in spite of the pain. Miss Mattie stayed over, "to be of what help I can, Clay. She is such a young girl." Fine lot of help. At the first sign of the baby, she takes to her bed. Aletta spoke: "You sure you don' want to get in the bed, Missus? Is you painin' bad?"

"There's no need for all this commotion. I've had a couple of pains. There's no reason for Miss Mattie to get so excited that she has to lie down."

"Oh, she mo' than excited, Miss Elizabeth. She done fainted dead away. She all right now, though. She sippin' brandy. She be jes' fine bye and bye."

Elizabeth could hear Clay coming up the stairway two steps at a time. "Come back later to make the bed, Aletta." Clay burst into the room. "Are you all right, Elizabeth?"

"I'm fine, Clay, just fine. This house has gone crazy. I've had a few pains that were more severe than yesterday and the day before, but I only sent for you because Dr. Barnes insisted. It's foolish, but those were his orders."

"Why didn't you tell me? We could have had him here."

"Here? Here, to sit around for a couple of days? There was no need, Clay, and probably there's no need now, but the pains I had this morning were very real, and I felt we should do as he asks. I've asked Hiram to fire the boilers on the *Mary Ann* so you should be able to go to Darien soon."

"Should I stay? Byron could go to Darien."

"Go to Darien, Clay. You'd be as much help as your Aunt Mattie is. She's taken to her bed with a measure of brandy. You might try the brandy, too. You look quite pale to me."

"Don't try to be funny. My boy must have every chance."

"In that case, Clay, get Lulu to stay with me while you're gone. Go fetch the doctor."

"Shouldn't you be in bed?"

"No, Clay. I'm fine, I tell you. Now, off with you."

Clay came to her side and took her hand. "Be brave, Elizabeth. I'll be back as soon as I can."

"Be brave? I needed bravery all along, even a week ago, Clay. I was really afraid then. But, now, I'm truly ready for the birth of my child." She didn't know why this was so, but it was true, and maybe he needed to hear it, so she said it again. "I don't know why, Clay, but I'm not afraid now."

"You are a surprising woman, Elizabeth," he said. "You get excited over little things, and you ignore the big ones."

"No more lectures. On your way. The steam must be up."

"Goodbye, darling." He kissed her hand and left.

As he walked down the hall, she thought: I'm a surprising woman, am I? And you, dear husband, are a paradox. You are a businessman at times, and also a fool; you are a tender lover, and a mean-tempered lout; you are a man of intelligence, and a spoiled child. Life with you has been all I could have hoped for, and none of it.

And you call me surprising.

Chapter Thirty-Nine

From her window, Elizabeth watched the *Mary Ann* as it moved away from dockside and down the river. A billow of wood smoke followed in its wake. As it receded, she could see only the superstructure. In time, the boat appeared to be a giant bug crawling through the reeds.

There was a knock at her door. It was Lulu. "Lordy, Miss Elizabeth, you done start them pains?"

"Too much is being made of this, Lulu. I sent for you because Mr. Greenleaf was overwrought. I think it's way too early, but I'm glad you're here. Most times, I know about my health. This time I just don't know what to expect."

"Don' you worry none, Miss Elizabeth. The doctah be here bye and bye." Lulu rolled her black eyes as she spoke. "But, 'till he get here, I be here. And I done sent for Birdie. Birdie, she be the best midwife anywhere. She got such tiny hands. She help many a woman. We both be here."

"Well, you're both going to be premature. I've had a couple of pains, that's all. I sent Mr. Greenleaf only because the doctor, himself, made such a point of it."

There was a knock. "Miss Elizabeth, it's Birdie."

There were no more pains during the next half hour. The three ladies sat around gossiping as if they had been friends for years. Birdie's bright eyes looked Elizabeth over carefully as they sipped their tea.

"When be the las' time you had a pain, Missus?"

"Oh, Birdie, you're as worrisome as Dr. Barnes."

"You 'bout ready. I know. I see many healthy women like you who think they not ready, but they is. It jes' creep up, and the next thing you know, they has a chil'. I know 'bout these things. You is close."

"Nonsense!"

"You had sharp pains this mornin'?"

"Yes, Birdie, a couple, but that was hours ago."

"And when you wake up, you had the backache?"

"Yes, but it's bothered me for weeks now."

"You ain' complained 'bout it, but today, when you has sharp pains, you be thinkin' about how your back hurt?" Birdie took her hand. "You is close, Missus, you is close."

Before Elizabeth could answer, a sharp pain wracked her body. "Oh," she said, holding her breath. "Oh, Lord."

"Good thing you sent Mistah Clay, Miss Elizabeth," Birdie said. "It be today, that sure. Ain' it, Lulu?"

"Now, ladies," Elizabeth said, "let's be calm. It's gas pains, nothing more. We'll know more when Dr. Barnes gets here. But now, I'm hungry. Gerda can fix our lunch."

"You bes' eat light, Miss Elizabeth."

"Miss Mattie ordered chicken salad. That's not heavy."

"No, Missus," Birdie said firmly. "Gerda, she boil the chicken for the chicken salad. That broth be good for you. But you bes' leave the salad alone."

Before the meal could be brought up, Elizabeth felt another pain. It was subtle at first, but then, without warning, it turned sharp. She winced. "Another one, Missus?"

Elizabeth held her breath until it eased. "Yes."

"You sure you want the broth, Missus?"

"Of course I'm sure. I'm hungry."

Elizabeth had a cup of the chicken broth. It warmed her insides. "That's what I needed," she said. "I had pains because I was starving." At the end of those words, she felt the next pain. Her hand went to her stomach.

"Missus, you'd best be in bed. No need sittin' up. You is painin'." Elizabeth started to protest. "No talkin'. You say Birdie know more 'bout this—an' she do. So Birdie say it be the bed for you. I don' want to call Miss Mattie, but if I have to—"

She hesitated. She could see Elizabeth was not anxious to have Matilda Greenleaf called in. "Come on, Lulu. Let's help her to the bed."

As Elizabeth settled herself in the billow of the feather tick, the next pain came. There had been no pattern to the pains earlier, but there was now. Elizabeth watched the clock. Her pains occurred on a regular basis. The last three had been equally spaced. This was more pain than she expected. Her hands tightened around the binding of her coverlet.

Before the onset of the next pain, Birdie, put her hand on Elizabeth's brow. "These is healin' hands, Missus. You ain' got no cause to fret. I done deliver more healthy babies than that Darien doctah ever thought about. We don' need him, do we, Lulu?"

"She's tellin' you right, Miss Elizabeth. This woman is the bes' friend a birthin' mother could ever have."

"I thank you both for being here." But the child was not to be put off by conversation. Elizabeth felt another pain, this time sharp and insistent. "I hope I can wait—"

"Ain' nothing you can do 'bout it, Miss Elizabeth," Birdie said. "The baby know when. Them pains be natural. You is getting ready; you is dilatin' now. It's the good Lord's plan, Missus. The baby do the mos'. You do your part, and when the time come, Birdie be with you." Birdie pushed the hair back from Elizabeth's brow, and then laid her calm, warm hand low on the damp forehead. One finger lightly touched Elizabeth's eyes. Now, she could not see the clock, but Elizabeth knew what time it had to be. Another pain wracked her body, another contraction. She wanted to expel the offender. And then the pain was gone.

"How long, Birdie?" Elizabeth hesitated. "How long?"

"No one know, Missus. You don' decide; I don' decide. Only the good Lord and the baby know. When the time come, you be ready all right. The baby do that. Hit know when."

The pains were closer and more intense. "Oh, now," Birdie said, "the water done broke. The baby comin' soon."

"Take my hand, Miss Elizabeth," Lulu said. You gonna help this baby. When the pain come, it be the chil' wantin' to come into the world. You mus' help it. Push. Your body jes' natural know how, but you, this first time, you got to learn 'bout it. You jes' squeeze my hand and push."

"I don't know—" A sharp pain stopped her.

"Yes, you do, Miss Elizabeth. You is learnin' right now. Squeeze my hand. You won' break no bones."

The contraction came again, sharp and demanding. Elizabeth felt the need to expel the cause of it. She pushed. As Lulu said, she knew what to do. "Good," she heard Birdie say, "tha' be jes' fine." There was pain and the need to expel, but it was only partially real to Elizabeth. Then she heard Birdie say, "The shoulder be fine now." Then she said, "We done got a beautiful baby."

The pain and the contractions were still going on. Elizabeth wept. "Am I all right? Am I all right, Lulu?"

"Yes, Missus, you is jes' fine. It be a fine child."

"Come tie the cord, Lulu. The job ain' done till the mother be easy, and the baby by her side."

The pains eased. Elizabeth's pillow was wet with sweat. The day must have been hotter than she knew. But, she thought dreamily, it's late July.

Her mind eased. She was only half aware of the two women in the room until they were both by her side. "Here you is, Miss Elizabeth," Birdie said. "It's a fine girl chil', the first in the Greenleaf house for many a year. Glory be."

The baby, wrapped in wool flannel, was placed beside her. She touched its face gently. She was sure it moved toward her, that it was reaching for her. She examined the tiny hands, the delicate little fingers. My own, she thought, a baby of my own. I can't believe it.

Clay and Dr. Barnes arrived an hour after the baby's birth. Elizabeth heard the *Mary Ann* come in and all the commotion downstairs. She expected to hear Clay's boots coming up the steps, two at a time, but the knock at her door was Dr. Barnes.

"I'd like to examine you, Mrs. Greenleaf," he said. "I understand you have a nice, healthy child, although I haven't seen her yet."

He opened his satchel and removed his stethoscope. "An examination isn't strictly necessary, but Mr. Greenleaf wants to be sure you're in good health."

"I'm just a little tired, that's all."

"I'm sure you are, Mrs. Greenleaf. This examination is more to calm a worried husband than it is for you. I won't be long." His examination was brief. "Ah, yes," he said, humming a tuneless song. "Birdie has done a competent job. You'll be all right. But, I mean this, stay in bed, Mrs. Greenleaf. You have plenty of help here, so don't exert yourself."

And, then he was gone.

Clay arrived five minutes later. "You're all right, Elizabeth. Thank God for that at least."

"Have you seen her, Clay? She's lovely."

"Not yet, my dear. The nursery is full. I'll wait until later to see her."

Wait? He's going to wait until later? What kind of a man is he? It's his first child and he shows so little interest. "I thought you would have seen her."

"I wanted to see you first, my dear, but I wanted the doctor to see you before I did. Just to be sure. I know Birdie has done this many times before, but—"

"I'm sorry it's not a boy, Clay."

"So am I, Elizabeth," It was matter of fact. "But there will be a boy. There has to be. The Greenleaf name and the Greenleaf lands need to be carried forward." He leaned over the bed and kissed her on the brow. "Rest, Elizabeth. You look pale."

Her eyes were shut as he let himself out of the room, and she listened as he walked down the hall. He passed the door of the nursery without stopping.

Closed eyes didn't stop the tears.

Chapter Forty

The doctor ordered Elizabeth to remain in bed for the two weeks following the birth of Helen Mary. In her own mind, she felt the inactivity was doing more harm than good. Each day she felt weaker.

At the start of the second week Elizabeth was ready to rebel, even though she could still remember Clay's slap. She had not forgiven him, nor had he asked for it. Still, she knew he had little tolerance for disobedience. He had demanded that she follow Dr. Barnes' orders to the letter, but staying in bed was tedious.

"Tess," Elizabeth said, "we are friends, aren't we? Oh, I know you're supposed to fetch for me, and you do the sewing, but beyond that, I believe we're friends. We are, aren't we?"

Tess was disturbed by the question. She had never thought of her relationship with the wife of her owner as a friendship—indeed, she had never had time for a friendship.

"Tess," Elizabeth said, "I've been talking to you. We are friends, aren't we?"

"Yes'm, I guess we is." What could she say? She loved Elizabeth. She had never before been respected or encouraged. Elizabeth had done this for her. She was not a field hand, an important distinction, one that was not lost on Tess.

"If we are, Tess, I want to strike a bargain with you. I'm tired of this bed. I want to get up, I want to stretch my limbs. I can't do it unless you help me. Will you?"

"Miss Elizabeth—"

"I won't let you get caught. If someone comes, I'll scoot over to the commode. That's a reason for being up. I need your help. You could cut your material over there by the door. You could bolt it so no one could come in and move the pieces. And while you're working, I could move about." Tess said nothing. "What could it hurt? I'm getting weaker staying in bed. When the baby cries, you go to her. When she needs feeding, you bring her to me." Elizabeth waited. Tess remained silent. She didn't look directly at Elizabeth. Her eyes rolled from side to side. "Are you afraid?"

"Yes'm. Mr. Clay, he have me beat if I do that."

"He won't know."

"He find out."

"How can he? We'll have the door bolted. You'll be cutting a dress." Tess rolled her eyes to all the corners of the room and licked her lips. "Don't you trust me, Tess?"

"Yes'm."

"Then help me do it."

The rest of the week the dress cutting ruse worked. Elizabeth was up for an hour or two at a time. No one tried the door and no one knocked. It wasn't necessary to make Tess a part of a lie. By the end of the second week, Elizabeth was strong enough to again follow Matlilda Greenleaf's edict that they should all dine together at the evening meal.

In an effort to make Clay pay more attention to his daughter, Elizabeth abandoned the double name. Helen Mary was simply called Mary, Clay's mother's name. The sop to Clay made no difference in his attitude.

The change in plans had been unexpected in June when Aunt Mattie announced that she would be staying until after the baby was born "to be of what help I can." It was equally unexpected when she announced one evening at dinner that she would be leaving the following week for Philadelphia.

"It's final. My mind is made up. I'm ready to go back to my own house. While she's been most generous, this one, after all, is Elizabeth's."

My house? Elizabeth was amused. The remark was made for the benefit of Clay and Byron. Both ladies knew all the houses belonged to Matilda Greenleaf, whatever name appeared on the deeds.

Miss Mattie simply assumed authority. She didn't need permission, especially from Elizabeth. There was never a problem with Clay because of her control of the money he always seemed to need, and, in such matters, Miss Mattie didn't bother to give Byron a thought.

Clay spoke. "Shall I arrange for your passage?"

"Byron already has, haven't you, dear?"

"She'll be leaving on Tuesday. The *Altamaha* to Savannah, and then the *General Oglethorpe* all the way to Havre de Grace. And the train, of course, on in to Philadelphia. I have written George. He can meet the train. I've also arranged a cabin for Aunt Mattie for the bulk of the trip. We were lucky to find the space available."

"Well, I'm glad to be informed about it before it was a done thing." Clay was piqued. "You two work quickly."

Elizabeth was aware of Carlotta's apprehension the morning after Aunt Mattie's departure. She knew she had to quell it at once.

"Carlotta, if you will, please continue with the day-to-day affairs of the household. I'll assist you, but, for now, I'd prefer to spend as much time as possible with the baby."

"Yes, Miss Elizabeth," Carlotta said.

Was that a hint of a smile she saw? Elizabeth could not be sure, but the moment passed. Little Mary had vomited down the front of her new dress.

"Oh, what a naughty girl you are," Elizabeth said. "Tess, quickly, a warm, damp rag, and a fresh dress."

Tess reached for the baby. "No, Tess, I'll do it. I caused the problem; I'll take care of it. I was too rough with you, wasn't I, Love? I bounced you around too much."

After the birth of their child, Clay stayed away from the house during the day, but at night he always found his way to Elizabeth's bed. When he was ready for sleep, he walked to the end of the hall where he continued to maintain the separate bedroom he had begun to use after Mary's birth.

"You get up every single time the baby cries, my dear. There's no need of it. I can't stop your maternal instincts, but I must have my rest. I have work to do." It was true. Clay was busy with Mr. Barnwell and he made frequent one-day trips to the rice island. He never stayed there for the night, because of the insects on that low-lying island.

"I know, Clay. It isn't fair to you, but she's so small. She needs her mother. Later, when she's stronger, Tess can look after her, but for now—she's such a baby."

"Which is the bigger baby, Elizabeth? You act addled."

"Had it been a boy, would you have said the same thing?"

"It wasn't a boy."

His remark cut, but she held her tongue. "The next one may be, my love," she said. "I'm not sure, but I think I may be pregnant again." Clay said nothing but she had his attention. "I've talked with Lulu and Birdie. They say a woman can be erratic following a first child."

He smiled. "Lulu said a woman can be 'erratic'? That doesn't sound like Lulu."

"Well no, Clay, she didn't say that. She said, 'Most women don't have no period for six or eight weeks after the birth of a first child, 'specially if they is breast fed.'"

"Well, that's your answer."

"I wouldn't think too much of it, Clay, except it has now been over ten weeks since little Mary was born—"

"And you are breast feeding her."

"Well, it's more, it's other things. I've been having nausea. It's been every morning this past week or two. That, combined with the length of time—"

"I hope you're right, Elizabeth."

"The delay bothered me. Both Birdie or Lulu know more about all this than I do. They think I may be pregnant again, but they hope not. Birdie said, 'I hope you ain't caught, Missus. It's not good for a woman to have two babies that close.' Lulu is more dire about it than Birdie. Lulu says a second child will cause your teeth to go bad."

"Oh, for goodness sake, Elizabeth. That sounds like what you hear in the quarters. There's nothing to that."

"She said, 'A child suck away her mama's teeth to make bones. Ain' good to have babies too soon.'"

"I'm going to have to keep you away from those women. Next thing I know you'll be wearing charms to ward off evil."

"Well, it's been over ten weeks. I'm not sure, but—"

"Elizabeth, my dear, I hope so, I truly hope so. You can't know how much I hope it."

"I think I do, Clay."

In a short period of time, Elizabeth was sure. Morning sickness became a constant companion. The second pregnancy was beset with discomfort. A visit to Dr. Barnes confirmed it. She was pregnant.

When they went to Darien to see Dr. Barnes, or to attend the newly completed church, Elizabeth spent time with the Coopers while Clay attended to his business. The Coopers were old friends of Clay's parents, although they were only slightly older than he was. Sam Cooper had been an overseer at Greenleaf before he opened a general store in Darien.

Staying with Elsie Cooper was a help to Elizabeth. She now had someone to answer questions, other than Lulu and Birdie. And she especially liked their thirteen year-old daughter, Dolly. From the beginning Dolly could do wonders with little Mary. If the child was colicky, Dolly could amuse and soothe her, and soon the fretful whine would stop.

In those weeks after she became pregnant again, Elizabeth spent as much time as she could with Mary, but her own health prevented her from giving the child the attention she felt it deserved. With the help of Tess, Elizabeth could tolerate her own personal discomforts because she knew Tess was a good nurse to little Mary. The child was being given loving care.

Clay did not come back to their room. Elizabeth's restlessness and discomfort disturbed him. Gradually, he shared the bed with her on fewer and fewer occasions. Many nights she was more at ease sitting in her rocking chair at the window. The upright position caused fewer problems.

As time passed, as she got closer to the birth of her second baby, Elizabeth spent more time sleeping in her rocking chair. All of it, the abdominal pain, the heartburn, the nausea, the problems with urination, and the ever-present backache, was less distressing when she was upright.

The period of confinement had been easy with little Mary, but this new child sapped Elizabeth's strength. The distress was constant, and she looked dreadful, too. She had it all: nausea, bloat, back pain, and self-pity. She felt she was fat and she knew she was tired. The difference in the confinement made her wonder: Is this one going to be a boy? Are they that much different?

"It might be a boy child this time, Miss Elizabeth," Lulu said one day. "You is carryin' this one different and it sure pull at you. Men do dat. Before they is born and after they is born. They pull a woman down."

Late one night in April Elizabeth was once again in the rocking chair. Clouds partially obscured the sky. The light from the quarter moon cast eerie shadows on the ground below the giant oaks. There was a wind. As Elizabeth watched the shadows dance on the bare earth, she saw a movement. Was it one of the dogs? Could it have been a wild animal in search of food? It might be a human figure, not an animal. She wasn't sure. She wasn't able to see it clearly in the weak moonlight. Her view was obscured by the large oaks and the disappearing moonlight as it played tag with the clouds.

She did not see the figure again, but she saw a dim light from the door of Carlotta's cabin when it was opened and then quickly closed.

Oh, my, she thought, Carlotta is having a caller. I wonder who it is? Wait until I tell Clay.

Chapter Forty-One

But Elizabeth did not tell Clay of Carlotta's nighttime caller. That was her intention, but the time was never right for such a conversation. She thought that such a bit of gossip would be something they could talk about without having a row, but it never happened. Anymore, Clay seemed to be constantly unhappy with her because of her condition. Yes, he was glad she was pregnant again because he wanted a son, but he was impatient with her.

"You use any excuse to take to your bed, Elizabeth. When father brought my mother to these islands, life was not as easy as it is now. Women have had babies throughout time. You're making too much of this one."

"I've no doubt it was more primitive then, but Mary Greenleaf didn't give birth to you here, did she, Clay? She went to Philadelphia."

"You could go there."

"He went with her; will you?"

"That's impossible and you know it."

"You had good cottom crop last year. Money isn't the reason."

"Don't argue, Elizabeth. Keep it up, and I'll spend even less time in this room. I'll not bicker with you while you're carrying a child. You're not carrying it well, you understand, but carrying it all the same. Your complaints never stop, and you look more like a bloated cow every day."

She turned. Tears filled her eyes. She didn't want him to see how hurt she was.

Clay came up behind her. "I'm sorry, my dear, I should not have said that." His hands were on her shoulders. "But you give in to every little pain, and you've put on too much weight, and you do pick at everything I say."

"I can't help how I feel, Clay."

"I know you can't, my dear." His hands slid off her shoulders. It was as much of an apology as he was prepared to make. "I must be on my way. I'm going to the rice island today with Barnwell. We're getting such a late start, we may not be able to make it back before nightfall. Don't worry if we're not here by then. We'll just stay over."

It was after the midday meal the next day when she heard the noise of the *Mary Ann* as it came in. Elizabeth had started spotting again and the ever-present back pains were worse. This was the way her labor had started with little Mary so she had sent for Lulu and Birdie.

"Tess, child," Elizabeth said, "run down to the docks and tell Mr. Greenleaf to load on some more wood and go back to Darien for Dr. Barnes."

"Ain' no call, Missus," Lulu said. "You ain' due yet."

"You told me the baby comes when the baby decides to come, Lulu. I think it has decided."

"No, ma'am. Not yet. What you think, Birdie?

"You spottin', Missus, but you spotted before."

"But the backache—"

"You jes' worrin', thas' all. But, Miss Elizabeth, if you want the doctah, you go on and send Mistah Clay. Ain' no use you worrin' your head none, and thas' what you doin'."

"Get on the way, Tess," Elizabeth said. "If you tarry, he'll be in the fields before you get there. Scoot."

The baby was born late the following night. Dr. Barnes was with her, assisted by Birdie. The pains that had started two days before did not go away. It was a long period of labor, and when it finally came to an end with the birth of little Ann Francis, Elizabeth was spent.

Again, bed rest was prescribed by the doctor. For several days Elizabeth did not rail against the bed rest Dr. Barnes had ordered. She felt wobbly. But by the beginning of the following week, she was ready to conspire with Tess. She needed exercise. Her muscles felt like jelly. Tess was more confident the second time. She bolted the door and laid her pieces of cloth into a working pattern on the floor.

Elizabeth gained strength. Her walking became more stable, but recovery was slower than she had imagined it would be. Five weeks after the birth of Ann Francis, she was still unable to sleep at night. Her back ached and she was weak.

It was a busy five weeks in the rest of the household. Aunt Mattie arrived for her yearly visit and the routine of the family eating the evening meal together was reinstituted. When Matilda Greenleaf was in residence, the plantation and the activities at the main house revolved around her. She saw no reason for Elizabeth's failure to recover, just as she had done with her first child.

"You must not give in to these things, Elizabeth," she said one day. "Childbirth is a very natural thing."

"What would you know about it?" It was sharp. It was out of Elizabeth's mouth before she could think about it. There was a stunned silence at the table.

Clay spoke first. "You will apologize at once, Elizabeth. Your behavior is inexcusable."

"I'm sorry, Miss Mattie," she said quietly.

"We didn't hear you, Elizabeth," Clay said. "If you have something to say, speak up." She had heard that strident sound before. It spelled trouble.

With her eyes on her plate she said, "I am sorry, Miss Mattie. You did not deserve a sharp word from me. I hope you will forgive me. I've not been myself lately."

"Your apology is accepted, dear child," Matilda Greenleaf said. "You're right. I know nothing about childbirth, but I do know you can give in to your minor problems. If you do, they become major problems. I could give in to this sciatica of mine. If I did it, I wouldn't be able to walk. I just won't do it. That's all I meant."

The incident was forgotten, but Elizabeth's physical problems did not go away. The back pain persisted, and the sleepless nights kept her in the rocking chair at the window. Clay made one attempt at coming back to their room for a night, but Elizabeth's restlessness, her discomfort, caused him to abandon the effort well before morning.

Elizabeth had forgotten Carlotta's nighttime caller, but as she sat at the window on this moonlight night, with clouds partially obscuring the sky, she saw the figure again. It was a man. Who might the young buck be? Who had the courage to pay court to the imperious Carlotta? He would have to be exceptional.

There was something familiar about the movement of the man. Who was it? Was it Anson, the wheelwright? He was tall and carried himself with the same kind of arrogant pride. She saw him again. No, this man was not as tall as Anson.

Elizabeth tried to find an angle where the oak limbs did not obscure her vision. The man was near the front of Carlotta's tabby house. In a short time he would be inside and she would not know who Carlotta had invited to her bed.

There was one patch of moonlight left. Elizabeth had it clearly in sight before the slow-moving figure arrived. Then, he was there. Moonlight gleamed on a boot. On a boot? Which of the slaves might be wearing boots? She had never seen one in boots. Boots were handmade. Too expensive for a slave. Perhaps Clay had given an old pair as a reward for a job well done. But wouldn't she have seen them? On Sundays the slaves wore their best and brightest. If a young man had a pair of Clay's boots, he would have shown them off, both as the treasure and as a show of the owner's esteem.

She had one last glimpse. The walk was so familiar. She knew this man. And then the thought came. He walks like Clay. Like Clay? That was not possible.

She found a robe, opened her door and moved down the hallway to his room. Light from his window showed a rumpled bed. She had to be positive. She moved to the bed, her eyes straining in the darkness. At last the search was complete. He was not in bed, he was not at the commode, and he was not concealed by the clothes press.

Clay was not in the room.

The blood drained from her head. Her eyes dimmed. She knew she was going to faint. She made it to his bed before the blackness overtook her. And then it came.

When she finally became aware of her surroundings, she brought herself to an upright position on his bed. She sat there as she she waited for her strength to return, waited for reality, waited for the dream to be over.

She was numb. She was unaware of how long she had been lying on his bed, but now she was able to move. She must get back to her room. It would soon be time to feed Ann Frances. If Tess were to come looking for her, Elizabeth knew her absence would be hard to explain.

She did not want this scandal made public It was enough for her to know of Clay's infidelity without making it common knowledge.

Elizabeth made her way back to her own room, her eyes overflowing with tears.

Chapter Forty-Two

Elizabeth cried. Tears may keep you from bursting inside, but they solve no problems. Toward morning the salty well behind her eyes had gone dry. It was time to decide what she intended to do. If she confronted Clay, he would deny it, or ignore her. In the end, he would do as he pleased.

She had no power. She was Clay's wife. In the year of our Lord, 1845, that was the beginning and the end of it. The children were his. He was their sire, but, more than that, they were his by the custom of the land. Children belonged to the male in the household, the provider.

If she confronted him, she would lose the girls. She would have satisfaction, but it would solve nothing.

The second possibility was to stay with Clay, hiding what she knew. She could pretend it never happened, as she had done before. But, could she do it this time? What he had done was a grievous offense. It was utterly intolerable. If she tried to bury the knowledge of his liaison with Carlotta, the last bastion of her own self-respect would be gone.

She could leave him, but she knew full well that such an idea was a poor choice. It would mean the certain loss of her children. And there was a further danger: What if he wouldn't let her go? He could take the cane to her and lock her up. What would her life be like if she were held on the island against her will?

As she examined the possibilities, two things stood out: leaving him was essential if she were to maintain her own dignity, and she could not consider leaving without her children. She must do both.

Elizabeth's plan evolved slowly. She needed to find a way to take the children at least as far away as Savannah before Clay became aware of her departure. She remembered the trip to Greenleaf from Philadelphia. She could imagine what it would have been with two small children, one only a few weeks old. She would have to have help.

Her only ally was Tess, but Tess was black. If it were possible to take Tess on to New York, it would have been the perfect choice. The problem was Papa. Her father would not be happy to see her and the children; he would explode if she were to arrive with the children and Tess, a slave his daughter had stolen from the rightful owner. He would not hold with thievery. The Reverend Mr. Medlock would take her in, even with children, but he would turn the four of them from his door. Tess was not the answer.

As she pondered her dilemma, Clay decided they would all go to Darien on business and then spend the night so they could attend services at the new church he had helped finance.

On that day, the waters between the island and Darien were choppy. Little Mary was fretful. By the time they got on solid footing on the docks, the child had vomited on Clay. He was furious. "Can't you keep that spewing child under control?"

It was worse in the rig going to Sam and Elsie Cooper's house. Mary wailed. People on the streets stopped to look, as though they were beating the child. "Shut her up, Elizabeth. I don't care if you choke her, but shut her up."

Young Dolly Cooper heard the crying and rushed to the front door. "Baby girl, baby girl," she cooed to Mary, "what is the matter? Come to Aunt Dolly." And the child, as she had done so many times before, stopped crying and held out her arms.

Elizabeth had her answer.

Dolly would be ideal. She could never be an ally, but she could handle either child, and she had a magical touch with

Mary. Elizabeth would take Dolly as far as Baltimore and then send her back to Darien. She would put her in the charge of the captain, and by the time Dolly got back home, Elizabeth and the children would be safely in New York.

In their room on the Cooper's second floor, Elizabeth washed the spittle from Clay's shirt. As she unpacked a fresh shirt, she said, "What a way Dolly has with Mary. I wonder, Clay—if it's all right with Sam and Elsie—I wonder if she could come and spend the summer with us at Greenleaf Island? I could use her help, especially since I've not completely regained my strength from Ann Frances."

"You have Tess—"

"Yes, darling, and Tess is wonderful, but, in these early years, it might be better for Mary to have a white person—"

"Elizabeth! I'm surprised to hear that from you." He was smiling. She had used the best possible approach; it was exactly right. "But, my dear," he said, "the Coopers might not want their daughter away for the summer."

"I'll talk to Elsie, Clay, if you agree. It would be good for Mary."

Elsie Cooper listened. She really didn't want her daughter gone the whole summer—although Greenleaf was not that far away—but Dolly could be of great help to this young mother who had had two children much too close together. She could imagine what it must be to have one child just barely weaned at the time a second is born. Poor girl. She listened to Elizabeth's proposal, and then she talked to Sam. They agreed to let Dolly go for the summer.

Elizabeth bought yards of new material while she was in Darien. She knew she could have a problem. Above all, she didn't want to hurt Tess' feelings about the children so she decided to load her with work.

"Now that I have my figure back, Tess, I need some new things for summer," she said, as she displayed all the new cloth.

"I know it isn't summer yet, but, I declare, most of the things that still fit me are too heavy."

The lie worked with Tess. At first, there was a quick flood of fear in her eyes, but she watched Elizabeth closely and decided she was not being replaced by this little white girl. She might can look after young'uns, Tess thought, but she can't sew. Elizabeth was relieved to see her fear fade.

She had the help she needed. Now Elizabeth had to devise a way to go to Savannah without Clay. Something Aunt Mattie said gave her the key. "I shall be going home next week, Clay, but before I come back in the Spring, promise me that you'll have something done to the draperies in the public rooms of this house. My goodness, they're threadbare."

"I agree, Miss Mattie," Elizabeth said. "The sun rot on those in the salon is disgraceful."

Clay looked at them both. There was rarely this much agreement. He shrugged. "What you're saying may be true, ladies, but before we spend money, we must talk to the exchequer. What about it, Byron? Can we afford it?"

"We had a good year, but I had hoped to retire debts. The interest is dear. It's chopping into our profits."

This was a perfect reason for going to Savannah, and the trip would not interest Clay. She must not let it die. She spoke quickly. "If I may offer it, I think I have a solution," Elizabeth said. "I have some funds. The monies from my mother, Clay. You said I might use them on little extras for our house. This is a good time, it seems to me."

"That kind of expense should be something from the plantation, Elizabeth. What you and Aunt Mattie are suggesting can run into quite a cost. When I said you could spend it on extras, I was thinking of a trinket, a vase, a piece of silver. Incidental items."

"Miss Mattie, I need your help," Elizabeth said.

"I think what Elizabeth proposes is excellent. She has a right to be proud of her house. You two men may pay little attention to it, but when the ladies of the house have guests in, we want it to look right. Don't we, Elizabeth? Look around you—both of you. Surely you can see the need."

"But," Clay said, "I'm thinking of the cost—"

"If she bought a trinket, the money would be gone, Clay," Aunt Mattie said, "and if she bought several of them, it could use the same amount. What's the difference? If this is money for Elizabeth—her mother's trust—why can't she spend it in a way that will give her pleasure, and, I might add, a measure of pride?"

"I don't know, I just don't know," Clay said. "What do you think, Byron?"

"If this is Elizabeth's money, Clay, if you lay no claim to it, then why can't she do with it as she wants? We are all too constrained by time and circumstances. It always does one good to be able to soar once in a while. I think she should do as she pleases. Such opportunities come too infrequently."

"Then the vote is in," Clay said. "What I say is being ignored. But, my dear, you have a real job before you."

"Oh, thank you, Clay. And my thanks to the two of you," Elizabeth said to Aunt Mattie and Byron. "I'd like to have a Burgundy in the salon, as Clay's mother had, but the rest of the rooms—" She turned. "Miss Mattie, will you help me?"

"Yes, but we must get on it, Elizabeth. I'll be leaving shortly. We will begin the planning tomorrow."

The colors were decided the next day. Elizabeth would not have chosen blue for the great hall, but, since she had no intention of ordering the draperies, what difference did it make? She let Aunt Mattie lead her at every step.

After Matilda Greenleaf was on her way home, Tess and Elizabeth made measurements, and spent hours making drawings of each festoon, each swag, each bit of braid and fringe.

Elizabeth dallied over details. Her trip to Savannah must take place during the rice harvest. Clay would be occupied. There must be no possibility of his deciding to accompany her.

She would have one chance to get away from Greenleaf with her children. She must not rush. It was necessary to choose a time when she knew where Clay was and what he was doing.

She knew nothing could keep him from the rice harvest. It was a perfect time.

Chapter Forty-Three

On board the *Altamaha*, Elizabeth was deliriously happy. Her plan had worked with precision. The day before her scheduled departure, Clay had come back from the rice fields. He knew she would be in Savannah for four days on the drapery buying trip, so, yard cock that he was, he was in her bed, randy as ever, on the eve of her departure.

I pray I'm not pregnant again, she thought.

The *Mary Ann* had departed the main island at daybreak to take Clay back to the rice ponds. The extra time for Clay had added two hours to her journey to Darien, but it gave peace of mind. This way, she would actually see him get off on the island, ready for work.

She would know where he was. He could not follow her, because Hiram would not make the return trip with the *Mary Ann* until the following day.

Now, safely aboard the *Altamaha*, Elizabeth smiled, recalling how smoothly her plan had gone.

She remembered the pains she had taken with all the measurements and drawings. There was never an intention of buying the materials or having the draperies made. She knew all the time that she needed every penny of her mother's money for the journey.

Elizabeth hated lying to so many people. Not Clay. His liaison with Carlotta was the worst kind of lie. But, she hated what she had done to Tess—especially to Tess—and to the

Coopers. And, what Dolly would think of her once she knew their true destination?

Someday when the girls are grown, I'll apologize to everyone, but today I must make my way cautiously. I'm safely on board the *Altamaha*, I'm on my way, but I'm far from New York.

In Savannah, she deposited Dolly and the two girls at the hotel, and then hurried to the bank and the steamship office. She obtained passage all the way to Baltimore, and paid extra for a cabin. It bit into her funds, but it was worth it. She dared not be seen on the *General Oglethorpe*. She might be recognized by a passenger.

She was grateful for her luck so far. Their departure was scheduled for 3:00 o'clock in the morning. It was an ungodly hour to rout Dolly and the girls from their beds. Still, it was a plus. It was an earlier departure from Savannah than she had hoped to get, and it was a wretched hour, but because of that wretchedness, passengers would not tend to mingle. She would be able to get on board as quietly and then hurry Dolly and the children to the cabin.

"Wake up, Dolly." she said, shaking the girl's shoulder. "We're going on to Charleston to have the curtains made. The boat will be leaving in about an hour." Dolly looked sleepy-eyed. "Get up, Dolly. We have to get the girls ready and hurry along."

Dolly rubbed her eyes. "To Charleston?"

"Yes." Elizabeth was calm. She must not excite the child. Her parents had not agreed that Dolly could go to Charleston. "While I was out yesterday," she said, "I ran into Mrs. Hollister. You know her."

"Yes," she mumbled, "I know her."

"She said we'd get better needlework in Charleston. I didn't mention it, Dolly, because I wanted you to sleep as much as you could. But, we're late. Help me with the girls, please. You dress Mary and I'll see to Ann Frances."

When they arrived in Charleston, Elizabeth knew the lies must cease. She must tell Dolly the truth.

"Dolly, please come and sit here beside me. I need to have a talk with you." There was something about Elizabeth's tone that brought a serious look to Dolly's face. With solemn eyes, she did as she was told.

"I've not been altogether truthful with you, Dolly. And I want you to understand that I was not lying to hurt you. I've been lying, Dolly, to protect the girls, just as I know you would have done had you been in my place."

Dolly's eyes were riveted to hers. The child was frightened. "I'm leaving my husband, Dolly. The reasons are unimportant now, but you must believe it, there's no other way." There was no change, no comprehension, in Dolly's expression. "You must believe, also, that the children are my only concern. I lied because I had to take my children with me. I had to lie to you and to so many other people that I wonder if God will ever forgive me, but perhaps one day you will forgive me, even if He can't."

"What kind of lies?" Elizabeth could still see fear in Dolly's eyes. She was not making the child understand.

"We're not staying in Charleston, Dolly. I'm taking my children to New York, and perhaps on to England. I'll do whatever is necessary to keep them with me. When Clay finds out, he'll follow me. By then, they will be safely hidden."

There was a tear in the child's eye. "But why—"

"Why, Dolly? Why? Because I needed you to help with the girls. That's why I lied to you and to your parents."

The tears were now flowing. "But this is unfair," Dolly said. "I want to go home."

"And you shall go home—"

"Now."

"It can't be now, Dolly, but I will see that you get safely back to your parents. Please believe me!"

"Why should I believe you, Mrs. Greenleaf?"

The question cut. The child's eyes were full of tears, and so were hers. "There's no reason you should. I can only hope you will." She put her arm around Dolly's thin shoulders. "You know I love both my girls, Dolly. I'd do anything to keep them with me—even lie."

"But why, why?"

"Because I can no longer stay under the same roof with Mr. Greenleaf. Truly, Dolly, there are good reasons. Very good reasons. You must believe that. I would never have gone to such extremes—I would not have lied to you—had it not been the only way. You must understand. It was the only way. I had to have your help."

"But if you wanted to leave him, if you wanted to go back to your daddy, why couldn't you take the girls and go?"

"Life is not like that, Dolly. You can't always do as you please. I married Clay, and when I did, I gave up the part of me that could do as it pleases. When you marry, Dolly, your husband becomes the head of the household. It's what *he* wants, not what *you* want. That didn't occur to me back then. I was in love. I wanted to marry Clay more than anything in the world. But, when you marry, you cede a part of what is yours to your husband. You lose the right to make your own decisions. If you have children, they are his children. That's the law. A woman, without a source of money, cannot care for children adequately; those same laws give the custody of any money a woman may have at the time of her marriage to her husband."

"That's not fair."

"Perhaps not, but that's the way it is. That's why I had to lie to you. I didn't think you'd come with me to help with the children if you had known the truth. Your father would never have permitted you to come to Greenleaf, or on this journey, had he known."

"I'm afraid, Mrs. Greenleaf, really afraid. I'm so far from home. I might never see my mother again." Dolly clung to her and her tears flowed. As she held Dolly, Elizabeth knew she could count on help with the children if she could calm the poor girl's fears.

"Of course you'll see your mother. I promise you, and I promise you that I'll never lie to you again. I'll see that you get safely home. You believe me, don't you?"

Dolly clung even more tightly. It was a long time before Elizabeth heard the mumbled reply, "Yes'm. I believe you. But how—how will I get back? You're going to New York and maybe to England. What about me? How will I—"

"When we get to Baltimore, Dolly, I'll arrange for your return to Darien. Wives often travel with the boat captains. We'll find such a boat. You'll be in the personal care of the captain, and his wife will be there for you to talk to, to take tea with. I promise you, Dolly, I'll not leave Baltimore until I have you safely on board a steamer that will take you home. How does that sound?"

Dolly pulled back. Her eyes sought Elizabeth's. She was looking for a hint of betrayal—or another lie. But, for the first time in many weeks, Elizabeth was telling the truth. Fresh tears joined the stains on Dolly's cheeks. "Promise you'll stay with me and take me to meet the captain's wife and that you'll stay until I'm on the boat?"

"I promise, Dolly. You need have no fear."

"Then I'll help you with the children, Mrs. Greenleaf, but when I get home, I'll tell the truth."

"Yes, Dolly. That's what I want you to do. You should not lie. I'm ashamed of my lies, but I couldn't leave Greenleaf without the children, and I couldn't have them without lying. Please understand that."

They sat on the side of the bed with Elizabeth's arm around Dolly's shoulder. The girl was in shock. It was a lot to comprehend: the loss of trust in Elizabeth, the stealing of children, an even longer journey to Baltimore, where she'd be alone on the return trip. Could she believe? Finally, Dolly spoke. "Can we get off here in Charleston? Do we have time? Mother says it's a beautiful city."

"There is time, Dolly. We won't be leaving for two hours, but we cannot get off the boat. Clay and your father are well known here. We can't take the chance."

"You told the truth, didn't you? There is time."

"Yes, Dolly, there is time. Perhaps you'll be able to see Charleston on the way back. Please understand—"

"Yes, Mrs. Greenleaf. You're afraid to be seen."

"I am, Dolly. I must get the children safely to my father's house. But after everyone has gone ashore, perhaps we could walk out on the deck. You could see a part of the city from there. I did that as we were coming down. It was my first glimpse of Charleston. As your mother said, it is a beautiful city. Some say the most beautiful in the South."

Chapter Forty-Four

Elizabeth was grateful it was late when she arrived in New York City. Darkness masked the spectacle of her arrival at the manse.

She knocked on the front door while the driver unloaded her minimal luggage. When she lifted the knocker again, she heard footsteps. The door opened a crack.

"Elizabeth! What in the world—"

"Papa," she said. "Oh, Papa." She gave him a quick hug. "But before we create attention, please help me to get the bags and the children inside."

"What are you doing here? And where is Clay?"

"I left Clay, Papa."

"What," he sputtered, "you did what?"

"Before I tell you about it, Papa, I must get the children to bed. They're exhausted."

After the children were bathed and settled in the beds, she went down to his study. "Yes, Papa, you wanted to talk."

"Don't be impertinent, Elizabeth. It's you who needs to do some talking." She knew they were off to a bad start.

"I'm sorry, Papa. I didn't mean to be impertinent."

"Well, you were." He didn't speak for a full minute. Letting the silence build was his way of intimidating her. Then he spoke: "You have a good deal of talking to do. It's my opinion the explanations for this unfortunate turn of events can only come from you."

"You're right, Papa. I'll try to make it brief. I left Clay. I left him because he was sleeping with one of the servants, a girl named Carlotta."

"A black girl?"

"Yes, Papa, a slave. A girl who couldn't say no,"

"Oh, my." he said. "Oh, my."

"Yes."

The old man leaned back in his chair. He looked stunned. Finally, he spoke, "You are sure?"

"Yes, Papa, very sure."

He was silent for what seemed like forever to her and then he said, "The fault is yours, Elizabeth. This would not have happened if you had been a proper wife."

She couldn't believe it. "Papa, doesn't the good book say, 'Judge not—'"

"Don't try to preach to me, Elizabeth."

She had heard that tone before. She bit her tongue to remain silent. "If we're going to look at this from a Biblical viewpoint, Elizabeth," he said, "we can only say that you are a wayward wife. Worse than that, you have stolen a man's children from him."

"Papa!"

"He will come for them and claim them. He has that right."

Elizabeth could not see nor could she hear compassion. Not the first ounce of it.

"I don't know what will become of you, Elizabeth. You'll never be able to marry again, that's certain. A widow may have a small chance to remarry, but not a woman who has done what you have."

"I've taken myself out of an intolerable situation."

"Intolerable? What is that, Elizabeth? Clay may have had a moment of indiscretion—and with two children hanging at your teats, he may have had reason—"

"I expected understanding from you, Papa, not vulgarity. I knew you'd be upset, but I was sure you'd understand. You've always opposed slavery and all it stands for. You lent the rooms of the church, you made it a meeting place for those who oppose it. You've heard the stories of maltreatment. By your actions, you've always been firmly against slavery."

His face could have been carved from stone. She saw no understanding, but she did see a coldness in his eye that she had seen before. She tried to appeal to him.

"If I understand what I hear now, you're taking Clay's side. If you have no pity for me, surely you have it for Carlotta. She is a slave, Papa, a chattel. She has even fewer rights than I have. She may have been a victim. She could not say no."

"The fault, Elizabeth, is yours. No amount of talking will change that. A woman's place is at her husband's side. Clay may have been indiscreet, but that's all."

"'Though shalt not commit adultery.'"

"You are not versed in the Bible, Elizabeth. I've always despaired of that. Don't try to quote it to me." She could see his anger. The Bible, apparently, was his private province, a source only he could use. At last he spoke again. "You will not be staying here."

"But, Papa—"

"You will not be staying here. It would cause a scandal. I can't have that. I won't have it." He waited. He wanted his words clearly understood before he continued. "But even if I were to permit it, what good would it do? Clay knows of your duplicity. I suspect he's on his way here, coming to fetch his children. He won't want you back, that's sure. No man would."

"What am I, Papa? Damaged goods?"

"Don't try to cover your sin, Elizabeth. It's on your conscience, or should be. You're wayward. Any man might have done what you say Clay has done But you left him. You chose to abandon him, to steal away with his children. Your chances for remarriage are nil. Remember, my girl, you're no longer a virgin. When this scandal is known, the world will know how willful you can be. Don't expect marriage."

"I don't know that I'll miss it."

"Impertinence again."

"Look, Papa, I may be only a woman in your eyes, but I am a thinking person, just as you are. I know when I've had injustice done to me. I'll take no more of it. If that precludes another marriage, so be it!"

"That's enough, Elizabeth. I'm your father, and I'll not listen to such talk, not for a moment."

"You have little choice."

"Oh, but I do. I do have a choice. Fortunately, no one knows you're here. The servants are off on Tuesdays. Even they don't know you've come crawling back. No one knows. No one will. I'll find a cab. I'll take you to the station, and you'll be on a train before daylight breaks."

"But, Papa—" She felt tears coming. "Where will I go?"

"I don't know. I don't want to know. If you put your mind to it, you'll find a place."

He paused. "But under no circumstances do I want to know the decision you reach." He was speaking slowly and emphatically. "You will buy your own ticket, and you will be on your way. I'll give you what money I have in the house, but that's the only part I'll play."

"Papa, how can you? There are two small children upstairs—"

"You should have thought of that before you left the South, my girl. You made your bed—"

"I have no other place—"

"You've just told me you're a thinking person, Elizabeth. Think your way out of this, but do it alone. I'll take you to the station. No more. I don't want to know where you go, or why. When Clay comes—and he will—I'll tell him in honesty that I don't know where you are. That's the most I'll do for you. It's the only way I can maintain my own integrity."

"Integrity?"

"If you want the money, Elizabeth, watch your mouth."

Her father had made up his mind. She would need the money. She had no idea where to go, and her own funds were slim. Her mother's people were in the same city as Papa, and the scandal would soon be out. She was in despair.

He spoke again, this time with a trace less rancor. "Now, get the children ready. Put your grips at the door while I go find a cab."

At two o'clock the next afternoon the cab brought Elizabeth to the house in Charter Street, Boston. A maid answered Elizabeth's knock. "Please tell Miss Medlock that her niece, Elizabeth, is at the door," she said. Oh, how I must look, Elizabeth thought. She wouldn't even ask me in.

The door was opened an inch, and then thrown open. "Elizabeth! I can't believe it. Ethel told me what you said, but I was wary. Bring the children and come in, dear."

Elizabeth was near tears and ready to collapse. Was it all behind her? Tears rolled down her cheeks. "Oh, thank you, Aunt Florence, thank you. I am so weary."

"Come in, dear. You look as though you might not be able to stand much longer. Come in." She turned to the maid. "This is my niece, Ethel. She may look like a worn rag doll, but she is my niece all the same. Call Charles. He can take those bags. Put her in the west bedroom. The small room next door will do nicely for the children."

An hour later, after the children were in bed, after she had taken a bath, rearranged her hair and washed the railway grime from her own body, she joined her aunt for tea. What she was handed was not a cup of tea, but a steaming mug. "I've given you the Florence Medlock remedy, Elizabeth. Tea alone is not enough. That mug is tea laced with brandy. Sip it slowly. It will bring life back to your limbs."

"I do need to explain—"

"Yes, my child, you do, but explanations can wait. For now, just sip the tea and get yourself together."

"Thank you, Aunt Florence."

"You're done in. Even now, you look a fright." Miss Medlock's cool gray eyes missed nothing. "Have you eaten?"

"There was a butcher on the train hawking his wares. I tried a sandwich, but I just wasn't able to eat it."

"You need a cup of good strong broth." After she had made these arrangements, she turned back to Elizabeth. "I see you're feeling better. The brandy is bringing life back to you. When you're able, I'll need to know more than you've told me. Of course you're welcome here, but that aside, I need to know what you are doing wandering around the face of the earth with two children—two very small children—and virtually no luggage. What is the meaning of it?"

As she sipped the tea, Elizabeth told Florence Medlock of her marriage to Clay and of the circumstances that led to its demise. Aunt Florence listened without a word until Elizabeth got to the part about her arrival in New York City.

"You can't mean it, Elizabeth! Chester did that? He is such a pompous fool. He always has been. Forgive me, Elizabeth, I know he's your father—he's also my brother. He's learned nothing with the passage of the years. He was a fool, and he is a fool. Even so, I can't believe he left you and the children at that dirty station after midnight. What a disappointment he is. All because he didn't want a scandal. What an insipid reason for such treatment. You are his only daughter, and those two babies upstairs are his grandchildren! Even knowing him as I do, I just can't believe it. He was afraid of the scandal. My God! He was spineless as a young man. He still is. He calls himself a Christian, too. It's so like him, but I still can't believe it."

"But he's right. Clay will come to fetch the children."

"That may be. But Chester could have hidden you—or sent you here. You thought of me and he could have. There's no excuse for him. None. He offered no help, not the first measure of it."

"But the money, he gave me—"

"You needed more than his money, my child. You needed his understanding. He didn't know how to give it because he doesn't have an ounce of it. He is a buffoon masquerading as a clergyman. Oh, my poor girl, the journey—your escape from that hell-island of slavery was bad enough, but my brother's behavior—his treatment of you. I don't know, I don't know. I shall never be able to forgive Chester for this."

"Maybe the fault is mine—"

"Not another word, Elizabeth."

"But, Aunt Florence, as Papa said, I was Clay's wife."

"I don't believe in slavery, Elizabeth—not in the South, or the slavery that women are shackled with. One day we will all get sick of it. We will begin to think, to decide for ourselves, and, when it happens, it will be a better world. A human being, black or white, male or female, has a right to at least a measure of freedom."

"Men will never let it happen, Aunt Florence."

"The pot simmers, Elizabeth."

"Those who have control will keep control."

"It may seem impossible, but it's not. One day women will simply say 'No more.' They will say it loudly, they will say it firmly, and they will mean it."

"You are one voice, Aunt Florence."

"True. I'm only one voice. But I scatter seeds. Maybe one will germinate. And I'm not alone. There are other voices, other women who are fighting against this kind of slavery. As long as I breathe, I'll fight our injustice, Elizabeth, just as I fight against the injustice brought about by the other kind of slavery. I may never live to see the end of it, but I'll know I did what I could."

Chapter Forty-Five

Elizabeth felt safe and comfortable in Aunt Florence's home. They knew each other, of course, but Miss Medlock's visits to the manse had always been brief and sporadic. "I could stand Chester only for a day or two," Aunt Florence said.

Florence Medlock did not find it a burden to be without a husband. "I didn't marry because I never found a man strong enough to allow me to be my own person," Florence Medlock said one day. "I don't regret it. It's been a good life for me."

And it had been. Miss Medlock lived in a handsome, well-ordered house, and she had shrewdly invested her small inheritance. She was now comfortably well-off. "I do as I please," she often said, "as I damned well please."

It did not take long for Elizabeth to comprehend what a rabid abolitionist her aunt was. Florence Medlock did not embrace anything as a half measure. If she cared about a person or an idea, it was with every ounce of her energy. She hated the idea of slavery. "It's a damnation," she would say. " If anything will bring this country down, it will be one human being's subjugation of another. You mark my words, Elizabeth, one day we will have to march down there and straighten this out. It's unthinkable, completely, utterly unthinkable. Slavery must be abolished."

Miss Medlock wanted to know all about living "cheek by jowl with slavery, that abomination from hell." She never tired of asking about it. "You lived it, Elizabeth, you know what I can only surmise." She wanted to know the smallest detail. And she asked about Clay. Did he beat the slaves?"

"No, Aunt Florence. I don't think he felt it was his job. He copied his father to the letter so I suspect his father did not personally use the whip." Beatings were given, Elizabeth explained, but that was a job for an overseer, or for one of the other slaves. It was more effective that way.

"But, he was the puppet master. It was he who pulled the strings."

"Well, yes, he could have stopped it."

"He didn't beat the slaves—but he did beat his wife."

"Be fair, Aunt Florence. He didn't beat me. Never. He slapped me, he threatened me with the cane, but he didn't—"

"Stop it, Elizabeth! Not another word. Clay threatened you from the day you married him, even on your honeymoon."

Aunt Florence was visibly angry. She could build a rage in an instant when she thought about slaves or about Elizabeth's life at Greenleaf Hall.

"He intimidated you, Elizabeth. He raped you virtually in the presence of others—it could be called nothing else. Don't defend him."

"Maybe I wasn't the wife I could have been."

"A wife is not there to be maltreated, beaten and raped. A woman is no less human than a man, Elizabeth."

They both knew Clay would search for the children so in Boston she became Elizabeth Burnside, a widow with two girls.

One day they were having tea in the garden. Florence Medlock put her teacup on the table and turned to her niece. "I want you to do something for me, Elizabeth," she said. "Remember the story about Carlotta having the other black girl beaten for some kind of imagined disobedience?"

"That was Racy. How could I forget? I caused it."

"No, you didn't. But it's Racy I'm thinking of. I'd like you to write it out for me, just as you remember it."

"I'm not trained, Aunt Florence. I can't write."

"Yes, you can, my child. Just write it the way you told it to me. I've tried to repeat the story and I can't. Do it for me. Keep it simple. Set it down the way you told it."

"I'm not sure I can—"

"I see you writing in your journal. Do it as though you were writing it for your journal. I'm sure you didn't write about it while you were at Greenleaf."

"No, I didn't. The journal might have been read—by Clay or by someone. Clay would have been furious with me. I have it in my mind but not in my journal."

"Then write it now, write it for your journal. Think of it as a late entry. Let it be your remembrance, just as you might have done it for the journal."

"If you'd like to have it, I'll try."

"Thank you, Elizabeth. Then, rather than try to tell it, I can read it. I'll at least have it straight."

Elizabeth thought of Racy. The memory filled her mind. In that moment she was back on Greenleaf Island. She could see Racy and Robert and the place behind the barn where the beating had occurred. What had become of them? What had she done to all of them? What had become of Tess? Tears formed. She blinked and looked away.

Two days after Elizabeth gave a copy of the journal entry to Florence Medlock, there was a visitor for tea. He was tall and distinguished looking. "Oh, I'm sorry to be late. I didn't know we had a guest," she said.

"Elizabeth, this is Spencer Chadwycke, a dear friend. Spencer, my niece, Elizabeth Burnside. Spencer is the publisher of *The Black Advocate*. Perhaps you've heard of it."

"I'm afraid not. Please forgive me, Mr. Chadwycke."

"My fault, dear," Aunt Florence said. "I should have given you a copy of it before I asked Spencer to tea. It's a paper for those who think that slavery is an abomination."

"It's not as well known as *The Liberator*," Mr. Chadwycke

said, "but Garrison has been at it longer. Mine is a labor of love. I'm losing money at it."

"It's very good," Aunt Florence said. "Spencer hits harder than Garrison. It will find a readership."

"Well, my dear Florence, I hope you're right. At the moment *The Black Advocate* is being supported by our other publishing activities. Edward—my assistant, Edward Dalton—is against this waste of money. That's what he calls it. In a way it is, I suppose. I'm sensible enough to know it can't go on forever, but—"

"Give it time, Spencer. As a part-owner of Chadwycke & Company, I'm not complaining. Subscriptions are building."

"Florence allowed me to read your story of Racy's flogging, Mrs. Burnside. It's the sort of thing I'd like to have in *The Advocate*. Would you consider letting me run it?"

Elizabeth's reply was prompt and firm. "No, Mr. Chadwycke, I don't think it would be a good idea."

"But it's an excellent piece. It goes to the heart without preaching. I beg you, Mrs. Burnside, reconsider."

"I'm sorry, Mr. Chadwycke, I cannot."

Florence Medlock saw the fear in her niece's eyes. "Elizabeth, my dear, Spencer is a trusted friend. With your permission, I think we should take him into our confidence. Trust me. Spencer is as dear to me as you are. Over the years we have become friends and allies. I'm sure we can safely bare your secret to him."

"It's the safety of the girls—"

"I know, dear, but you have my assurance it will stay a secret with Spencer. It may give you a way to fight the injustice you've suffered. May I tell him? I think it will clear the fog he's in."

"If you think it's the right thing, Aunt Florence, I'll abide by your decision."

"You see, Spencer," Florence Medlock began, as she poured fresh cups of tea, "Elizabeth is not a widow with two children. She is a woman who ran away from her husband for good and valid reasons, reasons we won't discuss, but they are bona fide. I've introduced her in Boston as Elizabeth Burnside. It's her mother's maiden name. Her married name is Greenleaf, but to use it would be to allow that scoundrel to trace her more easily, perhaps to find her, even here."

"So, my dear Mrs. Burnside, you think the story is so personal that the author of it might be recognized?"

"I'm sure of it, Mr. Chadwycke. Right now, I'm not sure Aunt Florence should tell the story about town. It's been a concern since I gave her a copy of my journal entry."

"But, Mrs. Burnside, there must be other stories, stories that are not so personal, things you have seen—"

"I'm not a writer, Mr. Chadwycke."

"You write better than you think, Mrs. Burnside. You've done this so well only a fool could miss the point. "

"But, sir, it cannot—it must not—be used."

"I understand. We can't use it. But what about some of your other recollections, things you have seen at first hand?"

"I'm not a writer—"

"Let me be the judge of that, Mrs. Burnside."

"It's too dangerous, Mr. Chadwycke. It could be seen by Clay and recognized. We saw *The Liberator* in Darien and at Greenleaf Hall. Your paper could find its way South, too. The idea is dangerous. Even if I didn't use my name, even if I used Burnside, Clay is aware of my mother's family. I just couldn't take the chance."

"Don't use Burnside or Greenleaf. Use an assumed name or a mythical name. Call yourself Cassandra. That would be fitting. Wasn't it Cassandra whose prophecies—whose warnings—were always disregarded? The name is a message."

"I like the name." Elizabeth hesitated, and then she said, "but I don't think I could do it."

"Try it, Mrs. Burnside. If it doesn't work out, who will know? The very fact that you are not accustomed to writing for publication is an asset. You write without guile. It's insidious. I felt it from the moment I read this piece. What about it? Will you try?"

"I just don't know, I don't know—"

"Say you'll try. That's all I ask. Try a couple of pieces. Things you've seen, either where you lived or elsewhere; experiences you've had; conditions under which these poor souls live in bondage. Say you'll try it, Mrs. Burnside. Please. We could call it 'Echoes from the South.'"

"Warnings by Cassandra," Aunt Florence interjected.

"Marvelous," Mr. Chadwycke said, "that could be a subtitle to the column."

"I'm still not sure—"

"Well, my dear, Mrs. Burnside, I have enough confidence for both of us. This could get *The Black Advocate* moving. It always takes a flame to ignite a paper. So far, we haven't had it. Your regular contribution could well be the stuff we need to get it going."

"Oh, Elizabeth, I'm thrilled," Florence Medlock said. "You know the hardships those poor people have. You've been there. What you write will have the ring of truth. This could help to bring political change. God knows we can't expect much from President Polk."

"The President aside," Spencer Chadwycke said, "the only thing that will bring change is to get the people behind abolition. Garrison's been at it for over ten years, and it's high time he gets some support—our support. That's why we've spent money on *The Black Advocate.* We can't depend on Polk. We have to put pressure on Congress." There was a lull in the conversation. Each of them seemed to be involved in private thoughts.

Then Spencer Chadwycke spoke again, "Remember this, ladies, a politician won't do anything but talk unless he is forced into action—unless we shove his feet to the andiron. We do need to stir it up. We need to light a fire. We have to make them listen to the people at home. We can't depend on the President, and that's true whether it's Polk, or whoever we may get next time."

"Those are true words, Spencer, true words."

"And now, ladies, I must get back to work. I want to re-think the new issue of *The Black Advocate*. I want to see that Mrs. Burnside's piece gets a prominent place."

"Not too fast, please, Mr. Chadwycke. I may not be able to do it."

"You'll do it, Mrs. Burnside, and you'll do it well. The sooner I can have the first piece, the better."

"She'll start tomorrow, Spencer. I'll see to the children while she takes pen in hand."

"Oh, dear," Elizabeth said. "I'm not sure of this. I think my life is taking another turn."

Chapter Forty-Six

Elizabeth sat at her desk with paper and pen, but she wrote nothing worth reading. She could only think of the flogging Robert was forced to give Racy, under Carlotta's direction.

She spent the morning in this solitary occupation and ended up with a wastebasket full of crumpled paper. When she wasn't looking at ink scratches that meant nothing, she looked at the fall weather outside her window. It was bleak out there, but it was better than thus stuffy room and this impossible task.

As she crossed the foyer to the closet, Florence Medlock came out of the library. "Are you finished, child? So soon?"

"No, Aunt Florence—far from it. It's an impossible task. I cannot write. I can't even think straight."

"Nonsense, Elizabeth. The Racy account was sparely written, but every word told the story in shocking detail. Of course you can write. You're making a bogeyman of this."

"I can't do it," Elizabeth said. Her voice betrayed the tears behind her lids. "I'll walk to The Common, and I'll think of how to tell Mr. Chadwycke that I'm not up to this job."

"The Common? It's too cold. This is foolishness, Elizabeth. You'll catch your death."

"Not likely, Aunt Florence. I come from strong Medlock stock. My father's blood ran a little thin, but yours didn't." There was laughter in her voice now. Her depression began to subside. She put on her heavy coat and pulled the muffler close about her neck. "If it's too cold, I'll come back. In any event, I'll be back for lunch."

At Florence Medlock's behest, Elizabeth agreed to give the writing one more try in the afternoon. This time she fashioned a lap board from a large book and a pillow and sat at the window. Write as though it were for your journal they had both told her. Her mind raced back to Darien, to Greenleaf, and to the sea and the marshes. She began to write.

Hours later, when she heard the bell for tea, there were a dozen pages strewn around her chair. She didn't know if *any* of it had *any* relevance. She remembered nothing that might be of even passing interest to Mr. Chadwycke or *The Advocate*.

After tea she gathered the papers from the floor. She wept as she read the stark honesty she had been unable and afraid to put in her journal. It was painful, but it gave her the strength to look at what her life had been. As she read, she found two segments that might make good columns for *The Black Advocate*, at least, as she understood what Spencer wanted.

Both incidents were intensely personal. They would not do, not as she had written them. Clay would know she was the author. They would have to be modified to protect the girls.

She moved to her desk. This time she was able to write. Elizabeth was so intent on hiding her own identity that she forgot she was writing for publication. Within the hour she had two articles written for Spencer Chadwycke.

That was how it began. As the years passed, she never altered her method. She began with an extended and honest journal entry, and then she selected parts of it for "Echoes from the South — Warnings by Cassandra." She modified, she altered, she eliminated anything that would tie Elizabeth Greenleaf to the piece. Then she sent it to Chadwycke & Co.

As Spencer Chadwycke predicted, with the publishing of her column, the readership of *The Black Advocate* began to grow. Cassandra was widely read and discussed. Speculation as to the real identity of the author was on every lip, but the secret was known only to three people. It stayed a secret, which added to the success of *The Black Advocate.*

Elizabeth was paid for the column. It was a small amount. Spencer called it her "stipend," but it was welcome pin money since her only income was her mother's trust. Regular payment for her writing made her feel less dependent on Aunt Florence. As *The Black Advocate* began to bring a return on its investment, Elizabeth's "stipend" grew.

In addition to her work for *The Advocate*, other newspapers and magazines contacted Chadwycke. He did not divulge her name or give out any information. He laughed about it. "You're becoming a celebrity, Elizabeth—or at least Cassandra is. They persist, so you must decide if you wish to write for others, and you must decide if such endeavors could put you or the children at risk."

"It would be a risk. No, Spencer, I think not. If they paid me, of necessity I'd be known to them, wouldn't I?"

"Oh, that part of it can be handled, my dear. The monies can be paid to Chadwycke & Company. Only I would be privy to your identity. The question is, do you want the burden?"

"I wouldn't call it a burden. I sometimes don't like writing, but I do like having written. In a way I'm simply writing a more honest journal and along the way I choose topics for the weekly column. I wouldn't call it a burden."

"The decision is yours, Elizabeth."

"Then I'd like to accept these assignments. Maybe, in time, I could be self-sufficient. Aunt Florence doesn't mind having me and the children here, but it is her house. It would be nice to have a cottage somewhere, a place I could call my own, just for the children and me."

"Well, how much you could earn—whether these requests are isolated—I can't say, Elizabeth, but I know of these two. If you like, I'll negotiate for the best possible payment."

"Please do, Spencer. Is there a time requirement? You didn't say."

"That wasn't discussed, my dear. I was uncertain of your reaction. I'll find out."

"You're a good friend, Spencer."

"I'm a businessman; you're a writer who makes money for my firm. It's as simple as that."

"You're a friend. The other may be true, too, but it's clear we like and respect each other. That's an asset."

"You're an asset."

"I may be a liability if you have to negotiate for me."

"If it should become onerous, you may be assured, Chadwycke & Company will charge for services rendered. Eddie Dalton is a trusted assistant, but he also has an accountant's mind. At first he was against *The Black Advocate* because we had losses. He wants all our endeavors to pay for themselves, and that would include you. He runs the profit-and-loss part of the company and he does it well."

"Good. I don't want to be a burden."

"There's something else, Elizabeth. There's a group opposed to slavery who would like to have Cassandra speak."

"Oh, no, Spencer, I couldn't. I wouldn't dare, because of the girls. Besides, I couldn't talk before a group."

"There's money in it, Elizabeth."

"Perhaps, but the risk is too great."

"There's nothing that can't be done if you want to do it enough."

"But the risk—"

"The risk can be minimal. I gave it some thought as I rode over here today. I didn't expect you would be willing to do it, but I do like a problem, a puzzle, so I mulled it over in my mind. It could be done."

"How, Spencer? How, keeping the risk in mind?"

"You're already a mystery, my dear. Become an even bigger mystery. Become the most talked about speaker in all of

New England. Because of the mystery, you could be difficult to get—and expensive."

"But, dear Spencer, I wouldn't be a mystery long. One time on the platform and everybody would know I'm Florence Medlock's niece. The mystery would evaporate."

"No, my dear. You could be heavily veiled and padded, wearing all black: black dress, hat, veil and gloves. You could depart after nightfall and in a closed carriage. As you leave each engagement, you could go to my house—everyone knows I know Cassandra. Later, you could leave by my back door in another closed carriage for the return."

"You make it sound exciting."

"It could become more exciting. There will always be those who will want to unmask the elusive Cassandra. You will be followed. We may even have to change your route. My house may not be the only answer necessary."

"I love the idea of it. It's a child's game for adults. You must have loved games when you were young, Spencer."

"I loved them then and I love them now. I've grown adept at games, my dear Elizabeth. Life's circumstances sometimes require you to be wily. You may not have been aware of it, but you, too, have played little parallel games."

"Not that I know of."

"Put your mind to it. I know something of your life. You are adept at games, just as I am. What your life appeared to be was not always what it was."

"I declare, Spencer, that's the most foolish—"

"Is it? Did you not play a parallel game when you planned your departure from Greenleaf Hall?"

"That was different?"

"Oh, was it? Think about it, Elizabeth. We all do it. Some of us play the game on grander scale than others, and some are able to play it better, but when we are faced with some unpleasant part of life, we retreat from that situation by playing games that are more to our liking, or games that will hide the facts while we prepare to take another direction." Elizabeth said nothing. "You did it when you went to Savannah to have curtains made for Greenleaf Hall—or, do you deny that, too, now that it's all behind you?"

Elizabeth remembered the deceit. Spencer was right, she had played a role—he called it a parallel game—and if she were bone-honest, it wasn't the only time she had played such a parallel game. She was never completely herself with her parents. She played a parallel game with them, too. Finally, she spoke. "It was, as you say, Spencer, a parallel game when I left the island."

"And, my dear Elizabeth, that was not a single example, was it? Don't bother to answer. I know."

"It would be easy to dislike you, Spencer."

"It's always easy to dislike your friends. And, I am your friend—and you know it. If I were not, I would never talk to you in such an intimate way. It exposes too much of myself."

Time passed swiftly. Elizabeth wrote regularly for *The Black Advocate*. She wrote for many periodicals in addition to *The Advocate*, and she was in demand as a speaker.

During the summer of 1852 she found a small house and she hired Lucy to care for the children. Elizabeth loved having a place of her own. It was her first.

She had always lived in a house that belonged to someone else. The manse belonged to her father; the Greenleaf house in Philadelphia belonged to Miss Mattie, without question; the house on the rice island was more Carlotta's than it was hers; and, Greenleaf Hall was Miss Mattie's or Carlotta's. While she had every comfort where she had been living, it was Florence Medlock's home. Now, Elizabeth thought, I have a place where I can "do as I damned well please," too. Aunt Florence was right in fighting for the privilege.

Elizabeth enjoyed the speaking aspect of her life, especially the "parallel games" Spencer devised. He was right. As the mystery of Cassandra grew, the unmasking of her became more intense. It was sometimes necessary to go to three locations, staying a varied amount of time at each, and leaving by another doorway, before going home.

The more Elizabeth spoke, the more she wrote, the more rabid Florence Medlock became. "You should do the speaking, Aunt Florence. You're more passionate about it than I am."

"I would, my child, but no one would listen to me. It takes Cassandra to get their attention."

Life settled into a pattern randomly punctuated with the elaborate games that surrounded the speaking engagements, but there was a pattern to her life. Both children were in school. After Elizabeth sent them to class, she began her day.

Late in May, in the year of our Lord, 1853, there was a knock at the door of her cottage. There stood Clay. "I've come for the children, Elizabeth."

The sound of his voice, the words he said, brought instant terror. She was, once again, the young girl he married, ready to obey, ready to do his bidding. The strength she had acquired by running away from Greenleaf Island, the unqualified help Aunt Florence had given her, the support Spencer had at her constant disposal, all seemed to fade. She could only see the handsome blue-eyed man she had married, with the wry smile he always had when he knew she was at a disadvantage.

"Did you hear me, Elizabeth? I've come for the children. Get them ready for the journey."

It was the same smile, the smile that said I am strong and you are weak, and you will do as I tell you. The smile was there again. It had always infuriated her, and it did now. With her fury came the strength she had acquired—a little each day—since leaving Greenleaf. "You've come to a goat's house for wool, Clay. The children are not here."

"I'll not force myself into your house, Elizabeth. I'll not be making a disturbance before your neighbors. They're watching; I've seen the curtains move. But, let me make this clear: I've been to my attorney; I know my rights. I'll return for the children in the morning. Have their trunks packed."

He smiled again. He was so confident. "And, Elizabeth, when I return, it will be with the constable. I won't be barging into your house, but, if necessary, the authorities will. For your own sake, have the children ready." He turned and walked back down the little gravel path to her front gate.

Tears filled her eyes. She could hear the squeak of the gate, she could see a figure walking toward a waiting carriage, but the scene was blurred by a cascade of tears that continued long after the sound of the carriage had faded.

"I'll return for the children in the morning," he had said. "Have their trunks packed."

Chapter Forty-Seven

Elizabeth's tears did not last long. If she were to keep her children, she had scant time to take action. With the help of Aunt Florence, she would devise a plan.

She began packing the trunks. When Lucy returned from taking the children to school Elizabeth said, "Take the market basket as you do every morning, Lucy, but this time it will be different. Leave the basket in the market. Go out the back door and hurry to the hack stand. Tell the driver to take you to my aunt's house. This is a note I have written for her. Take it to her as fast as you can."

"But, Mrs. Burnside, I don't understand—"

"You needn't understand, Lucy, just do as I say. Pretend you're going out to do the marketing. Simply leave the basket there in the store, go out the back, and take a cab to Charter Street. That's all there is to it. You can have the day off once you've given Aunt Florence this note. Now, on with you, girl. Don't gape at me. Get the basket and go."

"Oh, Miss, I'm not sure. You say I'm to pretend to go shopping, but I'm to leave the basket, slip out the back and take a cab to Miss Medlock's house? Is that it?"

"Exactly, Lucy. That's it. Take her this note."

As she waited for Florence Medlock, Elizabeth finished packing the girls' trunks and then she pulled them out on the back porch so Charles could pick them up after dark. Her mind fumbled with a plan. She knew running was futile. She was sure Clay had the Pinkerton men on her trail. How else could he know her every move? He had walked right up to her door, arrogant and confident as usual.

As Elizabeth packed her own trunk, Aunt Florence arrived in her closed carriage."What are you doing with the trunks, Elizabeth? You can't run forever."

"I know, Aunt Florence, but what else can I do?"

Over tea it was decided. The children must be hidden. Florence Medlock had dear friends in Chelmsford. It was far enough outside Boston to make them safe from Clay, but close enough for Elizabeth to see them. Being sure she was not followed was a game Cassandra knew how to play.

"You must stay to face Clay, Elizabeth. You are a woman. It's past time for you to take charge of your own life."

"I am in charge, Aunt Florence. I left him years ago."

"No, my dear, you're not in charge. You left him, you were out of his physical presence, but he was with you all the same. You are afraid of him, Elizabeth. Fear can bind you to another person, just as love can. Once and for all, you must stand up to him."

"But, I met him this morning. I stood my ground."

"Did you? Did you, really? Tears are not a sign of victory. You stood your ground, did you? Is that why you are putting your own clothes in a trunk? He still controls you, Elizabeth. That must stop. He has forced the issue; you have no choice. Every animal, particularly a female with children, will turn to fight, no matter how big the opponent."

It was decided. Aunt Florence would take the children to Chelmsford and Elizabeth would stay to face Clay.

Miss Medlock said her goodbyes at the door and went to her carriage. Charles drove toward Charter Street.

In ten minutes, Elizabeth, dressed for the autumn weather, set out for the school on foot. Clay would expect her to try to take the children and run so she knew the house and her every movement was being watched. That sure knowledge was part of the plan.

As she opened the gate in front of the school, the headmistress saw her and met her at the front door. "I've come to pick up the children," Elizabeth said.

"Come in, Mrs. Burnside. That wind has a nip, doesn't it?" She opened the door wider. "Could you wait for just a few minutes, please? The children are having milk and cookies." Elizabeth entered and the door was closed.

According to the plan, during the ten minutes after Florence Medlock's departure, and during Elizabeth's walk to the school, the Medlock carriage would proceed toward Charter Street, and then double back to the school. It would come in from the alley, and while Elizabeth was walking to the school or in front of it, Aunt Florence would have explained the situation to the headmistress, dressed the children for the weather and loaded them into the carriage. Long before Elizabeth's delayed reemergence from the school, Aunt Florence and the two girls would be on their way.

The plan worked perfectly. In twenty minutes, Elizabeth emerged from the school and walked home. If you are watching, she thought, I'll bet you're in a quandary. Where are the children? Too bad, Clay. I've had help from Aunt Florence, and I'm still one step ahead of you.

In less than an hour Clay was back at her door. "What have you done with the children, Elizabeth?"

"At school, Clay. Lucy won't fetch them until two."

"Don't play games, Elizabeth. You can't run forever. I'll have you watched every minute, day and night. If you go to them, I'll be right behind you, and I'll take them, even if it's in the middle of Boston Common. I'll get a constable, and I'll take them, just as I have every right to do."

"You're such a bastard, Clay—"

"Watch your tongue, Elizabeth."

"What will you do, dear husband, hit me again? Don't try. As you said earlier, all the curtains are pulled back. You'll be seen striking me. That's not your style, is it? You'd never want to be seen."

"I'll be provoked just so far, Elizabeth."

"So will I, Clay. Please go. You're on private property. I'm asking you to leave."

"You're still my wife. I still have rights."

"If you step one foot in this direction, I'll scream so loud I'll be heard in Cambridge."

He shifted from one foot to the other. He changed his tack. "So you are the famous Cassandra." It was a statement.

It was a shock. "Don't be silly, Clay."

He was back in control. "Yes, my dear, you are Cassandra. That's how we found you. You've been clever, Elizabeth, but not clever enough."

Clay moved closer to her. He had to intimidate her or he wouldn't have control. "The Pinkerton men were first to connect it," he said. "I was certain it couldn't be. They persisted. Finally, I read it all—all the drivel you spouted—and as I read, I became convinced. I agreed to put on more men, to have Cassandra followed. We lost you many times, but eventually you were followed to the Medlock house in Charter Street. And you, my dear Elizabeth, are a Medlock. In time you were seen leaving your aunt's house, and you were followed here. Oh, yes, my dear, you are Cassandra."

"Will you leave now, Clay? Please leave."

"I'll leave, my dear, but this is not over. I'll find the children if it takes forever, but, even before that, I intend to file for divorce. That will stop you. I'll have custody of the children, with the full force of the courts behind me. You can put money on that. And when I do, you'll never see them again."

"I'm their mother. You wouldn't do that."

"Yes, my dear, I can, and I will.

Chapter Forty-Eight

That afternoon in May of 1853 was the last time Elizabeth saw Clay alone. The second day after the children were taken to Chelmsford, Clay sent a message asking for a meeting the following afternoon.

Elizabeth was wary. She dared not see Clay alone. It had been more than seven years since he slapped her, but he was angry enough to hit her when he was last on her doorstep. Her words might inflame his passion, and she was aware of his quick temper.

Elizabeth was surprised when Clay arrived with his solicitor and he was surprised to see someone standing at her side. Florence Medlock had not seen Clay since the wedding, but his lascivious behavior with a slave made her want to see him again. She was certain she would see debauchery written on his face, but he was as handsome as ever. He's a villain, she thought. Too bad he doesn't look like one.

In the presence of his solicitor and Aunt Florence, Clay was polite and reasonable. But, under that civilized patina, Elizabeth could see his disdain. It was over for her, every vestige of love.

Her reverie was shattered. She heard Clay say, "We can take the girls back to Philadelphia, to Haverford Place. We can enlarge the quarters there for the three of you—"

"Philadelphia?" What was he talking about?

"Yes, my dear. I'm sure you'd prefer Philadelphia to Greenleaf Hall. Aunt Mattie's home is more than ample.

"To Philadelphia?" What was he saying?

"Mrs. Greenleaf, if I may intercede," Mr. Godbold, said, "Mr. Greenleaf is making a very reasonable offer. He knows you want the children with you. He is suggesting that you resume your wifely duties, and that you and the children return to Philadelphia; that the family be reunited."

"Miss Mattie's house? Oh, Clay—"

"Well, Elizabeth, I know how irrational you are about Aunt Mattie. We could get a house, if it would suit you better. It's an unnecessary expense but it could be done."

"I'm not sure of that either."

"A wife's place is at her husband's side, Mrs. Greenleaf," Mr. Godbold said.

"But, I'm not a wife—"

"Yes, you are, Elizabeth. You may have been wayward, you may have abandoned me, but you're still my wife. By law, I have jurisdiction over the children. Don't forget that. Don't think only of yourself. Think of them."

Yes, she thought, I was thinking of myself. He knows me too well. "Yes," she managed to say, "yes."

"You can stay with Aunt Mattie until we find a suitable house. That way, you can keep the children with you."

"Not at Aunt Mattie's—"

"Don't be unreasonable, Elizabeth. It'll only be a short time, until I can find a house. She's not a monster. She won't eat you or the children." He turned to Aunt Florence. "Speak to her, Miss Medlock."

"Elizabeth has made her own decisions for some years now, Mr. Greenleaf. I dare say she's still capable."

"But, she seems addled—"

"I'm not surprised, Mr. Greenleaf. You're here proposing a reconciliation and yet you have an attorney at your side. That would be enough to addle a young girl."

"I brought Mr. Godbold for *her,* Miss Medlock, not for me. I asked him so she would understand how untenable her situation is. They're my children; I'm responsible for them. And, I expect to assume that responsibility."

"Oh? Have they been located?"

"Miss Medlock," Mr. Godbold said, "the whereabouts of the children is not important. Mr. Greenleaf is their sire. His rights will be upheld in court. The judge will demand that Mrs. Greenleaf produce the children."

Elizabeth began to cry. She could not face life without the girls, and she seemed to have no chance of retaining them if it were to go to court. She dried her eyes and spoke.

"It's all right, Aunt Florence. Perhaps, for the sake of the children, returning to Philadelphia would be the best answer."

"It's a wise decision, Mrs. Greenleaf," Mr. Godbold said. "Any other course of action would be foolhardy."

"I'll find a nice house, Elizabeth. I'll do everything I can for the girls, but you'll have obligations, too."

"What do you mean? What sort of obligations?"

"You will be a wife to me." Clay could see her spine stiffen. "It need only be in appearances at first, but I've been embarrassed by your behavior, and I'll not tolerate it. You'll live the quiet life of the mother of two girls whose husband, because of his work, lives elsewhere. There will be no more speeches, no more tract writing, no more anti-slavery actions or affirmations of any kind. You will not so much as write letters to these so-called friends of yours who have fueled your hatred of the source of my income."

"But, Clay—"

"No buts, my dear. You'll be a housewife and nothing more. All abolitionist activity will cease. You will learn to curb your tongue. If you can't speak positively of our southern economy, you will not speak of it at all."

Miss Medlock was appalled by what she saw. Elizabeth was as limp as a sawdust doll. Her shoulders were pulled forward, her head down. She was what Florence Medlock could never allow herself to be. Elizabeth was defeated.

"I don't wish to belabor the point, my dear," Clay continued, "but you must understand the conditions that I demand before we both alter our lives for the sake of the children. Not many people know you are Cassandra. That's the way it will stay. You will forget you ever wrote those lies, all designed to inflame more than enlighten."

Elizabeth's mind was numb, but she heard the word "demand." It was always a demand. Arrogance from a man who had betrayed their marriage bed with a slave girl.

"What else do you demand, Clay?" she said quietly.

Clay failed to hear her anger. "As I said, my dear, you will forget you were Cassandra. But, if it should ever be discovered—and I pray to God it won't—you will admit you wrote lies, nothing but lies, and that you were being manipulated by a pack of Yankee abolitionists."

"They were not lies, Clay," she said. The voice was still very low, but firmer.

"They were lies, Elizabeth. You will admit it here and now, and you will continue to say it or I will take the children and you'll never see them again."

This was the Clay she knew. This was the man who slapped her, who raped her, and who was content only when she was a shadow in his presence. He wanted her to know who was in control.

"Take the children, Clay? Why don't you do that now? Why don't you take them today?"

"Don't be insolent, Elizabeth. My patience is thin."

"You tell me I talk too much. Well, dear husband, the same could be said of you. You talked so much this time that I remembered the dark side of your character."

"I'll not get angry, Elizabeth. It won't work. The law is on my side. You'll submit, you'll become a wife to me, or you'll never see your children again."

"Take them now, Clay."

"Mrs. Greenleaf," he said. "Mr. Greenleaf is offering a

solution. You can stay with your children. His household allowance will be very generous. I beg you to be reasonable. He is absolutely correct. The law will take the children from you. The law looks to their welfare and nothing else. I beg you to think about this."

"But, Mr. Godbold," Florence Medlock said, "the law is not blind, justice is not blind. All aspects will be considered by the court. There are circumstances about which you may not know. My niece did not leave her husband out of willfulness. Mr. Greenleaf's conduct, his affair with one of the slaves, was reprehensible. The law will take that into account, too."

There was complete silence. Florence Medlock's words echoed in their heads. Mr. Godbold was confused by them, but the others understood the words Aunt Florence wished she had never uttered.

Clay was first to recover.

"More lies. You start with one, a small one, and they multiply. The lies must stop, Elizabeth. That one is the worst of the lot."

"That is not a lie, Clay. I discovered your trysts with Carlotta well before I left Greenleaf Hall. That's why I left you. It's not a lie, Clay, and you know it."

"It is a lie," Clay persisted. He was bold. "And I warn you, Elizabeth, if you put that into print, I'll have you in court so fast it will twirl you in the air."

"It is a fact, Clay. I know it and you know it, but never fear, it won't be in Cassandra's column—not because of your threat, dear husband, but because of the girls. That part of their father's life I'd prefer to bury with the past."

Mr. Godbold did not like the turn his case was taking. He had to prevent complete disaster. "Ladies, please—and I beg of you, sir—let's not take this conversation further," Mr. Godbold said. "Our purpose is to benefit the children, is it not?"

"Our purpose, Mr. Godbold, may not be what we see on the surface," Elizabeth said firmly.

"If I may suggest, madam, perhaps it would be well to conclude our meeting for the day. We all need to think our goals through." Mr. Godbold had regained his composure. If the thought of sexual misconduct between races bothered him, it was under control.

He waited. No one spoke. Clay was angered by what Florence Medlock had said and furious with Elizabeth for not denying it.

Elizabeth was angry, too, not because of Carlotta. That had ceased to hurt; she was angry with herself for how close she had come to going to Philadelphia where she would have lost control of the children and her own life. Clay had been conciliatory; she had forgotten how well he could be whatever was required for the occasion. From now on, she must be watchful and wary.

Miss Medlock was angry with herself. She had interfered. But, she cooled her ardor with the thought that someone had to bring a modicum of sense to Elizabeth's irrational behavior. Philadelphia indeed! He wanted her on *his* territory, where *he* would set the rules.

Mr. Godbold began again. "Mr. Greenleaf, ladies, can we set a time for another meeting? No good will come from angry words, words we will all regret. Suppose we meet again on Monday? How would that day be for you, Mrs. Greenleaf and for Miss Medlock? Would Monday be agreeable?"

"I'm not sure I see the purpose, Mr. Godbold—"

"The purpose, Mrs. Greenleaf, is to allow the four of us to do something—not for ourselves, but for the children. I am sure, madam, that you do not want notoriety—you have implied as much. I am certain the children come first in your life, and I respect that. We need a little time, each of us, for contemplation. With that one thought in mind, would Monday, at about this same time, be suitable?"

"Monday will be fine, Mr. Godbold."

Chapter Forty-Nine

Clay and Mr. Godbold came to the cottage on two more occasions. Each time Elizabeth's words caused Clay's mantle of righteousness to come unraveled a little more. As Mr. Godbold had advised, she had taken the time between their meetings to think. Florence Medlock was pleased. Elizabeth was reasoning now, she was reluctant to bargain away the freedom she had acquired as a single woman.

The fourth meeting of this ill-fated series was the first Monday in June at ten o'clock. As Aunt Florence walked up the garden path, the second carriage arrived. Elizabeth watched from the window. Only Mr. Godbold got out. Oh dear, she thought, this spells trouble.

She brushed the thought aside. Florence Medlock was at the door before Mr. Godbold had finished instructing his driver. "What could this mean, dear?" she said under her breath. "Clay was angry the last time, but this seems to say we are at the end of something—or is it the beginning?"

Elizabeth had no time for a reply. Mr. Godbold walked briskly up the bordered path. "Good morning," Elizabeth said. "You're both on time. I have the tea things ready."

"I won't be taking tea, madam. This will be a business meeting and nothing more."

"Oh my," she said, "that sounds so dire, Mr. Godbold. Surely we can stay friends through this. You've always cautioned the rest of us to keep our emotions under control."

"I only meant, madam, we will keep this meeting on a businesslike level, without the social amenities."

"As you wish, sir. But, let me take your hat, and please sit down. Surely we can be that sociable."

"I'm not your adversary, Mrs. Greenleaf."

"No offense meant, sir. Please do what you came to do."

"Thank you, madam. As you ladies know, I represent Mr. Greenleaf. I have his final offer of reconciliation. Please allow me to give the proposal to you in its entirety. If we stop to carp over each point, the meeting will fall apart, just as others have."

"Proceed, Mr. Godbold. We will not interrupt."

Mr. Godbold took a paper from his valise. "Mr. Greenleaf is willing to take you back as his lawful spouse. He will see to the education of his children and he will provide you with a home in or near Philadelphia." He looked directly at Elizabeth. "Mr. Greenleaf, madam, is a very generous and compassionate man. He is aware that you now have an income from your tract writing and speaking, so he will provide you with an income from a trust, one that can be revoked only by your failure to abide by the terms of this agreement. The amount of the trust is a generous six hundred dollars a year."

"A trust?"

"You were not to interrupt, madam."

"My apologies, sir."

"In exchange, you will cease all writing and all speaking engagements. You will sever all your connections to the abolitionist groups here in Boston. You will agree not to consort with people who, even passively, object to slavery. You will, in short, become the wife of a southern planter who, if she has objections to slavery, will never speak them. Mr. Greenleaf will permit you to maintain the relationship you have with your aunt, Miss Florence Medlock, if you both, on your honor, agree never to discuss slavery. Mr. Greenleaf is confident of your honor, madam, and he is equally sure that Miss Medlock would abide by any agreement she is a party to."

How generous he is, Elizabeth thought. He will "permit" me to maintain a relationship with my aunt.

"Is that all, sir?"

"That is essentially it, Mrs. Greenleaf. It can be drawn up in precise detail, and then you can sign it."

"Does my aunt have to sign, too?"

"You test a man's patience, Mrs. Greenleaf. But no, your aunt's word is good enough for Mr. Greenleaf."

"Well, Mr. Godbold, I'll try to be equally businesslike and brief. And, I will be careful not to test your patience, as you phrase it. You may tell Mr. Greenleaf that I intend to stay in Boston, or in any city I choose; that I intend to continue writing about the abominable conditions in the South; that I will consort with whomever I please, whatever his or her politics; that I will keep my children with me, even if they have to stay hidden until they are of age; and, that I am not now nor will I ever be ready to resume conjugal relations. Have I covered all the points you mentioned, sir?"

Mr. Godbold's face grew pink.

"You know what this means, Mrs. Greenleaf. Mr. Greenleaf will have to sue for divorce. Let me assure you, he will have no problem with his suit or in obtaining custody. He was abandoned. It is well known that you plotted to steal away with his children when they were mere babes. Your children's welfare is not first in your mind, madam, that is evident. The court will know that you took them on a perilous journey when the eldest was barely a year old, and the youngest was still in swaddling clothes."

"I have no doubt Clay has grounds for divorce, Mr. Godbold. Let him file for it. But—and I want to make this point very clear to you and to him—if he attempts to take the girls from me, as much as I would like to keep his relations with a slave in the background, it will become a major issue."

"That is a threat."

"Call it what you will."

"But, madam, you know it's an empty threat. What proof have you? Do you have a single shred of evidence? It's folly. This ploy simply won't work."

Elizabeth chose her words with care. Mr. Godbold must understand and be able to repeat them. "If I were Mrs. Greenleaf, a simple housewife, Mr. Godbold, your point would be valid. But I'm not. I am Cassandra. I read a line of Scott's that I feel is appropriate here, sir. You would favor me by quoting it to Mr. Greenleaf: 'I will make you famous by my pen, and glorious by my sword.' I may not be good with the sword, Mr. Godbold, but I am adept with my pen."

"An empty threat. In a court of law you'll need proof."

"All battles are not won in a court of law, sir. That is your arena and I don't question your abilities there. But I know Clay. He is not unhappy that I am no longer his wife; he is unhappy because his pride has been wounded. He thinks he is a laughingstock, and he may be. That, Mr. Godbold, is the only reason he's here to claim the children. It's malice, not love. He paid them scant attention when they were born. And why? Because, dear sir, because they were born girls. Girls! He was furious with me when I didn't produce a son."

"Spare me, madam. It has nothing to do with the case."

"I think it does, sir. I think it does. I believe Mr. Greenleaf might have different instructions for you once he knows that I fully intend to fight for the children in whatever way I can. If you intend to represent him, Mr. Godbold, tell him that he may have the law on his side, both for the divorce and for the custody of the children, but if he persists, his name will be famous—or perhaps infamous—both in the North and in the South."

"There are laws against slander."

"And if he sues for slander, I may lose that suit as well, but, without my children, what kind of life will I have? It's not an empty threat, Mr. Godbold. You would serve your client well if you made the point abundantly clear. My name, once it's out in the open, and Cassandra's reputation, will bring someone from every newspaper. The word will spread—not only in my columns, but in all the newspapers in the country. Scandal always makes news, and this is more than scandal. I need not tell you, Mr.Godbold, feelings run very high in all quarters of our nation on the question of slavery. Oh, sir, you can wager your last cent safely: That scandal will attract more than enough attention. You can tell Clay that."

"I believe I understand your position, madam," Mr. Godbold said stiffly. "Is there more, or is that it?"

"That is it, Mr. Godbold. Tell him I'll not act, but I certainly will react."

Without the girls, Elizabeth could see no point in maintaining the cottage, so she moved back with her Aunt Florence. Her visits to the children were rare because of the circuitous routes she had to take to Chelmsford. She dared not be followed.

She continued her work as Cassandra. Seeing Clay and being harassed by him, reminded her of details of life in the South. Clay's visits prompted her mind even better than her journals. Ideas for new stories were endless and the identity of Cassandra continued to be a mystery. This was a surprise. She discussed it with her aunt.

"If Clay is as proud as you have painted him, Elizabeth, if it's spite because of the embarrassment he feels—"

"Of that you may be sure, Aunt Florence. It's vanity. His vanity has been wounded, his stupid southern pride."

"—then it's no wonder you've heard nothing. He doesn't want further embarrassment. Think what a laughingstock he'd be if the world knew his wife was Cassandra."

"Oh, I hope you're right. I hope that's the reason."

"He must have instructed Mr. Godbold not to say a word."

In the middle of December, 1853, Elizabeth thought about the clothing she would need for a longer stay in Chelmsford.

Christmas was a dangerous time to go there. She would be doubly watched because of the season. Clay would increase the number of Pinkerton men.

"You can't wait until Christmas Eve, dear," Miss Medlock cautioned. "Leave early. The closer we get, the more dangerous it will be."

"But I've agreed to speak. I didn't think of the Holidays. The engagements exist. The last one is only a few days before Christmas. Wait, let me get my book."

"Cancel. Wherever and whenever it is."

"I couldn't do that."

"Then you can't go to the girls for Christmas."

"I must go to Chelmsford, Aunt Florence. I want to hold them in my arms and hear all about what they've been doing—about how Mary is doing in school, and how Frannie is mastering the alphabet. Whatever the cost, I must go."

"You must not be careless, Elizabeth. Spencer can cancel for you—after you're out of town. We can't alert them in advance. I'd suggest you pack and go at once. To delay is to multiply your problems."

"I can't. I haven't shopped. I'll need presents."

"Shop in Chelmsford, child. It's not Boston, but as the poet Heywood said, 'Beggars should be no choosers.'"

Ethel tapped lightly on the door. "Beggin' your pardon, Miss. Constable Kennedy is at the door. "

"You may tell him I'll be right down, Ethel. Thank you."

As the door closed, Elizabeth said, "My Christmas present from my dear husband. He wanted it to arrive on time."

Chapter Fifty

When she returned from Chelmsford on the second day of the new year, 1854, Elizabeth made arrangements to meet with Spencer Chadwycke and his attorney to discuss the before-Christmas summons that had dampened her spirits every day of her visit with the girls.

She had been able to forget Clay when she romped with the girls in the snow, or when she told them stories at bedtime, but her return to Boston brought the return of her heavy heart. The dead snows on the cobbled streets, the filthy gutters, reminded her of the summons.

The meeting with the attorney was even more debilitating. Mr. Marquant offered no comfort. He read the law to her; he explained it. With each word her position deteriorated. They were all laws by men and for men. Women were no more than chattel, no more than a good plow horse or a fine mare. Where was justice for a woman? As Oliver Marquant cited case law, as he warned her what she might expect in court, her spirits crumbled. At last she was reduced to tears.

Spencer touched her shoulder. Neither man said a word. When the tears dried, determination began to seep back into an empty heart. "You present a bleak picture, Mr. Marquant."

"We must be realistic, Mrs. Greenleaf."

"But, it's so unfair. I've been writing about this—I've been writing about slavery for years. It's not limited to the blacks in the South, is it? Women are slaves, though no one will speak those words. If women ever realize the position they're in under the laws you cite, there will be rebellion."

"I'm sure women are not blind to the law, Mrs. Greenleaf. Our laws protect women. Women can't work. The laws makes sure men support wives and children. That's as it should be."

"Rot, Mr. Marquant, pure rot. Forgive me for being blunt." With shoulders back, she faced him squarely. "Am I—are my children—being protected? By every law you cited, I am the victim. Women don't know how unprotected they are, and they never will know until they are in a situation where they are face-to-face with it. And when that happens, Mr. Marquant, when one of us finds out how great the injustice is, we've lost the battle before it begins. Women learn of their lack of protection one-by-one, just as I have. One woman can't fight the whole battle, can she? We need a new paper, Spencer. We need one called *The Woman's Advocate*."

"You're overwrought, Mrs. Greenleaf."

"Perhaps, Mr. Marquant, but I'm not stupid. I've written about injustice. I know it when I meet it in the pathway."

"I agree, Mrs. Greenleaf, given your own circumstances, you are at a disadvantage, and that is injustice."

"Thank you, Mr. Marquant. Spencer respects you, but I wasn't sure you were the one to represent me."

"You intend to fight the action?"

"I certainly do."

"In that case, we will be with you all the way, won't we, Spencer? We had to be absolutely positive you understood the risks. If you fight it—if you do not agree to go back under your husband's roof—you could lose your children. This is a point you must understand at the outset."

"I understand it fully, sir. Clay's attorney made the point. I didn't doubt his veracity. And, even more graphically, you have made me see my hopeless position under the law. But, as I said to Mr. Godbold, I'm banking on the fact that Clay will not want the Greenleaf name dragged in the mud, that his custody threat is all bluff and bluster."

"It's a gamble, Mrs. Greenleaf."

"It is, sir, but it's a gamble I'm ready to take."

They left Boston for the rented house in Philadelphia on a cold, gray morning in February. There was Elizabeth and the two girls, Aunt Florence and the staff, which included Mrs. Duffy, the cook, and both Charles and Ethel.

Spencer Chadwycke stayed in Boston. He would come down when the trial was over. Aunt Florence made the point. "After all, dear, if there is a scandal, and there will be if Clay doesn't back down, the brush can smear the tar both ways. How would it appear if Spencer's presence were noted? I know there's nothing between you two, but what fun they'd have with the headlines: 'Husband's Dalliance Causes Wife to Flee to Arms of Publisher.'"

"You're right. We mustn't drag Spencer into this. He's done so much for me. I couldn't sully his reputation."

"I wasn't thinking of Spencer's reputation, Elizabeth. A man's peccadilloes are rarely frowned upon, but a woman must be careful. If Clay persists, you'd surely lose custody of the girls if such rumors were abroad."

The divorce and custody proceedings went badly from the beginning. Clay intended to take the children. Judge Watkins followed the letter of the law. Both the first and the second day of the hearing gave every promise of a decision for Clay. The next move was hers.

She remembered Spencer's last words to her. "What you do to Clay, my dear, is justly deserved, but it will hurt others. The girls will be drawn into it. Think it over. Those of us who love you will not think less of you if you back down."

"There will be no backing down, Spencer. If I lose the girls, I'll do all I can to ruin him."

"I only ask you to think, my dear. The choice is yours."

"Not only will I reveal his liaison with Carlotta, but I'll bend every effort to bring his world down around his ears. Without the children, I'll have only two goals: the end of slavery and the end of Clay Greenleaf."

"All right, my dear. But, if you should need someone in Philadelphia, call on Bart Driggers. He's a trusted friend. He'll see that your story has coverage. In the meantime, I've written him. He knows of your problem with Clay."

The next day Elizabeth knew it was time to talk to Mr. Driggers. Clay's smirk was even more pronounced. He was winning the custody battle, and proving to himself that Elizabeth's threats were empty puffballs. His smile was more than she could bear. When the hearing recessed for the day, she took a hack to the address Spencer had given her.

Spencer's letter had made Mr. Driggers aware of all the details. He had only one question: "Are you sure, Mrs. Greenleaf, are you really sure? Is this what you want? Once the box is opened, we can't put the demon back in."

"Very sure, Mr. Driggers. But, is it possible—" Elizabeth hesitated. She didn't know how to say it. She began again. "I'd like to give Clay one last chance to withdraw. Is it possible—could we get a story in print that would only hint at the scandal? Could we sound a warning shot? I'd like for him to be able to back down—not for his sake, but for the sake of my children."

"When scandal is in the wind, Mrs. Greenleaf, it blows in all directions. No matter how gently it may blow at first, you can't contain a zephyr."

"Could we just say," Elizabeth said, 'In an interview with Mrs. Greenleaf, the defendant in the custody action, she stated that there were valid reasons why the two children should not be given to their father. When pressed on this point, Mrs. Greenleaf would only say it would all come out in the courtroom in due time.' Couldn't that, or something like that, be printed in tomorrow's edition? If so—if he knows my intentions are still valid, perhaps he will back down."

"I can do it, sure, but it won't be the end of it. By the time you leave the courtroom tomorrow, you'll be surrounded. You'll have a hard time turning away the questions."

"You forget, Mr. Driggers, I've been turning away questions for years. As Cassandra, I've successfully kept my identity hidden. It won't be easy, but it can be done."

"As you wish, Mrs. Greenleaf. The story will be in the morning edition. I'll see to it, but you will have to be responsible for keeping the scandal hidden until you know whether or not the ruse has been successful. If Mr. Greenleaf backs down, you'll still have to fend off questions."

"Put the story in, please, Mr. Driggers."

By ten o'clock the following morning it was clear that Clay had read the story. In the hallway on a brief recess, he said, "We must talk, Elizabeth."

"If you have something to say, Clay, say it here."

"But, this is a public place."

"It's safer for me. I can't risk being slapped again."

"You bitch."

"You can be heard, Clay." She wanted him heard. She hoped her remark would sharpen the ears of all the people in the hallway. "We could walk to the window, but I will not go into one of these rooms with you, not without Mr. Marquant."

He took her arm and steered her toward the window. "The libelous stories to the paper must stop, Elizabeth."

"There will be no more stories, Clay, providing I get custody of my children. The divorce itself is a matter of no importance to me. I want nothing from you."

"They're my children as well, Elizabeth."

"You were never a father to either of them. Drop the custody action and the newspaper stories will die before they are born."

"You'd do this to the girls?"

"I'd do it to *you.* I want my children, Clay."

"I'll see you in hell first. Do your damnedest, Elizabeth. I'll take the children, you can depend on it."

There was a sharp rap on the floor. The bailiff said, "Ladies and gentlemen, please return to the courtroom. His Honor, Judge Watkins, is ready to continue."

Inside, Elizabeth saw more people than she had seen earlier. Was Mr. Driggers right? Were these people from the press? And what had they overheard? She could not remember the exact words that either had said; she only knew that Clay would not back down.

When the day was over, a cluster of men with pads and pencils surrounded Elizabeth. Mr. Marquant and Mr. Folgar pushed a pathway through the crowd. The reporters swarmed after her with questions: "What are the valid reasons, Mrs. Greenleaf?" "Why shouldn't the children be in their father's custody?" "Do you have the resources to care for them?" "What has he done?" " Should a man be deprived of his own children?" "Is this being done for spite?"

In the carriage, jolting over the cobbles, Elizabeth said,"Oh, my. That was more than I bargained for."

"Get used to it, Mrs. Greenleaf. You'll have no peace until you meet with them, but isn't that your intention?"

"Yes, Mr. Marquant, it is."

"Then, Mrs. Greenleaf, the sooner it's done the better."

Elizabeth sat quietly for a moment. Was this being willful, as her father had so often said of her? Then she spoke: "Please make the arrangements, Mr. Marquant."

"I suggest you meet with them at my hotel. Both Mr. Folgar and I will be there, but you must be ready for some pointed questions. They are little more than jackals, those newsmen, and they sniff the blood of this story."

At that moment Elizabeth felt the children slipping from her grasp. Her eyes were dry, but her heart wept. "Make the arrangements, Mr. Marquant. I'll be there."

Chapter Fifty-One

Mr. Marquant said the meeting with the reporters should take no more than fifteen minutes, but it ran well over an hour. Both of the attorneys had counseled her to tell only the bare bones of Clay's indiscretion, but that was not her intention.

Clay's action while they were still sharing a marriage bed was blatant infidelity; it defiled her marriage and her trust; it was the personification of the many shades of mistreatment that all women shared.

This was her moment. She would expose all of the injustices while she had the opportunity to be widely read in something other than her own column.

By some, Cassandra's "Echoes from the South" was considered a biased and slanted antislavery tirade, but these men, these gentlemen of the press, had no sword to hone. Her message would take on more credence because it was not written by Cassandra, because it was not in *The Black Advocate*.

The direction of the interview appalled Mr. Marquant and Mr. Folgar, but it followed Elizabeth's plan. She was experienced with an audience, even one that was cold at the outset. There was no sympathy here. She overheard whispers: "Poor bastard, he could lose his kids." She saw a man jab another fellow in the ribs and say, "A wife that looks like that and his pick of the darkies. I'd trade for either one."

They were ready for the scandal it promised to be, but she sensed the hostility that was also there. Her answers would have to ring true. Her mind took the high road. She spoke clearly. As she answered the questions, she saw the ice melting.

She knew she had them when one of their number, a small man with a sparse, untrimmed mustache asked a bold question: "What did you do to provoke your husband, ma'am? A man doesn't wander from the hearth if there's a fire there."

She heard a grumbling from the reporters. They had warmed to her, they were no longer adversarial. She was relieved. It was time for her move.

"Gentlemen, please," she said. "The question is impertinent, but I will answer it. I'm not here to hide anything from you." And then she proceeded to let them see what an innocent she had been. How, even when he was drunk and loud, even when he publicly embarrassed her, she had been a loyal and loving wife.

When she finished the detailed answer, she knew they were on her side. The stories in tomorrow's papers would roast Clay to a fare-thee-well.

Now, it was time to sink the blade into his heart; it was time to embarrass him in his own backyard. The men of the South would pay scant attention to a dalliance with a black—it might rate a joke or a snide remark at the cotton gin, but nothing more.

If she meant to hurt Clay, it could not be by something that was universal and therefore easily forgivable; it would have to be by something beyond the pale, something beyond the forgivable.

It was time to tell these gentlemen that she was the notorious Cassandra, that Mrs. Clay Greenleaf of Greenleaf Plantation, Darien, Georgia, was the author of "Echoes from the South."

"Gentlemen," she said, "I have been frank and honest. I have not avoided a question, even those that were either poorly phrased or deliberately insulting." She paused. She wanted that preamble to have an effect. "I have one more statement to make before this interview is over. I want each of you to understand why I have given such frank answers. I may have appeared bold. Many women of my age and upbringing would have fled from the room. And, it has been an ordeal for me, but I have not been offended. I gave you the story without subterfuge. There is a reason. In one sense of the word, I am one of you. I, too, am a journalist. I know the importance of getting the story—all of it."

Pencils stopped.

She dabbed at her brow with a linen handkerchief. They were quiet. "I am Cassandra." She waited. The effect was dramatic. "Some of you have read my column, 'Echoes from the South.' It appears regularly in *The Black Advocate.*"

At first there was silence. She could hear the sharp intake of breath by Mr. Marquant and Mr. Folgar. Then there was pandemonium. The reality of the situation dawned on the newsmen. This was more than titillating scandal; it was more than a white man's dalliance with his slave; this was a major story. There was a wild rush to the door. Each man wanted to get back to his newspaper. The few hacks at the door of the hotel would be snapped up quickly, and each man wanted his story to be the headline for the morning edition.

The room was empty. Only Mr. Marquant and Mr. Folgar remained. "My God! This will create more problems than we can ever solve. I dread court tomorrow. Now you've done it."

"Yes, I have, haven't I?"

Court was to begin at ten. By then, banner headlines were all over the streets of Philadelphia. The courtroom was full. The hallways were packed. Cassandra was a personality because she had been a mystery for so many years and now she was revealed. They wanted to see her, to touch her.

Elizabeth expected her meeting with the newsmen to create a stir, but this was more than she had anticipated. Four newsboys hawked the banner headlines outside the courthouse. The crowd made any movement toward the courtroom door hazardous. The remarks she overheard were mixed. Regular readers of Cassandra were supportive, but some, it was clear, thought she was a hussy, a woman who had forced her husband to face the scandal of divorce in order to protect his own children.

As the courtroom door closed behind them, Mr. Marquant said quietly, "You see what you've done, Mrs. Greenleaf. The tiger is loose. You'll be lucky if it doesn't eat you alive."

At ten, Elizabeth heard the sing-song of the bailiff, beginning with the familiar words, "All rise." Judge Watkins' face was stern. The Greenleaf divorce was no longer routine. Elizabeth had created a problem. Justice required very little thought, but this procedure had become partisan and political.

With the rap of his gavel, the proceedings began.

"The bailiff will clear the court of all persons who are unable to find seating," he said firmly. "This matter may have become a circus on the outside, but it will not be a circus in my courtroom."

The grumbles, the shifting of feet, the whispers grew louder as the people standing at the back were asked to leave. Judge Watkins picked up his gavel again and rapped it sharply. "There will be order in this court." His glance swept the room. Elizabeth felt his disdain as he paused at the table where she sat with counsel. "If we have to, we will make arrests. I will not have disorder here. Mr. Bailiff, if anyone hesitates, you will shunt him aside for booking. Do you all understand that?" The last remark was louder than the room required, and he glared at each person as he spoke.

"We're in for a bad time," Mr. Marquant said.

"Order!" His gavel echoed in the room. "Order! The talking will cease. There will be order in my court." His cold blue eyes seemed to dampen the noise. When the overflow had been ejected, he rapped his gavel again and said, "Gentlemen, you may proceed."

The next two hours were the slowest and most agonizing of Elizabeth's life. Even before the trial's close, it was clear: The fate of her children had been decided. She had sensed the loss each day of the trial, but, today it permeated the room; it hung like a shroud above her head. She was not prepared for it.

Your mind may tell you the battle is lost, that the time has arrived for the back-alley fighting, but your heart is never ready for the loss.

It was the same when Mama died. She told herself how Mama would be in the arms of Jesus; how her mother's suffering would be over. Her head knew, but when Mama sighed the last time, Elizabeth was not ready. The same empty feeling gnawed at her entrails.

She heard herself accused of not being a fit mother, because she had deliberately exposed her children to scandal; she heard herself called a wayward wife, a wife who had abandoned her husband when his fortunes were at low ebb; she heard herself described as loose, a woman who may have consorted with an overseer while still virtually a bride; she heard how she forced a young girl to go with her as a nursemaid as she stole his children from a brokenhearted father. She heard the word "objection" over and over again, and she heard the judge saying "overruled" or "sustained," but none of it had any meaning to her.

The cold feeling in the depths of her stomach grew. She could sense the ordeal was coming swiftly to a close.

At her request, Mr. Marquant had insisted upon having the divorce and custody matter heard before a jury. Elizabeth believed she would be treated more fairly if she were judged by more than one man. "I don't mean to revile men in general, or your profession, Mr. Marquant," she had said, "but Clay will try anything, even bribery. I'll feel safer if this is heard in an open court before a jury."

Mr. Marquant touched Elizabeth's arm lightly. He wanted to be sure she showed proper respect as the judge instructed the jury. She straightened her shoulders and turned her eyes toward the jury box.

"Gentlemen," she heard Judge Watkins say, "you have heard the testimony brought forth in this action. . ." Her mind let the voice fade. She heard him say, "Now, I will instruct you as to the law. . ."

His voice faded once more.

None of it was real. She sat erect, eyes unseeing, ears barely functioning. At that moment reality ceased to have a bearing. The moment was suspended, the voices in the courtroom lost meaning. It was a chorale, with sounds running the scale, with point and counterpoint, with rhythm and pattern, but with words that had no meaning.

Then it was over for the day.

"Mrs. Greenleaf," Mr. Marquant said, shaking her shoulder, "are you all right? Folgar, a glass of water. Quickly, Folgar. She seems faint."

"I'm all right, Mr. Marquant. This room is so warm, so very warm. For a minute it all seemed to go black."

"Take a sip of water, Mrs. Greenleaf." The attorney didn't like what he saw. She was pale as a specter.

He handed her the glass. "Can you hold it? Yes, you're doing fine. We will stay here for a minute, until you get to feeling better."

He watched her as she sipped the water. "We'll leave through the rear of the building, Mrs. Greenleaf. I want to avoid those vultures, but we'll wait until you are feeling able."

Elizabeth sipped the water. "I'm fine, Mr. Marquant. I just—well, I don't know how to explain it."

"We'll wait a few minutes, Mrs. Greenleaf. Let those damnable newsmen and the curious be gone before we leave." Mr. Marquant gathered his papers and put them in his satchel. "I hope you heard the judge's instructions, Mrs. Greenleaf. I am to see that you are in the courtroom tomorrow at ten. You are to bring the girls with you."

"But why? I don't want them involved in this."

"It's Judge Watkins' order, Mrs. Greenleaf. He is more than irritated with you. I would suggest we bring them."

"I don't like the sound of it, Mr. Marquant; I don't like it at all."

Chapter Fifty-Two

Two days later, Elizabeth became aware of the world around her. At first it wasn't clear and then she realized she was in the bedroom of the house Aunt Florence had leased in Philadelphia. A woman stood at the window.

"Who are you? What are you doing in my room?"

"I look after you, Miss. I'm Sarah Milgrew."

"There's nothing the matter with me. I'm fine."

"Of course you are, Miss, but you've been a bit under the weather, that's all. You just stay where you are. I'll go get Miss Medlock."

Elizabeth could hear the skirts in motion as the two ladies hurried down the hall. Aunt Florence paused at the threshold.

"Thank heaven! Oh, thank heaven!" she said. "I can't tell you how glad I am to find you with your eyes open and seeing. We've been so worried, Elizabeth."

She touched Elizabeth's forehead lightly and smoothed the hair back from her brow. "Oh, my dear child," she said, "I thank the Lord for sending you back to us."

"I'm getting out of this bed." Elizabeth swung her feet to the floor and stood up. The room and everything in it lost focus. She sank back down on the bed and fell over on the pillow. "What is this? What's the matter with me?"

"You're all right, Elizabeth. You're weak. You haven't eaten in three days, and very little before that. We tried broth, but we got precious little of it in you. Of course you're weak."

Elizabeth began to cry. She didn't know why but she couldn't stop. Sobs racked her body, even though the eye sockets were dry, spent of all their tears.

Elizabeth's eyes were closed and the sobs grew lighter and finally ceased. She slept. "Thank you, God," Aunt Florence whispered. "Stay with her, Sarah. I'll make fresh beef broth. She needs strength. If she awakens, call me."

When Elizabeth opened her eyes, she saw Sarah Milgrew. "You know me now, don't you, love?"

"Yes," Elizabeth said. "You're Sarah Milgrew."

"I am, love. I'll call your aunt."

Sarah returned with Aunt Florence and Spencer Chadwycke. "Oh," Elizabeth said. "I thought—"

"You thought I was in Boston, and I was, my dear, until I heard from Florence and Oliver."

"But I'm fine. I'm just weak for some reason."

"You've been through an ordeal, Elizabeth. The doctor says you are physically well, but your spirit was too heavily burdened. That spirit simply shut down. At least, that's how Dr. Howerton said it to me. 'A person can take just so much,' he said, 'and then the mind shuts down. It takes a holiday.' With what you've been through, Elizabeth, with Clay, and the trial, and the children—"

"The children," Elizabeth said,"I want to see them."

Florence Medlock looked quickly at Spencer Chadwycke, but she could see he had no experience to guide him, either. Their eyes came back to Elizabeth. "What is this? I saw the look that passed between you. Where are the girls? I want to see them."

Spencer Chadwycke took her hand.

"The girls are with Clay, Elizabeth. Surely you remember that?" He saw no comprehension. He tried again. "Clay has custody of the girls, Elizabeth. We'll try for a new hearing; we'll—"

"Clay took them?"

"Yes, my dear. That was the decision—"

"That bastard!"

"Elizabeth!"

"I don't care, Aunt Florence. He didn't want them; he never wanted them. He did this to punish me."

"We'll get them back, Elizabeth," Spencer said.

"What does Oliver Marquant say?"

"You're punishing yourself, Elizabeth. Don't—"

Elizabeth closed her eyes. With her eyes shut, they were all gone: Spencer, Aunt Florence, Sarah Milgrew, and the memories—memories that were just behind her eyelids, memories that refused to take shape. It was all so much better with her eyes closed.

The past returned in bits and pieces. Everything was a fragment of something larger. In time she made the pieces fit; she made a quilt top of colored bits. They formed a pattern only after she stitched them together.

One day, more than a week later, she could see it all. Everything. Her own ill-fated arrival in Philadelphia weeks before, the courtroom, the hallways, Judge Watkins, the news people, the headlines, and finally the jagged bits that made up the last day when the girls were awarded to Clay.

"Clay took them, Aunt Florence. Damn him! I was happier when I didn't know. Now I have nothing. Nothing."

"My dear child, it's not the end of the world—"

"Oh, isn't it, Aunt Florence? How would you know? How could you know?" Elizabeth's voice was cold. Florence Medlock turned to leave the room. "Oh, come back. Come back. I'm sorry, Aunt Florence," Elizabeth said. "I should never have said that."

"The famous Medlock tongue," Aunt Florence said. "It's often dipped in the acid of truth, and truth is seldom enjoyed." She paused, as though remembering something from her own past.

"You're forgiven, Elizabeth. It's something I might have said, given the ordeal you've had."

She moved closer to the bed. "My remark was gratuitous, Elizabeth, a platitude, an inane politeness. You were right. How could I know what losing a child would be? It's I who should ask you for forgiveness. And, I do. I'm sorry. I should never have said that."

"You are forgiven, Aunt Florence. Am I?"

"Shakespeare said it for us, Elizabeth, '...to thine own self be true.' That's all we're trying to do."

"He said more than that, Aunt Florence. He said, 'to thine own self be true, and it must follow, as the day the night, thou canst not then be false to any man.' He was a man, speaking as a man, Aunt Florence. Such freedom does not extend to women. If we are true to ourselves, we get into all kinds of trouble. Had I been less true to myself, I'd have been loved by my father; had I curbed my tongue to a point where I might have strangled on it, I'd have a husband; had I been a good little girl and gone back to him, I'd be permitted to stay with my children. But, I spoke my mind."

Elizabeth stopped talking, but her mind continued to churn Then she said what had been hurting her all along: "And, as Cassandra, I also spoke my mind. What has it earned for me? Think about it, Aunt Florence. The children are gone. I've been true to myself, but to what purpose?"

"I don't know, child, but I do know *I* must be my own person. That may be why I'm not married, but, when I look in the mirror, I see a woman who needn't castigate herself for being a weathercock, twisting in the wind."

"I may feel the same one day, but not today. Today I'm a woman who lost her children by her own willfulness. The price is too great."

From that day on, Elizabeth's spirits grew even weaker. She had no desire for food, no need to read or to write, no wish to see anyone, including Aunt Florence and Spencer. Her body recovered, but she would not leave her room.

Sarah Milgrew stayed on, although there was little she could do. "I want someone to be with her at all times, Sarah," Miss Medlock said. "Try to talk to her."

Spencer spent hours with Elizabeth. He told her of the new edition of *The Black Advocate*; he told her they were re-running her past columns, and that people were clamoring for new work by Cassandra. His words about the column brought a little animation, but it came and then was gone.

"Would you like to go home, Elizabeth?"

"Home? I have no home."

"I meant back to Boston, my dear. Your two experiences here in Philadelphia have been bad. I talked to Florence. We wondered if you felt well enough—" he hesitated and then went on "—well enough for a journey to Boston?"

Elizabeth looked directly at him, but she didn't seem to hear. That was something neither Spencer Chadwycke nor Florence Medlock could cope with. It frustrated them. At times both of them had felt like grabbing her by the shoulders and shaking some sense into her vapid brain. This was such a time for Spencer.

"You're being a baby, Elizabeth." He meant it to be unkind. He wanted the flint of his words to strike a spark, but she said nothing. Had she heard him? His voice took on a colder edge as he tried to bludgeon her into reality. "I can't stay here wet-nursing you, Elizabeth; I have a business that needs my attention."

"Go to Boston, Spencer."

She had heard his words. It was a response. "I need to go, my dear, but it's not essential. Eddie Dalton has the situation in hand I know, but I'd like to be there."

"Go."

"I'll stay until you can travel. When I go, I want you and Florence with me. Wouldn't you like to go to Boston?"

"I don't care, Spencer," the voice faded. "I just don't care. Please leave me alone." She turned toward him. "You pick at me; Aunt Florence picks at me. Leave me alone, both of you. Send Sarah in. At least she has the good sense to stay quiet." It was a momentary burst of spirit, but the lethargy came back.

Dr. Howerton had told Spencer the only thing they could do was to let her rest. "Let her mind come to grips with the reality around her." Spencer had mentioned the trip to Boston to him. Could she travel, or should they wait?

"It could all be over tomorrow," Dr. Howerton said, "but it could be years in coming. Melancholia is not something new to the medical profession. We have little ability to treat it."

"Could she safely travel, Dr. Howerton? Would the rigors of a trip in this miserable March weather cause further problems?"

"We don't know, Chadwycke, we just don't know. You say that once before, years ago, she had an unhappy experience in Philadelphia? That could—" Dr. Howerton stopped. His fingers rubbed at his bewhiskered face. And then he continued, as though he were thinking aloud. "It seems remote, but, yes, I believe the other experience could have an effect, especially when it is coupled with the deep loss she had while in Philadelphia this time."

Dr. Howerton stared out at the dreary Philadelphia winter. At last he turned back to Spencer.

"A trip?" He seemed to be thinking it over. "Well, yes," he said. "It might be good to get away from Philadelphia and its memories. She would have to be aware of the changes occurring. The weather itself would make her take notice. Even the rigors of the trip might be good for her. It would be a change, a decided change. You must know, Chadwycke, the room she's in and the world around her is all bleak and unchanging. That's what melancholia is, as best we understand it. Yes, Chadwycke, as I think on it, I believe taking her back to Boston might be a good idea."

Chapter Fifty-Three

The journey back to Boston was as rigorous as Spencer had hoped it would be, but it did not change Elizabeth. Rigors were external; she found reality only inside her own head.

The jolting of the carriage had no effect. She was aware of the near blizzard conditions they had encountered after leaving Philadelphia, but these things did not intrude upon her thoughts of the girls, of what might happen to them without her guidance.

Cold feet and slippery roads were not sufficient to override these agonies, especially when she knew these agonies were all of her own making.

Within her thoughts, Elizabeth had a collection of never-ending fantasies. They were a kaleidoscope—changing, shifting, vivid, and wildly real. The terror in her mind did not reflect on her face. The expression never changed. The other occupants of the carriage saw only the waxen skin, the unblinking eyes—eyes that seemed to be unaware of the physical conditions which grew steadily worse as they made their way toward New York.

Aunt Florence, Spencer, the driver and Ethel, the maid, were all beyond the metes of her inner world. They were not allowed to interfere They were no more than the winds that whipped the two carriages, the ice on the roads and the hardships that seemed to occupy the minds of her traveling companions. They were nothing to her.

She was aware of the worsening conditions, but she didn't care about the wind, the ice or the cold. She didn't care about her aunt, or Spencer or Ethel. They were a callous lot. Their own comforts, their own fears, were all they thought about. It dominated their conversation. What fools they were. She was riding in a carriage with three fools. What a commotion they made over trivial details.

These idiots didn't seem to comprehend that her girls were in the care of virtual strangers. Poor babies! How frightened they must be—in the care of slaves who could not teach them. They could grow up ignorant. Byron might help with their education, but would he be willing? Would Clay permit it? Or, would the girls be punished because of their mother?

She looked at her companions. Fools, three fools. Nothing interests them but the winds, the blowing snow, the ice and their own cold feet. Elizabeth did not consider those external things, she didn't care about them or her own discomfort. Her thoughts were with the girls.

The slippery roads, even the occasion when the carriage slipped into a ditch, could not break the chains that bound her to her two lost children. They were torn from her, just as she had seen families torn apart when slaves were taken to be traded.

For the first time Elizabeth could truly understand the anguish that eroded the tear-stained faces of the slave women whose children were being taken. This was reality; cold feet and icy roads were not.

The last half of the journey to Boston was by train. With the deteriorating weather conditions, Spencer decided the attempt to shake Elizabeth back into reality was not working. He and Florence Medlock agreed the train would give welcome protection from the stinging cold.

The blizzard passed long before they reached Boston, nevertheless, Florence Medlock was glad to be home. Elizabeth didn't care. It was warmer in her room with a coal fire in the grate, but nothing took her mind off the girls except sleep. Sleep had become a friend.

Florence Medlock had Dr. Beardsley in to see Elizabeth. He pronounced her physically fit, just as Dr. Howerton had done in Philadelphia. He, too, used the word melancholia. He prescribed an herbal tea, but nothing else. "Time is the healer, Miss Medlock. Let her sleep. At least when she is sleeping, she is at peace."

But this was not altogether true. Florence Medlock had heard Elizabeth when she slept, both in the daylight hours and at night. Sleep may be a salvation, but it did not always bring peace. Elizabeth must still be in turmoil. How else could you explain the moans, the cries of anguish and the tears?

More than a month had passed since their return to Boston. It was now late April. Someone was always with Elizabeth: Florence Medlock or Ethel or Ethel's daughter, Lucy. In the afternoons, Spencer would arrive. From the first day after their return, Spencer made it a practice to stay with Elizabeth from three to five every day of the week.

On occasion, Florence Medlock listened at the door. There was always talk in Elizabeth's room, but most of it was Spencer. He gave Elizabeth a report of the day; he told her of the latest gossip; he described each new issue of *The Black Advocate*, but he got few replies. Elizabeth's answers were monosyllabic at best.

Spencer Chadwycke was undaunted. "She hears me and understands me, Florence, I know she does," he said. "One day I'll say something that will arouse her. What will it be? It's like trying to awaken Sleeping Beauty."

In the first week in May, Spencer arrived at three in the afternoon, as he always did. He had a copy of *The Advocate* in his satchel, along with two of the Cassandra columns they were planning to rerun. He also had a letter from Clay, sent in care of *The Advocate*.

"I have some interesting things today, Elizabeth, and I want your approval on the squib I've written to go with the rerun of your columns." She heard him; there was a slight wave of her hand. "And I have a letter to you from Clay—I think it must be from Clay—there is s large G on the seal." He watched her as he spoke. He had her attention. She had not moved, but there was something about the eyes, a light, a flicker. Spencer was sure she was ready to listen.

"Do you want to read it, Elizabeth—" he waited. When there was no reply, he said, "—or shall I?"

"Read it," she said. He could barely hear her.

He broke the seal. The impression in the red wax was elaborate and handsome. With his penknife he carefully slit the envelope. Elizabeth watched. Spencer could see that she knew the seal and the handwriting, but she made no effort to take the letter or read it.

"You should read it, Elizabeth. It may be personal."

"Read it," she said, this time in a clearer voice.

He began: "*Elizabeth,*" it said, without salutation, "*after your behavior in Philadelphia, we have nothing more to say to one another, but for the sake of the girls, I have a proposition to make to you. If you will stop writing Cassandra, if you will withdraw all the columns you have written in the past, if you cease all anti-South rhetoric and renounce your affiliations with all the anti-South organizations, I will permit you to meet with the girls, once a year, for a one-week period. This meeting will be in Philadelphia at Aunt Mattie's house. You will find accommodations nearby, and you will be permitted to visit each morning and afternoon for two-hour periods. This, of course, will be under the strict supervision of Aunt Mattie, who has graciously consented to the arrangement.*

"*You profess to love the girls. If you do, you will readily abide by the terms of this arrangement. After all you have done, I am being more than generous in making this offer, but it is my last. I am keeping a copy of my letter, and if the terms are not accepted at once, be assured our daughters will see for themselves how much you love them. I will show them this letter, just as soon as they are old enough to comprehend it—"*

"The bastard. The bloody bastard."

"That's becoming your favorite word, Elizabeth. I'm glad Florence didn't hear it this time."

"Aunt Florence knows," she said in a firmer voice. "There is no other word for him. He is a bastard, a bastard, a bastard." As she spoke her voice trailed off.

"There's more, Elizabeth. Shall I read the rest?"

Her hands were first to move. They gripped the arms of the rocking chair she liked to sit in when she was not in bed. The muscles of her arms tightened. At last, sitting straight in her chair, her eyes flashing fire, she said, "There is no need to read the rest, Spencer, I have already made up my mind."

"Do nothing in haste, my dear."

"Haste? Do you call this haste? I've had nothing else on my mind. I must have known what I had to do, but I couldn't find the mettle for it. Well, I have it now. He is a bastard, and I would shout it from the rooftops if I could, but since that way is not open to me, I'll use the only one that is."

She turned to look at Spencer for the first time since his arrival. "You've been wanting a new column from Cassandra, Spencer. Well, you shall have it. I'll send it tomorrow morning before ten. And, it will be a scorcher. Now, Spencer dear, clear out of here. I have work to do. I have a column to write."

"But—"

"No buts, please, Spencer. I have work to do, and I can't do it if you stay here to tell me who was seen with whom. The gossip you bring is delicious, but it can wait. Now out with you."

He gathered his papers together and walked toward the door. "And, Spencer, if you will, please go by the kitchen. Tell Mrs. Duffy I'll be needing a pot of tea—hot, strong tea."

Chapter Fifty-Four

The following morning at ten Elizabeth dispatched the first of the new Cassandra columns to Chadwycke & Company.

A few minutes before twelve, Spencer Chadwycke came to the house. "I received the manuscript, Elizabeth, and, as usual, it's good, but—"

"'But,' Spencer, you said, 'but.'"

"But, my dear, "Echoes from the South" has changed. You've change it. I'm not sure your readers are ready for the new Cassandra."

"You underrate my readers, Spencer dear. Shall I show you the correspondence admonishing me for not going after those rascals with more vengeance? My readers are an informed lot, but if you're timid, I could find another publisher."

"Don't take your pique out on me, Elizabeth. I know how you feel. I share those feelings, but—"

"There! I heard it again. I heard you say 'but.'"

"I only meant, my dear, you have not dipped your pen into politics this heavily in the past. It's dangerous, and, it's a new avenue for you. Perhaps you should—"

"Shall I quote the man who helped me get started with my writing, the man who gave Cassandra the courage to speak? You were that man, Spencer. You said, 'What I like about your writing, Mrs. Burnside, is its purity. You speak of the South with authority. You know it first-hand, and you say it with a minimum of words. You speak it honestly, and that's the way the reader will perceive it.' That's what you said, Spencer. You gave me the courage to think I might make a difference. And now—I'm not sure what I'm hearing now, Spencer. Are you saying it would be wise to be a little less honest? And, if I were to be, wouldn't the reader perceive that as well?"

He had to admit, her words were too accurate.

"I'm sorry, Elizabeth," he said. "I simply thought the politics of slavery might somehow hurt your effectiveness. But, since you use my own words to chastise me, I'll concede I was in error. What I said then was true. It's your honesty that makes you effective. If that includes politics, so be it."

"The system in the South must end, Spencer. Slavery must go. The sooner the better. When I first started writing, slavery was a slow-bleeding wound in our country, but now it bleeds freely. When will the loss of blood be too much?"

Spencer didn't try to stop her. Elizabeth was herself again. Pray God that it will last. He just listened.

"Now, there's a new force emerging," she said. "The new Republican party is the one to watch. It's not effective enough—not for me—but it does propose at least to put a cap on slavery. The new Republicans, God bless them, are a group without cohesion, but watch them. They're better than the mealy-mouthed Whigs who don't want to offend anyone, or the Northern Democrats who are, if you could look into their hearts, either pro-slavery, or willing to abide it."

"It's a political as well as a social problem."

"I can't keep politics out of what I write, not now."

"I've conceded, my dear."

Elizabeth did not listen to his words. She was prepared for his sure objection. She'd given the bad situation a good deal of thought. She had a point to make, and nothing could stop her.

"The situation in the Kansas territory grows worse, and what is President Pierce doing? He shilly-shallies, hoping no one will press him into a corner. Mark my words, when his true colors show, he'll knuckle under to the South. And, Henry Clay's

Compromises aren't worth a grain of sand. He may have meant well, but, in the end, they were pap, pure pap, and nothing more."

She was right, and he knew it. "That's true, Elizabeth. The situation is serious, and Franklin Pierce is not going to allay it. I apologize for trying to change your mind. I'd have had more luck going to the entrance to Boston harbor trying to stop the tide."

This time she heard him. She stopped and smiled. "When you are sensible, Spencer, you can be such a dear. And, since you are being sensible now, and, since you are here at noon, perhaps I can persuade you to stay for lunch. If you accept, I'll have another column for you to take back. But you must know, my dear Spencer, it is a column larded with politics. It's completed, except for the final copying. This column tells our befuddled President what he ought to be doing in Kansas."

"Please remember, Elizabeth, people are afraid of war. What you write could be thought of as sedition."

"It should be thought of as honest. Everyone has the right to speak. I may not be permitted to vote, but the government can't seal my mouth or dry my pen.".

"You're going to be the death of one or both of us—"

"Not likely. We're both such sinners that we'll have to stay around for years, trying to atone. Papa still can't believe I'm divorced, or that I'd be a party to the pillorying of Clay. I'm told the papers in New York were full of it. He has little hope for the salvation of my soul. But, enough of this. Will you stay to lunch? I'll avoid politics."

Elizabeth's recovery from the shock of losing her children started with Clay's letter, but it was not given credence by either Spencer or Aunt Florence. They had seen her rally, only to slump back into the mire of depression.

By the time she had completed her third piece, she decided to enlarge her own personal battle against slavery.

Since the divorce, the identity of Cassandra was well

known but, she decided, when speaking, the black attire, the weeds of mourning, would stay. They were still appropriate. She was in mourning for her children and for the nation.

Two hours later she was in the offices of Chadwycke & Company. She asked to meet with both Spencer and Edward Dalton. Dalton saw to the coffers of the company. Elizabeth wanted to be sure that her plans were financially sound.

"I'm glad you could both be here," she said. "I don't know who handled my speaking engagements in the past—"

"I did, Mrs. Greenleaf," Edward Dalton said. "Spencer concerns himself with the writing end of it."

"Then it's to you I speak, Edward. I've decided that I'm ready for the fray. In the future, I want to accept every possible engagement—every single one. I have things I must say, and the more people I can talk to, the better."

"Well," Spencer said, quietly clearing his throat, "I believe you should begin the speaking engagements slowly, Elizabeth. Being before an audience has always taken a lot of your strength."

"I'm well, Spencer. I'm full of vitality. I've rested a long time—perhaps too long. The men of this nation are never going to say what must be said—at least, not those in politics. Cassandra is ready to speak bluntly, and she is ready to say it to anyone who will listen."

"But, you can wear yourself out—"

"No more 'buts,' please, Spencer. You persist in using the word. My path is clear. There are things I must do. I'm sick to death of our so-called leaders and their mealy-mouthed ways. I should have spoken out when the Kansas-Nebraska Act was passed in our miserable Congress several years ago. I can't rectify the past. Perhaps I can't put the torch to anyone else, but I can fire up my own resolve. For twenty years the question of extending slavery was at least restrained by the Missouri Compromise. The unbridled presidential ambitions of Stephen Douglas and the self-interest of Southern Democrats has gutted the

Missouri Compromise. It wasn't only the Southern Democrats; there were more than a few right here in Boston who preferred trade at whatever cost. Now, of course, slavery is on the move in Kansas. It's close to a civil war out there. It's scandalous. Vote trading on the floors of Congress. Vote trading! It's in the open. The shenanigans in Washington may not be illegal, but they are immoral."

"We understand your desires, don't we, Edward? We agree with all you want to do. But, are you physically able?"

"Who should be the judge of that? Neither of you know how I feel, what I can do." She looked directly into Spencer's eyes until he looked away. She turned to young Edward Dalton. "And you, Edward, have you anything to say?"

"What do you want from us, Mrs. Greenleaf? We didn't know of these plans. It's all new to us. You've had time to think it through. Suppose you tell us what you have in mind."

"Thank you, Edward. I can now see why Spencer finds you indispensable. You're right. I have thought it through—I've had months for that. I do have plans. One of them involves you, Edward."

"I'll do anything I can, Mrs. Greenleaf."

"I'd like for you to arrange a tour. Line up speaking engagements—one, two or three a day in the larger cities, whatever is possible. I want to go to every state even remotely anti-slavery, all of them. The East, of course, and the other abolitionist states, all the way to Illinois—"

"But 'Echoes from the South' has only a few columns on hand, not enough—"

"Not a problem, Spencer. Edward will schedule the engagements, he will know how long it will take. Before I leave, you'll have enough columns to cover my absence."

"Such arrangements will take time—several weeks."

"That time will be productive. I'll write for Chadwycke & Company, of course, and I'll write for other publications. You do have requests, don't you, Spencer?"

"Yes, my dear. You'll be over your head in work, if that's what you want."

"It is. It's exactly what I want. Since Clay has taken my children, I'll use my time to rip down his precious South. It's evil." She paused a moment to contemplate those changes, then she continued, "And, Edward, please arrange for as many close-by speaking engagements as you can while we wait for the tour to begin. I'll use this fallow period for writing and for preparing myself for the world out there."

She was rushing ahead too fast for Spencer. "We will both help with your plans, Elizabeth," he said, "but with one proviso: If this gets to be too much, you are to tell us. If you agree to that, we will give you full cooperation. Won't we, Edward?"

Spencer Chadwycke waited for Edward Dalton's nod of assent. "But, Elizabeth—and this is the essence of it—you must, at the first signs of fatigue, allow us to alter the schedule. Will you agree to that?"

"I will. It's a fair bargain, but don't think it will happen, don't expect me to tire. I have much to do. Our country is in serious trouble—our Union could fall apart from the pressures that rip at its seams, and most of that comes from slavery. To go on as we are will only prolong its agonies. The gored flesh already bleeds too freely."

It was more than a month before the arrangements for the tour were completed. Elizabeth wrote from early morning until time to leave for her speaking engagement. There was venom in her pen. Every article contained a political message, even though it was cleverly hidden.

Elizabeth continued to wear the black dress, gloves and hat—Cassandra's trademark—but the veils were gone. She still told of slavery and plantation life, but with something added—now there were political shadings carefully inserted into her talks. On the platform, Elizabeth dared not directly speak her mind on all subjects, so she played a little game with herself. She found clever ways to bury her ideas into something that seemed anything but political. She planted the seed without appearing shrill.

In her writing, she was more direct. Experience had taught her that the double standard would not allow her to speak her mind as a man could—not from the platform. But, in her writing she could say it. It was her opinion that her *nom-de-plume* allowed her to be much more open than she could have been if she used her own name.

It was unfair. But, righting that kind of double standard was not her mission of the moment. For now, she must content herself with causing enough public furor to alter the conditions existing in the South.

And then at last, the long-planned for tour began. City by city, Elizabeth appeared to grow stronger as she worked through her busy schedule of talks. With each meeting, the essence of what she had to impart crystallized even more. She hit hard at the evils of slavery and the South, and she was gratified to find that people were more concerned now than she had ever seen them. She hoped she was a part of the growing awareness of what must be done. The question of slavery was causing talk of "marching down there and doing something about it," just as Aunt Florence had predicted years ago.

Each appearance added to the success of the last. She was having a truly wonderful effect. They were listening.

The speaking tour that had started on a crisp day in mid-June was now near its terminal point in Peoria, Illinois. From there, she would drop south to Springfield, and then begin an easterly course back to Boston.

As the carriage approached the city, Elizabeth reviewed the itinerary. She would stay with the Bradford Whites in Peoria and make talks at Eureka, Farmington and Elmwood.

Her hostess in Peoria, Hannah White, was a smiling, big-bosomed woman who seemed to exude starch and cleanliness.

"Come on in, child. Let me show you to your room. I know how you must feel with all the grime of the road on you. Its been dusty here. We just haven't had enough rain. Not even enough to dampen the roads. It won't be doing the harvest any good, I can tell you. Come along now. Brad, please ask Hascal to bring Mrs. Greenleaf's trunk up. The front bedroom."

At the top of the stairs stood a man waiting for them to ascend. Elizabeth, listening to the chatter of Hannah White, had not seen him standing there.

She caught her breath when she looked up for the first time into the face of Jonathan Rigby.

Chapter Fifty-Five

"Mr. Rigby!" Elizabeth gasped. The horror of the encounter in the barn swept over her.

"Oh, do you two know each other?"

Mr. Rigby was calm. "Yes, Mrs. White. We've met."

"But, I thought you were from inland Georgia, Mr. Rigby. I understood Mrs. Greenleaf lived on the coast."

"I live upriver from Greenleaf Plantation, Mrs. White. Years ago I managed rice fields on the coast. That was before Mrs. Greenleaf came there to live, but I had the pleasure of meeting her before I moved upriver."

"You know each other. How delightful. We had no idea."

Elizabeth had managed to recover from the shock.

"Mr. Rigby and my husband have business together, Mrs. Greenleaf," Mrs. White said. "He's been a visitor here before. When I volunteered to have you, I didn't know he would be coming again. I was a little worried by it, even though the house is large enough, but now—now that the two of you know each other—I consider it a fortunate happenstance. It's like a reunion—though, possibly, you're not on the same side on the question of abolition."

"I know nothing of Mr. Rigby's politics, Mrs. White," Elizabeth said. "My interest is in keeping the Union whole."

"We share that interest, Mrs. Greenleaf."

"I'm pleased to hear it, sir."

"If you ladies will excuse me, I'll be on my way."

"Of course," Mrs.White said. She turned to Elizabeth. "Come along, dear. I know you'd like to wash up and maybe change into something more comfortble."

As Elizabeth followed Hannah White to the bedroom, her mind was filled with the terror of her situation. Rigby had worn the same half-smiling leer that she had encountered at Greenleaf Plantation.

She would have to be careful for the next three days. She must not, under any circumstances, be alone with Jonathan Rigby. But, she reasoned, if this stop on the itinerary is anything like the others, there will always be a crowd, little clutches of people after every talk. On other occasions, when she was weary from the rigors of speaking, she had resented the crowds who kept her from the rest she needed, but not tonight. Tonight she would welcome them.

Then she thought of the lock. She had stayed in places where the locks were flimsy—a twisting wooden button or a hook and eye. Surely not here, she thought. This grand house should have good locks. It was a large brass lock, mounted on the inside of the door, a lock that turned a tumbler, sending a rod with a heavy brass bolt into a brass-lined hole in the floor and a brass receptacle mounted above the door. She touched it. Thank God.

Elizabeth and Hannah White dined alone. Mr. White and Rigby had been delayed. They would meet the ladies at the farmer's union hall. Elizabeth did not know if she could keep from showing her loathing of Rigby, but he was a guest, as she was, and good manners demanded that she make the best of it.

She longed to tell Hannah White about Rigby, but there was no opportunity. Mrs. White was full of questions and the conversation was never intimate enough—the feeling between the two women never warm enough—to permit Elizabeth to tell the truth about Rigby. So it never happened.

"Will Hascal be driving us?"

"He'll hitch up for me, but I'll drive." Elizabeth turned. "You seem surprised. Women out here in Illinois frequently drive—"

"Oh, I didn't mean that. I've driven—not a buggy, but a cart—although not for ages."

"I don't mind telling you, dear," Hannah White said, "I just couldn't do the work you do. I feel as you do about slavery—the thoughts of it just tears me up inside—but I just couldn't go around making talks. I'd be terrified."

"It terrifies me, too, Mrs. White, but there's a real danger of the Union coming apart, all because of slavery. The idea of human beings being bought and sold like beasts of the field revolts me. Little by little—and much faster recently it seems to me—it's undermining our country. How slavery could have started here in a land settled by people seeking freedom is more than I can fathom. I must speak out, especially now that my girls have been taken from me. Without the writing and the speaking, I believe I would go quite mad."

"Come, dear, get your shawl and your case. Hascal is at the door with the buggy. We'd best be on our way."

All the seats were taken at the farmer's union hall. Elizabeth's talk was going well. She knew it was dangerous to speak of the situation in the adjacent territories. Emotions were on the ragged edge because of the slavery question in that newly-settled region, but she also knew she must speak out. These times called for forceful words. She felt it at every stop. The nation was fragmenting.

There was strong sentiment against slavery here in Illinois, but she sensed a fear of trying to quell it. Strong and powerful words were required because of the lawlessness and turmoil in adjacent Kansas. President Pierce would say nothing, so she must.

Then it was over. She heard the applause and saw people coming toward her. There were always questions. If she had not made the point in her talk, she had to explain the black dress, gloves and hat, but she tried to remember to speak of it. Being in mourning for the Union was such a good line.

Hannah White pushed her way through the cluster of women. At last she was close enough to speak. "Excuse me please, Betty Ann," she said, addressing the woman who had Elizabeth's attention."I know you're anxious to talk to Mrs. Greenleaf, but there's something I must tell her. It's urgent."

She took Elizabeth's hand. "Mrs. Greenleaf, I'm sorry. I've just had word, My sister has taken ill. I must go to her."

"Of course, Mrs. White. I'll go with you."

"No, Mrs. Greenleaf, it wouldn't be fair. These ladies have been anxiously awaiting your arrival. They should not be deprived of the chance to talk to you. Please stay. Mr. Rigby will see that you get home. Brad has spoken to him. He'll be happy to drive the buggy for you."

"Oh, no."

"He doesn't mind, Mrs. Greenleaf. He'll be happy to see you back to the house." She turned. "I must go."

From that moment on Elizabeth was operating on two levels of consciousness. Her mind was filled with terror, but she looked serene. Her answers, her discourses on plantation life, were quiet and coherent, but fear gripped her entrails.

When the questions slowed, she usually seized the opportunity to bring the session to a close with a stock statement she had devised. This time, she made no effort to end the questions. She needed every minute to forestall the ride home with Rigby.

She had no solution to this dire situation; there was no reason not to accept a ride home with such a fine gentleman as Rigby appeared to be.

When there were only three people left, three she had already spoken to, he stepped forward. "Are you ready to be taken home, Mrs. Greenleaf? I've brought the buggy around to the front."

He turned, addressing the others. "We'll be going," he said, "unless you folks have something further."

"Oh, no," an older lady in blue said, "she's already been delayed too long. She's been most gracious. "Take this poor child home, sir. After traveling all day, she still came here tonight to be with us. She must be at the end of her tether."

"I'll stay until all the questions have been answered."

"You've done that, child. Now, run along. It'll be late before you get any rest. On with you." Elizabeth made no move to go. "Shoo, shoo. Let this nice gentleman take you home."

There was nothing she could do. "Good night to you all. You have been a most responsive and gratifying audience. I thought I might get a little dissension when I spoke unkindly of your Mr. Stephen Douglas, but there was only a murmur. Perhaps his courting of the Southern Democrats, his sponsorship of the repeal of the Missouri Compromise, was not the political bonanza he thought it would be."

"Mrs. Greenleaf, I know how much this issue means to you," Mr. Rigby said, "but you can speak of it in detail when you are in Elmwood tomorrow."

"I'm not tired, Mr. Rigby."

The lady in blue spoke again. "You may not feel tired, my child, but you've had a day. Now, go get the rest you deserve."

Rigby took her arm and directed her toward the door.

They followed the last few buggies from the farmer's union hall toward the main road back to town. When Rigby turned left instead of right, Elizabeth had a moment of terror, but she knew of her own inability to remember directions so she tried to calm her rapidly beating heart.

As they rode on, the thought nagged at her. The road back to town was to the right. Finally, she could stand it no longer.

"Mr. Rigby," she said, "I thought we turned right to go back to town."

"That's one way, but Brad showed me a way to avoid Main Street, and, from the farmer's union, it's actually closer."

Elizabeth did not reply. The silence between them was foreboding. The only sounds were the night noises of summer, and the crunch of the iron-rimmed wheels on the gravel of the roadway.

A late moon rimmed the horizon.

"Well," Rigby said, "I'm glad to have a little light. The lamps on this buggy are a poor excuse." Elizabeth made no reply. "You're very quiet, Mrs. Greenleaf. It's a noticeable change from all you had to say at the meeting."

Elizabeth said nothing. She only wanted the safety of her room at the Whites' house and the comfort that big brass lock would give her.

Rigby appeared relaxed and impersonal. His demeanor only added to her fear. She had not forgotten the look he had given her earlier in the day at the top of the stairs; she had not forgotten how he had been thwarted at Greenleaf, and that he could be rough. She glanced at him quickly.

"Do you like what you see, Elizabeth?" My God, she thought, it's no longer Mrs. Greenleaf. "Yes, my dear," he continued, "I saw you take a look. I saw that look the first time when I met you in Darien, when Clay brought home his bride. You thought I was handsome then, and you do now."

Now, she was truly frightened, but she dared not show it. "Mr. Rigby, turn this buggy around. I don't care if it is the long way, I want to go home through town, the way Mrs. White brought me. Turn around and take me home now, or—"

"Or what, Elizabeth?"

"Mr. Rigby, take me home without any further delay."

"I have a score to settle first, my dear."

"Lay a hand on me, sir, and I'll have you horsewhipped.

"Oh, will you now? You who paled at the sight of Racy's lashing? You're going to have me horsewhipped?"

"I will." She spoke clearly and firmly. "I promise you, I will. Take me back now, Mr. Rigby. Now!"

"I like to see a little spirit in a filly."

There was a clearing ahead. She could see it in the moonlight. "You can turn around right there, Mr. Rigby. I want to be taken home. Please, turn around."

"Oh, now it's 'please,' is it? Your tone changed, Elizabeth. Not enough, but it did change. I'll pull the buggy to one side, but we're not ready to turn around—not yet. We have some talking to do, you and I."

He entered the clearing she had seen, but he drove on beyond the patch of moonlight into a clump of trees. "This is more private, my dear. We'll have our little talk."

"Mr. Rigby, I implore you, don't do anything we'll both regret for the rest of our lives. Take me home, I beg you."

"Oh, now the high and mighty Mrs. Clay Greenleaf begs. Much better, my dear. You're not begging for the right thing, but you will. All in good time. Before we think of going, I want to recall the old times—the day in the barn when that damned pickaninny came hunting for you. As I remember it, Elizabeth, the struggle was beginning to subside. Then Tess arrived. You wanted me. Your body leaned into mine. We'll try again. You may say no, but you won't fight long."

Rigby touched her shoulder. She jerked backward. "Take me home, Rigby. Take me home right now, or—"

"Or, you'll get out and walk?"

"Yes, by thunder, that's just what I'll do," she said. By the time she had dismounted, he was out of the buggy and in front of her. He jerked her to him. His beard scratched her face and then his lips were on hers—not the lips of a lover, but the slobbering lips of a man gone wild.

Elizabeth wrenched free. "No you don't, my lady. Not so fast. You're here at my pleasure and far from the nearest house. The choice of what is done—and when—is not yours; it's mine. There's no loud-mouthed pickaninny this time."

She jerked free again. She felt a jacket button pull loose. He pulled her back. "If you don't want your widow's weeds torn to hell, Lizzie, you'd better take them off—now!"

"I will not."

"Won't you? We'll see. He drew back his fist. With one short jab, he knocked the breath out of her. She fell. Her body ached. At last she got a small amount of air into her lungs. "You bastard," she muttered. "You bastard."

"And I'm looking for a bitch, a bitch in heat. Can you fill the bill, or do you want another punch?"

"I'll be black and blue, Mr. Rigby. And, I will show those bruises. You truly will be horsewhipped."

"Oh yes, back to the whipping. That's a good idea, Lizzie. Perhaps I should take the buggy whip to you. Perhaps it will make you come to your senses."

"It will leave marks, Mr. Rigby. You can't afford that."

"I can afford to do anything I damned well please. You're not dealing with Clay, Elizabeth. You're dealing with a man now. I'll do anything I damn well please. There will be no marks on your face—just on your body, and you won't show that. You'll be too ashamed to show that. The truth is, you'll show nothing, you'll tell nothing—not to anyone. You will either enjoy your little walk in the woods with me, or you won't, but you won't discuss it. I know your kind. You won't say a word. Now, take your clothes off."

"I certainly will not. I will not!"

"What will it be? A jab in the gut or the whip?"

"You wouldn't dare!"

"Save it. I'm not impressed with your southern-lady talk. Get those ugly black clothes off—now! Your widow's weeds, you call them. You're in mourning for the Union! Such bullshit. You're trying to interfere with the way we live. It won't happen; we won't let the likes of you spoil it." Rigby punched her with the butt of the whip. "Get those goddamned clothes off, or while I'm in a rage I'll beat you to a pulp. Did you hear me? Take them off. Now!" As he spoke he broad-handed her below the breastbone. Gasping, she fell to the ground. "Get up, damn you, and get those clothes off."

Rigby walked over to where she was lying, trying desperately to get her breath. He nudged her with the toe of his boot, and when she didn't respond quickly enough, he kicked her in the ribs. "I'm through playing, Lizzie. Get it through your head. Get up and get those clothes off, or I'll beat the shit out of you and rip them off."

She got to her feet. Her ribs ached and her stomach was a mass of pain. She started with the buttons on her jacket. "You are smart enough to know when it's over, aren't you, Lizzie? Your campaign against the South is over, too."

He watched the jacket fall to the ground, and then the skirt. "You and those Northern rabble-rousers are fighting a lost cause. Right now, while you're in Illinois trying to undermine the South, I'm here buying guns."

She stopped undressing. "Surprised, are you? Hannah White may be ready to free the slaves, but Bart don't give a damn one way or the other. He's out to make the dollar. He can get guns, and I have money. It's business with Bart. In a short time, we'll have another shipment on the way to our friends in Kansas. The influence of the South is spreading. Slavery is good for the South; it'll be good for the West, too. They're going to need cheap labor. We showed them how it's done. The South blazed the trail. There may be a few in Kansas who don't want slavery, but we'll kill a couple, and the rest will tuck tail."

Elizabeth had stopped undressing. Rigby was lost in his own thoughts, but he sensed her lack of movement.

"Get'em off, Lizzie. All of them. That corset, those lace-trimmed bloomers—everything. I want to see you in the flesh. I've waited a long time for this, and I don't intend to settle for half measures."

She hesitated. He wanted her to stand naked in the moonlight. Would that be the end of it? Fear chewed at her stomach. "Get'em off, Lizzie." She didn't move. He stepped closer and gave her a strong jab below the ribs. The pain and the loss of breath brought the reality to her situation.

His eyes were on her, but still she hesitated.

His arm moved toward the buggy whip."Don't slow down, Lizzie," he said, and the whip struck her across the buttocks. "Get'em off." The whip struck again. She quickly removed the last few garments.

"Much better. And, my love, aren't you something to see? Moonlight dappling your body. A forest nymph. Dance for me."

"I can't dance, Mr. Rigby."

"You will call me Jonathan, my love, Jonathan, sweet Jonathan. And you will dance! You'll go to that patch of moonlight yonder, and you'll dance. Take the pins out of your hair. I want to see you wild and free." She didn't move. "Shall I teach you the steps, my love? Shall I use the whip?" As he spoke, the whip grazed her thigh, and the back stroke brought a flash of pain to the opposite calf. She moved. Perhaps it was not a dance, but she moved. "That's it, love. You know how to dance. Get out there. Dance for me."

He raised the whip. She skipped into the moonlight clearing. As Elizabeth danced, making up the steps as she went along, she could not see Rigby. He was in the shadows of the grove of trees. She knew he was watching. She thought of running. But, where would she go? If she tried the road, he would surely find her. Then the beating would be done in earnest. Where do you run when you are naked?

She danced for him, and she wept for herself.

"You may quit dancing now, my love. I'm bored with it, though it was a pretty sight—one very few men have ever seen. Come back in here. I have more ideas of what a pagan night should be."

She continued dancing. "Don't make me use the whip again, Elizabeth. Come in here, now! And, I want to see a young woman who is eager for her man. Don't come in here sniveling. Wipe your eyes, and come to the man you first looked at with something close to lust. Come to the man who is ready to return your lust." She heard the snap of the whip. She stopped, wiped her eyes and walked to the trees.

She didn't see him. It was dark under the trees. Gradually her eyes adjusted. He was naked, sprawled on a bed of moss at the foot of a large tree. She saw his white skin and the dark hair of his body. She stopped.

"This way, my dear. Come lie with me."

"Mr. Rigby," she said, "this has gone far enough. You have embarrassed me, you have humiliated me, you have repaid me for whatever insult you feel I may have caused. Put your clothes on, please. I promise you I will never tell a soul of this incident, so you'll be perfectly safe. I have been properly chastened, Mr. Rigby."

She did not see his arm move, but she felt the sting of the whip. It lashed around her waist and the tip of it dug into the flesh of her breast on the other side. "You will call me Jonathan, and you will come over here and kneel before me. Your hands will caress my body. You will lean forward to kiss my lips. You will let your breasts lightly skim my chest. You will tell me that you love me—that you love me—that you love me." His lips were wet with spittle, his voice trailed off.

This is a madman, she thought. He uses a whip, he hits me with his fists, and then talks of love. He is both mad and dangerous. For the first time she wondered if she were going to be able to escape with her life. He would fly into a rage with no provocation. Foolish tears streaked her face.

She felt the whip again. He struck her from the right and then from the left. He was not just teasing with the whip. She felt warm blood run down her belly. "Get over here." The whip struck again.

She moved toward him. She saw him lean back, content that she was obeying. The whip was out of sight. She kneeled. Her fingers touched his chest. She saw his eyes close.

"Tell me you love me, Lizzie. Call me Jonathan, sweet Jonathan. Call me lover..."

Chapter Fifty-Six

Elizabeth remembered little of the ride back to town, but she was aware of a change in Rigby. That change began the moment they both had their clothes on. He didn't speak on the way back to Peoria, but at the front door he was calling her Mrs. Greenleaf once again, not Lizzie. His voice was unnaturally loud.

"I'll see to the horse, Mrs. Greenleaf, if you're sure you can manage getting to your room in the dark."

"I can manage, Mr. Rigby, thank you."

It was incredible. Her voice was as calm and stilted as his. They spoke to be overheard, not for each other.

Once inside her room, she turned the heavy brass lock, stumbled to the bed and began to cry. Only now that she was safe could she begin to think of the horror of the past hour.

Reality was slow in coming but as time passed, maybe for the first time in her life she truly knew the meaning of humiliation and degradation. I'd like to kill him, she thought. The idea of shooting him helped to allay her shame.

She saw the whole scene again. He taunted her, slapped her, whipped her, and knocked the wind out of her body, but this time it was different, at least in her mind. This time she managed to reach into her reticule and pull out a derringer. As he approached, eyes shining, mouth heavy with spittle, she shot him once. A dark red stain appeared on his white shirt. He reached for her as he stumbled and fell.

But, that was not the way it had happened. Dreams of what might have been were soon shunted away by reality. She knew the truth; she knew the horror. But, I will get a gun, she thought. I must get one. I will not continue this tour without one.

When the weeping was spent and the tears ran dry, she let practicality seep back into her bones. She was alive. There had been more than one time when she was not sure he would permit her to live to tell the tale. But, I am alive, she thought, and I *will* tell.

She got up, removed her clothing, and hung them. Then with the provided china pitcher and bowl, she tried to wash the horror of the night from her body.

Bradford and Hannah White did not return until ten o'clock the next day. Mrs. White knocked. "Are you awake?"

"Do come in, Mrs. White. Yes, thank you; I've been up for hours. I've been writing letters."

That was a lie. She had been awake; she had been at the window; she had watched the dawn, but she had been careful not to unlock the door. Why did she lie? Why didn't she tell Mrs. White what had happened?

"I'm sorry, Mrs. Greenleaf, but I must trade you off to another hostess. My sister is no better. We were there all night, Mr. White and I, and we must go back."

Elizabeth started to speak, but Mrs. White continued. "Hascal can take you to Beulah Morse. Please understand."

"Of course, Mrs. White. You must do what you can for your sister. I can be ready in short order."

And so the opportunity to speak passed again. Rigby's words came back to haunt her as she looked at the soiled and torn black dress. "The truth is you will tell nothing—not to anyone. I know your kind. You won't say a word."

With Beulah Morse at her side, Elizabeth completed her stint in Peoria, Eureka, Farmington and Elmwood. She saw

Rigby in the audience, but that was not surprising. Others traveled to hear her speak again. He was always with people from Peoria and on one occasion he was with Brad White.

Elizabeth never went anywhere alone. Mrs. Morse turned out to be the older lady in the blue dress and she was delighted to be the official hostess. She clung to her guest avidly. Elizabeth felt more secure knowing her blue angel would be her constant companion.

At last the four days in Peoria environs were over. Elizabeth packed for Springfield. There would be no danger from Rigby and no smothering from Beulah Morse. She was delighted to look out of the carriage window and see the last of Peoria fade in the distance.

The first talk in Springfield was in a church basement. It was sparsely attended.

The second, in the courthouse, was to a capacity crowd. People stood at the back. Halfway through her talk, she thought she saw Rigby. When she looked back, he was gone. Gone? Or, was he ever there?

The following day she moved to Decatur. This time, in the bright light of midday, there was no mistake. Rigby stood at the back of the church, and he was in the group who came forward after the talk. Her hostess, a Mrs. Passmore, said, "Come on up here, sir, and meet our guest. And, what's your name? I'd like to present you."

"Rigby," he said. "Mrs. Greenleaf and I have met."

"You know each other? That's wonderful. How nice for you both. I'm having a reception for Mrs. Greenleaf later. Perhaps you'd care to come."

"I'd be delighted," he said.

"That's my husband." She pointed to a man near the door. "Over there, the one with the cane. He can tell you how to get there and when." She turned back to Elizabeth. "Isn't this a lucky surprise? I can't believe it, finding someone you know so far from home?"

Rigby walked away and the questions began again. Elizabeth had no trouble answering, but fear was cold in her belly. She felt nausea rising and falling. Her chest felt numb. What could she do?

The reception was from five to six. He was there. Elizabeth went through the motions. She deported herself as the guest of honor. Nothing about her demeanor betrayed animosity toward Rigby or any other guest. When he looked at her, it was with a discreet leer. He seemed to be saying, "I'll see you later, Lizzie. The moon may have dimmed, but my ardor hasn't." It was clear to her, the ordeal was not over.

Elizabeth vowed to stay *with* people, even if she had to expose Rigby and humiliate herself. She would not—she must not—be left alone with him. Elizabeth knew she had to make a friend of Mrs. Passmore. She had to have an ally.

When the last guest left, Mrs. Passmore said, "You seem tired, Mrs. Greenleaf, and you've grown pale. Are you ill?"

"Yes, I am, Mrs. Passmore. I feel faint. The church this afternoon was too warm. I haven't been feeling well since then."

"Would you like to go to your room? I could brew some tea. Better still, I could bring a light supper up to you. I'm sure you'd like to take off your corset."

"I don't want to be a burden."

"It's not a burden, dear. I'll fix a tray. Mr. Passmore won't be here. When I have him fed and gone, I'll be up with a nice soup for the two of us. We can talk. Lands alive, I truly haven't had a minute with you. There are so many questions I want to ask."

Elizabeth knew what she must do. When the sordid tale had been told, Mrs. Passmore was ready to help with Elizabeth's plan of escape. The next stop on her itinerary was for several talks in and around Urbana. Elizabeth had one day for travel and rest.

Mary Ella, one of the two maids in the Passmore household, was Elizabeth's size. She would dress in the black outfit with the veil and gloves. She would take the carriage to Urbana, a decoy for Mr. Rigby. After Mary Ella was well on her way, Elizabeth, in another carriage, would head north to Bloomington. From there, she would make her way back to Boston. The speaking tour was over. Later, when she was safely on her way, she would send a message to Spencer by telegraph to cancel all engagements after the one in Decatur.

Aunt Florence and Spencer met her train. They were full of questions, but Elizabeth passed them off with, "No, my dears, I'm not ill. I simply became so exhausted I couldn't continue. Now, please, no more questions. I just want to sleep for three days. I'll never try a journey of that length again. Edward, bless his heart, tried to discourage me each time we discussed the itinerary, but I was firm. It turned out to be more than I could handle."

That explanation satisfied Spencer, but, at every opportunity, Aunt Florence renewed talk of the tour. At tea she would say, "Just what was it, Elizabeth, that finally made you decide to come home? Not just being tired surely, for I've seen you press on when others would have wilted," Or she would say, "Was it because you were passed from one hostess to another without a moment for yourself? Was that it? Was that what finally brought you back to us?"

Gradually, Elizabeth resumed a normal schedule. The political tone of her writing became more accented and she blasted the lack of strength President Pierce exhibited, even when she spoke in New Hampshire, his home state. She was aware of the irony: She could speak against him, but she hadn't the right to vote against him. Voting was a male prerogative. She resented it.

Her work, especially "Echoes From the South," took on a stronger social expression. When she wrote of the degradation of a slave, she spoke from the heart. She understood. She had been beaten into submission, defeated by the whip and the fist. When she spoke, her words lighted every dormant heap of abhorrence in New England. To a degree, she had expressed the same theme in her earlier work, but she had experienced it only as a woman in a man's world, in a world where women had no rights other than those that might be generously extended by a husband. But now, now after the horror of her experience at the hands of Jonathan Rigby, she knew what slavery was, and knowing it, she was even more determined to eradicate it.

Elizabeth never went to a speaking engagement without her driver and at least one other companion. It was Aunt Florence or Spencer or Edward.

One afternoon, an hour before she was to leave for Newton, Aunt Florence was taken ill. It was too late to arrange for Spencer or Edward, so Elizabeth decided to go alone. There had been no sign of Rigby. Was she was making too much of her fears?

As she dressed, Aunt Florence came in with a second round of apologies. "I'm so sorry, dear. I hope you understand. I just don't think I can possibly go with you. I'm so unsure of my stomach, and I have the skitters."

"Skitters?"

"The runs, my dear. I'm just not sure of what my bowels might do. I'd best stay home."

"It's all right, Aunt Florence. Charles will be with me. I prefer company, but I can manage. Skitters, as you call them, can be most unpleasant."

"I could send Ethel with you," Aunt Florence said as she walked uncomfortably around the room. She stopped at the dresser.

"Elizabeth! What is this? A gun?"

It was a small derringer, bought on the way back to Boston. She kept it in a drawstring pouch, but she had changed bags, and it was on the top of the dresser.

"Yes, Aunt Florence. I bought it while on the tour."

"But, why, Elizabeth? Why? You needed a gun?"

Elizabeth closed her eyes and put her fingers to her forehead. She had tried to avoid the situation now at hand. She did not want to think of the moonlight night in Peoria with Rigby, but the terror stayed. She thought of it when she avoided questions from her aunt and Spencer; she thought of it when she wrote about slavery; she dreamed of it—that brutal night was never far from her thoughts.

"As you seemed to have sensed, Aunt Florence, there was more to the cancellation of the tour than I told you or Spencer. I'll tell you all of it, but when I do, I want the story to die. I do not want Spencer, or anybody else, to know. It's just too personally humiliating."

Elizabeth picked up the gun. "Yes, I have a gun, and one day I may use it. If Rigby should follow me to Boston—if he ever makes one move toward me, I can assure you I will kill him without blinking an eye."

"Rigby?"

"The overseer Clay had when I first went to the rice island. I'm sure I told you something of him." She sat on the arm of her chair at the window. "It's such a long story, Aunt Florence. I can't even start it now, but I promise to tell it all when I get back from Newton."

"I knew it! I knew there was something."

"I must go now, or I shall be late."

"Wait. I'll send Ethel with you."

"There's no need. I'll be fine."

"You will take the gun, Elizabeth, and you will take Ethel, or I won't permit you to take one step out of this house."

Chapter Fifty-Seven

Florence Medlock heard the story of Jonathan Rigby from the beginning at Greenleaf Plantation through to the last, the most brutal part of it, in Peoria.

At the end of it, she decided that Elizabeth's career as a speaker must come to an end. The dangers were too great.

"No, Aunt Florence. I must not quit."

Florence Medlock opened her mouth to speak.

"No, Aunt Florence, I won't let fear of him stop me. If I'm going to hold my head up, I must fight against everything Rigby stands for. I won't cower, but I will be watchful, and I'll have people with me when I venture forth to speak, but I won't be terrorized. I don't expect I'll ever meet Rigby again, but if I do, I will not be menaced—not ever again. I know it's wrong to kill, but I'll do it without giving that sin a second thought. When the time comes for me to account for my life on earth, I don't believe I'll be judged for killing a brutish swine; and, if I am, then the God I thought was in heaven has deserted me."

"Elizabeth! That is sacrilegious."

"I don't mean it to be. There is no justice for a woman. None. I didn't see it in England or New York, or Darien—or in that wooded copse outside Peoria. Neither I nor my children got justice in the courts in Philadelphia. But, I do expect justice in heaven. If it's not there—"

Elizabeth took a deep breath and then said, "If the God I look to turns out to be a man, then I don't care if I have been disrespectful. If I find injustice in heaven, I will speak my mind, even if I have to endure the flames of hell."

"We shouldn't blame heaven for what we find on earth. It's our task to change what we find."

"Now, you're speaking on my side, Aunt Florence. You're absolutely right. That's why I speak and write. I'm trying to make a change. I'm trying to eliminate slavery of every kind, but I've started with the most obvious, the slavery, the bondage in the South. When that is over—and it will be one day—there's the other kind of slavery. Women are enslaved all over the world."

"Women are enslaved, dear niece, only because they allow themselves to be. I'm not."

"Can you vote, Aunt Florence? Can you throw out that nincompoop from New Hampshire we have as our head of state? Can you do anything about that? Are you permitted to vote?"

"Well, no."

"You've made a place for yourself, Aunt Florence, but not an equal place. You've done it because you have money. Money is a ring of protection. It may allow you to live without bondage, but are you equal? Be honest. Are you? What about women who have no money? They are forced to toe the line in order to live. They are bossed by fathers, by brothers, and then one day, with high hopes, they marry. What then? They have a new master. Nothing more, nothing less. Marriage is all we have, and we accept it, even if it is a subtle form of slavery."

"You're logical, Elizabeth, and at times, obnoxious."

"So Papa tells me. But, you, Florence Medlock, *are* second-class, just as I am. And, we will be until we stand on an equal footing with men."

"You'll never see that day."

"But, I will see the end of slavery in the South?"

"Yes, I think that will happen."

"That's my battle now, but it won't be my last battle."

"It's quite impossible to argue with you, Elizabeth."

"Then you agree that I should continue with the speaking and the writing?"

"You've worn me down. Yes, I suppose you should. You're making an impression. Our cause grows stronger, and one day the South will feel the weight of our opposition. But, Elizabeth, you will not go to speak alone. You will go nowhere alone. And that is final!"

The days passed. Elizabeth's schedule was full with her writings and her speeches. She supported the new Republican party, but there were misgivings.

"I'm so disappointed in them, Aunt Florence. They're opposed to slavery, but it's the only thing that gives them cohesion. Except for that, they're of a dozen minds. Our Republicans are a raggle-taggle bunch. But, what can we expect from dissidents from the anti-slavery Whigs, from anti-Nebraska Democrats and from Free Soilers, plus who knows what? They're for abolition, but will they ever really be a real party?"

"They are now, Elizabeth. They're becoming more aligned as time passes. All the strife out in Kansas—"

"Strife? It's civil war; that's what it is."

"Yes. I just hated to say those words. I hate to think we're fighting and killing each other. But, Kansas has a lot to do with the cohesion the Republican party is developing. Differences are fading. I think Fremont has a chance against Buchanan."

"Nonsense. Complete nonsense. John Fremont made a name for himself out West, but he's not known in the East. The Democrats are formidable. I'll support Fremont, but I think he'll end up chewed into little pieces."

"You underestimate the party, dear. Many, who may not yet call themselves Republicans, will stand up for Fremont."

Florence Medlock was right. When it was over, Fremont managed to get 114 electoral votes against James Buchanan's 174. The Democrats put their man in office, but Elizabeth had to admit the Republicans were now a party.

When it was clear the Republicans were capable, there was increased talk of secession. Talk of "disunion" was heard both in the North and the South. Elizabeth believed the Union must be preserved, even if it took troops.

She raged over the injustice of the Dred Scott decision. She believed in the rightness of Scott's original suit and she hoped fairness would come out of the Supreme Court, but the majority decision there was a travesty.

"How could they do this, Aunt Florence? He was a slave in Missouri, but when he was taken to Illinois, and then on to the Louisiana territory, why didn't he have a right to freedom? Illinois was a free state. And out in that vast, purchased land, slavery was *specifically* forbidden by the Missouri Compromise. That was federal law!"

"But, dear, the Missouri Compromise had been scuttled by the time the Supreme Court acted. Stephen Douglas scuttled it with the Kansas-Nebraska Act."

"Nevertheless, Aunt Florence, Scott was taken to a place where he was a free man. And, later, by federal law, there could be no slavery in the territory. That was the situation when the suit was filed. The case should have been decided under the laws that existed at the suit's inception, not as the law presently exists."

"Right or wrong, it's something we must live with."

"Well, it's not something I must live with. It's wrong. The court is wrong. I read every word of the decision. It's so patently unjust that I'll never let the issue die. The stupidity of it. How could anyone say a Negro slave—or any descendant of a slave—could *never* be a citizen of the United States? Never is a long, long time. I can't change Chief Justice Taney's decision, but I can oppose it, and I will."

"It won't change a thing."

"Do you think I should drop it?"

"When have you ever done anything because I thought it? You're tilting at windmills, as poor Don Quixote did."

"It's injustice. I will not let it pass. I may fail, as Don Quixote did, but I'll fight it."

1857 was also the year of the Lecompton Constitution in the Kansas Territory. It was unabashedly pro-slavery. The South was jubilant over the Dred Scott case and the Lecompton Constitution. Elizabeth was inflamed by both, but the Lecompton Constitution frightened her more. There would be more killing in the Kansas territory. She remembered the guns Jonathan Rigby and Brad White were sending there.

Elizabeth's pen pricked the political career of Stephen A. Douglas at every opportunity. He proposed the Kansas-Nebraska Act which nullified the Missouri Compromise. He was willing to play the politics of slavery with his fellow Democrats for his own ambitions so he was grist for her mill. One chink in his armor was his ready acceptance of the Dred Scott Decision. Some Northern Democrats were offended. She was well aware of that fact and she tried to rub the wound raw.

Elizabeth never wrote specifically of the debates between Lincoln and Douglas, but the Douglas inconsistencies were inserted into column after column. She wanted to blast Douglas in the South and she was well aware that she had done him considerable harm in the North.

Spencer called on Elizabeth unexpectedly one morning. "I knew it was your habit to stop for tea about ten. I also knew this was the morning for Florence's meeting with the Boston Literary Guild. I wanted to see you alone."

"Alone? Am I due for a reprimand? Have I been too hard on Stephen Douglas? Do you think I might be sued?"

"Nothing of the sort, though I do think some of the things you say are close to slander."

"Oh, pooh! He deserves even more. Slander, indeed!"

After Ethel left the tea and closed the door, Elizabeth poured and said, "All right, Spencer. You've managed to stop my writing by your presence at this unseemly hour. What is it, since it's not a reprimand?"

"I'm not sure how to say this, Elizabeth. I've been trying to think of a way, but, now that I'm here, every thought seems to come out wrong."

"Oh, my. Spencer Chadwycke speechless?"

"Don't chide me, or I'll never have the nerve."

"Oh, poor boy. I'll be very quiet. I'll sip my tea like a lady, waiting for you to speak."

The next minute crept by. Each of them made an elaborate ceremony of the tea. Spencer sipped it slowly, looking at some faraway spot past her left ear, and she pretended to be busy with the cream pot. Spencer, always so sure of himself, was unable to explain his mission.

At last he spoke. "We are such good friends, Elizabeth; we have so much in common, and we support each other so perfectly that it might work out well for both of us if we got married."

She was aware of the words, all rushed and jumbled, but she was not sure of what she had actually heard. Married? Had he said *married*?

"I want you to think about this, Elizabeth. I know you are self-sufficient now because of your writing and speaking, but I also know you have no great reserves."

She spoke. "Did you say marry, Spencer? Marry?"

"I'm off to a bad start, my dear. I had it all worked out on the way here, but, somehow, it didn't come out well."

"In that case, my dear Spencer, let me relieve you. For whatever reason, you seem to have impaled yourself on a lance of your own making. Let me take you off." She paused. "Marriage, I'm afraid, is out of the question for me." He moved forward on the chair. "Don't interrupt, please. There is something I must say, and I don't think I'll be able to do it any better than you have, if as well. As you were, I'm not sure how to phrase what I must say."

She walked to the cabinet below the pier glass and selected a bottle. "I'm taking a dollop of brandy in my tea, Spencer. Would you like one? Maybe then I'll find the words I need." She poured the brandy. He waved it away. "You needn't find the words, Elizabeth. If the answer is no, it's no. No explanation is required."

"Yes, Spencer, I think one is. Just be quiet and let me do it in my own way." She put her cup down and looked directly into his eyes. "I love you very much. I want you to know that, but I cannot marry you. I love you too much to simply dismiss your proposal. For that reason, I must explain."

"An explanation is not necessary. You needn't bare your soul to me."

"*You* may not require it, Spencer, but I do. You are the dearest man, the best friend I've ever had, barring Aunt Florence, of course. I must say this—for myself, if not for you." She told him of the experience with Rigby in Peoria, holding nothing back.

"Oh, my dear," Spencer said when she had finished, "I'm so sorry. I revived all this. I could see the pain of it on your face. Can you ever forgive me?"

"There's nothing to forgive, Spencer. You deserved a reason for my answer. It was I who wanted to—indeed it was I who *had* to make it. But, now— Well, now you know why I cannot marry you, even though you are the dearest man in the world."

"I'll take the brandy now, please, Elizabeth. We both have some things to say, and while I've begun rather poorly, you've shamed me with your own honesty. I, too, have a confession. Maybe it will make a difference, and maybe it won't, but you felt you had to bare your soul, and so do I."

"Oh, my. This does sound ominous."

"No little jokes, Elizabeth. I am serious about this. What I have to say must be said if we are to preserve the integrity that our relationship has always had. It's not something I want to talk about, either—just as you didn't—but, like you, it's something that must be said if you are to consider my proposal, even for a moment."

"But, Spencer dear—"

"Let me tell it, Elizabeth, in my own way. I did not interrupt your account of the horror you had in Peoria, and I must have the opportunity to pick my way through my own difficult confession."

Elizabeth started to speak, but she was silenced when he raised a hand in protest. "I am considerably older than you; I am 43. An unmarried man of my age is always considered to be just outside the pale. He is a question mark. He has not conformed. He dares to break the pattern. He is a cipher, an unknown, even a threat. He is viewed, at least in some quarters, with suspicion. I am sure you have heard gossip, speculation—

"I know who you are, Spencer."

"Perhaps you do, my dear, perhaps you don't. But, let me continue. There has been talk, partly because I am honest with myself. I go to the theater and concerts because I want to go, not because I must, as some men pretend. I consider myself civilized, and I conduct myself as though I am. I am fastidious about my person and in my work. My dear mother's repetition of the little saying about cleanliness and godliness was impressed upon my mind so well that it cannot be obliterated."

As far as Elizabeth was concerned, none of this was necessary. A part of what she had always admired about Spencer was how thoroughly civilized he was, how considerate, how well-dressed, how urbane. She was ready to speak. Once again he raised his hand in protest.

"As I say, there has been talk, and some of it, to my shame, has involved Edward. I have never felt I had to conform just to be accepted, but now—now that Edward's good name is being slandered—I wonder if it would not be wise—" He was unsure of how to continue. Then he found his voice. "I wonder if it's not time for me to play the game, for surely it is a game, that is being played elsewhere, and in the City of in Boston as well. Once we talked of parallel games, Elizabeth. This is one of them."

He placed his teacup carefully on the table in front of them. And then he continued.

"I did not know of the personal violation you experienced in Peoria until today, but I believed, from what you've said, what you've written, and from my talks with Florence, that it was unlikely you would ever marry again. I knew, or thought I knew, that you would not want a traditional marriage. That's not what I am offering you."

"This would be a business arrangement?"

"I wouldn't say it so bluntly, but, yes, you might see it that way. I don't."

When Elizabeth started to speak, he raised a hand. "I think what I offer is a great deal more than business. In my own way, I love you, Elizabeth. I think you know that. I enjoy your company, I know how capable you are in social situations, and I admire your intellect. We live in a time when women are supposed to be silly and useless, but that was never my opinion. I believe women are as capable as men. I have two excellent examples of it closely entwined in my life: you and Florence. You have both managed to make a life for yourselves, under conditions that have been less than ideal. Florence has turned a small inheritance into a sizable fortune. She didn't do it without brains. She's a shrewd investor. You, a runaway wife with two children, have made a name for yourself in a world where a man must push his way forward or be shunted aside—a woman has almost no chance at all. That, too, took brains, and not a little courage."

"But, a marriage, Spencer—why a marriage?"

"You wouldn't consider less—"

"Of course not, but—"

"We have much to offer each other, Elizabeth. I'd like to come home to an intelligent woman at day's end. I would adore having a hostess who could preside over parties that would be the envy of all of Boston. I would savor being known as the husband of the famous Cassandra."

"I don't believe, Spencer—"

"You have less to gain, Elizabeth, but I can offer you a security you've never known, and I can offer you the freedom to do whatever it is that would make you happy."

"But, Spencer, I don't—"

"I love you, Elizabeth, perhaps not in a carnal way, but with a love that is as deep as the respect I think you have for me. Am I wrong?"

"You're not wrong, Spencer. I love you, too. You are dearer to me than I can ever say. I think you've known of my love, as I have. But is it enough for a marriage, even one that is not traditional? I just don't know."

"I didn't expect an answer, my dear. I can only hope you will give it consideration." He looked directly into her eyes. "Please, Elizabeth, give it your serious consideration. It would mean so much to me, my dear, more than I can say."

"I will, Spencer, I will. But, you must give me time. This is such a radical change for me. I've grown happy here with Aunt Florence. I just don't know. I don't know."

Chapter Fifty-Eight

Elizabeth did not mention Spencer's visit, but every household has a reporting system of its own. When Elizabeth was not involved with speaking, she took her afternoon tea in the parlor with Florence Medlock.

"Ethel said Spencer dropped by. Sorry I missed him."

"Yes," Elizabeth answered. "He took more of my time than I could spare, but he's such a dear."

"Spencer always lifts my spirits with his bits of gossip and his banter. It was probably good for you. You're so intent on blasting poor Mr. Douglas—"

"Poor Mr. Douglas? You know he'd sell his soul to the South for a chance to become President."

"You're getting red in the face, Elizabeth so let's talk no more of Stephen Douglas." She poured a second cup of tea. "Let me tell you what I heard this morning about Minnie Pritchett. What a highly proper lady she appears to be. But, since she moved here from Waverly, I've felt there was more there than meets the eye. This is what I heard. I got it from Emma Peabody, and she'd know if anyone did..."

And, thus, Elizabeth was allowed to drop the subject of Spencer's morning call. She did not want to lie, even by indirection, but she was not prepared to discuss the proposal.

The following week Elizabeth had no contact with Spencer, but he was always in her thoughts. She hated herself for her own avarice. Financial freedom would mean not having to worry about the cost of a new dress or hat; it would mean having a carriage and driver at her disposal; and a home with gleaming silver and English china. These thoughts always started with money and ended with money. How could she think of marrying Spencer with these ideas in her head? But, they were there, she could not deny it.

Spencer was one of the most eligible bachelors in the city and it would be wonderful to have a husband who treated you as an equal; but, when she considered his proposal, were these her reasons, or were her reasons more tainted? Were her thoughts guided by Eros or by Plutus?

And, the girls? Such a marriage might be of considerable social value to them. She had little hope of taking them from Clay, but one day they might come to Boston to live. If she were mistress of Spencer's handsome house, would it help her to make amends with the girls? It was a consideration, but wasn't that avarice as well?

She tried to give meaning to the marriage he had proposed, but in the end, it came back to what she had previously called it: a business arrangement.

She loved Spencer but she would not be a wife to him in the accepted sense of the word. She would be living a lie. Could she do it and still maintain her self-respect? And, was it truly a lie? Were there not legions of marriages, even here in Boston, that were based on less?

She knew Spencer. She had worked with him. He had been with her when she was distressed, angry, outspoken and childish. He accepted her many moods as no man had ever done before. He stood at her side through the ordeal when Clay had taken the girls.

Isn't this what a good husband would do? Were they not, in every sense, closer than the brides and grooms who peopled the churches of the city? They had a deep and abiding love. Was this not a cornerstone for marriage, even if it did not meet with the common idea of such a union?

And, she was aware of the seamed side of his personality. One could not have been through the ordeal in Philadelphia and the close quarters of the trip back to Boston without having seen the raw edges. He was not all urbane charm. She had seen him when he was angry, when he was petty, when he was a thoroughly-spoiled child, but she could accept him as he was, just as he seemed able to accept her. He was not flawless, but neither was she. If they could love each other, knowing of these imperfections, tolerating them, was that not a basis for a lasting relationship?

The questions, the recriminations, the tears, the moments of despair, pummeled her brain each night until at last, weary from the onslaught, she would fall asleep.

Spencer had agreed to accompany her the following evening to Brookline where she was to speak, but he wanted to leave a little early.

When he helped her into the carriage, he said, "I hurried you out of the house at four, Elizabeth, because I wanted time for a leisurely drive and a quiet dinner. I know a place, beyond Brookline. You'll like the atmosphere and the food.We'll be back in plenty of time for your talk."

"A week ago I might have been annoyed at leaving so early, but this has been such a hectic time. I've worked like a drudge, and still I'm behind on my commitments. I welcomed the chance to get away."

"We've had a great deal on our minds, my dear. We can talk later, after we've had a good dinner. For now, let's just ride along, happy to be in each other's company."

He lowered the carriage window to let the breeze in. "It's been warm all day, but just occasionally there's the hint of winter in the air. Do you feel it? It's always been a time of year I especially like, when the seasons themselves are as confused as we are."

"I'm not confused—"

"Not another word. Lean back and watch the colors as we pass. Or, rest your eyes, if you wish, but let your mind go back to a time when life was not so complex for either of us."

He spoke quietly and his eyes looked beyond the window. He relaxed. As his tension was released, Elizabeth caught the spirit of it. She leaned back, her neck muscles no longer tense and her eyes closed against the light of the afternoon. He took her hand in his. They were not asleep, but it is all either of them remembered until they arrived at the country inn beyond Brookline.

It was a place of simple charm, a farmhouse now converted to an inn. It was operated by a man and his wife who enjoyed the company of their guests.

"It got too lonely for us," the man said as he led them to a quiet alcove in what had once been the parlor. "I had hoped my son would have chosen to stay on the farm, but young people have lost the sense of their own tomorrows. We lived close to the earth, all my family, and Erna's, but he's gone to Boston, my son has. My only boy A lawyer, he is. And, God bless him if that's really going to make him happy."

After they had been seated and served, Spencer spoke. "You have decided to marry me, haven't you, Elizabeth?"

"Yes, Spencer, I think I have."

"You decided yesterday morning, didn't you, my dear?"

"Yes, but how did you know?"

"My week was as much in turmoil as yours must have been, Elizabeth, but my mind found peace yesterday as I sat having coffee with Edward. When your man arrived with the note, it was as though I knew he would be there. I slept well last night for the first time in over a week."

"That could have been exhaustion. I know I was near it."

"No, my dear. It was as though I knew your mind. I knew you had decided to accept me as I am." He touched her hand. "You are close to impossible sometimes, Elizabeth, and sometimes I think I love you because of your faults not in spite of them. You say and do things that I keep under restraint. I can never be totally free. I'm so careful; you're a madcap. But, my dear, you have compassion, the greatest of all gifts. That's why I love you."

"You must be sure about this marriage, Spencer. You have been a bachelor all your life; you've lived alone since your mother's passing. It's a decided change. Is that house large enough for a woman?"

"Yes, my dear." He touched her arm. He wanted her full attention. "This is not an idea that came without thought, Elizabeth. It's been teasing my mind for several years. I admired you and believed you felt the same, but in those earlier years when we worked together, I knew admiration would not be enough. Time has passed, Elizabeth. We have endured a great deal together. It's more than admiration. When I say I love you, Elizabeth, I mean it in its purest sense. I want to do all the things for you a man has a right to do for those he loves."

"And, I love you, Spencer. It's not the kind of love I felt for Clay. We neither one want that. Perhaps you said it the only way it can be said: it's love in its purest sense."

"You have made me very happy, Elizabeth. You'll never regret your decision."

He withdrew a ring box from his pocket. There, in a simple mounting, was the most beautiful pale yellow stone Elizabeth had ever seen. "I want you to have it, my dear, as a symbol of our betrothal. It was my mother's ring."

"Oh, but I couldn't. Not your mother's—"

"Of course you can. If she were alive she would give it to you herself." Spencer took the ring from the box and slipped it on her finger. "The man who runs the inn was upset because his family had lost continuity when his only son chose the law. I can understand his feeling. This ring represents continuity in my family. My mother, rest her soul, would be the first to want you to have it."

"It's lovely. It's a most unusual stone.What is it?"

"A yellow diamond. They're not all that rare, but this one is flawless and beautifully cut. My father had it made for her in Amsterdam. Mother had many jewels, but this one was her joy. I hope it will be your joy, too."

"You are a sentimental and thoughtful man, Spencer. How could anyone not love you?"

"When, Elizabeth? Only you must be the judge of that."

"Since there's no doubt in our minds, Spencer—not in mine or in yours—then I think it's best that we marry soon. Perhaps it could all be arranged by the end of next month, if that's not too soon for you."

"I'd welcome the ceremony tomorrow."

"Tomorrow has an element of haste to it. We'll plan it for the end of next month."

"A large wedding, the largest Boston has ever seen—"

"A small wedding, my darling. A large wedding would not be proper. I am a divorced woman." He moved to protest, but she kept on speaking. "We'll keep the wedding small, only family and the dearest of friends, but the reception can be open to the whole of Boston, if you like."

"I'd like a real party to celebrate the fact that I'm now the happiest man alive. I want my friends there, and not a few of my enemies. I want the world to know how lucky I am."

"Now, it's my turn to protest. I think you may have gone too far with the compliments, dear Spencer."

"Not one word of it! A brilliant mind that has unleashed a fusillade of fury on the South and on slavery."

"A brilliant mind that couldn't control a bold mouth, so I lost my children—"

"Not now, Elizabeth. Not on this day. You did what you had to do. It wasn't you, or anything you did; it was the law. One day, when abolition is a fact, we will work for another kind of emancipation—the emancipation of women. If we can change the South—and we are succeeding—we can change a few laws."

Chapter Fifty-Nine

They were back in Boston at midnight. The house was ablaze. Florence Medlock and Ethel were on the doorstep before the carriage came to a stop. "We've been so worried."

"Worried, Florence, when Elizabeth was with me?"

"Well, I knew she was with you, Spencer, but, I worried about—" Florence Medlock hesitated, she didn't want to betray a confidence—"I was worried about other people. These are dangerous times, sir, and Cassandra is always at risk because—"

"We were delayed by the audience in Brookline, They were wonderful." Elizabeth said. "There's such an interest now in politics and in what the Republicans might do about abolition."

"Well, you're both safe, thank God for that. Come in—you, too, Spencer. We'll have a nice cup of tea. I'm freezing in this night air." She turned to Spencer's driver. "And you, Mr. Dawkins—take the carriage around back. Ethel will see that you have a cup of tea, won't you Ethel?" Then in her bustling way, she herded them inside.

After tea was served, Elizabeth glanced at Spencer. He nodded. She turned to the older woman. "Aunt Florence," she said,"we do have something to tell you, Spencer and I." Florence Medlock glanced up from the fruitcake she was buttering. "Spencer has asked me to marry him, and I have accepted his proposal."

Florence Medlock carefully put the fruitcake back on the plate. "I knew it; I knew there was more. You were never able to keep anything from me, Elizabeth. I can tell when you are harboring something. So, that's why you're so late."

"No, Florence. That's not the reason," Spencer said with a chuckle. "Our late arrival was politics, just as Elizabeth said. It was the crowd and the questions. Elizabeth accepted my proposal before her talk, not afterward. We had a quiet dinner in the country, out beyond Brookline. I plied her with viands and wine, and she foolishly said yes."

"I don't know what to say. I'm both surprised and not surprised. You've been thrown together because of your work, so it's no wonder you grew fond of each other."

She took Elizabeth's hand in hers. "And, since Spencer is the only man I would ever have married--had I known him when I was younger—how can I ever blame you for learning to love him?"

"Thank you, Aunt Florence. We wanted your blessing."

"You have it. My two favorite people, married! Oh, there will be so much to do. I'll be up early. I'll see Mrs. Mullineaux first thing. She's so good at these things, and we'll need help, won't we, Elizabeth? I'm the only family you have here. Arrangements will be my responsibility."

"You must remember, Aunt Florence, I'm a divorced woman. The wedding will be small and very private. Anything else would be unseemly."

Florence Medlock frowned with disappointment. "Yes, Elizabeth, I suppose you're right, but for the moment, I had forgotten—"

"I wanted a large wedding, too, but we must stay with the judgment of the bride," Spencer said. "Elizabeth has agreed to a gala reception. Perhaps you can plan that."

"Oh, lovely, lovely. We'll still need Mrs. Mullineaux. She arranges the most beautiful parties."

"It will be my party. We'll spare no expense."

Florence Medlock's spine stiffened. She turned toward Spencer. "That is the prerogative of the family of the bride. I'll not permit you to meddle in tradition."

"We can talk about it, Florence; we have time." He stood, cane in hand. "It's late, ladies. It's already tomorrow. I have work to do. The piper must be paid."

"I'll go to the door with you, Spencer." Elizabeth turned to her aunt. "Tell Ethel to send Mr. Dawkins around with the carriage, please, Aunt Florence. This poor man must have sleep or the house of Chadwycke & Company will suffer.

Elizabeth and Spencer were married on the cold and overcast afternoon of October 29, 1859. The quiet ceremony was held in the rectory, and it was rigidly correct. Three members of Spencer's family were there: a sister, a nephew and an elderly aunt. Her family was represented by Aunt Florence and a cousin from Amherst. Papa sent his regrets. She expected his reaction. Papa did not believe in divorce, but, to his everlasting credit, his note made no mention of his beliefs.

The reception was everything Spencer and Aunt Florence had hoped it would be. Mrs. Mullineaux, as Florence Medlock had promised, was good at arranging parties.

At ten the next morning, under lead-colored skies and in a cold rain, the bridal couple finally got a moment to themselves as they huddled together in the carriage that was to take them on a week's trip to an undisclosed destination.

Elizabeth did not like the weather. Was it an omen? Could any good come from this marriage? She decided not to speak of omens. What would Spencer think of her childishness?

The rest of the year swept by for Elizabeth. It was exciting being married to Spencer. It was a dream come true. From the beginning, the bachelor who had maintained Chadwycke House withdrew completely. He introduced her to the staff, and that was the last time he issued an order concerning how the house was to be run. When a party was planned, or a dinner, Spencer discussed it with Elizabeth, and then left all the details to her good judgment.

Her bedroom adjoined Spencer's. The door between was never locked, but each had a deep respect for the privacy of the other.

She had three rooms in the suite she considered her own private domain: a sleeping chamber, a sitting room, and, beyond that, her office, a smaller room that had once been the trunk room.

Spencer's office was more remote and quieter, since it was more toward the back of the house.

Because the rooms were larger, he prevailed upon Elizabeth to take the room next to his office for her own, but she preferred the cozy, private space the trunk room afforded, and she liked the view of the Charles River from its lone window.

Just a few days before the marriage, Elizabeth was distressed by the news of John Brown's raid on the arsenal at Harper's Ferry, not because it was an illegal act, but because it was not successful.

John Brown and his men had failed to make good their escape and were captured.

As her editor and publisher, Spencer very rarely felt the need to discuss Elizabeth's writing, but he felt he had to do so in the case of John Brown.

"I know how you feel, Elizabeth," he said, "but, personal feelings aside, Cassandra would not condone lawlessness."

"She has always expressed my feelings."

"Don't be petulant, Elizabeth. The column has influence; it's making an impression—you must not dilute its power."

"They were after arms to fight against slavery."

"The raid was led by a fugitive from the law. Surely you don't condone the murders he committed out in the Kansas Territory? Murders, Elizabeth, the bloodiest of murders."

"The killings were wrong."

"He killed deliberately. Slavery is wrong, but it's no excuse for murder. I beg you, my dear, don't write of it."

She wrote it, but it went in the trash basket.

As Elizabeth prepared for a gala New Year's Eve party the last frigid day of 1859, she reviewed the year in her mind. Sentiment against the South had mounted. You could read it, hear it, see it, and almost feel it in the streets. The growing demand for abolition warmed her heart, as did the strong interest in Abraham Lincoln as the Republican standard bearer. Lincoln had been brilliant in the debates, and she believed he was opposed to slavery. She hoped he could wrest the nomination from Seward.

She remembered the omens on her wedding day. How silly she had been. She remembered the trip with Spencer to New York City. She had seen Papa without a single unpleasant moment. Papa liked Spencer, which was a surprise. And, she had seen the debut of Miss Adelina Patti in "Lucia di Lammermour." That alone made the trip memorable.

Elizabeth missed Florence Medlock, but it was the only thing she missed about her life before the marriage to Spencer. It was not as though Aunt Florence was at a distance. She was only five minutes away, and she frequently dropped in. "I know your habits, dear," Florence Medlock would say. "It was the time you stop for your morning's tea so I just had Charles bring me over."

Florence was delighted with the Republican party and Abraham Lincoln. "He's not much to look at, Elizabeth, but he's our great hope. We're going to win this one."

The ladies had watched with joy as the Democrats planted the seeds of their own undoing. After fifty-seven ballots, the first convention failed to nominate a candidate and finally deteriorated completely. They reassembled in Baltimore on June 18, but still could not resolve their differences. In the end, they nominated Stephen A. Douglas, but, because a pro-slavery platform was not included, the South bolted the party. The dissenters met on June 28 in Baltimore. They called themselves the National Democratic party and they nominated John C. Breckinridge of Kentucky as their candidate.

To further divide the votes the Democrats might hope to receive, there was a third group, individuals from the old Whig party, the Know-Nothings and others who seemed to like neither Democratic faction. These unlikely allies nominated John C. Bell of Tennessee.

"They've done it this time," Aunt Florence cried with delight. "We are a walk-away. We'll win it. They don't have a chance."

Florence Medlock was right.

Lincoln easily bested Douglas in the North, and Breckinridge and Bell drained Southern votes in such numbers that Douglas had little support there.

Lincoln, with only forty percent of the popular vote, managed to carry state after state. In the end he had 180 votes in the electoral college to 72 for Breckinridge, 39 for Bell and only 12 for Douglas.

Elizabeth was pleased with Lincoln as the president-elect, but she was even happier with the results of the electoral college. Douglas had only managed to get 12 votes. She felt the loss handed him was her own personal victory.

Hopes were high for the coming year when Lincoln would take office. "He'll stop slavery once and for all," Florence Medlock said. "Next year will be full of action."

Action came earlier than Florence Medlock anticipated. In the waning days of the Buchanan administration, on December 20, 1860, South Carolina, unhappy with the results of the election, and despising Lincoln, voted to secede from the Union. President Buchanan did nothing.

Whether or not it was the President's desire, the wound began to fester. By February of 1861 the states of the lower South had also decided to secede. With the secession of Mississippi, Florida, Alabama, Georgia, Louisiana and Texas, the Congress of Montgomery was held, and the Confederate States of America was born.

"We are heading for a confrontation," Spencer said, "It's serious. We cannot allow this to happen."

"And, what can we do to stop it, Spencer?"

"We must quickly put this thing down."

"You don't think Buchanan will, do you? He's shown precious little concern, and I doubt he could influence anyone now. In a few scant weeks he'll be out of office. Why should anyone pay any attention to what he might propose?"

"We'll have to wait for President Lincoln," Florence Medlock said.

"I agree with Aunt Florence," Elizabeth said. "Wait until he's inaugurated. Then you'll see it happen."

The day arrived. Lincoln was inaugurated on March 4. There was no change in Washington. Lincoln chose his cabinet carefully. Too carefully some said. He appointed William Seward, his former adversary, as Secretary of State. It seemed a foolish choice. Could he expect loyalty from a man he had beaten on the third ballot? His other choices seemed equally perverse. Lincoln seemed to be offering a bone to every faction under heaven. He was off to a poor start.

"We had such hopes for Lincoln, didn't we, Aunt Florence? His cabinet is ridiculous. He toadies, he mollifies, he languishes. So far, he's no more effective than Buchanan. He waits. Does he think the situation will improve?"

"Yes, dear, he's a disappointment. Such a bright mind. I do declare, he seems addled in these first few days."

The action they wanted was not long in coming, but it was not instituted by President Lincoln. Fort Sumter was the thorn. South Carolina considered itself separated from the Union, and it was not happy seeing Fort Sumter, a bastion of a foreign government, in the middle of Charleston Harbor. They began a blockade. Supplies ran low at the Fort. It urgently requested provisions. Lincoln hesitated. He still harbored hope that the Southern states might be brought back into the fold. The situation at the Fort continued to deteriorate.

South Carolina, emboldened by the weakness of the new administration, decided to overpower the garrison. On April 12, 1861, the battle for Fort Sumter began.

"Lincoln must move. Can't he see that. They're tweaking our noses."

"Yes, my dear, they are. He must put a stop to this."

It happened. When Lincoln called up the militia for a period of three months, sufficient time to bring order back to the nation, he consolidated his enemies. When the order went out, the border states were put to the test. They had to choose sides. Arkansas, Virginia, North Carolina and Tennessee chose to secede, going with the Confederate States. Delaware, Maryland, Kentucky and Missouri stayed with Lincoln.

The strengthened Confederate States of America moved its capitol from Montgomery to Richmond. Elizabeth believed the rift was too great to expect the two sides to find common ground. The first phase of the war was a reality.

"I'm glad it's here, Aunt Florence," she said. "There was no other way. I've lived in the South. They're a pig-headed lot."

"I can't believe it! You, a minister's daughter. You know there will be bloodshed."

"Oh, now, Aunt Florence, we both knew it would come to this. You pushed for this moment as much as I did. Now you're straddling. Blood will be spilled, but there's already been bloodshed. Maybe it won't be as bad as you think. We have over 22 million people on our side. They have only about eight—maybe nine—and half of them are slaves."

"Surely not half."

"Perhaps not half, but a large number. We'll overpower them. It's not all bleak. Lincoln has begun a blockade, from

South Carolina to below Jacksonville, I've read. If they can't sell cotton, they can't buy supplies, so they can't last. Cotton is their money, and otherwise they're not self-sufficient. They buy what they need, as we did at Greenleaf."

"Their backs are against the wall, Elizabeth. They will fight and it won't be an easy victory," Florence Medlock said.

By the summer of 1861, it was apparent once again that Miss Medlock was right. One of the administration's objectives was to overrun the Confederate capitol at Richmond, but the Battle of Bull Run ended in defeat. Richmond held.

"I don't know if it's true, Elizabeth, but I heard today that Lincoln offered an olive branch to those madmen down South," Florence Medlock said. "He proposed a gradual emancipation, with compensation for the slave owners."

"Yes, Spencer told me about it. It's another of the President's attempts to mollycoddle the South. And, who's going to pay for it? Where will the money come from?"

"You can't take property without compensation—"

"Property? They're not property, Aunt Florence. They are an enslaved people, but they're people just the same."

"But, Elizabeth, don't you see, the owners do have an investment. It can't just be confiscated."

"Can't it? Why not? What do you think will happen when we win? Do we beat them in conflict and then pay them? If they persist in this—and they will—we must maul them."

"You *are* bloodthirsty."

"I have a great deal of compassion, but we must get this over quickly, with whatever force is needed. To drag it on, as the President seems to be doing, will result in the deaths of tens of thousands. If I were in power, I'd show you how it should be done. It must be quick and decisive."

The war dragged on without measurable results through the remainder of 1861. 1862 followed a similar pattern. The second Battle of Bull Run brought another defeat for the Union.

McClellan's attempt to take Richmond by moving up the peninsula between the York and James rivers lasted from March to July, and it failed. In sight of Richmond, he withdrew when reinforcements failed to arrive.

Elizabeth read of small victories along the way, but she wanted an all-out fight. She wanted to use the Union's superior manpower in one consolidated effort.

The victories at Fort Henry early in the year and at Fort Donelson a few weeks later were not enough for her. Nor, were the victories at Roanoke Island, Jacksonville and New Orleans. She threw up her hands in despair when McClellan forced General Lee to retreat at the Battle of Antietam in September and then failed to pursue the fleeing Lee.

"Thank God there's incompetence on both sides," she said to Florence Medlock. "If it were not so, Lee would be marching into Philadelphia and New York right now. It's impossible to believe these blunders, and I dare say, we only know of those disasters that can't be kept hidden. What is President Lincoln thinking? Our armies have no head. Our generals go off on individual expeditions. There's no plan."

Elizabeth had been brought to a belief in Lincoln slowly. Initially, she thought him to be an unpolished lawyer from Springfield who had an interest in politics. She couldn't take him seriously. But, in the debates with Douglas, she started to see him as the real hope for the nation.

As his term of office dragged on, her faith in him faded. Her original dislike of Lincoln found its way back into her mind.

By the Battle of Antietam, Lincoln had been President for over a year. He shook her faith further when, shortly after McClellan forced Lee to retreat, the President issued his Emancipation Proclamation. In her mind, he was playing politics, not fighting a rebellion.

The statement that on January 1, 1863, he would declare "forever free" all slaves in the states which were still in arms against the authority of the federal government was politics and nothing more. He was trying to garner the good will of England, while trying to frighten the South.

With this kind of stupidity, victory for the Union did not seem likely to Elizabeth. Or, she wondered, did Lincoln believe those freed slaves would rise up against their masters, thus ending the war with the stroke of his pen? The President was good with words, but this time, she felt, if an insurrection were truly his aim, he has made a grievous error in judgment.

She knew the men of the South. They were not easily frightened. If they had been, there would be no Confederate States of America. South Carolina would never have brashly chosen to secede, or fire on Fort Sumter. No, Mr. Lincoln, she thought, you can't frighten them, nor will the slaves revolt. How could they? Could they fight guns with sticks and stones? If you, Mr. President, cannot form a competent army, how can you expect it from a group of people who have known only subjugation?

"He has blundered again, Aunt Florence."

She was right. The Emancipation Proclamation did not alter the course of the war. If anything, it solidified the resolve of the South.

January 1, 1863, the "forever free" day came and went. It was all but unnoticed in the nation, both North and South.

Chapter Sixty

There was wide support for abolishing slavery, but there was little heart for it when it meant sending sons to battle. As the weary days of the war passed, there were fewer subjects Elizabeth could write about short of sedition. She did not approve of the conduct of the war and she had lost respect for Lincoln. She believed politics prevented an easy victory. If she wrote what she felt, even Spencer wouldn't publish it.

As time passed, the columns grew fewer. On the day Mr. Lincoln's Emancipation Proclamation became effective, on January 1, 1863, she let Cassandra quietly die.

Under her own name, she continued to write on assignment, and for Spencer, but her articles were sporadic. "It's a good thing I married Spencer when I did," she told her aunt. "I'm earning precious little these days. What would I have done?"

"Stayed with me. There never was a need for you to earn a living, but you were lost when you came to my doorstep," Florence Medford said. "Writing put steel in your spine. You're the better for it. This is only a breathing spell. I dare say abolition is not your last crusade."

Elizabeth might have been mollified by her aunt's kind words, but not in the early months of 1863. The war had been going on two bloody years and still the South was an entity. It was a stalemate. The rebels amazed her with what they could do with so little manpower and so little ability to produce for themselves. Neither side had achieved an advantage, and the unity of the populous North was eroded by the endless and hopeless killings. Paradoxically, the Southern forces appeared to grow stronger with every defeat. Their right to self-determination was tempered in battle.

Elizabeth smoldered under the defeat of the Union forces at Chancellorsville, and then, in the early summer of 1863, General Lee actually began an invasion of the North. He had made one successful foray into Maryland the year before, a foray thwarted by his defeat at Antietam.

This time it was not a foray, it was an invasion. Bypassing Washington, Lee boldly led his men up through Northern Virginia and Maryland and into Pennsylvania. He was audacious, fast and clever. He made no attempt to take Washington or Philadelphia, although it was a fear Elizabeth heard openly expressed in Boston.

From early June until near the year's end, General Lee moved across Pennsylvania. He went as far as McConnellsburg to the west and Wrightsville to the east. He edged toward Harrisburg, and was already as close as Carlisle.

"When are we going to stop him? Why are they waiting? If we know what's happening, why can't those idiots in Washington see it, Aunt Florence?"

"I know how disappointed you are in Lincoln, Elizabeth, but I still have faith in him. I'm sure he has a plan. Lee will spread himself too thin, and when he does, when the moment is right, the President will send our men in."

"In the meantime Pennsylvania is being terrorized."

"We will prevail, Elizabeth."

"How many must be slaughtered first?"

The following week Spencer brought the news of a battle in a small town in Pennsylvania. "Gettysburg," he said. "No one knows much about it. It's farm country, they say, about fifty miles north and west of Baltimore. Lee is in retreat."

"Are we in pursuit?"

"I don't know, Elizabeth. That wasn't in the dispatch."

"Well, I'll wager we're not. How many times have we done this? Every opportunity we've had has been bungled. This is a golden opportunity. He's in our territory, not his. We should pursue him; we should eliminate the threat he's been from the beginning. I wish he were on *our* side."

"Elizabeth!"

"Well, I do, Spencer. He's been brilliant. That much is clear. And we're not hearing all of it, either."

"At least today's news is good." He patted her on the shoulder. He knew she could not discuss the war without becoming enraged. He worried for her health. "I shan't be joining you for supper, my dear. It's been such a hot day. I spent a part of it in the plant and it was like a furnace. I'm drained. If you don't mind, I'll go to my room. Ask Margaret to bring a tray of cookies and milk. If I eat and have a good rest, I'll be able to face tomorrow. I hope it's not as hot as today."

"Yes, it has been warm, Spencer," Elizabeth said. "I'll see to your tray myself. You go on upstairs and lie down. I won't be long."

The next day was even hotter. The thermometer reached ninety before ten o'clock. Because of the heat, it did not surprise Elizabeth when Spencer knocked on her sitting room door at least an hour before he usually arrived home. His face was flushed, just as it had been the day before.

"Oh my, you do look distressed," she said. "Come sit here by the window, and I'll help you off with your boots."

Spencer's face was florid. He was over-heated, but sweat did not stand on his brow, and his breathing, she thought, was shallow. "I'll get a basin of cool water, Spencer. That will help more than anything else. Later, we can ask Arthur to draw a tepid bath for you. By dinner time, you'll be as good as new. So, my darling, off with the shirt."

"Now, Elizabeth—"

"Take it off, Spencer. You need this cool cloth on your face, neck and upper torso. Take the shirt off, please."

It was plain she would permit no deviation. He removed the shirt. As he leaned back in the chair, she administered the cool cloth to his nape, his face, and gradually she moistened his chest and back. "Lean back, Spencer. I'll get fresh, cold water. I'll be right back."

When she returned, his eyes were closed, and his breathing seemed better. She anointed his face and scalp with the cool cloth. "That's better, isn't it?"

"Yes, my dear, much better."

"You were in the plant again today, weren't you?"

"I spent some time there, but the ride home, even with the windows fully open, seemed only to make me feel more uncomfortable. I don't understand it."

"Perhaps you should see Dr. Ferguson—"

"Don't be an alarmist, Elizabeth. It's been hot for four days. It's just that I got too much of it today."

"Lean forward, please. I want to do your back."

"You've made me forget the reason I came home early."

"It wasn't the heat?"

"The news is all over Boston. I read the dispatch at the newspaper office. We've had another tremendous victory."

"They've captured Lee."

"No, my dear. The victory today is on the Mississippi. Grant has finally taken Vicksburg."

"At last."

"Yes. They were dug in. They withstood the best we could muster for months on end. But, some weeks ago the final siege of the city began. Vicksburg has fallen. We control the Mississippi. Our luck has changed. We heard of Meade's victory yesterday and now Grant's today."

"It's wonderful news, Spencer. The rebels are cut in two. Perhaps it will soon be over."

"I hope so, but they're a tenacious lot."

As she dipped the cloth in the basin and wrung it out, she said, "Control of the Mississippi! I just can't believe it! It's a greater victory than the one in Pennsylvania."

"Until we know just how much we've crippled them, who can say? In the end, Gettysburg may be considered the greater victory. The number of Southern men killed in the encounter at Gettysburg was enormous."

"And, we lost none?"

"We lost many, Elizabeth, you know that."

"I know it and you know it, Spencer, but the dispatches are always chary of that kind of information. We are lied to by omission. The dispatches embroider the good parts and hide the bad. There's no honesty in war, that much is certain."

During the night the heat spell was broken. A rain began around midnight and by morning it had gone out to sea leaving refreshing weather behind. Elizabeth was up early to breakfast with Spencer. She was grateful to see how well he looked. His color was normal. There was a spring to his step as he prepared to leave for the office. At the door he turned. "It might be a good idea, Elizabeth, to have another of your pieces for the magazine. These two days of good news would make a nice addition to the next issue. We can easily make room for it."

"You're going to throw the old dog a bone?"

"Elizabeth, what gets into you? You know that was never my intention. I gave you no excuse for a sharp tongue."

"I'm truly sorry, Spencer. I don't know why I spit out such venom. I suppose I miss having deadlines to meet."

Spencer walked back into the room. "It's true you haven't been as busy as you like to be, Elizabeth, but isn't it your own fault? Long ago I asked you about writing a book for Chadwycke & Company. An account of your experiences in the South would sell. Once the war is over, there will be a real desire to read once again. Edward agrees. A personal account of what brought about this disaster might very well find a wide audience. Think about it. And, now I must hurry. We're relocating a couple of the presses into the new part of the building. I want to be there." He kissed the top of her head and left the room.

She sat for a while over a second cup of tea. She knew she had been beastly to him. He didn't deserve it.

From her desk, Elizabeth watched as the sky continued to clear from the west. Write a book? She was sure she could not. The idea of it overpowered her. She had paper in front of her, and the pen close at hand, but the thought of writing a book made her mind go to jelly. I can't write a book! That's impossible. Writing a column is easy enough, but a book, hundreds of pages? It's impossible.

Florence Medlock arrived at ten. "I came by to have tea with you, Elizabeth dear. I hadn't planned on coming this morning, but I just had an impulse—"

She saw the paper on the desk, and the pen. "Oh, dear," she said, "I've barged in at an inconvenient time. You seem to be ready to write."

"No, Aunt Florence. Please stay. The paper is as pristine as it was when I put it there hours ago. I'm not writing anything. Spencer suggested I might write a book. I think he believes it would keep me quiet for a while. But, I can't do it. I can't! I could never write a book."

"And, why not?"

"I don't have anything to say."

"Neither have ninety percent of the people who write, child. Either that, or I choose all the wrong books."

"I just can't do it."

"I've heard that lament before, Elizabeth. I remember a little girl who came to my doorstep years ago. She couldn't write, either. But, she became well known in the North and South as Cassandra. Perhaps you've forgotten her. I have not. That was a girl without the advantages you now have, Elizabeth, and she managed. So can you—if you have the mettle for it. Write the book or leave it alone—it is all the same to me—

but don't say you can't. Others may, but I won't put up with your nonsense. Now, do I get a cup of tea or don't I?"

Elizabeth listened without comment. "Yes, Aunt Florence, but I can't tarry over it. I have some writing to do." As she sipped her tea, as she listened to the bits of gossip Florence Medlock brought, Elizabeth's mind was at work.

The writing began the moment her aunt closed the door. There was no question about where to begin. The beginning—not the one she would ultimately use, perhaps—had suggested itself, and her pen flew across the page. The breeze through the window was cool. How easy it is to work today, she thought. I hope Spencer is having a better day. Poor dear, this past week has been hard on him. The last two days of it, before the rain broke the heat, were almost too much.

She wrote rapidly. The first chapter was completed by three o'clock in the afternoon. After the writing, she needed water, not tea. As she started for the kitchen, she heard a carriage stop at the front door. Who can that be? Not Aunt Florence—not at this hour—and I'm expecting no one. Instead of going down the back stairway, she chose the front.

As she got to the door, Spencer opened it. "Spencer! I'm surprised. You're early." And then she saw his face. He was pale, the skin had a gray pallor, and the wrinkles in his brow cut deeply into his forehead. There was a set to his jaw.

"Yes," he replied. "I've not felt well since eleven. The equipment is moved. I came home to lie down."

"You're ill. I'll send Dawkins for Dr. Ferguson."

"No, Elizabeth. I'm weary from the move; I'm not ill."

"Are you sure?"

"Quite sure."

"Then go on up to your room, Spencer. I'll see to a pot of tea with a dollop of rum in it."

"No tea. I just need to lie down."

He crossed the foyer, unsteadily she thought, and started up the stairs. He had gone up no more than ten steps when he turned toward her. "Elizabeth," he said, "Elizabeth—" His voice trailed off to a whisper. She saw a desperate look on his face, followed by a grimace. His hand went to his throat. As if in a dream, she saw him crumble to the stairs and roll slowly downward until he came to rest at her feet.

The scream that grew inside her head seemed never to come out. And, then she could hear it, echoing from the corridor upstairs. She knelt and lifted his face in her hands. "Spencer, Spencer," she said. "Oh, my darling, you are ill. I should have known, I should have known."

The pain was gone from his face, but there was a pallor that frightened her. She removed her shawl.

As she raised his head to make him more comfortable, she knew: Spencer was dead.

Chapter Sixty-One

The widow's weeds Cassandra wore had been given to charity the first of the year, on the day Emancipation Proclamation became effective. Elizabeth decided Cassandra's purpose had been served. Now, with Spencer's death, she needed to buy new black dresses. This time she was truly a widow.

The wake was in Chadwycke House in the large, oval, formal foyer, with its marble floor and curving stairwell, the room where Spencer died. Papa arrived for the funeral although he had not been able to come to the wedding. He stayed with his sister, Florence. If he meant it to be a rebuke for what he considered his daughter's adulterous relationship with Spencer, Elizabeth didn't know of it. The subject, however, was mentioned to Florence Medlock.

"In the eyes of God, she was never married to Spencer," Chester Medlock said. "It's a pity. He was a most likable chap."

"Their marriage was perfectly legal."

"We were not discussing legality, Florence."

"No, I suppose we weren't. You were deciding what was right and wrong in the eyes of God. Do you truly believe, Chester, you have access to God's inner thoughts? Sheer rubbish! How dare you make a decision for the Almighty?"

"The marriage vows say 'til death do us part,' Florence."

"Are they the words of God, Chester, or of man?"

"It's no wonder you never married. You're willful and headstrong. And, you passed it along to Elizabeth."

"You're her father, Chester. Perhaps being willful and headstrong are Medlock characteristics. You have it. You willfully close your mind. It's your values or none."

"That is your opinion."

"Yes, it is. But, if you believe you have special insight into God's mind, dear brother, then you need watching over."

Elizabeth managed a widow's public duties with quiet dignity, but she was unprepared for those times when she was alone. She missed Spencer in a thousand ways. He had been gone most of each day attending to the business of Chadwycke & Company, and he had often been out at night, but his presence was everywhere. She missed the tap on her door when he said good night, the animation that came over the house with his arrival home each afternoon, his laugh, his touch, his little jokes, his bits of gossip. She wept. Spencer was beyond tears. Elizabeth wept for herself.

"I feel so selfish when I cry," Aunt Florence. "I keep thinking, Why me, Lord? That's so selfish. It's nothing but self-pity."

"Yes, child, it is. As I said to your father, it's arrogance. Chester didn't care for the word, and I dare say you won't either, but it *is* arrogance. What makes you think you're so special that God would choose *you* to punish? Your father decides what God means; you're deciding who God punishes. You both need to pray more and speak less."

Her words brought tears. "You didn't have to say that."

"Yes, dear child, I did. I know your loss is great, but you seem to forget that I loved Spencer, too. He was my dear friend. I know you have need to weep and grieve. You can count on me. I'll weep with you or hold your hand. But, in my opinion, you are no more privy to God's plans than your father."

"You think I should dry my eyes and get on with life."

"That's not what I said, Elizabeth. Let the tears flow, lament your loss, let your suffering come out. I share it. But, there must come a day when you will do with your life what you were put on earth to do. Many of us never find out what that is. You were more fortunate."

Spencer's majority interest in Chadwycke & Company was left to Elizabeth and Edward. There was a note: "*My will outlines the facts that surround my bequests, Elizabeth, but I wanted you to be aware of my reasoning. You are a writer, but you have no interest in the day-to-day business side of writing. For that reason, and because he has earned it, I leave control of the company to Edward. With the other properties and securities, the income from your share will give you adequate resources. You will be free to write the truth as you see it. I know you cannot compromise your beliefs. It will never be necessary to do so. It is my hope that Edward will consult with you as concerns the affairs of Chadwycke & Company. He is a man of honor. I have been fortunate to have known and been loved by two such as you.*"

The date of the note shocked her. It was written only a month before his death.

Tears washed down her cheeks. But, as though he had spoken to her, she dried her eyes and went on with the business of going through his personal belongings.

She put his clothes in order for the poorbox box at church. His jewelry had not been mentioned in his will. She put the case aside for Edward.

Life went on at Chadwycke House. One day Elizabeth took a fresh piece of paper, picked up her pen and wrote, "This book is dedicated to my beloved Spencer." She put it on the top of her one completed chapter.

The writing progressed and so did the war, but both moved much too slowly.

The rebellion, as Elizabeth preferred to call it, should have been over with the defeat of the Army of Northern Virginia at Gettysburg or with the fall of Vicksburg. But, this was not the case.

Meade stupidly failed to pursue, and Lee's retreat was orderly and successful.

In the lonely months after Spencer's death, Elizabeth tried to write every day, but the numbness she felt in her limbs extended to her brain. She completed pages, but she wondered if they had any value. It was lonely in that big house by herself, but she couldn't go back to live with Aunt Florence. Such a move, she believed, would thwart something Spencer had in mind when he first proposed marriage.

Her brain played hurtful tricks. At times, late in the afternoon, she would think she heard Spencer in the foyer. His voice would float up to her room with sparkling clarity. One time she walked to the railing and looked down. The foyer was empty. She ran back to her room and wept.

Even the accounts of the successes of Grant, Sherman, Sheridan and Thomas meant nothing. Her interest in everything diminished with the loss of Spencer. Aunt Florence brought news of the win at the battles of Lookout Mountain and Missionary Ridge. She listened. She was happy the war was at least turning around, but she really didn't care.

When Sherman invaded Georgia in the spring of 1864, she was still in a deep depression. After he captured Atlanta and started his march to the sea, she gained a new interest. This was no longer just a war being brought to the South; it was a war going toward Greenleaf Plantation. Her girls were there. Victorious men are sometimes hard to control. She had read accounts of rape and pillage.

These were Union soldiers, Sherman's men. There was probably nothing to worry about, but the thought would not die. She had seen more than enough of brutish men, bent on having their own way. She could not shake the feeling of danger; she worried. Her daughters would be young ladies, Mary almost twenty now, and little Frannie nineteen. Vulnerable ages. Where were they and how were they? If the girls were at the plantation, there was real danger. News dispatches interested her again. She read them avidly. Sherman slashed his way southeast, in the direction of Greenleaf. When he marched into Savannah a few days before the Christmas of 1864, her heart ached with fear.

"Clay is a bastard," she told Florence Medlock, "a bastard, a pluperfect bastard. If the girls are safely in Philadelphia, he could have written."

"Clay is furious with you, Elizabeth. He wouldn't write to you if he were facing Judgment Day."

"I suppose you're right. But, Byron could have written, that old lady could have—"

"Clay's aunt?"

"No. I suppose that's expecting too much, too. Miss Mattie never had any love for me then, and the scandal must have caused a world of talk, especially since it all happened in Philadelphia."

"You'll not get word from any of them."

"Oh, I can hear Papa now, Aunt Florence. 'Ye shall reap what ye sow.' He always smiled when someone got what he called 'their just rewards.' Or is that my imagination?"

"No, dear. That is Chester."

One sunny Spring morning in 1865 Elizabeth said, "I'd almost decided we'd never try to take Richmond again, but I read that we're on the move towards Petersburg. That's good news, and isn't it about time? We've been thrusting and parrying in that area for nearly a year now with no results."

"War isn't a move on a chessboard, dear. It's a dirty, muddy, and bloody business. The President didn't send our boys to be slaughtered. They went to quell a disturbance—"

"Disturbance? Disturbance, Aunt Florence? You underplay it, just as our President does. It's a rebellion, a civil war, and our boys are being slaughtered. And, why? Because of the posturing of our generals and our President's leadership."

"I used the wrong word, Elizabeth. But you know full well what I meant. Perhaps my word was too weak, but yours, all of them, are too strong. War cannot be done quickly. We've seen that. If Lee had been successful in Pennsylvania, he might be on our doorsteps right now. Can you imagine how we'd fight? My hat pins would be lethal weapons, my tea or coffee would be laced with arsenic.We mustn't judge. Lincoln is trying to quell a rebellion, and it's clear, they believe in their cause with the same fervor we do. They're fighting as we would fight. War is even more difficult in winter.

"It's spring now, Aunt Florence. It's April."

"And the troops are on the move. You just told me of a battle for Petersburg. It will be Richmond next."

"Petersburg could remain untouched. Richmond has up to now. It's been four long years, Aunt Florence. Everyone is losing heart. They're weary of it and sick of seeing the casualty lists."

"We'll take Richmond, Elizabeth. Mark my words."

At that moment a battle was raging beyond Petersburg. Confederate General George Pickett was unable to hold his position. When he was forced to retreat, the defenses of Petersburg crumbled. Word of the defeat reached Richmond. General Lee advised the Confederate President of the situation. Jefferson Davis and his cabinet escaped in the darkness of the night of April 2.

Before the troops left Richmond, the order was given: "Destroy the city. Leave nothing of value. Blow up the bridges, burn the cotton, fire the buildings. Let them have a victory without substance."

At dawn on April 3, 1865, the Union forces found Richmond still burning.

A *Boston Journal* reporter wrote: "I entered the town soon after sunrise and found our troops pouring in from all quarters, cheering, swinging their caps, helping themselves to tobacco, rushing upon the double-quick, eager to overtake Lee."

She reread the account for the fourth time. She liked the sound of the last four words: "...eager to overtake Lee."

The two ladies decided that from then on neither would open their newspapers until they could meet at Chadwycke House. "It's the only way, Aunt Florence. This has meant so much to both of us. The war is in its closing days. We'll share the news. When Lee is captured, it will be over."

There were news dispatches of the fires being quenched in Richmond, and of President Lincoln arriving to survey that devastated area. News of the rebels' defeat at Little Sayler's Creek, where 6000 prisoners were taken, and, sadly, news of Lee's safe westward retreat.

"Here is something interesting on the second page, Elizabeth. It purports to be a copy of a proclamation made by Jefferson Davis from his capitol in Danville. It says: 'We have entered a new phase of the struggle. Relieved of the necessity of guarding particular points, our army will be free to move from point to point to strike the enemy. Let us but will it, and we are free.'"

"Read it again, please, Aunt Florence. My ears refuse to give credence to it. That cannot be right."

"You read it, Elizabeth. Second page, first column of *The Boston Journal.*"

She watched as her niece found the article and read it. "Your lips are moving," she said. "You are so astonished that you're sounding out each word."

"My lips are, but my brain isn't. This must be a joke. Davis couldn't have issued such an insane proclamation."

"It may be false. We've seen that before, but if Jeff Davis wrote this, we're far from a truce, dear, whether or not Lee surrenders," Florence Medlock said. "He makes the defeat at Richmond sounds like a new opportunity, '...our army will be free to move from point to point to strike the enemy.' Patent nonsense!"

"It's no worse than, 'Let us but will it, and we are free.' It requires more than will alone to gain the freedom they want so badly for themselves but deny to others."

"We are dealing with a madman, Elizabeth. I feel sure Lee will be forced to surrender soon. But, this power-crazed idiot won't know when he's beaten."

"When Lee surrenders, Jefferson Davis will see the cause is lost. This is bravado, nothing more."

"I hope you're right, Elizabeth. In my bones I don't think you are, but I pray that you are."

The two ladies continued to meet. One day they read the dispatch they had been hoping for. Very early in the morning of April 9, 1865, Lee sent a note to Grant. Well before noon, Lee surrendered.

By ten o'clock p.m. of the same day, the news was delivered to President Lincoln in Washington. It spread across the nation with the speed of sound—the joyous sound of voices echoing and reechoing in every town and village.

Chapter Sixty-Two

The next day Elizabeth and her aunt read the text of Lee's farewell to his troops. "A gentleman to the end," Elizabeth said, lowering the paper. "What a leader! His words exactly right. It's too bad he wasn't on our side."

"If only the President of that rag-tailed bunch were as perceptive as General Lee," her aunt replied. "If so, the killing would be over. But, unfortunately, Davis hasn't the intellect of Lee. Our problems will continue, Elizabeth. Hear what I say."

"This will be in their newspapers, too, Aunt Florence. Once the reality of it is known, we'll be sued for peace."

"Men's minds are not easily penetrated, and the minds of defeated men are harder than oak."

Two days later they read the full text of a speech Lincoln had given. "Look at this, Aunt Florence. He's an ass. It took four long years, and now when we are finally victorious at Richmond, when we have driven them to Danville, he speaks of reconciliation. Reconciliation, for God's sake! Where is his mind? It's time to raise the cudgel high; it's time to seize the main chance, especially if the battle for Richmond is not the end of the rebellion."

"I read it, Elizabeth. He chose his words with care. Mr. Lincoln thinks it through before he speaks. We weren't in this to punish the South; we were in it to give freedom to all the citizens of the South—"

"Blacks are not citizens."

"Not now, but when the rebellion is quelled, it should be the President's first thought. I'm sure it will be."

Elizabeth laughed. "You call me an optimist, Aunt Florence. What about you? You're worse; you're a dreamer. I've followed Mr. Lincoln's public remarks, and what has he said? He's made no public statement that convinces me he's a staunch supporter of giving the slaves citizenship."

"He will, Elizabeth. I'm sure he will. He chooses his words. He can't afford to inflame large segments of the populace, even here in Boston, but Mr. Lincoln is fair."

"He's a politician. He'll do the expedient. He has never had any real fire for abolition. He toyed with us, he wooed us, but where is his clear declaration?"

"We differ, Elizabeth. We must each stay with our beliefs and remain courteous. We must lower our voices and lower our ardor."

"You must lower your expectations."

"Perhaps, my dear, perhaps."

In the days that followed Lee's surrender, the newspapers carried the account of the 28,231 men who marched into Appomattox Court House to lay down their arms. Mr. Coffin wrote of it in *The Journal*. "As the defeated Southern soldiers marched by, the men of the Union army brought their arms to the salute position. The shocked Army of Northern Virginia recovered quickly and returned the salute. With that gesture, the battle for Richmond was finally over. The rancor that burned in the hearts of these men, North and South, began to wane. It was a simple salute; it was one army acknowledging the bravery, the valor, and the honor of the other."

The two ladies continued to meet for what they called the War Watch. Elizabeth fought with herself to keep from peeking at the newspapers before Florence Medlock arrived. Since Lee's surrender, the dispatches told of Major General William T. Sherman's defeat of Raleigh on April 13. The following day

Brevet Major General Robert Anderson raised over Fort Sumter the same tattered and torn U. S. flag he had taken down in defeat four years earlier. Those were stories she savored.

On April 15 Elizabeth peeked. She opened the newspaper before her aunt arrived. She had worked all morning. Her hands ached from holding the pen. I need a rest, she thought. I need a cup of hot chocolate. When she rang for Margaret, no one came. She waited. There was no sound. I'd better see to this, she thought. As she stepped into the hallway, she saw Margaret making her way down the passage.

"Oh, there you are, young lady. What kept you?" Margaret's large blue eyes were flooded with tears. "What is it, child? What's the matter?" Elizabeth listened but the blubbering made no sense. She recognized the name "Lincoln," but little else, so she went down the stairs to the kitchen.

The news of the assassination of Abraham Lincoln covered the city like an ice shower. From household to household, it raced across the town, but she had not heard it. She'd been busy writing. In the kitchen, Elizabeth found everyone in tears. Cook was most in control. "Mr. Lincoln has been shot," she said, honking her nose loudly into a handkerchief. "He's dead, they say. Oh, what will we do?"

Elizabeth raced back up the stairway. She opened her paper. It was there. Large black headlines, the paper bordered in black. It was true. "My God," she said aloud."My God in heaven. What have we come to—" And then she heard the carriage at the front door. It was Aunt Florence.

Before the day was over, Andrew Johnson, a Union supporter from Tennessee, was sworn in as President of the United States of America. His troubles began. Talk of vengeance was rife.

On that same day a group of men came to see the new President, demanding harsh treatment for the South. Those loud-talking men, led by Senator Wade, seized upon the death of the President to push their own views.

President Johnson attempted to stand with one foot in each camp, but he was not so politically adroit as President Lincoln had been. Finally, when there seemed no other way, Johnson said, "I hold this: Robbery is a crime; rape is a crime; treason is a crime; and, crime must be punished."

Even before Lee's surrender, the quiet voice of Abraham Lincoln spoke of forgiveness, of reconciliation. Elizabeth did not agree, but now the point was moot. The President's assassination, at the hands of a Southerner, stopped all talk of compassion.

Talk of punishment grew stronger. Ralph Waldo Emerson felt the war was a necessary purge to rid the social system of "great evils"; he thought the men of the Confederacy were "enemies of mankind"; and, that the war itself was a "battle for Humanity."

From lesser men she heard: Free the slaves! Punish the insurrectionists! Take their lands! Take away their rights! Occupy the whole area, put the army in full charge until we are sure they can behave! They lost the war; they are the vanquished!

Was this what she wanted? Her mind whirled. Treason should not go unpunished, but how much of the current uproar was malice or vindictiveness; or, worse yet, how much of it was a ploy to move in behind the winning side to gobble up lands and assets while the frenzy of winning the war and losing a President had the whole world in a cocked hat?

The war, itself, wallowed along. In large areas of the South the fighting was over. Defeated Southern forces went back to their plows. But, to some, it would not be over until the last man lay dead.

Mosby's Raiders, a scant forty miles from the nation's capitol, did not surrender until a week after Lincoln's death, and more than ten days after Lee's surrender. General Johnston's men, further South, continued to hold out against Sherman. In some parts of the Confederate States, little credence was taken of Lee's surrender, so the war continued.

"It's like killing a snake," Elizabeth said. "You cut off it's head and it refuses to die."

"What do you know of snakes, child?"

"I know, Aunt Florence."

"Well, if that's the way snakes behave, then I agree with you. The South is beaten. And, still, they won't sue for peace. It's the stubbornness of Jeff Davis, that's what it is. "

"Where is he hiding while his forces are being pummeled?"

"He's been reported in Greenville, in Charlotte, and God only knows where all else. He must now have a hard time finding a new place, with Atlanta destroyed, and Columbus burned, and with Mobile and New Orleans in our hands. Where can he be? What can he be thinking?"

"He's not thinking of his people. The killing goes on. This is no longer a battle; it's a rout."

"Not a rout, dear," Aunt Florence said. "That's what you would prefer it to be. But, a rout, at least to me, implies flight. They're not running, even if their cause is lost." Elizabeth started to speak, but her aunt, raised a hand. "I know it was a Southerner who killed Mr. Lincoln, Elizabeth, but it was the act of one man. My sympathies are with Southern women who must stand by and see this carnage."

The two ladies read of the Lonesome Train that carried the body of the slain President on a journey of 1654 miles. Five days after the final journey began, the man who killed Lincoln was tracked down. When he refused to surrender, the barn he hid in was set on fire. John Wilkes Booth was shot.

On the morning of May 10, Florence Medford said, "I don't know what it is, Elizabeth, but just as I was leaving, Ethel asked me to remind you to pay special attention to the articles on the second page of *The Journal.* I was curious, but she just said, 'Tell her to look there.' And, that's all she would say. Open it, dear, or I shall die of curiosity."

Elizabeth read the long statement by William Lloyd Garrison aloud. One line caught her attention: "The year of jubilee is come; slavery is now a thing of the past." She put the paper down. "I'm afraid Mr. Garrison is not thinking clearly. I'm not so sure the year of jubilee is here yet."

"Read the rest, Elizabeth."

Wendell Phillips' reply made more sense to her: "The system of slavery stands, in the eyes of the law, untouched."

"Oh, goodness," Florence Medlock said, "I do hope not."

"He's absolutely right, Aunt Florence. What has changed? The war is not over, and not one law has been revised. Changing the laws will not be easy, even when the war is won. Not without Lincoln."

"Not without Lincoln? What are you saying, Elizabeth? You've always said he was weak on abolition."

"He was, Aunt Florence, but he was well above the crowd we now have in Washington. Expect nothing from Johnson."

"You have a new man to champion, Elizabeth. You have Mr. Phillips. Perhaps your column will start again."

"No, Aunt Florence. Cassandra is no more. And, Elizabeth Chadwycke is busy writing a book. There will not be a column again, under any name. Besides, what Mr. Phillips said this time does not—at least in my mind—negate the fact that he displays little fervor for the rights of women. There was talk of merging the Women's Rights Society with the Anti-Slavery Society, but he would have none of that."

"You're sure? Wendell Phillips?"

"Quite sure. I appreciate the help he's been on abolition, and I appreciate the pioneering of Mr. Garrison, but the years seem to have taken a toll on him. Garrison doesn't have the bite he once had. Perhaps he's too old."

"He's only about sixty, maybe a little more."

"He's slowing down."

"Well, my dear, if I'm any judge, so are you."

Elizabeth laughed. Florence Medlock had hit a mark.

"Yes, I have lost my zest for it. Spencer buoyed me up in so many ways. Why do we always learn these things too late? I didn't realize it, but he was the wind that filled my sails and he was my rudder. Now my only interest is the book Spencer suggested I write just before he died. This fight is not mine. Let others pick up the standard."

"That doesn't sound like you, Elizabeth."

"Well, it is me. When I finish the book, maybe I'll help with Susan Anthony's cause, but I'll stay independent of her organization. I work best alone."

"Not work with her? A woman's right to the vote has been a never-ending theme with you."

"I'm not sure I'd fit in her organization. I don't like what she said recently. Wait. I have it. I clipped it from the newspaper. Let me read it.

She fumbled through the papers on the table."Oh, here it is, right under my nose. You are not going to like what you hear, Aunt Florence. Listen to this drivel: 'Of what good is Negro suffrage, as proposed, to Negro women? There is—there can be—but one true basis, that taxation and representation must be inseparable; here our demand must go beyond women...' and I don't disagree with her to that point, but then she goes on to say, '...We therefore wish to broaden our women's rights platform and make it in name what it has been in spirit, a human rights platform.'"

"I see nothing wrong in that. You want equality for women, equal justice in every way, and that is human rights. It's not men's rights or women's rights."

"It will set us back twenty years, Aunt Florence. We've only begun to make a mark. People are beginning to take the rights of women seriously. But, when Susan Anthony changes the direction of the Society, she tries to force men to bite off a larger mouthful. They will fight it. No, we must take one step at a time."

"Yes, but in the end, it's human rights."

"This is a war women will have to win by attrition, not by a direct assault."

"You *have* changed."

"Yes, I've grown older. Perhaps, if I lived nearer to Papa now, I would distress him a little less."

Peace did not occur. With the capture of Jefferson Davis, President Johnson issued another proclamation. "Armed resistance to the authority of this Government in the insurrectionary states may be regarded virtually at an end." His words rang hollow. Within days the paper reported the dead and wounded at the Battle of Palmito Ranch in Texas.

But, Johnson's proclamation was taken seriously in some quarters. There were two days of parades. The spectacle was called the Grand Review. Elizabeth saw nothing grand about it. It was posturing, boys playing soldier, a public display to assuage the hurts of women who had lost their men in battle.

The first day honored the Army of the Potomac, and the second honored Sherman's men from the west. With fighting still going on, with killing still a part of it, the parades were hollow. Worst of all, in Florence Medlock's mind, was the poor taste shown in playing the war song, "Marching Through Georgia" as the troops passed in review.

"Victory parades, indeed! There has been no peace."

That was true.

In some parts of the South, the fighting went on. There had been neither peace nor amnesty.

Florence Medlock continued to come for tea, but the War Watch was allowed to quietly fade out of existence.

"President Johnson's proclamation granting amnesty and parole for all the rebels if they would take a loyalty oath and support emancipation would make more sense to me, Aunt Florence, if he had not, on the very same day, issued a second one. The first one sounded like a man offering an olive branch. The second one tainted the first. Politics. Nothing else."

"It was clumsy of him to put both thoughts into the one document, dear. You are suspicious of everybody's motives."

"I've learned to be suspicious."

On June, 2, 1865, well after the "parades and posturing" in Washington, the men of the Trans-Mississippi Department of the Confederate States of America surrendered.

"It drags on and on," Elizabeth said. "The snake lost its head when Lee surrendered and still it writhed. We hit it again and again. Finally, there was one mighty blow when he put Jefferson Davis in chains, but the tail still lives."

"As Shakespeare said, 'Time will one day end it.'"

"You and Papa, Aunt Florence! The Medfords can always come up with words for the occasion. Words tend to sweep it all into a corner. This won't sweep. Nothing will end it. We'll go on hacking at this serpent forever."

There was a third "Grand Review" for Sheridan's men. It was a hot day in June and the sun was merciless. Along the parade route men fell from heat and exhaustion.

"It's a debacle. It's in the worst taste possible." Elizabeth said. "Silly parades by stupid men. A woman would never permit such a thing! Where is their compassion? Strutting won't bring amnesty or heal the nation's wounds."

"Yes. Washington pulls in two directions."

"Would that it were only two, Aunt Florence. We might be able to cope with only two directions. It seems to me every man there is looking to his own personal power."

"Judge not, Elizabeth, lest thou—"

"Oh, rubbish. I was given a brain to use."

The rebellion, like a pot that had been pushed to the back of the stove, continued to boil. A bubble would form, rise to the surface and pop. Brigadier General Stand Watie, a Cherokee and commanding general of the Territorial Division, finally surrendered late in June of 1865 on behalf of the Cherokee, Creek, Seminole and Osage units of the Confederate States of America.

In the last days, the dying throes of the South were all

senseless and empty heroics. The vainglorious flight, the self-imposed exile of the group of men who crossed the Rio Grande into Mexico seemed especially sad to Elizabeth. They chose July 4, 1865, the anniversary of the defeat of the South at Gettysburg.

It was an empty gesture. "More of the boys playing soldier," she muttered to herself. It astonished her to read the names of some of the men who had been in this motley band of losers: Confederate officers Stanley Price, Jo Shelby, John Magruder and Kirby Smith, as well as two Confederate governors, Henry Allen of Louisiana and Pendelton Murrah of Texas.

The winter of 1865 was severe. Elizabeth and Florence Medlock were happy to see the arrival of spring in Boston. With each spring rain another layer of the winter's soot was washed from the cobbles, and with each washing, Elizabeth's spirits rose. The book Spencer had suggested was completed. She wanted to reread it before taking it to Edward for his opinion, but there was nothing more to do, save choosing the exact words for the dedication page. It would be to Spencer, of course.

And then, to shatter a life finally being put into perspective, came that day in May: The day she received the letter from Byron, the day Gordy came to Boston.

Chapter Sixty-Three

Elizabeth received Byron's letter scant hours before Gordy arrived. In the days that followed, her anger subsided. She saw to Gordy's enrollment at Harvard and arranged for tutors.

That was the first step. Then she read every paper, every deed, every document Byron sent. Most of it was easy to comprehend. It was information she would need *if* she were to allow Byron to will her his part of the Greenleaf Plantation, but, once he began his recovery, she would put a quick stop to that absurd notion. Her life had been reconstituted in Boston, and in Boston it would stay.

She could not grasp the financial situation of the estate, with its mortgages and factored accounts. She sent that bundle to Edward. Her note said, "*Edward, be a dear and go through all these documents for me. They were sent by my former brother-in-law who is ill. If anything needs to be done, I will try to do it for him. Together we can determine how best to do whatever needs doing, if anything.*"

The contents of the satchel Gordy brought her from Byron were discussed with Florence Medlock, but only in a general way. Elizabeth spoke of some of Byron's neatly bound packets, but without elaborate detail; some bundles were not discussed at all.

She did not mention Byron's wish that she take his share of the Greenleaf estate after his death. Her life had been rebuilt in Boston; she had no intention of accepting his absurd proposal.

She would not be going back to Greenleaf Plantation so Elizabeth saw no point in discussing that subject with her aunt.

She told Florence Medlock of Byron's illness, of Clay's death in action, and, of course, she told her how the girls had been sent to Philadelphia before Sherman took Savannah.

"At least, my dear," her aunt said, "that's a large worry off your mind. You have not mentioned the girls in months. That omission disturbed me. I knew you were worried about the girls."

"Not knowing was the worst of it. It was all so uncalled for. Byron, damn his soul—"

"Elizabeth!"

"I mean it. Byron could have written."

"You have word of the girls now."

"Because he wants a favor. His conscience bothers him. It's the Greenleaf cheek. They expect to get anything they ask."

"Well, dear, you're doing it, everything he asked. You've taken Gordy in, and you have him enrolled in school."

"I'll do what I can for Gordy. Perhaps it's for the part I may have had in the downfall of the South. Byron blistered me with that. I don't remember his exact words, but he clearly said, 'You must share in the responsibility for your part in bringing down a system that was at least working.'"

"He said that? He *does* have cheek. But, dear, at least you know the girls are safe. Your worries continued until Byron sent Gordy to Boston Be grateful. Try not to damn Byron. Be wary when you damn, Elizabeth. It's a double-edged sword."

"He gave me pitifully little news of them, but, yes, he told me enough to put my mind at rest. But, just think of it, Aunt Florence, instead of Matilda Greenleaf, he could have sent the girls here, where they should have been. Still, I thank God they're safe. Which brings me to the reason I asked you over this morning, Aunt Florence. I'd like a special favor."

"Did a little of the Greenleaf cheek rub off on you?"

Elizabeth laughed. "You have a right to ask. But, let me tell you what I have in mind and then you be the judge. Gordy now seems to be settled, his studies are progressing from all I can see—"

"Get to the point, Elizabeth."

"I'd like to go to Philadelphia. I want to go see my girls. I may not meet with a welcome there, but Matilda Greenleaf must be a toothless crone by now. She may claw me, but she can't eat me."

"And you want me to look in on your house from time to time; you want me to keep Chadwycke House running, is that it?"

"Yes. How quickly you see through me."

"We Medlocks don't have a lot of cheek, child, but we're not without brains, and you're transparent, almost from the start."

"Then you'll do it?"

"Yes, of course. Now that Clay is dead, I know you should at least try to see the girls, try to reestablish what you once had. When do you plan to leave?"

"I'll take the train to New York this afternoon, stay over with Papa for a day, and then go on to Philadelphia."

"And, you already have your ticket." It was a statement.

"I've sent Mr. Conroy to pick it up for me, yes."

"Well, dear," Aunt Florence said, "let's hear no more talk about the amount of cheek the Greenleaf family has."

The Reverend Mr. Medlock seemed distant, removed, even annoyed to find Elizabeth on his doorstep. The coolness of his welcome brought a moment of uncertainty, even regret, that she had decided to come to the manse, but it didn't bring the kind of pain she felt during their conversation after breakfast the next morning.

"I'm on my way to Philadelphia, Papa. I've recently found out that the girls are with Matilda Greenleaf. I may find that I am not welcome there, but I have to go, I have to see them, talk to them, hold them."

"How did you find that out, Elizabeth?"

"From Byron. He told me they were safe."

"Yes. They're safe."

She looked directly at him. Had she heard correctly? Red crept up from his white shirt collar. "You knew, Papa?" He said nothing. "Papa, are you saying you *knew* they were safe? You didn't tell me? How long have you known?"

Mr. Medlock had not meant to say anything about what he knew or his visits to his granddaughters. It just tumbled out, and Elizabeth was quick to pounce on it. She waited.

The truth was written on his face. "You needn't answer, Papa. You knew. You've known for a long time I dare say."

At last he spoke. "Yes, Elizabeth, I knew. But, my child, I was sworn to secrecy. Lavinia Custer is Matilda Greenleaf's sister, as you know. She knew of the girl's whereabouts and their welfare. I was worried, of course. She told me they were safe. Later, she arranged for me to see them, but I had to give my word that I would not breathe so much as a hint of it to you. It was a condition Matilda Greenleaf insisted upon. I gave my word, Elizabeth. I could not tell you."

"You were under duress, Papa. The promise you made was unfair. Matilda Greenleaf is a wicked woman. Why did you feel you had to comply?"

"You have no right to suggest that I should have broken my word." Her father was angry. "That's what you're saying. That's exactly what you are saying. If you have no morals, Elizabeth, that is a concern that you must face with your Maker. You have no right to demand that I descend to your level."

What he said stunned her. It should not have. She knew how he felt, and yet hearing it brought more pain than she could endure without answering him in a way he would find willful.

She tried not to speak at all, but the words came slowly to her lips. "You are right, Papa. You owe nothing to a daughter, to a fallen woman, to someone you feel has deeply sinned by not cleaving to a philandering husband—to a woman who has been divorced! But, Papa, it relieves my heart to know—because I heard it in your church—that Jesus did not feel so unforgiving toward Mary Magdalene."

In Philadelphia, she resisted the urge to rush to see her children. She needed a night's rest. She had not expected to find scorn and pain at her father's house, but she was fully prepared to find that and more at her meeting with Matilda Greenleaf. She had to be ready for it.

It was just past ten the next morning when the carriage brought her to 12 Haverford Place. As she mounted the steps, she added the years since she had been at this house to Matilda Greenleaf's age. She must be almost ninety now, she thought. What could there be to fear? As she raised the knocker, she wondered if George were still in service. He, too, must now be quite old. Not as old as Miss Mattie, but not far behind. She brought the knocker down sharply.

She heard the knock echo in the entryway. The door opened. It was George. He was smaller. Had he shrunk? His hair was white as winter snow, but the smile was still warm. "Miss Elizabeth," he said.

"George! How nice to see you. It's been a long, long time." She took a step forward. "May I come in?"

"Yes, come in." Elizabeth heard the strong voice of Matilda Greenleaf. "I've been expecting you. I didn't know when you'd arrive, but I knew Gordy was sent to you, so I knew one day you'd be here."

George stepped aside. Behind him, Elizabeth saw Miss Mattie in a rolling chair. She had been small and bird-like when they had first met, but now Clay's aunt was a bundle of bones with brown-spotted skin drawn across the parts where the flesh had fallen away. She sat erect in her chair, with a robe across her lap. "Come on in, girl. Don't stand there. It may be summer but the wind has a chill to it. Come in, so we can close the door."

George stood behind the chair waiting.

"You want to see Byron," Matilda Greenleaf said, "but before you go up, I must have a word with you. Come into the parlor."

The furniture had not changed, but the colors had faded. The parlor was too warm, the windows were closed, and there was a fire in the grate. A fire, Elizabeth thought, in summer! It added to the oppressiveness of the musty room.

Miss Mattie pulled the shawl closer. She needed to warm her body. Her blood was not enough. She had a fire, the lap robe and a shawl. "Sit down, Elizabeth. There, where I can see you."

"I'll sit here, not so close to the fire."

"Fire didn't bother you when you helped turn Atlanta to ashes—and Richmond, and Mobile and Columbus, and Salem, and all the others."

"The war is over, Miss Mattie."

"Yes, Elizabeth, I suppose it is, but the havoc it wrought is not. It hangs like a pall over the South."

"There were losses on both sides, Miss Mattie."

The tea arrived.

"You will pour for us, please, Clarisse. I'm too old for it, and Elizabeth should not be forced to be a hostess in this house."

Elizabeth let the remark pass. "It's nice to see you again, Clarisse," she said to the maid she had not seen since that morning in 1844 when she and Clay left for Greenleaf Plantation for the first time. "The years have treated you kindly."

"You lookin' good, too, Miss Elizabeth."

Matilda Greenleaf did not wait for Clarisse to finish serving. "Elizabeth, I asked you in for a cup of tea so we could establish an understanding before you see Byron."

"I want to see Byron and I want to see my daughters."

"All in its own good time. This is my house, and I will decide the order of things."

"It wasn't my intention—"

"I'm sure it wasn't." Everything in the room seemed to stop. Even Clarisse stood quietly, the pot in her hand. Elizabeth looked directly into Matilda Greenleaf's small black eyes. They are alive, she thought, even if that body seems ready for the grave. "As I was saying, Elizabeth, we must have an understanding—or your trip will have been in vain."

"I have no cards to play, Miss Mattie."

"Oh, I'm not so sure that's truc, Elizabeth, but we will have to see how wisely you play them."

"Then, Miss Mattie, perhaps I should hear what you have to say."

"Very sensible."

Matilda Greenleaf waved Clarisse out of the room. When she heard the latch click, she said: "I'll be direct, Elizabeth. I want no misunderstanding. Byron told me of his plans for his part of Greenleaf Plantation if he should fail to recover. What I think of his decision does not matter. I have only one concern: the welfare of my two grandnieces. You can play a role in that—even if Byron has to buy your cooperation with his half of the estate."

The insult was too much. "Let me make one point at the outset, Miss Mattie. Perhaps it will clear the air. I came here to see my children. Nothing more. At the same time I hoped I could see Byron. I intend to tell him, in person, that I want no part of his plan to convey his one-half of the estate to me. I have no desire to own any part of Greenleaf Plantation—or to ever go there again for any reason."

"Oh, Miss High and Mighty."

"No, Miss Mattie, but you implied that I came here to get something that wasn't mine. I have not. I have no interest in Greenleaf Plantation or Georgia—not any part of it. I am not interested in Byron's proposal. You need have no fear, Miss Mattie, I'll never return to Greenleaf Island."

"Never?"

"You heard it clearly, Miss Mattie. Never!"

"The sole reason for your trip was to see your children?"

"Yes."

The old lady leaned forward. Her black eyes were alive. This was what she wanted to hear.

"You love your children and you want the best for them, is that it?"

"That's right, Miss Mattie. I want nothing from Byron or any of the Greenleafs. I want to try to make up to my children for the years they were taken away from me by their father."

"If you want the best for them, you're going at it in a strange way. Their inheritance hangs in a precarious balance. Their father was an officer in the Confederate army. There's talk of war reparations, of punishment. What is left of the plantation may not come to them at all, not even their father's share; it may be taken as booty, as the spoils of war. From what I've been able to determine, amnesty comes in all stripes."

Matilda Greenleaf tried to put her teacup back on the tray, but it slipped from her fingers with a crash. She appeared not to notice.

"Do you want your daughters to come into their rightful inheritance or don't you?"

"Of course I do. My girls mean everything to me."

"If that's so, then your animosity toward me does nothing to help them. You don't seem to know the damage you and the other abolitionists have done to this county. It's in chaos, particularly in the South. Land is being taken from rightful owners, and I see no reason why our family should receive special treatment, unless—" Matilda Greenleaf stopped abruptly.

"Unless what?"

"Unless you get off your perch. Try to make amends."

"What could I do? I have no friends in Washington—"

"I'm not so sure of that, Elizabeth. I think you might make the difference. Listen to me. I've thought this through. Hear what I have to say."

Miss Greenleaf dabbed at the corners of her mouth, wiping away spittle that had collected as she spoke. Then she began again. "I expect Greenleaf Plantation will not fare well because of our strong support of the Confederate States—"

"That's what I was saying—"

"That would be the case, except for one thing: *You* were not living in the South—*you* were on their side. You were in the thick of all that mitigated to bring the South down. You were there, Elizabeth, rallying the rabble who brought about the end of it. *You were Cassandra.* In light of all that—"

"You are an opportunist, Miss Mattie, a callous—"

"Don't preach to me, girl! Take a good look. You must know that I am no longer interested in what happens to me. I've been on earth too long right now, but I believe we're placed here for something. Perhaps my role in these last days of my life is to keep a foolish woman from her own stupidity. Your daughters' rightful inheritance is being snatched away because their father was a Confederate officer. You can prevent that, Elizabeth."

Elizabeth knew from experience that whenever they were together in private, Matilda Greenleaf had always spoken her mind. Clay had never heard it, but she knew, because she had been the brunt of it. This appeared to be no exception. The old lady continued.

"Listen to me. If the confiscation of Greenleaf Plantation were not about to happen, I would never have invited you into my house this morning. If it were just the two of us, young woman, I wouldn't give you and your sorrow a passing thought. Yes, Elizabeth, I still remember the scandal you caused. I'll never forgive you for it."

No, Elizabeth thought, I don't think you would have asked me in.The scandal must have been hard for you to take.

Miss Mattie's arrogance melted. Her voice was calmer as she continued: "It's time now to put grievances aside, yours and mine; it's time to do what we can for Mary and Ann Frances.

If you want as much for them as you profess, then you'll consider Byron's bequest. In that way, Cassandra and her daughters would be the rightful inheritors of Greenleaf Plantation."

Matilda Greenleaf was silent. It was as though she were waiting for a slow child who could not comprehend quickly. Finally, she continued.

"If you fail to exercise the opportunity Byron offers you, you will snatch your daughters' inheritance from them as surely as you're sitting here. By your willfulness, you will allow the estate to go to the first greedy man who tries to wrest it from us."

"You are a wicked woman, Miss Mattie."

"Save your breath. What you think of me has never been a concern—not yesterday, not today. My concern is the Greenleaf girls. If you have bat brains, it will also be your concern."

What was left of the fire still glowed in the grate, but it was turning to ashes at the edges, just as Matilda Greenleaf seemed to turn gray now that she had expended such effort in forcing her will on Elizabeth.

"I'd like to see the girls, Miss Mattie."

"What is your decision, Elizabeth?"

"I need time to think it through. I just don't know—"

As she watched the old lady, renewed strength came back to Matilda Greenleaf. She rolled her chair forward.

"There's no time left, Elizabeth."

"I must think."

"Think? About what? There's only one way to go. Cassandra will have a strong voice, even though the war is over, but as time passes, her voice will be less effective. You are a heroine of sorts now, Elizabeth, but it will pass."

"I want to see my daughters. We can talk later."

"You'll see them when I say you can."

"I didn't know you hated me that much."

"You, young woman, are inconsequential to me. You think only of yourself. But, selfishness aside, you can't see the girls; they are not here."

Elizabeth gasped. What had she heard? The old lady continued in a matter-of-fact voice: "That was a precaution I had to take. I knew you'd come. I didn't know whether you'd try to see them without my permission, but with your boldness, it was a chance I could not take. The girls have gone to the shore, perhaps for the summer."

The heat of the room was even more oppressive, or was it the heat of Matilda Greenleaf's passion. Her hatred filled the room. Elizabeth seemed unable to breathe. Seconds passed. The tiny old woman in the rolling chair sat bold and upright. Elizabeth saw determination in the set of her jaw.

"They're at the shore," Miss Greenleaf repeated. "How long they remain there depends on you. Think about that."

Chapter Sixty-Four

The musty, sour smell of the closed and over-heated room pressed against Elizabeth like a coiling snake. She tried to pull fresh air into her body. She wanted a lungful of life, of anything to sustain her, even the fetid atmosphere that surrounded her. She heard the hiss of a puff of gas as it escaped from one of the burning lumps of coal. She did not look at Matilda Greenleaf, but she could feel the old lady's eyes, waiting for the defeat she expected to see on Elizabeth's face.

It would be sensible to arrange for transportation to Darien. Elizabeth knew land holdings were being taken. What Matilda Greenleaf said was true. The old lady had given the matter serious consideration, and she had a mind that could comprehend complex matters. The affairs of Greenleaf Plantation had been guided by this wicked old woman, the only Greenleaf who did not own an acre of it. Clay had been the head of the farming operation, but the brains behind it came from this house, just as was happening now.

"I'd like to see Byron, Miss Mattie," she said in a voice that sounded calmer than she felt inside.

"First, you must agree to go to Darien, Elizabeth."

Matilda Greenleaf's words were not unexpected, but Elizabeth's reaction to them was.

Since Miss Mattie's greeting at the door, Elizabeth had been beaten down by this old lady, and now, even though it might be irrational, she could take no more. Anger boiled in her veins. Her voice was controlled and firm. The words she said surprised her. She hadn't thought them out, they simply came as they were required. "You'll get an answer when I'm ready to give it, Miss Mattie. You said I might have cards to play. You're right. I didn't realize how strong my hand was, but now I do. I have at least one card that will top anything you have. I don't intend to squander it foolishly. But, you, Miss Mattie, have been so confident you misplayed your hand."

"Don't talk nonsense, girl. If you wish to see your daughters, now or at any time in the future, the game will be played with my set of rules."

"Will it, Miss Mattie?" Elizabeth dabbed at the perspiration on her forehead. "The girls are grown young ladies, Miss Mattie, and you can't keep them hidden forever. That will not be a problem anymore. On the other hand, I do have something you want. You gave me the card I needed, but I failed to see it at the outset."

The old lady hunched forward. "Nonsense, utter nonsense." She spoke in a bold voice that seemed too powerful for the rack of bones in the rolling chair, but she was wary.

"You said you want nothing for yourself, Miss Mattie, and I believe you. You said the only thing of any real value to you at this late time in your life is the welfare of your grandnieces. To a degree, I think that's true, but to a greater degree I see something stronger, something I know well. I see the Greenleaf pride here, in all its bright colors. You want to keep Greenleaf Plantation alive. You want it held together, at whatever cost." The empty teacup Elizabeth held was no longer being gripped as though it might fall. She was no longer afraid.

"When we first met, Miss Mattie, when I came to your hotel room, I was really nothing to you, either way. I was a passing annoyance. You would have preferred that Clay not marry at all; you thought such an arrangement might claim some of the attention you demanded for the forty pieces of gold you doled out on a regular basis.

"Later, when I lived here in this house, I was a mild source of irritation to you, but nothing more. In those days, it was all by your rules. Clay was a chess piece you moved across the board, and I was less than a pawn.

"It was only when I fought for my children, in the only way I knew—when I created the scandal—that the Greenleaf pride came roaring out of the cellar. I bathed the Greenleaf name in public scandal—your name, Miss Mattie—and for that you can never forgive me. I didn't know how strong your hatred was. I thought Clay kept me from the children. But, today, as you tried to bully me one more time, I saw who had kept me from the girls: you are the culprit, Miss Mattie. It was because I caused the Greenleaf name to be sullied."

"Nonsense, Elizabeth. I don't like you; I never have. You were a ninny when Clay married. When you left, I was glad to see you go. But, when it came out, when it became public knowledge, that you were Cassandra, when you insisted on telling that wild story about Clay and one of our servants, I grew to hate you with a passion I have kept alive all these years. I don't deny it for a moment. I wouldn't spit on you if you were standing at the gates of hell."

The wary look was gone from Matilda Greenleaf's eyes. She had regained control of herself, and she intended to regain the upper hand with Elizabeth. She wheeled her chair closer, her voice was cold. "The fact is, you want only the best for your daughters. I believe you. That's the reason you're here. You want to win them back." She smiled as she spoke, but there was no mirth in the grimace. "You will go to Darien, Elizabeth, and you will do whatever is required to protect your children's assets there. You won't do it for me, but you will do it."

"Do you think so, Miss Mattie? Can you be sure? Think about it, I beg you. Consider all sides of the situation, all the possibilities. You have never leapt to conclusions. So, Miss Mattie, consider this: All through my life I've been called willful--you said it today. The spite you have shown me deserves at least an equal dose in return, don't you think? If I choose to do so, I can ignore your plea for the welfare of my children; I can let Greenleaf Plantation be ripped apart by the many who have already started South looking for opportunities in the ashes of its defeat."

Elizabeth had the upperhand, but Matilda Greenleaf fought to keep that fact from showing on her face.

"So, Miss Mattie, think about it," Elizabeth said. "If I am as willful as I've been told I am, why shouldn't I place my own feelings first in this unsavory encounter? Why shouldn't I let Greenleaf Plantation come to its own well-deserved demise? I hadn't fully realized it before, but I am aware of it now. I have no feeling for you but revulsion. I feel the force of your hatred, but don't forget, I am fully capable of returning it. I may have to give something; I may have to pay for what I get. But, let me remind you, even without Greenleaf, the girls will not be destitute, so I have a free hand to be as vengeful as you are, and I am just as capable of it. I may have been a ninny when I met you, but I'm not now. I have the key. I know what you want. You want the monument of Greenleaf. You want it kept intact for the sake of some strange kind of family pride. Well, Miss Mattie, I have your pride in my hands. Why shouldn't I burn you with it?"

"You won't do it because of your daughters."

"I'll do what I damned well please, Miss Mattie. I've been on my own now for over twenty years. I've had power; I have it now, the same kind of power you have wielded over the Greenleaf clan. I needn't tell *you* how warm it makes you feel inside, how strong, how arrogant. You already know that. So, understand this point right now: I will do as I please. And, when I'm ready to tell you what I intend to do—and when I intend to do it—it will be on my terms and in my way."

Elizabeth could see the effect her words were having, and for one brief moment she was ashamed of treating an old and obviously ill woman with such brutality, but she brushed the thought aside. She saw Matilda Greenleaf's eyes tear, she saw them lose the defiance that had been there since the two ladies had met in the entryway.

"And, now, Miss Mattie," Elizabeth said, "with or without your permission, I'm going upstairs to see Byron."

Clarisse showed Elizabeth the way to Byron's room on the third floor. She knocked. She could hear that familiar voice from inside: "Come in." Bittersweet remembrances of Greenleaf Plantation came flooding back. She took a deep breath, squared her shoulders and entered.

He was lost in his own dreams. Perhaps his mind is at Greenleaf, as mine was a moment ago, Elizabeth thought. He is not here. She spoke softly, "Byron—"

He turned at the sound of her voice. "Elizabeth! I can't believe it. I thought it was Clarisse." He was propped up in the bed with pillows behind him. "Aunt Mattie said you'd come, but I was afraid you wouldn't—not after the responsibility I thrust on you. But, thank God, you're here."

She wasn't sure what to expect of Byron's physical condition, but she was delighted to see that he looked surprisingly fit. He had lost weight and his face looked gaunt, but the bright blue eyes were alive with the joy of seeing her, and his brown hair had color and luster. "Oh, Byron," she said, "I'm so glad to see you looking well. You are recovering. Gordy will be so glad to hear it."

"I wish it were true, dear sister, but I'm less able to move about now than when I arrived just a few weeks ago."

"But—"

"I don't look as spent as I am. My deterioration is not visible. The problem, dear Elizabeth, is that I'm losing control of my limbs, my muscles will not obey. My breath is short. I can still get up, but when I do, I ask Clarisse to send her boy Pliny up to help me. I'm afraid of falling. I think a fall could break a limb; or worse, it could shatter what remains of my confidence. I have a rolling chair, just as Aunt Mattie has." He gestured toward the corner where the chair was half hidden, and as he did so he laughed. The sound of his mirth brought another quick glimpse of Greenleaf. "We don't have races on our wheels, Aunt Mattie and I, but if we did, I'm sure she'd win. Have you seen her?"

"Yes. She was at the front door. She hasn't changed."

"I hope you've forgiven her for keeping your daughters from you all these years."

"I have not. Perhaps I should for the sake of my own mental state, but I have not. I realize she's old, but, Byron, I cannot forgive her, or Clay. They meant to hurt me."

"'Forgiveness to the injured does belong—'"

"Spare me the platitudes, Byron. I've just come from Papa's house. He knows them all. I've been burdened with enough homilies."

"I'm sorry, Elizabeth. It's just that—"

"It's just that she's your closest kin, and you love her in spite of what she is. That's your right, Byron. But, don't ask me to love her or forgive her, at least not now."

"We'll say no more, Elizabeth. Tell me about Gordy. Will you see to his education? Will you go back with him to Greenleaf to bring some order there? Will you—"

"One thing at a time, please Byron. Gordy is fine. He is being tutored and he is enrolled at Harvard for the fall session. And, yes, I will continue to see to Gordy's education." She walked over to the windows, opened them wider to let the breeze come in. She had to be honest with Byron, but she didn't want to be too blunt since he was unable to fend for himself.

When she turned back, there were tears in his eyes. She heard him mumble a thank you, and she turned her head so as not to embarrass him further.

She sat on the padded window seat, waiting for the moment to pass. And then she spoke: "As for the other—" How could she say what she must say? "—as for inheriting your share of Greenleaf, Byron, your part of the Greenleaf estate, that must be forgotten. I shall never return to Greenleaf to stay. I know you offered your part of it with a pure heart, but it's a proposal I must decline."

"But, dear sister, you wanted to teach, you know the need. That need is multiplied now, because those people are free. Perhaps it's a boon; perhaps it's a burden. But, they need you. I saw it at first hand. There's no one to take care of them—and, my dear, you must know—you must remember—how woefully unprepared they are."

"I *wanted* to teach. That's in the past, Byron. It's over. Time changes people. It has changed me."

"But, you are still willing to help Gordy."

"Yes, I'll do all I can for him. I'll do that much for you, Byron, and for Gordy, and for his people. Gordy wants to go back. He wants to teach. He wants to help. Gordy has a mission. I do not. I want nothing that is—or ever was—Greenleaf. The exception is the love of my daughters. It may be an impossible task, thanks to your brother and your aunt."

"Elizabeth, do you know that land—entire plantations in the South—are being taken? As reparations. It's being reparceled. Has Aunt Mattie talked to you about what could happen to Greenleaf Plantation? It would certainly concern your daughters."

"Oh, yes. Her approach was direct. Of course I know her feelings in the matter. I also know the axiom of war: 'to the victor belongs the spoils.'"

Elizabeth walked to his bedside. She rearranged his pillows. Why do we do this? Why must women fuss at pillows in a sickroom? Is it to cover our feelings?

She continued: "I read the newspapers. Washington favors punishment of the South. More than that, my late husband's business partner spoke to me of war reparations before I began the journey to Philadelphia. I don't question it. Your aunt has assessed the situation correctly. She's aware that Greenleaf may not rise again. She doesn't want that to happen. What is Greenleaf to her? Is it a monument to her brother George, to the family name? I'm not sure. But, this I know: her pride colors it all."

"True," he replied. "Pride is a part of it."

"I hadn't thought of my own position, Byron, but, yes, your aunt is right again. As Cassandra, because of the work I did, I might be of some help in keeping the estate together, since I participated on the winning side. But, at this moment, I'm not sure now what I will do."

"What about the girls, Elizabeth—"

"I've made no decisions, Byron."

"You could make a difference."

"Perhaps. We can talk of it later. For now, though, let me ask, Byron, where are the girls?"

"They've gone to the shore with the Pennypackers. George and Ethel have two daughters about the same age."

"My daughters were bundled off to the shore, Byron, so I couldn't see them."

"How can you think that, Elizabeth? No one knew you were coming, or if you would ever come."

"She knew."

"When Aunt Mattie was younger, she may have been that clever, she may even have been that cunning, but she's an old woman now."

"Byron, you are naive. Matilda Greenleaf is as she was. She has not mellowed with age. She *told* me she sent them away. There was malice in what she did, just as there was malice in extracting my father's promise *not* to breathe a word of the girl's safety or whereabouts to me. She made her point clear: If he didn't promise, he couldn't see them."

"She asked for your father's promise?"

"She demanded it. Otherwise, he couldn't see them."

"My God. You have reason to feel—"

"Yes, Byron, I have."

"And, because of Aunt Mattie, you'd let Greenleaf go? You wouldn't help your daughters?"

"I've not said what I'll do, Byron. I said I'd made no decisions. With your help, perhaps I can make one now."

"Anything. I'm so grateful for what you are doing for Gordy. I can't begin to tell you how much. I'll do anything you ask."

"Even if what I ask is difficult?"

"Name it, Elizabeth."

"I'll tell you my decision, but only if I get from you the same promise Miss Mattie demanded of my father."

"I'm to deny all knowledge of your plans to my aunt?"

"Before you promise, Byron, think it over. She'll wheedle, she'll badger, she'll berate and revile you. But, if you promise, you must not breathe a word to her."

"I promise, Elizabeth."

"Are you sure, Byron? It will not be easy. I don't underestimate Miss Mattie, nor should you."

"I will do it, Elizabeth, and I wish you Godspeed."

"Godspeed, is it? You've decided what I'll do?"

"You are not a foolish woman, Elizabeth, but I can see that you'd cut off your own nose to repay Aunt Mattie. I think I now understand your reaction. Be assured, I will honor my promise."

"You were right. I'll do whatever I can for the girls, even if I must use the name of Cassandra."

"And, my part of the estate, Elizabeth?"

"I'll do what I can for you, too, Byron."

"Not for me." He reached for her hand. "Can't you see, Elizabeth, my breathing is difficult. Those muscles, too, are faltering. Take my land. Your case will be stronger if it's Cassandra and her daughters trying to reclaim their land."

"The answer is no, Byron. A firm and final no."

"But, you do see the strength of it? Your name will influence any Yankee administering the reparations."

"You may be right, Byron, but the answer is still no. I will not accept your offer, I will not start a school. You have my word that I will assist Gordy in every way I can. Leave your part of the estate to him if you wish, but don't try to burden me with it."

"That is final?"

"Yes, Byron, it is."

"When will you leave?"

"I'll return to Boston. I'll need a few days and then—"

"You could leave from here. Time is eroding the land."

"You are as persistent as your aunt. The Greenleafs never give up, do they? But, dear brother, the answer is the same. I will go to Darien, but in my own good time."

"Then, again, Elizabeth, I wish you Godspeed."

Chapter Sixty-Five

Two days after Elizabeth's return to Boston, a messenger arrived with a small package from Byron. She took it to her room and ordered a pot of tea. It contained information on the factored accounts, and three mortgages on acreage sold by Greenleaf Plantation before the war, each with substantial sums still unpaid. The last bundle was deeds for the various parcels of land that made up the remainder of the estate, all newly drawn, and made out in her name. Then she found the letter.

"*Dear Elizabeth,*" it began. "*First, I want to thank you for coming. I was not sure you would, considering the past, but you came. Seeing you once again has given me new hope.*

"*Secondly, I want to explain why I called in a solicitor and had these new documents prepared. I have given our conversation a great deal of thought since you left Philadelphia. This is the only way the estate can be saved.*"

There it is, she thought, the Greenleaf pride. Save the estate—at whatever cost! She glanced back to the letter.

"*No, my dear, this is not selfishness, as you believed to be the case with Aunt Mattie; it's being practical. One of us must be. When you discuss Aunt Mattie, you are simply not rational. So, in the quiet of my room, I am trying to think clearly—not just for you, but for Mary and Ann Frances.*

"*If half of the estate remained in my name, you would be able to make a practical case only for the part rightfully belonging to your daughters. You might speak for me, but it would lose its effectiveness. I was a part of the system in the South. I did nothing to modify it. It would be a hard point to overcome. I know you speak with power, but the task is not likely to succeed if the land remains in my name, even with your facility with words. I read all your columns. I kept a folder for Cassandra. If my house is still as I left it, you will find those clippings are in the bottom drawer of a storage file, the one farthest from my desk. They truly are 'Echoes from the South,' faded now, no doubt, but symbols of how much I believed in what you wrote."*

She put the letter down. The war had ended her column. If she could only go back, back to those happy days before Spencer died. She sighed and took up the letter again.

"The next possibility for the land is one you suggested. You said I could leave it—or give it—to Gordy. However good this idea seems, it is not sound. There is precious little support for the Emancipation Proclamation. If I deeded the land to Gordy, I would be giving it to someone who does not yet have full citizenship. God only knows when he will. You see the danger. The suggestion is impractical for a second reason: We both know there still is considerable prejudice abroad, even in the North. The Irish are incensed at the preferential treatment they believe blacks are receiving in some quarters. This situation is real. I can see it in Philadelphia, even confined to my room. The officer dealing with reparations may be named McGillicuddy. The point is valid, and you know it. I worried about Gordy's safety when I sent him to Boston. Your visit put my mind to rest.

"The strength of our case rests with you—and with Cassandra. Your daughters have a bona fide claim, and you will have, with these deeds. But, deeds won't validate your claim so much as the service you rendered the Union before and during the war. If a nation owes a debt to its fighting men, does it not also owe a debt to its fighting women? I believe it does and I am confident you can make the case.

"The ultimate question: Why should you bother? You do not want to return to Greenleaf to stay, and you have no desire to teach. I believe you. You agreed to upset your own life to help your daughters claim what is rightfully theirs.

"I have not said a word to Aunt Mattie, but, as you predicted, she stormed into my room after you left. She demanded to know what you intended to do. She called you 'willful,' and she said it with venom. I could imagine the tenor of your talk with her. She used other strong words, but that one sticks, because it came up so often. But, Elizabeth, on that one point she is right. You are headstrong when you are pushed into a corner, and you think I am doing it now."

You are trying, Byron, but you're not succeeding, she thought. Wild horses couldn't drag me back to Georgia to stay. She laid the letter on her desk.

I need more than tea, she thought, and I need a little brandy laced into it. As she began the second cup of 'fortified' tea, she picked up the letter again.

"My plea to you is not that you go back to Greenleaf to stay. I am convinced. That is not in your plans. My plea is that you save my part of those valuable lands for a nobler purpose. You will decide the purpose: give it to Gordy, parcel it out to the people who worked there, or dedicate it to public use. That choice is yours, but, please, Elizabeth, accept these deeds, save the land. Later you will know what to do with it."

That phrase again, she thought. In the future "You will know what to do—" Just as I "will know what to do" with the miniature of Clay. You have cheek, Byron, but you ask too much. You want no burdens for yourself, yet you have no compunction about dropping the weight of your burdens on my shoulders. With a sigh she continued reading:

"Do this for me, Elizabeth, consider it the last wish of a dying man. Take these deeds with you--deeds made out in your name. Use the influence you have earned with the Union. Don't let the land my father worked so hard to tame be torn asunder

by the carrion eaters that are flocking to the South for their own financial gain.

"It can be done, dear sister, but it can only be done by you. I have never said it, but before I leave this mortal shell I want you to know: I love you. I loved you then, and I do now."

As she read this last line, a tear fell, splotching the purple ink of the last carefully written word: *"Byron."*

On the dawn of the next day she left Boston for Darien.

the end